C1

D0207541

The Political Economy of Water Pricing Reforms

Edited by Ariel Dinar

Published for the World Bank
Oxford University Press

Oxford University Press

OXFORD   NEW YORK   ATHENS   AUCKLAND   BANGKOK   BOGOTA   BUENOS AIRES
CALCUTTA   CAPE TOWN   CHENNAI   DAR ES SALAAM   DELHI   FLORENCE   HONG KONG
ISTANBUL   KARACHI   KUALA LUMPUR   MADRID   MELBOURNE   MEXICO CITY   MUMBAI
NAIROBI   PARIS   SÃO PAULO   SINGAPORE   TAIPEI   TOKYO   TORONTO   WARSAW

and associated companies in

BERLIN   IBADAN

Published by Oxford University Press, Inc.
198 Madison Avenue, New York, N.Y. 10016

Oxford is a registered trademark of Oxford University Press.

All photographs by Ariel Dinar except for "Farm Water Works" (at bottom of cover), which is by Pearl and Harold Denner.

Cover and interior design by International Communications, Inc., Sterling, Virginia.

Manufactured in the United States of America
First printing April 2000

The findings, interpretations, and conclusions expressed in this study are entirely those of the authors and should not be attributed in any manner to the World Bank, to its affiliated organizations, or to members of its Board of Executive Directors or the countries they represent.

Library of Congress Cataloging-in-Publication Data

The political economy of water pricing reforms/edited by Ariel Dinar.
p.cm.
Includes bibliographical references.
ISBN 0-19-521594-X
1. Water-supply--Political aspects. 2. Water-supply--Economic aspects. 3. Water-supply--Rates. 4. Water-supply--Management. 5. Water--Prices. I. Dinar, Ariel, 1947–

HD1691.P65 2000
363.6'1--dc2I   99-059024

Text printed on paper that conforms to the American National Standard for Permanence of Paper for Printed Library Materials, Z39.48-1984Library of Congress Cataloging-in-Publication Data

To my beloved sons:
Roee, in whose steps I walk,
and
Shlomi, who follows my footsteps.

Contents

Acknowledgments

This book is based, to a great extent, on papers presented at the World Bank-sponsored Workshop on Political Economy of Water Pricing Implementation that took place in Washington, D.C. on November 3–5, 1998.

The World Bank Rural Development Department's training budget and the Bank's Rural Family Water Resources Management Thematic Team supported both the workshop and this book. Partial funding for the workshop was provided by the FORWARD project. Liliana Monk and Fulvia Toppin of the Bank's Rural Development Department helped me organize the workshop.

Although this book includes just some of the papers presented at the workshop, the remaining papers that were published in other outlets have added a great deal to our knowledge. I would like to take this opportunity to thank the other presenters: Mahmood Ahmad, Mohamed Ait-Kadi, Ra'ed Daud, Jennifer Davis, Antonin Dvorak, Peter Fiala, Frances Grey, Joshua Johnson, Tom Jones, Clay Landry, Ales Lisa, Michael Moore, Koussai Quteishat, Peter Sauer, Pierre Teniere-Buchot, Anantharama Vaidyanathan, and Christina Wood.

Three anonymous reviewers did a great job and their detailed comments undoubtedly helped me improve the final product. The World Bank Publication Committee and the Office of the Publisher provided careful guidance on publication details.

The "Farm Water Works" picture on the front cover was taken by Pearl and Harold Denner of Van Nuys, California.

Finally, I was fortunate to have a wonderful group of colleague authors who responded to all my requests, starting with preparing the workshop and concluding with the final touches to this book. It has been indeed a cooperative effort.

Contributors

Musa Asad, Financial Economist/Analyst, Water Resources Management Team, Latin America and the Caribbean Region, The World Bank, Washington, D.C.

Luiz Gabriel T. de Azevedo, Water Resources Engineer, Water Resources Management Team, Latin America and the Caribbean Region, The World Bank, Washington, D.C.

John J. Boland, Professor, Department of Geography and Environmental Engineering, Johns Hopkins University, Baltimore, Maryland.

Daniel W. Bromley, Anderson-Bascom Professor of Applied Economics, Department of Agricultural and Applied Economics, University of Wisconsin, Madison, Wisconsin.

Alfredo H. Cueva, Senior Environmental Engineer, Alpha-Gamma Technologies, Inc., Raleigh, North Carolina.

Xinshen Diao, Research Fellow, Trade and Macroeconomics Division, International Food Policy Research Institute, Washington, D.C.

Ariel Dinar, Principal Economist, Rural Development Department, The World Bank, Washington, D.C., and Adjunct Professor, Department of Economics, George Washington University, Washington, D.C.

Darwin C. Hall, Professor, Department of Economics, California State University, Long Beach, California.

Julie A. Hewitt, Economist, U.S. Environmental Protection Agency, Washington, D.C.

Karin E. Kemper, Economist, Water Resources Management Team, Latin America and the Caribbean Region, The World Bank, Washington, D.C.

Donald T. Lauria, Professor, Department of Environmental Sciences and Engineering, University of North Carolina at Chapel Hill, Chapel Hill, North Carolina.

Richard J. McCann, Partner, M.Cubed, Davis, California.

Warren Musgrave, Consultant and formerly Special Adviser-Natural Resources, New South Wales Premier's Department, Sydney, Australia.

Douglas Olson, Senior Water Resources Engineer, Rural Development and Natural Resources Sector Unit, East Asia and Pacific Region, The World Bank, Washington, D.C.

Gordon C. Rausser, Robert Gordon Sproul Distinguished Professor and Dean, College of Natural Resources, University of California at Berkeley, Berkeley, California.

Steven Renzetti, Associate Professor, Department of Economics, Brock University, St. Catherines, Ontario, Canada.

Terry Roe, Professor, Department of Applied Economics, University of Minnesota, St. Paul, Minnesota.

Jon Strand, Professor, Department of Economics, University of Oslo, Oslo, Norway.

Yacov Tsur, Associate Professor, Department of Agricultural Economics and Management, Hebrew University of Jerusalem, Rehovot, Israel; and Adjunct Professor, Department of Applied Economics, University of Minnesota, St. Paul, Minnesota.

Peter Van Humbeeck, Attaché, Social and Economic Council of Flanders, Brussels, Belgium.

Joseph Makwata Wambia, Senior Financial Analyst, Rural Development Sector Management Unit, South Asia Region, The World Bank, Washington, D.C.

Christopher Ward, Principal Operations Officer, Middle East and North Africa Region, Natural Resources Department, The World Bank, Washington, D.C.

Dale Whittington, Professor, Department of Environmental Sciences and Engineering, University of North Carolina at Chapel Hill, Chapel Hill, North Carolina.

David Zilberman, Professor, Department of Agricultural and Resource Economics, University of California at Berkeley, Berkeley, California.

1

Political Economy of Water Pricing Reforms

Ariel Dinar

As water becomes scarcer and its quality continues to deteriorate, policymakers have been compelled to explore new approaches to improve the management of water resources. Water pricing reforms are among various measures designed to encourage the efficient use of water resources. Documentation in the literature demonstrates that many countries have been engaged in such pricing reforms lately. For example, Jones (1998) and OECD (1999) report on recent water pricing reforms in 16 Organisation for Economic Co-operation and Development (OECD) countries, Ahmad (1998) presents information on pricing reforms in the water sectors of 7 Near East region countries, and Dinar and Subramanian (1997) provide information on experiences with water pricing reforms in 22 selected countries (table 1.1).

The prices reported in table 1.1 are the result of complicated reform processes that took place in each country over long periods of time and under various circumstances. Many countries have dealt with reforming their water sectors in the last decade, so there is a wealth of data on widely varying practical experiences. In addition, the interest in water management has led to a surge in theoretical and empirical research in this area, particularly in the fields of economics, political science, and institutional studies. Furthermore, an increased number of projects funded by international development organizations (for example, the World Bank, regional development banks, the Food and Agriculture Organization of the United Nations) in the irrigation and urban and rural water supply sectors include substantial water pricing reform components. A recent collection of studies in five Latin American

1

TABLE 1.1
Price Ranges for Various Sectors and Countries in the Analysis
(US$)

Country	Agriculture Fixed (per hectare per year or season)	Agriculture Variable (per cubic meter)	Domestic Fixed (per household per year or month)	Domestic Variable (per cubic meter)	Industry Fixed (per plant per year or month)	Industry Variable (per cubic meter)
Algeria[a]	3.7900–7.5900	0.0190–0.0220	—	0.0570–0.2700	—	4.6400
Australia[a]	0.7500–2.2700	0.0195	9.0000–162.0000	0.2300–0.5400	—	7.8200
Austria[b]	—	0.3600–0.9800	—	0.8500	—	—
Belgium[b]	—	—	—	2.0600–2.4700	—	—
Botswana[a]	—	—	—	0.2800–1.4800	—	—
Brazil[a]	3.5000	0.0042–0.0320	—	0.4000	—	—
Canada[a]	6.6200–36.6500	0.0017–0.0019	—	0.3400–1.3600	—	0.1700–1.5200
Czech Republic[b]	—	—	—	0.6800	—	—
Denmark[b]	—	0.7100	—	3.1800	—	—
Egypt, Arab Republic[c]	—	—	—	0.0700–0.0900	—	0.1200–0.5900
Finland[b]	—	—	—	2.7600	—	—
France[a]	—	0.1100–0.3900	—	0.3600–2.5800	—	0.3600–2.1600
Germany[b]	—	—	—	1.6900	—	1.0220–3.7040
Greece[b]	92.0000–210.0000	0.0210–0.0820	—	1.1400	—	—
Hungary[b]	—	—	—	0.8200	—	—
India[a]	0.1640–27.4700	—	0.8240	0.0095–0.0820	5.4900	0.1360–0.2900
Israel[a]	—	0.1600–0.2600	—	0.3600	—	0.2600

(table continues on following page)

Table 1.1 continues

Country	Agriculture		Domestic		Industry	
	Fixed (per hectare per year or season)	Variable (per cubic meter)	Fixed (per household per year or month)	Variable (per cubic meter)	Fixed (per plant per year or month)	Variable (per cubic meter)
Italy[a]	20.9800–78.1600	—	—	0.1400–0.8200	—	—
Japan[b]	246.0000	—	—	1.5600	—	—
Jordan[c]	—	0.0100–0.0400	—	0.2700–1.0300	—	0.1200–0.3500
Korea, Republic of[b]	—	—	—	0.2700	—	—
Lebanon[c]	—	—	8.7100	—	—	—
Luxembourg[b]	—	—	—	1.0100	—	—
Madagascar[a]	6.2500–11.2500	—	0.0750–0.2500	0.3920	—	—
			—	0.3250–1.2500	—	—
			—	0.9000–1.7500	—	—
Mexico[b]	33.0000–60.0000	—	—	—	—	0.0800–0.3500
Namibia[a]	53.1400	0.0038–0.0280	1.5400–4.2800	0.2200–0.4500	—	—
			—	0.3300–1.3800	—	—
Netherlands[b]	—	—	—	3.1600	—	0.5700–1.7100
New Zealand[a]	6.7700–16.6300	—	16.0000–164.0000	0.3100–0.6900	—	—
Pakistan[a]	1.4900–5.8000	—	0.2500–1.6300	0.0600–0.1000	—	0.3800–0.9700
Palestinian Authority (Gaza)[c]	—	—	—	0.3300	—	—
Palestinian Authority (West Bank)[c]	—	—	—	0.7900–1.1200	—	—

(table continues on following page)

Table 1.1 continues

Country	Agriculture Fixed (per hectare per year or season)	Agriculture Variable (per cubic meter)	Domestic Fixed (per household per year or month)	Domestic Variable (per cubic meter)	Industry Fixed (per plant per year or month)	Industry Variable (per cubic meter)
Poland[b]	—	—	—	—	—	0.2000–0.9400
Portugal[a]	—	0.0095–0.0193	4.4600–1937.0000	0.1526–0.5293	8.8600–2,705.0000	1.1900
Saudi Arabia[c]	0.9600–164.4800	—	—	0.0400–1.0700	—	—
Spain[a]	—	0.0001–0.0280	—	0.0004–0.0046	—	0.0004–0.0046
Sudan[a]	4.7200–11.2200	—	1.6700–3.3300	0.0800–0.1000	1.6700–3.3300	0.0800–0.1000
Switzerland[b]	—	0.3300–1.9600	—	1.2900	—	—
Syrian Arab Republic[c]	50.0000	—	3.2100	0.1100–0.5300	—	0.7100
Taiwan, China[a]	23.3000–213.6400	—	—	0.2500–0.4200	—	—
Tanzania[a]	—	0.2600–0.3980	—	0.0620–0.2410	—	0.2610–0.3980
Tunisia[a]	—	0.0200–0.0780	—	0.0960–0.5290	—	0.5830
Turkey[b]	—	12.0000–80.0000	—	—	—	—
Uganda[a]	—	—	—	0.3800–0.5900	—	0.7200–1.3500
United Kingdom[a]	—	—	152.0000–171.0000	0.0095–0.0248	—	—
United States[a]	—	0.0124–0.0438	—	—	—	—
Yemen[c]	—	0.0200–1.4500	—	0.1000–13.7900	—	0.1000–13.7000

— Not available.

Note: For sources a and c, prices are 1996 constant US$. For source b, prices are July 1997 constant US$. Range of prices depends on various factors and conditions. For more explanation see the sources.

Several countries are reported in two of the three studies. In such cases, only the earlier reference is presented in the table.

Sources: a. Dinar and Subramanian (1997)
b. OECD (1998a); OECD (1998b, tables 11 and 24)
c. Ahmad (1998).

countries provides the latest documentation of reform efforts of various types in the urban water sector (Savedoff and Spiller 1999).

With such widely varying water pricing reform experiences, there are likely instances of failure as well as success. Can we learn from these experiences? Can we, for example, explain why irrigation water pricing reform at the union (federal) level in India (Government of India 1994) failed to materialize after it was proposed in 1992? Can we contrast it to the successful water pricing reform that has taken place in the state of Andhra Pradesh in southwestern India since 1998 (Oblitas and others 1999)? Why is the Australian water pricing reform progressing in the right direction, although not at the same pace in all states (Musgrave, chapter 14 in this volume)? Finally, will the 1999 federal government initiative for bulk water pricing reform in Brazil (Azavedo and Asad, chapter 15 in this volume; Asad and others 1999) succeed?

This book attempts to respond to such questions by introducing political economy concepts into the analysis of water pricing reforms. It draws on theoretical contributions in the field of political economy of water pricing reforms as well as on quantitative studies that address certain aspects of the reforms. Designing and implementing pricing reforms is a complicated process affected by various forces, many of which are difficult to define and model. As theory alone may fall short of providing an adequate response to these questions, this book also relies on a variety of case studies that demonstrate a diversity of physical conditions, institutional settings, implementation approaches, and status of the reforms (see also Haggard and Webb 1996a for a similar reasoning as to the use of case studies).

This chapter starts by addressing, in the next section, major possible shortcomings of implementing normative economic approaches that may produce first-best pricing outcomes. What emerges from that discussion is a justification for the inclusion of political considerations in economic optimization approaches that are used for water pricing reform designs. The third section offers a framework to help compare water pricing reforms. The fourth section documents the experiences of reforms in various sectors. The chapter continues with a review of the structure of the rest of the book, highlighting the research reported throughout the book. It concludes with a short review of the conditions for successful reforms and a summary of the main findings and of additional research needs.

Difficulties in Water Pricing Reforms

The classic analytical economic framework (market model) is supported, in most cases, by well-defined behavioral theory of the parties involved in the reform. This theory is based on individuals' rational behavior, on avail-ability of full information with no transaction cost, on a preference set that depends only on individual consideration, on maximization of welfare, and on freedom of choice. If the party is a group, it assumes that each group speaks with one voice.

Within such a framework, economists and water experts are comfortable with calculating efficient water pricing schemes. However, such schemes usually ignore the information and knowledge needed for their implemen-tation. The schemes also underestimate distortions arising from mis-specification of relationships (institutional structure and power) among individuals and organizations. Therefore, in most cases economists actu-ally produce second-best solutions. As a result, evaluating the consequences of these pricing reforms can be difficult.

Because of the differing physical characteristics of water systems and the various institutional and cultural frameworks within which pricing policies have to perform, considerable variation remains among reforms in different countries. Such differences include the pricing structures, the pace at which countries are moving toward implementing reforms, the level of full cost recovery, and the degree of targeting of environmental and so-cial objectives. As one would expect, political pressure frequently affects the process. Political influence on development in the water sector has of-ten led to unforeseen social and economic consequences.

Other researchers have also addressed some of these difficulties. For example, Shubik (1982) suggests that modeling aggregates as a single player presents difficulties, especially in situations in which the representation of a group by a single player can be dangerously misleading. In the case of reciprocal interests among parties, political considerations, which are usu-ally not incorporated in economic analyses, can hinder, or even block, the most efficient arrangement (Dinar and Wolf 1997). In such cases economic models, although extremely important as indicators of the magnitude of the reform process, may fail to explain the occurrence of frequent and large departures from first-best policies. In addition, social planner models can-not explain the differences between reform processes in countries with simi-lar economic conditions and resource levels (Alesina 1996).

Political Dimensions of Reforms: Design, Implementation, and Likelihood of Success

Institutional reforms associated with changes in the distribution of power and benefits inevitably create considerable political opposition. The con-ventional view of institutional change is that either it is in the interests of economic efficiency or it merely redistributes income (Bromley 1989). In this regard, interest groups form and attempt to influence the decision-making process so that the end result best serves their interests. Powerful political groups may slow, divert, or even stop a desirable reform. The larger the number of interest groups, the more complicated the implementation process is likely to be.

Political dimensions of reforms can be traced as early as the stage when the reform was originally considered, and as late as the postreform stage, when its implementation is being evaluated. This book presents a framework for evaluating and comparing reforms based on Haggard and Webb (1996b), Krueger (1992), White (1990), and Williamson (1994). The suggested framework is only one of many available for explaining reform success. Some aspects of the process may be over- or underemphasized, and others may be missing from the suggested framework. However, the list of issues addressed seems to fit the overall approach taken by analysts in other sectors and types of reforms. The individual chapters attempt to provide evidence to support the framework; however, in some cases this support relies on evidence from other studies.

Reasons for Reform

Reasons for reform can vary according to the particular situation. However, in most cases, pricing reform in a particular sector appears to be associated with a larger reform agenda. Pricing reforms are often complicated by financial crises and low cost recovery of the investment in the water system. Such a situation is described in the case of Pakistan (Wambia, chapter 17 in this volume), where the central government has to subsidize the budgets of the irrigation departments. Morocco is another case (Diao and Roe, chapter 7 in this volume) where the public budget used to be the sole source of funding of water services provided mainly by irrigation districts. The Republic of Yemen case (Ward, chapter 18 in this volume), in which macroeconomic measures accompanied the water reforms, provides a good example of the importance of having a wide-ranging agenda for reform. For the water sector to be targeted for pricing reforms after elections when a new regime takes over is also common, as occurred in Andrha Pradesh in India (Oblitas and others 1999). In such instances the new regime should consider a broader perspective for reform reasoning and design that takes many other issues, raised in its platform, into account.

Institutions and Reform

During both the design and the implementation stages of a reform, the institutions that govern the sector have to be accounted for cautiously. As

Bromley (chapter 2 in this volume) suggests, the water pricing and management reforms must be understood as part of the property regimes in which water users, water suppliers, and regulators are embedded. Existing bureaucracies have to be acknowledged and also engaged in the reform process, as has been the case in Brazil (Azevedo and Asad, chapter 15 in this volume). The various interest groups play a major role in both the design and the implementation stages of the reform.

The power system that comprises political parties, electoral systems, interest groups, and the dissemination of information has proven important in planning and implementing water pricing reforms. Tsur (chapter 5 in this volume) suggests that a social cost is associated with asymmetry of information that can affect power relations. As a result, a pricing reform can produce solutions that are suboptimal, that is, of a second-best type. Cueva and Lauria (chapter 8 in this volume) acknowledge such a possibility and offer a simulation to target possible difficulties and achieve third-best reform results. Rausser (chapter 3 in this volume) suggests that the objective function of the reform should account for the social cost of power as part of other transaction costs.

Another aspect of governance is the structure of the electoral system that provides support for or opposition to the proposed reform. The voting systems in water districts (McCann and Zilberman, chapter 4 in this volume) provide a good explanation for the differences in water pricing implementation levels.

Support for and Opposition to Reform

Because reforms change the status quo, one can expect both support for and opposition to reform agendas by various affected groups. As described in all the country case studies in this volume (see part 2), water pricing and institutional reforms generate active involvement by various interest groups that may be affected directly or indirectly. In some cases, as described by Hewitt (chapter 12 in this volume), the implementing agency may not have a reform agenda that coincides with that of the government which initiates the reform. Wambia (chapter 17 in this volume) analyzes instances in which certain agencies within the government that administer the reform may oppose it, because some reform outcomes may affect them.

Geographical characteristics (Bromley, chapter 2 in this volume), type of farm operation (McCann and Zilberman, chapter 4 in this volume), and farm size or wealth (Wambia, chapter 17 in this volume) can also determine reactions to water pricing reform.

An important explanation suggested by Israel (1987) for support for or opposition to a reform is the ability of each of the affected groups to comprehend the various reform components. Therefore, to increase public support, a carefully planned dialogue should be initiated prior to launching the reform.

The reform process frequently involves the creation of temporary coalitions by previously rival groups (Williamson 1994). In other cases, groups that support or oppose the reform early in the process change their positions later in the process (Dinar, Balakrishnan, and Wambia 1998; Haggard, Lafay, and Morrison 1995; Hall, chapter 9 in this volume; Stallings and Brock 1993).

Compensation

An important pillar of the reform agenda is the existence of a mechanism that addresses negative impacts of the reform on various sectors, or that allows a fair share of the reform outcome to be allocated to powerless groups. As Haggard and Webb (1996b), Krueger (1992), and Williamson (1994) have suggested, adequate compensation mechanisms are an important part of a reform. In the case of water pricing reforms, several sectors need more attention. Boland and Whittington, Strand, and Van Humbeeck (all in this volume) address the importance of adequate attention to the poor.

Postel (1999, pp. 235–36) describes a related aspect of compensating those affected by the water reform with regard to the pricing of irrigation water: "Actually, raising water prices, however, can be a politically high-wire act." She adds that "if water fees go to the national treasury rather than to a fund for maintaining that particular system, higher prices will not result in better service and so farmers will not support them. Many studies have shown that farmers are able and willing to pay more for their water, but only if deliveries become more reliable and service overall improves." The same is true also in the urban sector.

International Influence on the Reform Process

International influence may be critical in the reform design and implementation process. Such influence may take the form of pressure to comply with structure imposed by an international development institution as part of a large investment project. It can also take the form of incentives that come from regional cooperation through a trade agreement.

LOAN CONDITIONALITIES. These are common features in structural adjustment projects that enhance price reforms in various sectors (for example, agricultural pricing policies as described in Krueger, Schiff, and Valdes 1991). Other types of conditionalities can be found in big national water resource projects that include large components of institutional or pricing reforms, as was the case in Pakistan (Wambia, chapter 17 in this volume; World Bank 1996) and Mexico (Kemper and Olson, chapter 16 in this volume; World Bank 1997).

TRADE AND OTHER REGIONAL AGREEMENTS. Although not yet common or widely used in the water sector, several trade agreements that affect the agriculture sector may impose the restructuring of a price system in one country as part of a condition for that country to join the regional agreement. An example of such regional pressure is the recent initiative in Europe known as the European Water Framework Directive. This is the central legislative piece that will guide European water policies for the coming decade. Water pricing reforms, as part of that directive, are expected to follow common rules that the member countries agreed to.

Both global efficiency and the need for fair competition in the regional arena (Haggard and Webb 1996b) justify the use of regional external pressure to initiate price reforms in a country that might join a regional project.

Documented Experience from Other Sectors

The literature contains a rich set of studies that describe the political economy of institutional reforms in general (Azis 1994; Bromley 1989; Haggard, Lafay, and Morrisson 1995; Nelson 1992; Paul 1990; Rose-Ackerman 1997; Stallings and Brock 1993) and in the agriculture sector in particular (Bhalla 1991; Brandao and Carvalho 1991; Garcia 1991; Hamid, Nabi, and Nasim 1991; Nabi, Hamid, and Zahid 1986; Rose-Ackerman and Evenson 1985; Sturzenegger 1991). Few studies exist that address the political economy of reforms in the water sector. However, the available literature provides several leads about the affect of political pressures that can be used to introduce a number of hypotheses that are tested by evidence throughout this book.

Experience from reform implementation in other sectors suggests that political pressure may affect the successful implementation of water pricing reforms and create outcomes that vary considerably from the original objectives (Bokros and Dethier 1997; Krueger, Schiff, and Valdes 1991; Manor 1999; Nash and Takacs 1998; Patel 1998; van Zyl, Kirsten, and Binswanger 1996; Williamson 1994).

A few examples are provided here to justify the theoretical interpolation. Haggard, Lafay, and Morrisson (1995) describe the main issues of political feasibility of adjustment in developing countries. Their study addresses the broader issue of adjustment programs imposed on a country, including the involvement of international agencies and governments. Many of their find-ings, especially those associated with the tactics of reform implementation, the role of interest groups, and the behavior of the social groups, are relevant to the cases dealt with in this book. Stallings and Brock (1993) analyze the lessons that may be learned from the 1973–90 economic reforms in Chile. Referring to two reforms—trade liberalization and privatization—the au-thors found that in the case of trade reforms, the creation of coalitions that were opposed to the reforms could be expected. However, those who stood to lose from the reforms, and therefore had more reason to organize, had much less ability to do so. In the case of privatization, pressure for reform came from the government and from the business sector, whereas labor or-ganizations were not active in the process.

Finally, Sturzenegger (1991) describes agricultural price interventions in Argentina between 1960 and 1985, which may be a relevant example for water pricing reforms. Lobbying activities by interest groups on both sides of the issue of intervention took various forms, such as meeting with policymakers, conducting studies that supported the interest group's point of view, making monetary contributions to legislators, running public opin-ion campaigns, and directly participating in government. The author rec-ognized the relative advantages of various groups in organizing an effec-tive lobby, both in terms of the results and the associated costs of influencing the price intervention. The two interest groups—the agrarian lobby and the industrial lobby—differed in that respect. The industrial lobby was much more organized and efficient than the agriculture lobby.

One may generalize from this group of studies that reforms of any kind are likely to stir up either opposition or support among certain groups. The change in power of each affected group compared with the status quo, and the effect that the reform would have on the group's benefits, deter-mine the level of opposition or support. Reforms may create new coali-tions that were not previously in place, or even predicted. The ability of a group to influence the implementation of a reform is a function of many factors, and generalizing about the issue is difficult.

Williamson (1994) offers a framework to test preconditions for suc-cessful economic reforms. This approach is used here as a building block to the framework described earlier, and it is supported by a considerable number of studies.

Haggard and Webb (1996a) provide a rich set of case studies that confirm hypotheses for a general model to explain the politics of economic reforms. By reviewing various economic reforms (monetary and fiscal controls, and trade and exchange rate policies) in various countries, the authors develop a framework that allows them to evaluate the implementation of the reform.

This framework explains the outcome of a reform as a function of the interaction between politicians, bureaucrats, and interest groups.

Although reforms in the water sector are similar in many respects to reforms in other sectors, the water sector may have some unique characteristics and needs because of the highly political and cultural nature of water resources. This hypothesis is tested in this book.

The Structure of the Book

The book comprises two parts that attempt to explain the political economy of water pricing reforms. The three sections of part 1 provide the theoretical and empirical foundation to the approach of this book. Part 2 is a collection of five country case studies that individually and collectively attempt to support the framework and empirical evidence in part 1.

One thread that unites the chapters in part 1 (and, to a great extent, the country case studies in part 2) is the distinction between first-best, second-best, and third-best reform outcomes. Two major economic factors can impair the outcome of water pricing reforms: information deficiencies and the high transaction costs of necessary regulations. In such cases, reform outcomes may not achieve first-best efficiencies, but only second-best, or even third-best, if a solution must be achieved through a negotiation process.[1]

The chapters in section A of part 1 provide a theoretical framework that emphasizes the link between property regimes and pricing regimes, address the power and influence between and within water resource management organizations, and demonstrate the importance of asymmetric information for the implementation of efficient pricing reform.

Bromley, in chapter 2, argues that coherent pricing regimes for water resources must be understood as part of a larger concern for both the physical infrastructure of irrigation systems (channels, control structures, ditches) and the water that moves through those systems. Users are co-owners of both the infrastructure and the water. One of Bromley's messages is that sustainable pricing regimes should be based on the rule that all co-owners contribute to the integrity of the resource regime.

Rausser, in chapter 3, develops and applies two analytical frameworks: the Nash-Harsanyi and the Rausser-Simon multilateral bargaining models. These models allow the assessment and evaluation of processes that must take place to achieve sustainable reforms of water resource systems. Using the Rausser-Simon model, Rausser simulates various situations pertaining to California's

---

1. The suggestion to approach reform evaluation from this point of view came from one of the reviewers, and it is highly appreciated.

water sector and demonstrates the usefulness of a bargaining framework when full information is lacking. One of the most important issues to address regarding the political economy of water pricing reforms is that default options and admissible coalitions (which are able to implement a reform agenda) play critical roles, with stakeholder access to the collective decisionmaking process being one of the determinants of relative political power.

McCann and Zilberman, in chapter 4, develop a framework to explain the behavior of water districts (known in some parts of the world as water user associations), using the example of California agricultural water districts. Agricultural water districts have been identified as major obstacles to reforming the water sector in California. The chapter demonstrates how different governance structures are likely to influence the management of water resources. The authors suggest that the distribution of reform benefits may affect the success of the reform. Therefore, understanding how political power within the water district or water user association affects the distribution of benefits is a key element in the design of the reform.

Tsur, in chapter 5, investigates the effects of asymmetric information on efficient water pricing policies. Asymmetric information in the form of unobserved individual water intakes, or private information regarding water-yield relationship, affects efficiency and the implementation cost of pricing policies. Implementation costs alone change the performance of pricing regimes and hence may change their order of efficiency. The problem of unobserved water intake in itself might be overcome by output (or input) pricing. Asymmetric information regarding the water-crop response functions (the water-yield production function) requires the use of quantity-dependent (volumetric) water price functions to achieve efficiency. A combination of these factors requires the use of mechanism design theory to define efficient water allocation and to evaluate the efficient price schedule. Here again the author distinguishes between first-best and second-best pricing rules, and demonstrates how, by accounting for transaction costs, sometimes second-best rules may provide the same results as first-best rules.

Section B of part 1 demonstrates the applications of various political economy concepts in the evaluation of water pricing reforms. Main issues include the need to design the reform to account for the existing institutional and political setup; the advantage of either having a broad agenda for the reform or combining two reforms that address similar issues of economic efficiency, such as agricultural trade and water rights; the need to account for asymmetry of information through negotiation when dealing with private parties; and the need to account for the stochastic nature of the demand for and supply of water services so that compensation of less powerful, and often poor, parties can be assured.

Renzetti, in chapter 6, examines the structure of water users' preferences, as well as the structure of the cost of supply and the appropriate structure for prices. He incorporates these factors into management plans. Renzetti also argues that, because reforms are the result of public policy decisions, examining the political environment in which water pricing decisions are made is necessary.

Diao and Roe, in chapter 7, use an intertemporal general equilibrium model to analyze the far-ranging economic effects of the links between trade reform and water markets reform in Moroccan irrigated agriculture. The chapter focuses on the conflict between importers and domestic producers. The analysis finds a significant investment and growth response to the trade reform and a reallocation of resources to the production of fruit and vegetable crops, for which Morocco has a strong comparative advantage. The chapter shows that trade reform can actually create an opportunity for the introduction of water pricing reforms and suggests that creating a water user rights market not only partially compensates farmers for their losses in the era following trade reform, but also increases the efficiency of water allocation.

Cueva and Lauria, in chapter 8, apply a simulation model to analyze the results of a pricing reform that was pared back by political pressure and thus did not affect certain sectors. They challenge the use of deterministic models for water rate design, because such models do not take into account the stochastic nature of water supply and demand and do not indicate how much confidence can be placed in their results. An alternative approach, the Monte Carlo simulation, is used to address this problem. The chapter demonstrates the application of a deterministic net revenue model and its stochastic Monte Carlo simulation counterpart, which were developed and calibrated using data from a contingent valuation household survey from Dakar, Senegal. As was expected, the rate structure of the Monte Carlo simulation is both more economically stable and more politically acceptable, because it can account for irregularities in demand and supply and, therefore, better accommodate the needs of the poor.

Hall, in chapter 9, analyzes the political and economic aspects of the Los Angeles Blue Ribbon Committee for Water Rates reform following the 1986–91 drought in California. The chapter describes the standard microeconomic analysis of rate design for a natural monopoly; the process; and the political intrigue surrounding what happened, including the formative decisions of the committee. It highlights the important role of natural disasters in reaching the reform. The chapter employs public choice models (Peltzman type and Becker type) to help explain what occurred.

Section C of part 1 addresses various political economy issues of urban water pricing reforms. In addition to efficiency and financial issues, the chapters in section C address the equity and social preferences of various segments of society affected by the tariff structure. Three chapters in this section also discuss the political process that leads to the actual reform and the impact of the parties involved.

Boland and Whittington, in chapter 10, argue that decisions about tariff design require balancing multiple objectives, such as economic efficiency, equity, water conservation, management effectiveness, and financial sustainability. The chapter contends that, although increasing block tariff (IBT) designs is currently popular in developing countries, such designs fail to achieve the expected objectives, mainly because of asymmetry of information and political power regarding the first block of the tariff. In addition to reviewing the political obstacles and economic difficulties of implementing IBTs, the chapter concludes with a comparison of IBT and other tariff designs that combine volumetric charges with fixed payments. The latter designs, the authors claim, better achieve the objectives of economic efficiency, financial sustainability, equity, and water conservation, and they are also more politically transparent.

Strand, in chapter 11, explores water pricing policy options in Tegucigalpa, Honduras's capital, from a political economy perspective. Given that current water prices are too low and are significantly below long-run marginal cost, the chapter demonstrates that they must be raised significantly over the next ten years to balance projected demand and supplies. Because low water prices have a number of adverse allocation and distribution consequences, such a price reform will have political consequences as well. The chapter discusses the stakes that various groups (both internal and external) have in maintaining or changing the current water pricing regime, and suggests some mechanisms by which a more efficient and fairer price regime could be implemented.

Hewitt, in chapter 12, investigates utilities' choice of rate structures by looking at utility management decisions, particularly with respect to understanding the use of increasing block rates. This focus is due to the market mimicking nature of this rate structure. Two factors garner attention: the rationale (including the effects of weather) for water utilities to choose price discriminatory rates and utilities' reluctance to adopt rates that make revenue more variable. The analysis takes into consideration the effect of borrowing. The results demonstrate the rate structure that utilities may be expected to choose in the absence of government regulations or constraints imposed by lending agencies.

Finally, Van Humbeeck, in chapter 13, estimates the ex post impact of water and wastewater pricing reforms in the Flanders region in Belgium on various types of households. Political pressure brought about a reform in 1997 in which a social correction (accounting for family size) of the wastewater charge was replaced by a per person annual quantity of free drinking water for all households. The chapter analyzes the social welfare effects of the reform. Contrary to policymakers' expectations, findings suggest that the change increased the nominal purchasing power effects and made drinking water and wastewater services more expensive.

Part 2 of the book presents five country case studies. They should give the reader an impression of the complexity of water pricing reforms and of the types of policies that can succeed or fail.

Musgrave presents the case of Australia. His chapter reviews the ongoing, long-term water pricing reform in that country, examining the comprehensive reform agenda and summarizing reform efforts in the various states and territories. He performs a more detailed analysis in two particular instances. The first case, urban water pricing reform in the Hunter Water District, illustrates the value of a focused program of communication with the community to combat opposition to the implementation of a reform. The second case addresses the determination of bulk water prices in the state of New South Wales and the associated price reform. It provides a study of the problems (which can be overcome) in applying reform principles in a rigorously designed (yet publicly defensible), transparent, and consultative way.

In the second country case study, Azevedo and Asad review Brazil's experience. Brazil is on the verge of implementing wide-ranging water sector reforms, including the introduction of bulk water pricing at the national level. The case reviews the political process behind the development of the National Water Resources Management System and draws lessons from recent analytical work and practical experience in Brazil. The authors observe that the development of regulations and pricing mechanisms has been slow, sporadic, and poorly coordinated. They provide several reasons, including the political power structure, rigid institutions, recurring drought, information asymmetry, and a tradition of unrealistic water prices. They recommend the development of both water pricing and allocation policies, including establishing clear, gradual pricing objectives—cost recovery first, then economic efficiency—and creating conditions enabling water markets to evolve and facilitating the introduction of bulk water pricing throughout the country.

Kemper and Olson compare the reform process in Mexico and the state of Ceará in Northeast Brazil. Using an institutional economics perspective, they analyze the governments' experiences in implementing water resources management programs. The analysis emphasizes the rationale for the new water policies, summarizes the policies and the implementation process, and analyzes the outcomes. Although the reform in Mexico was at a national level, entailing complications stemming from the federal structure of that country, the Mexican case is similar in several respects to the state-level reform in Ceará. In both cases, the reforms seem to have been triggered by a government commitment to link water management to its economic agenda. In addition, the reforms linked changes in the overall water resources management framework with water pricing.

In the fourth country case, Wambia discusses the introduction of wide-ranging institutional reforms in the water sector in Pakistan under the recently approved National Drainage Program Project of the World Bank. The introduction of institutional reforms in Pakistan's irrigation and drainage system is instructive. This is because the nation's social structure includes unique land tenure characteristics and a range of stakeholders with varying roles in the reform process; its irrigation system is also the biggest in the world. In addition, the government's approach to the institutional reform process has been simultaneously comprehensive, gradual, and radical. Because of all these factors, a gradual approach involving negotiations with the affected parties may succeed in implementing a sound reform, although risks from opposition to the reform have proved to be high.

The Republic of Yemen case study by Ward traces how a weak government was able to subsidize both groundwater and surface irrigation heavily for 20 years. The government relied on the manipulation of the price of diesel, credit, and other agricultural input prices, and on the support of donors interested in helping with the rapid development of Yemen's water resources. The economic and fiscal crisis of the 1990s and the exploitation of groundwater resources have created pressure to reform the water sector. This has led to a structural adjustment that raises fuel prices and reduces government subsidies for various inputs. Thus, efficiency improvements will be necessary to keep irrigators' incomes stable, but as water prices increase the government is losing a way to provide patronage to powerful constituencies, thereby creating a political risk. The chapter examines the ramifications of these trends and the way in which irrigation water pricing has been determined by a delicate balance between the interests of farmers, politically powerful groups, and donors.

Conditions for Successful Reforms

The political economy literature surveyed in this chapter suggests a core of conditions necessary for successful economic reforms. While the successful outcome of a reform is not defined in comparative terms, the reform process and the variables that affect it are better understood. Theory suggests (for example, Haggard and Webb 1996b; Krueger 1992; Williamson 1994; and many others cited in the chapter) several factors that have to be in place to ensure a successful reform outcome.

According to Cordova (1994, p. 277): "A reform program will be successful if there is economic rationality in its design, political sensitivity in its implementation, and close and constant attention to political-economic interactions and social-institutional factors, so as to determine in each case the dynamics to follow." Many of this book's chapters support Cordova's statement.

The timing of a reform is also important. Two hypotheses (Williamson 1994)—the crisis hypothesis and the honeymoon hypothesis—are offered to account for the time factor in the reform implementation process. The crisis hypothesis suggests that public perception of a crisis is needed to create conditions under which it is politically possible to undertake the reform. The honeymoon hypothesis suggests that it is easier to implement a reform immediately after a government takes office. Both hypotheses were proven to be valid, depending on the particular country case study.

The recommendation for an implementation method (swift as opposed to gradual) is less clear in the literature. However, some of the studies in Williamson (1994) suggest a relationship between a country's political style and the pace of its reform implementation. Whereas strong regimes or dictatorships may be able to implement swift reforms, Williamson suggests that weaker regimes or democratic regimes use a gradual approach amended by a series of supportive and compensatory programs. The set of studies in this book does not include sufficient information to conclude which implementation method is preferable.

In many cases, water pricing reforms have been implemented on a subsectoral basis, for example, reforming only the irrigation subsector and leaving urban and industrial sectors unchanged. However, as Bromley (chapter 2), Diao and Roe (chapter 7), and others in this volume suggest, water pricing reforms that are designed and implemented in a comprehensive manner have a greater likelihood of succeeding. Because the irrigation sector in many countries accounts for both large volumes of the available water and a substantial share of employment or gross domestic product, reforming the irrigation subsector in isolation from the rest of the economy may be unsustainable.

Williamson and Haggard (1994) suggest additional factors to help implement successful reforms. These include the commitment of a strong government; the creation of an independent, dedicated, and professional reform implementation team; the use of the media to convey the reform messages; the use of alternative policy measures to allow for sustainable reform consequences; an efficient reform program leading to low transition costs; the implementation of safety nets for the poor and those who were ignored; and the introduction of compensation packages to those who may be hurt by the new policies.

The book attempts to examine the validity of these hypotheses. Table 1.2 summarizes the major reform factors highlighted in each chapter. All chapters address most of the following factors: institutions, fairness and equity, power, asymmetry of information, transaction costs, wide reform agenda, distribution of benefits, participation and education, coalitions, crisis, and compensation.

What Have We Learned and What Still Has to Be Done?

Can we predict the outcomes of water pricing reforms? Is a well-planned reform more likely than a less-planned one to succeed? Is the extent of the reform a good predictor for the likelihood that it will achieve its objectives? Crisp and Kelly (1999), using analyses of structural adjustment reforms in 16 Latin American countries, show that multiobjective reforms, even if thoroughly implemented, sometimes fell short of key objectives. Is the water sector different?

The evidence presented in this book suggests that the water sector is no different from other sectors when it comes to implementing reforms. Although water has several characteristics that make it different from other commodities, water pricing reforms are affected by the same factors as reforms in other sectors. However, some factors, such as the power of ownership effect, may have a larger impact on the water sector than on other sectors.

The analyses in this book are intended to add to the volume of knowledge of reforms in other sectors. Therefore, the lessons in this book are summarized in a set of recommendations that, although written in water sector terms, can be generalized to other sectors.

Water pricing reforms should be launched after extensive public awareness campaigns. Reformers should communicate a clear economic rationale, develop a broad reform agenda, adjust to institutional and political reality, and take account of traditional customs and social structures. Successful reform programs must include compensation mechanisms negotiated with stakeholders. Reformers should precisely identify their objectives. Reforms should be well prepared, because once they are implemented, they are hard to modify.

TABLE 1.2
Main Reforms Analyzed in the Chapters

Author (chapter number)	Institutions	Fairness and equity	Power	Asymmetry of information	Transaction costs	Wide reform agenda	Distribution of benefits	Participation and education	Coalitions	Crisis	Compensation	i-best efficiency[a]
Bromley (2)	•	•	•		•	•					•	1,2
Rausser (3)	•		•		•							2,3
McCann and Zilberman (4)			•									2,3
Tsur (5)	•			•	•		•					2
Renzetti (6)	•			•		•	•		•			1,2
Diao and Roe (7)		•		•	•		•	•			•	1,2,3
Cueva and Lauria (8)		•	•	•	•		•				•	2
Hall (9)		•	•				•	•	•	•	•	1,2,3
Boland and Whittington (10)			•				•				•	1,2
Strand (11)	•	•	•	•	•		•		•		•	2,3
Hewitt (12)	•	•	•	•	•		•		•			1,2
Van Humbeeck (13)		•		•	•		•				•	2
Musgrave (14)	•	•	•	•	•	•	•	•	•	[b]	•	1,2,3

(table continues on following page)

Table 1.2 continues

Author (chapter number)	Institutions	Fairness and equity	Power	Asymmetry of information	Transaction costs	Wide reform agenda	Distribution of benefits	Participation and education	Coalitions	Crisis	Compensation	i-best efficiency[a]
Azevedo and Asad (15)	•		•	•		•		•				2,3
Kemper and Olson (16)	•		•	•	•	•		•	•			2,3
Wambia (17)	•	•	•	•	•	•	•	•	•	•	•	3
Ward (18)	•	•	•	•		•	•	•	•	•		2,3

a. First-best, second-best, and third-best efficient outcomes from reforms.

b. Although not mentioned, drought events have been always a factor in reform pressures in Australia (see figure 14.1).

Source: Author.

The implementing agency must be sensitive to political events when putting the reforms in place. The agency should package and sequence the reform components to minimize opposition. It should be aware of other political events, such as elections; seek external support; and mobilize supportive stakeholders as much as possible.

Additional recommendations culled from several book chapters include the following:

1. Gains from reforms have to be shared.
2. Pricing reforms should acknowledge asymmetric upstream-downstream externalities, as well as the differences between water sources (groundwater and surface water).
3. Reformers should acknowledge the need for a set of institutions and not impose a generic process for reform implementation.
4. The social objective function should include the power and transaction costs associated with reform implementation.

What is still required in the way of additional development in the field of political economy of water pricing reforms? The work in this book clearly suggests a need for more research into the following issues.

First, collecting more data about ongoing water pricing reforms, especially in the form of case studies, is extremely important. The case studies should follow a given structure to allow analysis and comparison. Second, research should focus on several theoretical issues, including (a) defining and measuring the extent of water reforms; (b) defining and measuring reform objective achievements; and (c) defining status quo conditions and their impact on reform implementation, such as institutional setup, power structure, and physical conditions.

With the variety of pricing and other water-related reforms under way, the research agenda will fill up easily and produce much-needed knowledge.

References

Ahmad, Mahmood. 1998. "Water Pricing and Markets in the Near East: Policy Issues and Options." Paper presented at the World Bank–sponsored Workshop on the Political Economy of Water Pricing Implementation, November 3–5, Washington, D.C.

Alesina, Alberto. 1996. "Political Models for Macroeconomic Policy and Fiscal Reforms." In Stephen Haggard and Steven B. Webb, eds., *Voting for Reform*. New York: Oxford University Press.

Asad, Musa, Gabriel Azevedo, Karin Kemper, and Larry Simpson. 1999. *Management of Water Resources: Bulk Water Pricing in Brazil*. Technical Paper no. 432.Washington, D.C.: World Bank.

Azis, Iwan J. 1994. "Indonesia." In John Williamson, ed., *The Political Economy of Policy Reform*. Washington, D.C.: Institute for International Economics.

Bhalla, Surjit. 1991. "Sri Lanka." In Anne O. Krueger, Maurice Schiff, and Alberto Valdes, eds., *The Political Economy of Agricultural Pricing Policy*. Vol. 2: *Asia*. Baltimore, Maryland: The Johns Hopkins University Press.

Bokros, Lajos, and Jean-Jacques Dethier, eds. 1997. *Public Finance Reform during the Transition: The Experience of Hungary*. Washington, D.C.: World Bank.

Brandao, Antonio Salazar P., and Jose L. Carvalho. 1991. "Brazil." In Anne O. Krueger, Maurice Schiff, and Alberto Valdes, eds., *The Political Economy of Agricultural Pricing Policy*. Vol. 1: *Latin America*. Baltimore, Maryland: The Johns Hopkins University Press.

Bromley, Daniel W. 1989. "Institutional Change and Economic Efficiency." *Journal of Economic Issues* 23(3): 735–59.

Cordova, José. 1994. "Mexico." In John Williamson, ed., *The Political Economy of Policy Reform*. Washington, D.C.: Institute for International Economics.

Crisp, Brian F., and Michael J. Kelly. 1999. "The Socioeconomic Impacts of Structural Adjustments." *International Studies Quarterly* 43(3): 533–52.

Dinar, Ariel, and Ashok Subramanian. 1997. "Water Pricing Experience: An International Perspective." Technical Paper no. 386. Washington, D.C.: World Bank.

Dinar, Ariel, and Aaron Wolf. 1997. "Economic and Political Considerations in Regional Cooperation Models." *Agricultural and Resource Economics Review* 26(1): 7–22.

Dinar, Ariel, Trichur K. Balakrishnan, and Joseph M. Wambia. 1998. "Political Economy and Political Risks of Institutional Reforms in the Water Sector." Policy Research Paper no. 1987. World Bank, Policy Research Department, Washington, D.C.

Garcia, Jorge Garcia. 1991. "Colombia." In Anne O. Krueger, Maurice Schiff, and Alberto Valdes, eds., *The Political Economy of Agricultural Pricing Policy*. Vol. 1: *Latin America*. Baltimore, Maryland: The Johns Hopkins University Press.

Government of India, Planning Commission. 1994. *Report of the Committee on Pricing of Irrigation Water. Indian Journal of Agricultural Economics* 49(1): 107–133.

Haggard, Stephan, Jean-Dominique Lafay, and Christian Morrisson. 1995. "The Political Feasibility of Adjustment in Developing Countries." In Christian Morrisson, ed., *Political Feasibility of Adjustment*. Paris: Organisation for Economic Co-operation and Development, Development Centre.

Haggard, Stephan, and Steven B. Webb, eds. 1996a. *Voting for Reform*. New York: Oxford University Press.

_____. 1996b. "Introduction." In *Voting for Reform*. New York: Oxford University Press.

Hamid, Naved, Ijaz Nabi, and Anjum Nasim. 1991. "Pakistan." In Anne O. Krueger, Maurice Schiff, and Alberto Valdes, eds., *The Political Economy of Agricultural Pricing Policy*. Vol. 2: *Asia*. Baltimore, Maryland: The Johns Hopkins University Press.

Israel, Arturo. 1987. *Institutional Development: Incentives to Performance*. Baltimore, Maryland: The John Hopkins University Press.

Jones, Tom. 1998. "Recent Developments in the Pricing of Water Services in OECD Countries." *Water Policy* 1(6): 637–51.

Krueger, Anne O. 1992. *The Political Economy of Agricultural Pricing Policy*. Vol. 5: *A Synthesis of the Political Economy in Developing Countries*. Baltimore, Maryland: The Johns Hopkins University Press.

Krueger, Anne O., Maurice Schiff, and Alberto Valdes, eds. 1991. *The Political Economy of Agricultural Pricing Policy*, Vols. 1–4. Baltimore, Maryland: The Johns Hopkins University Press.

Manor, James. 1999. *The Political Economy of Democratic Decentralization: Directions in Development*. Washington, D.C.: World Bank.

Nabi, Ijaz, Naved Hamid, and Shahid Zahid. 1986. *The Agrarian Economy of Pakistan Issues and Policies*. Karachi: Oxford University Press.

Nash, John, and Wendy Takacs, eds. 1998. *Trade Policy Reform*. Washington, D.C.: World Bank.

Nelson, Joan M. 1992. "Poverty, Equity, and the Politics of Adjustment." In Stephen Haggard and Robert R. Kaufman, eds., *The Politics of Economic Adjustment*. Princeton, New Jersey: Princeton University Press.

Oblitas, Keith, and J. Raymond Peter, in association with Gautam Pingle, Halla M. Qaddumi, and Jayantha Perera. 1999. *Transferring Irrigation Management to Farmers in Andhra Pradesh, India*. Technical Paper no. 449. Washington, D.C.: World Bank.

OECD (Organisation for Economic Co-operation and Development). 1998a. "Agricultural Water Pricing Practices in OECD Countries." Document 66119. Group on Economic and Environment Policy Integration, Environment Directorate, Paris.

_____. 1998b. "Pricing of Water Services in OECD Countries: Synthesis Report." Document 69368. Group on Economic and Environment Policy Integration, Environment Directorate, Paris.

_____. 1999. "The Price of Water: Trends in OECD Countries." Paris.

Patel, I. G. 1998. *Economic Reform and Global Change*. New Delhi: Macmillan India.

Paul, Samuel. 1990. "Institutional Reforms in Sector Adjustment Operations - The World Bank's Experience." Discussion Papers Series no. 92. World Bank, Washington, D.C..

Postel, Sandra. 1999. *Pillar of Sand: Can the Irrigation Miracle Last?* New York: W. W. Norton & Company.

Rose-Ackerman, Susan. 1997. "Corruption and Development." Paper presented at the World Bank Annual Conference on Development Economics, April 30–May 1, Washington, D.C.

Rose-Ackerman, Susan, and Robert E. Evenson. 1985. "The Political Economy of Agricultural Research and Extension: Grants, Votes, and Reappointment." *American Journal of Agricultural Economics* 67: 1–14.

Savedoff, William, and Pablo Spiller. 1999. *Spilled Water: Institutional Commitment in the Provision of Water Services.* Washington, D.C.: Inter-American Development Bank.

Shubik, Martin. 1982. *Game Theory in the Social Sciences: Concepts and Solutions.* Cambridge, Massachusetts: The MIT Press.

Stallings, Barbara, and Philip Brock. 1993. "The Political Economy of Economic Adjustment: Chile 1973–1990." In Robert H. Bates and Anne O. Krueger, eds., *Political and Economic Interactions in Economic Policy Reform.* Cambridge, U.K.: Blackwell.

Sturzenegger, Adolfo C. 1991. "Argentina." In Anne O. Krueger, Maurice Schiff, and Alberto Valdes, eds., *The Political Economy of Agricultural Pricing Policy.* Vol. 1: *Latin America.* Baltimore, Maryland: The Johns Hopkins University Press.

van Zyl, Johan, Johann Kirsten, and Hans P. Binswanger, eds. 1996. *Agricultural Land Reform in South Africa.* Cape Town, South Africa: Oxford University Press.

White, Louise G. 1990. *Implementing Policy Reforms in LDCs: A Strategy for Designing and Effecting Change.* Boulder, Colorado: Lynne Rienner Publishers.

Williamson, John, ed. 1994. *The Political Economy of Policy Reform.* Washington, D.C.: Institute for International Economics.

Williamson, John, and Stephan Haggard. 1994. "The Political Conditions for Economic Reform." In John Williamson, ed., *The Political Economy of Policy Reform.* Washington, D.C.: Institute for International Economics.

World Bank. 1996. *Pakistan National Drainage Program Project.* Staff Appraisal Report no. 15310-PAK. South Asia Region, Country Department 1, Agricultural and Natural Resources Division, Washington, D.C.

_____. 1997. "Mexico Staff Appraisal Report: Water Resources Management Project." Latin American and the Caribbean Region, Country Department II, Natural Resources and Rural Poverty Division, Washington, D.C.

PART I

Theory and Empirical Applications

SECTION A

Political Economy Frameworks and Water Reforms

2

Property Regimes and Pricing Regimes in Water Resource Management

Daniel W. Bromley

The issues to be addressed in this chapter concern the relationship between property regimes and pricing regimes in managing water resources in agriculture. The chapter first discusses the water management problem in surface and groundwater systems and then turns to a discussion of property regimes in irrigation. This permits consideration of a pricing regime for improved water management. The chapter closes with an illustration of the water management problems in two villages in Gujarat state in western India.

Surface Irrigation

Consider an irrigation system in which a number of farmers extract water from a common distribution channel. The water management problem in surface systems is exacerbated by the fact that only the first farmer on the system is immune from the predatory water appropriation of the other N-1 farmers. All others have at least one upstream water appropriator, and usually several. A surface irrigation system epitomizes asymmetric externalities among independent economic actors. Consider an irrigation system that consists of only four farms, all of which sell their identical product (y_i) for the same price (p). If we invoke the simplifying assumption that crop yields are a direct function of water availability, we can write the four farmers' maximization problem as:

$$(2.1) \qquad \pi_1 = \max_{y_1} py_1 - d(y_1)$$

I am grateful to Ariel Dinar and R. Maria Saleth for helpful comments on an earlier version.

(2.2) $\pi_2 = \max_{y_2} py_2 - e(y_2, y_1)$

(2.3) $\pi_3 = \max_{y_3} py_3 - f(y_3, y_2, y_1)$

(2.4) $\pi_4 = \max_{y_4} py_4 - g(y_4, y_3, y_2, y_1)$

where the functions $d, e, f,$ and g are the costs of production for each farmer. We see that production costs for all farmers downstream from the first farmer are a function of the water use of upstream farmers. The greater the water expropriation from the common channel by upstream farmers (and hence the greater their production), the more downstream farmers will suffer. We might also consider the distributional aspects of this problem: production by upstream farms is to the detriment of production by downstream farms.[1] The solution to this independent (anarchic) production regime is given by:

(2.5) $\dfrac{\partial d(y_1)}{\partial y_1} = \dfrac{\partial e(y_2, y_1)}{\partial y_2} = \dfrac{\partial f(y_3, y_2, y_1)}{\partial y_3} = \dfrac{\partial g(y_4, y_3, y_2, y_1)}{\partial y_4} = p.$

All farmers along the system equate their private marginal costs with the product price, but farmers 2, 3, and 4 face the likelihood that they will suffer from reduced water availability. In a poorly managed system, for the farmer at the tail end to be unable to produce a crop because of a lack of water is not unusual.

Consider now the situation if all four farms were under one management system. In that case, the sole owner would face the following maximization problem:

(2.6) $\pi_{1+2+3+4} = \max_{y_1, y_2, y_3, y_4} p \cdot (y_1 + y_2 + y_3 + y_4) - d(y_1) - e(y_2, y_1) - f(y_3, y_2, y_1) - g(y_4, y_3, y_2, y_1).$

First-order conditions for the unified firm and its four subunits become

(2.7)   Farm 1: $\dfrac{\partial d(y_1)}{\partial y_1} + \dfrac{\partial e(y_2, y_1)}{\partial y_1} + \dfrac{\partial f(y_3, y_2, y_1)}{\partial y_1} + \dfrac{\partial g(y_4, y_3, y_2, y_1)}{\partial y_1} = p$

(2.8)   Farm 2: $\dfrac{\partial e(y_2, y_1)}{\partial y_2} + \dfrac{\partial f(y_3, y_2, y_1)}{\partial y_3} + \dfrac{\partial g(y_4, y_3, y_2, y_1)}{\partial y_2} = p$

---

1. Ostrom and Gardner (1993) present a bargaining game in which upstream and downstream farmers negotiate labor contributions to the system until the marginal product of labor at each end of the system equals its opportunity cost. In this model, the amount of water coming into the system each season is a function of the total labor supplied by the irrigators. The authors also discuss a family of rotation rules to overcome the asymmetric externalities discussed here.

(2.9)   Farm 3: $\dfrac{\partial f(y_3, y_2, y_1)}{\partial y_3} + \dfrac{\partial g(y_4, y_3, y_2, y_1)}{\partial y_3} = p$

(2.10)   Farm 4: $\dfrac{\partial g(y_4, y_3, y_2, y_1)}{\partial y_4} = p.$

System optimality requires that the three upstream farmers must be made to bear the costs of their imposition of marginal social costs on the downstream farms. The potential marginal social costs of farm i's behavior is given by

(2.11)   Farm 1: $\dfrac{\partial e(y_2, y_1)}{\partial y_1} + \dfrac{\partial f(y_3, y_2, y_1)}{\partial y_1} + \dfrac{\partial g(y_4, y_3, y_2, y_1)}{\partial y_1}$

(2.12)   Farm 2: $\dfrac{\partial f(y_3, y_2, y_1)}{\partial y_3} + \dfrac{\partial g(y_4, y_3, y_2, y_1)}{\partial y_2}$

(2.13)   Farm 3: $\dfrac{\partial g(y_4, y_3, y_2, y_1)}{\partial y_3}.$

Only farm 4 does not have any potential marginal social cost of its behavior, because there are no downstream farms on which it can impose costs because of its water-taking practices.

The above analysis can be generalized to n farms on an irrigation system in which all farms (excluding the one at the head of the system) are exposed to unwanted marginal costs by $N-1$ upstream farms. The apparent solution to such systemic externalities is to develop a management regime in which farmers have no incentive to take water that is not properly theirs; to do so would be to visit costs on downstream farmers. Equations 2.11 to 2.13 suggest a taxing regime in which water prices are set in an irrigation system to preclude the existence of external costs down through the system. In practical terms this could mean that there are $N-1$ water prices in a system, one for each farmer along the distribution system. Only with perfect compliance—the complete absence of external effects—would there be one price for water. The ideal system would thus permit a single price for water that achieves first-best outcomes.

While a useful heuristic, we should not underestimate the transaction costs (for example, information, contracting, and enforcement costs) associated with a system of water prices that would internalize the externalities in irrigation systems. Moreover, even if we managed to design irrigation systems in which the marginal social costs of water appropriation were fully internalized, the water pricing regime would not solve the related problem of system maintenance. Upstream farmers have the opportunity to shift costs onto downstream farmers by shirking on system maintenance. After all, once they have their water, why should they bother to make sure that the system is effective in delivering water to those farther downstream? This suggests that farmers' willingness to contribute to the maintenance of the delivery system increases as they move down the system.

The pricing problem in surface irrigation systems thus has two components: (a) to encourage efficient water use along the system, and (b) to encourage a regime of system maintenance that minimizes water loss as it moves down the system.

Groundwater Irrigation

The groundwater problem differs from the surface water problem in several important respects. First, groundwater does not show up at a farmer's intake from a collectively maintained distribution system. Rather, the farmer must invest in pumping to gain access to it. Second, unlike surface water that comes in a somewhat known quantity during each growing season, groundwater is a stock resource that is held in storage until it is extracted. Third, groundwater not used for one season is, for the most part, available for use during the next season. Fourth, unlike surface water, whose use, and therefore subtraction from the seasonal total, is easily monitored, groundwater use is difficult to monitor. Fifth, while externalities in surface water use are transmitted down the sequence of recipients along the channel, externalities in groundwater tend to be reciprocal.

In considering the groundwater problem, we borrow from a model developed by Provencher (1995). In this formulation, an optimal control problem is set up by letting the ith farm's net revenue from water use be written as:

(2.14) $\pi_i(q_{it} + s_{it}) - c(x_{it}) \cdot q_{it}, \; i = 1,\ldots, N$

where π_i is water-dependent revenue from a crop y; q_{it} is the water pumped (and used on crop y); s_{it} is the surface water used on crop y by the ith firm; and x_{it} is a parameter that indicates the condition of the aquifer, such as the depth-to-water table, which affects pumping cost per unit of water, $c(x_{it})$. If we preclude surface water from consideration, then equation 2.14 can be rewritten as:

(2.15) $\pi_i q_{it} - c(x_{it}) \cdot q_{it}.$

Let $v(x_t)$ be each farm's present value of net revenue from groundwater use given an infinite planning horizon and optimal current and future extraction from the aquifer. In the optimal control problem, $v(\cdot)$ is the value function where r is the recharge of the aquifer.

(2.16) $v(x_{t+1}) \equiv v(x_t - Mq_t + r)$.

Therefore, the water manager's problem is

(2.17) $Nv(x_t) = \max_{q_t} N[\pi q_t - c(x_t) \cdot q_t + \gamma v(x_t - Nq_t + r)]$

where γ is the discount factor. The solution to this problem must satisfy the necessary condition

(2.18) $\dfrac{\partial \pi}{\partial w} q_t - c(x_t) = \gamma N \dfrac{\partial v}{\partial x} x_{t+1}$.

We see that $\partial \pi / \partial w$ is the change in net revenue with respect to water use (marginal revenue), and $\partial v / \partial x$ is the marginal value of the stock of groundwater. The right-hand side of equation 2.18 is the social marginal user cost of pumping at x_{t+1}. That is, pumping a unit of water now by any farm reduces the present valued net revenue of all N farms by increasing the future costs of pumping.

Anarchy at the pump set—as opposed to along the distribution channel—finds each firm unconcerned with user cost. Therefore, the solution to equation 2.18 becomes

(2.19) $\dfrac{\partial \pi}{\partial w} q_t - c(x_t) = 0$

In this formulation, individual farmers are oblivious of the user costs to other farms as well as to themselves. In technical terms, a state equation is missing from the farmer's maximization problem (Provencher 1995). The problem for groundwater extraction is not materially different from the problem along a distribution channel, although with groundwater the externalities are reciprocal, whereas for surface water the externalities cascade down the distribution system. Of course when farmers on an irrigation system also pump groundwater, the potential for externalities is multiplied. In that case, we would reintroduce the "s" in equation 2.15.

In groundwater systems we find relatively wealthy farmers using pump sets so that they are not dependent on an unreliable irrigation system. For upstream farmers, the unreliability problem tends to consist of water deliveries to the system as a whole (say from government canals), whereas for downstream farmers it consists of both water deliveries and the predatory behavior of upstream farmers. Governments have a tendency to undertake precisely the wrong approach to these reliability problems. Rather than improving the reliability of surface irrigation systems, governments tend to give subsidies to farmers (both rich and poor) to buy pump sets so that they are not dependent on unreliable irrigation systems. Once pump sets invade a surface system, each farmer has a reduced incentive to make the surface system work better. With this proliferation of pump sets, the externalities in the surface system are simply shifted underground as water access is "privatized" by pumping. Yet the full costs of pumping are not at all private but are clearly collective—and reciprocal—in character.

The pressing question for water management policy concerns whether officials can devise a feasible pricing regime to bring efficiency to surface and groundwater irrigation systems. Before addressing that, we must first take up the issue of property regimes in surface and groundwater systems.

Property Regimes in Surface and Groundwater Management

Irrigation water in developing countries is used under a variety of property regimes. Often groundwater is the property of the state, at least in name if not in practice. In such cases, governments have declared ownership of an asset over which they often have no capacity to exercise judicious management. Because of this lack of management authority, groundwater becomes an open access resource and anarchy prevails. In some countries, ownership of land bestows title to subsurface water. However, given the externalities in groundwater extraction, this apparent private property right is an illusion and the groundwater remains an open access resource. The possible ownership regimes of water are shown in table 2.1.

The essence of a surface water system is that upstream irrigators are free to disregard the interests of those downstream (equations 2.1 to 2.4). In groundwater systems, each extractor is free to disregard the interests of others who pump from the same aquifer (equation 2.19). The individualization of groundwater appropriation from the central source is made possible by the advent of low-cost technology that is amenable to individualization. To understand this, imagine that water pumping technology were of such a scale (and cost) that a large group of farmers needed to pool their resources to acquire it.[2] In fact, we see this at work in surface irrigation systems. The technology of surface water distribution locks together a group of farmers in a system of mutual (though asymmetric) interdependence. If each farmer, regardless of location, could obtain irrigation water from a main canal without any cost, then the externalities that characterize surface irrigation would disappear, though they may well shift to the main canal.

So a government-provided distribution system becomes the indivisible pumping technology that brings water to each farmer. In doing so, it locks

---

2. Rather like a plow gang in medieval times.

TABLE 2.1
Classification of Property Regimes

Type of regime	Implications
State property	Individuals have a duty to observe use and access rules determined by the controlling (or management) agency of the state. The agency has a right to determine these access and use rules.
Private property	Individuals have a right to undertake socially acceptable uses and a duty to refrain from socially unacceptable uses. Others (nonowners) have a duty to allow socially acceptable uses and a right to expect that only socially acceptable uses will occur.
Common property	The management group (the owners) has a right to exclude nonmembers (a right sanctioned and supported by the same authority structure pertinent to private property), and nonmembers have a duty to abide by the exclusion. Individual members of the management group (the co-owners) have both rights and duties with respect to use rates and maintenance of the thing owned.
Nonproperty	There is no defined group of users or owners and the benefit stream is available to anyone. Individuals have both privilege (the ability to act without regard to the interest of others) and no right (the incapacity to affect the actions of others) with respect to use rates and maintenance of the asset. The asset is an open access resource.

Source: Bromley (1991).

together the farmers in a set of reciprocal relations that we find in common property regimes. That is, the farmers in the group have a right to exclude others from getting "their" water. That right is sanctioned and supported by the irrigation authority and the national government, and outsiders have a duty to abide by it. Individual members of the irrigation system have both rights and duties with respect to use rates and maintenance of the system. In essence, the individual irrigators stand united against outsiders, but they are bound together by the reciprocal obligations and expectations of the technological imperative that brings them the water they all need.

Of course, it need not be this way. Why, after all, should we worry about downstream farmers on an irrigation system experiencing unreliable water delivery? Why is it inappropriate that upstream farmers take as much water as they wish? After all, ensuring secure and equitable water deliveries throughout an irrigation system entails nontrivial transaction costs. Would it not be more efficient to allow for the survival of the fittest?

The answer to these questions arises from a recognition that competition on an irrigation system is different from other forms of acceptable economic competition. This is because the playing field is not level: farmers at or near the head of a system have an unfair competitive advantage over those who are downstream. Therefore, water allocation policy is driven by the desire to make sure that competitive behavior among farmers occurs in a domain in which all have an equal chance of success. Equitable water allocation within a system gives each farmer an equal chance to excel at growing crops, not at figuring out how to take as much water as possible from the neighbors. But efficiency issues arise as well. The assumptions of pure competition require that factors of production be mobile and available to all at the same price. If a few irrigators at the head of the system are able to monopolize water deliveries, then this factor of production ceases to be available to all members of the system at the same price.

What about groundwater systems? Why should we worry that those farmers able to purchase the biggest pumps and drill deeper will take the bulk of the groundwater and thus eventually destroy those farmers with less powerful pumping technology? We do not regulate the technology of harvesting, so why should we worry about the technology of pumping? One reason is that in systems that involve the conjunctive use of groundwater and surface water, groundwater is a complementary input to surface water and the same competitive ideas apply as if the system were exclusively reliant on surface water. That is, success as a farmer should not be predicated upon success in being able to take more water than one's neighbors.

If we are considering irrigation based exclusively on groundwater, then a multiplicity of extractors can serve as a source of essential information that is useful in monitoring total extractions. That is, if one individual does all the pumping from an aquifer, then that individual has an incentive to conceal total pumping. That individual's incentive structure is dominated by his or her own preferences. Despite the fanciful notion that a single owner will use a natural resource wisely and in the interest of sustainability, the iron law of the discount rate tells us that if the individual's rate of time preference exceeds the recharge rate of the aquifer, its destruction will be optimal from the individual's point of view. By contrast, if many farmers are pumping from an aquifer, a number of whom are situated over deep or shallow portions of the aquifer, these multiple extractors can be a valuable source of information about the management of the aquifer. Clearly each farmer, while having an interest in pumping, also has an interest in making sure that he or she is not put out of business by the pumping of others. Whereas individuals are inclined to ignore the costs of their behavior on others, they are not inclined to ignore the costs of others' behavior on them. Therefore a community of water extractors can actually become a community of water guardians. The challenge is to figure out how to instill that response.

Toward Solving Anarchy in Water Management

Let us now turn to the problem of trying to solve the anarchy that characterizes surface and groundwater irrigation systems. It is from this premise that pricing is addressed in water management. The usual starting point when we discuss water pricing is to make sure that water is used efficiently in agriculture, and that its use in agriculture in relation to other uses is optimal. That is, water pricing can be thought of as a way to ensure that irrigation water is efficiently allocated across all possible uses, as well as across regions, irrigation systems, farmers, soil conditions, and crops. Indeed, most models of optimal pricing regimes tend to see water pricing as a critical factor in assuring that irrigation water, along with other inputs, is optimally utilized on individual farms as well as throughout an irrigation system. When that occurs, all inputs will be efficiently combined to grow the optimal crops in the optimal proportions given the system's managerial attributes. This approach sees water management as an agricultural problem, and it seeks to make sure that the mix of water use in agriculture and competing demands is efficient. The argument will be advanced that because water is underpriced in agriculture—and it surely is in most settings—getting its price right would induce efficiency throughout a nation's (or at least a region's) water sector.

This chapter will contend that such an approach to water pricing, although desirable, expects a great deal of any water pricing system, particularly in the developing world.[3] Recognizing this difficulty, I will propose a somewhat more modest goal for water pricing regimes in developing countries. In particular, I will suggest that the purpose of a water pricing regime should be to ensure that water allocation within an irrigation system (or a community of irrigators) is optimal with respect to the efficient operation of the system as a domain of shared access to a scarce resource.

First, assume that a known stock of surface water is available for a cropping season and that this water is allotted to an irrigation system by a central

---

3. Note that few places in either industrial or developing countries manage to get water prices "right" to the extent necessary to accomplish these broad efficiency goals.

authority on the basis of one unit of water (w) for each unit of land (L) in each irrigation system. Second, assume that the community of irrigators is bound together by the recognized need to maintain the collective infrastructure represented by the distribution system and the drainage facilities.

Each unit of land in an irrigation system is entitled to a share of water for the season.[4] The farmer with L_i units of land can use all the water on all of the land under his or her control or can allocate it to just a fraction of the land. If the farmer wants to grow a crop that is highly water-intensive—perhaps rice paddy or sugarcane—then some of the land may have to remain dry. The farmer knows how many units of water are available for the season and decides how that water will be used. The allotment may be sold to others within the system, but not outside the system.

The irrigation system receives W units of water, where $W = w\Sigma L_i$. Assume that enough surface water is available for individual systems to receive, for a cropping season, W units of water. We can think of individual farmers as shareholders at the beginning of each irrigation system, with the shares to which they are entitled being their proportionate share of W. The management problem then becomes making sure that the available water (W) is allocated among shareholders in an optimal fashion.

The earlier discussion indicated the necessary surcharge applied to each irrigator to reflect the marginal costs imposed on downstream irrigators. We can use that heuristic formalized in equations 2.7 to 2.10 to suggest that an optimal irrigation system is one in which each irrigator along the distribution channel behaves in full knowledge of that marginal cost and acts to avoid imposing external costs on others in the system. That is, the goal of all farmers on the system is taken to be perfect compliance with a unified system as expressed in equation 2.6. We might think of this compliance in terms of each farmer's contribution to the public good that is the efficient operation of the system.[5] If that is attained, the extra terms in equations 2.7 to 2.9 will drop out and the water use externalities will disappear.

Drawing on the work of Baland and Platteau (1996), an irrigation system will be modeled as a problem of the optimal provision of a public good. The public good in this system has several components. First, it is

---

4. The government can influence cropping patterns in a general way by the number of shares of water it allocates to individual irrigation systems.

5. An irrigation system might be thought of as a "club good" in that one is either in the system or out of it. However, the term public good is used here to stress that compliance with norms of behavior—and the efficiency and equity benefits of that compliance—is the very essence of a public good for those in the system.

represented by the allocation of water through the system that solves the problem of marginal costs expressed in equation 2.6. Second, it is a program of maintenance of the system that involves all farmers in routine maintenance so that the level of water yield at each water intake on the system is optimal (see Chakravorty, Hochman, and Zilberman 1995 for a model of problems in water conveyance through an irrigation system). Finally, the public good is a schedule of groundwater pumping by individual irrigators that both is consistent with the sustainable yield of the underlying aquifer and makes each irrigator conscious of the marginal costs of the choice between using groundwater and surface water.[6]

The public good within an irrigation system is therefore the attainment of optimal behavior in four interrelated realms: (a) water allocation along a channel, (b) system maintenance, (c) groundwater extraction, and (d) conjunctive use of surface water and groundwater. The more of the public good that is provided, the better the system will perform in terms of water yield at each water intake, reduced externalities along the distribution channel, system maintenance, and the conjunctive use of groundwater and surface water. We can think of this as the outcome of the provision of the public good that farmers on the system call an efficient management regime. The essential purpose of water pricing regimes is to contribute to this end.[7]

In the Baland and Platteau model, the production function for the public good is given by

$$(2.20) \quad z = \beta \Sigma h_i$$

where h_i is the contribution to the public good of each individual farmer on the system, and β can be any algebraic form that maps h_i into z. We might imagine that the contribution h_i could be in the form of a financial assessment at the start of each season, plus the quantity of donated time for system maintenance over some defined period of time. Indeed, h_i could be thought of as a water charge to the ith farmer in that $h_i = cw_i$. The key here is that the parameter β converts the sum of the h_is into some management and behavioral outcomes that improve the operation of the irrigation system. The higher that z is, the better managed the system and the closer to 1 is the probability that all farmers will receive exactly the correct share of water as indicated by their area of land and their proportional claim on total water within the system (including both groundwater and surface

---

6. This brings together the two sources of water for optimal conjunctive use.

7. The effects of pricing upon irrigation technology and the shift to drip irrigation have not been considered.

water supplies). If we define $0 \leq z \leq 1$, then a poorly managed system will have z tending to its lower bound, whereas a well-managed system will have z tending to its upper bound.

If we assume identical preferences over system performance across all farmers on the system, we can consider

$$u_i = u_i(h_i, z) \text{ for } i = 1, 2, \ldots, N.$$

We then define $a_i(h_i, z)$ as the marginal rate of substitution between z and h_i. From this:

$$a_i(h_i, z) = \frac{\partial u_i / \partial h_i}{\partial u_i / \partial z} \text{ for } i = 1, 2, \ldots, N$$

where $\partial u_i / \partial h_i < 0$ and $\partial u_i / \partial z > 0$. We saw earlier that the production function for the public good is given by $z = \beta N h_i$.

The management problem is

(2.21) $\max\limits_{h_i} \quad u_i = u_i(h_i, z)$

s.t. $z = \beta \cdot [h_i + \sum\limits_{j \neq i} h_j]$

and $h_i \geq h_j \ \forall \ j \neq i$

The Pareto optimal solution to this problem is $a_i(h_i^0, z) = \beta N$, where h_i^0 is the contribution to the production of the public good (z) that the ith individual would most prefer everyone to make. This solution to the public good problem accommodates the preferences of all farmers on the system for efficiency in terms of net water yield at each farmer's water intake, system maintenance, conjunctive use of groundwater and surface water, and assurance that all farmers' water receipts exactly match their proportionate share or entitlement. As developed by Baland and Platteau, this follows from the structure of the maximization problem as follows:

(2.22) $\max\limits_{h_i} \Sigma u_i = u_i(h_i, \beta N h_i)$

If the irrigation system is characterized by anarchy, then the public good will be underprovided. In this case, individual contributions of h_i^* solve the maximization problem, and the irrigation system as a going concern will cease to exist. Instead, it becomes every farmer against all others. This follows from the management problem expressed in equation 2.21. When anarchy prevails, the solution to the management problem is $a_i(h_i^*, z) = \beta$ where $h_i^* < h_i^0$. Individual contributions to the public good can range as $h_i^* \leq h_i \leq h_i^0$. Under a regime of full reciprocity, every farmer does exactly as all others do. In the limit, this can range from anarchy (h_i^*) to full (optimal) individual provision of the public good (h_i^0). The management problem then becomes one of inducing each farmer to contribute exactly h_i^0.

The amount h_i^0 is the monetary value (or labor equivalent) of each farmer's willingness to pay to have the system function optimally. It is also the amount that each farmer will want every other farmer to contribute to the provision of the public good. That is, each farmer knows that unless all contribute this amount, the system will not perform as each farmer wants it to perform: some will receive less water than their entitlement, some will shirk on their maintenance obligation and cause excessive water loss for others, some will extract too much from the groundwater aquifer, and some will not make the efficient choice between using surface water and groundwater.

We might regard this contribution problem as the mechanism necessary to overcome the advantages (and disadvantages) of differential positions along an irrigation system, as well as differential access to complementary groundwater resources. Consider that all farmers were made to agree to a constitution governing all the decision variables, and that agreement were exacted behind a Rawlsian veil of ignorance in which the farmers could not know their individual positions or situations (their "endowments") until after the constitution was adopted unanimously. Under risk neutrality, we might expect the farmers to agree to a constitution that would make each indifferent to the particular endowment they might control once the system became operational. That is, farmers would be indifferent between ending upstream or downstream because the constitution (assuming perfect compliance) would assure them an equal situation with respect to the choice variables under consideration here.

This model builds on Sugden (1984). To Sugden, the principle of reciprocity requires that each individual contribute to the public good—efficient and equitable operation of the system with no free riding—exactly that amount that each would prefer every member of the group to make. The idea of obligation arises from this principle. An equilibrium exists if for any vector of contributions h by the group of irrigators on the system, and for any member of that group i, individual i is meeting his or her obligation to the group if and only if (a) h_i exceeds or equals the utility maximizing level of h (h^0); or (b) for some other person j in the group, h_i exceeds or equals h_j. We say it is in i's self-interest to contribute h_i^0 because this will maximize his or her utility given the contribution of all $N-1$ others in the group. Sugden argues that because self-interest within the limits of reciprocity are being assumed here, the irrigators have an obligation to themselves to contribute at least as much as self-interest requires.[8]

In operational terms we might think of this optimal contribution (h_i^0) to the public good as "earnest money" on the part of each farmer. It must be paid before an irrigation season starts. This payment would not go to the irrigation administration for the delivery of water to the system. Rather, it is the annual fee required of each farmer to receive water during the coming season. That is, the contribution is required before the irrigation season starts. The charge must be understood to encompass maintenance of the system as well as the water made available to the farmer by the community of irrigators, not by the national water authority.

Note that the community of irrigators, which we can call a water users association, cannot avoid anarchy unless it assesses such charges *before* the growing season gets under way. If liquidity before the crop season is a problem for some poorer farmers, the system can have some built-in slack that will cover necessary costs for them during the irrigation season.

Case Studies from India

The following discussion concerns two irrigated villages in the Junagadh district of Gujarat state in western India.[9] In one village, Amrapur, continued groundwater pumping threatens agricultural viability over the long run as the underlying aquifer is degraded. When the monsoon fails or is inadequate, many residents of the village are forced to leave in search of fodder for their livestock. In the second village, Husseinabad, pumping brings saltwater intrusion from the Arabian Sea. The salinity of wells not only threatens continued agricultural activity in Husseinabad, but it has started to destroy domestic water supplies in the village. Some villagers must now haul in domestic water over great distances.

---

8. A reviewer notes that: "Sugden's principle would seem to apply only if farmers are homogeneous (which seems inappropriate in the context of head and tail farmers)." However, this confuses the issue of farmers having similar preferences with respect to their production prospects, with farmers being "similar" in terms of their water endowment. The Sugden approach requires similar preferences, but it is meant to address precisely the other problem: differential endowments. If all farmers were similar in terms of both preferences *and* endowments, then we do not have a problem in need of a solution.

9. These draw upon the author's work in the villages of Amrapur and Husseinabad in 1989 on a project for the Aga Khan Rural Support Programme.

The Case of Amrapur

Amrapur is a village of approximately 850 families located over an aquifer that is largely coincident with the land area of the village. Such coincidence is helpful—though not sufficient—for effective collective management of the aquifer under a common property regime. In Amrapur, the aquifer consists of a number of subdivisions that complicate management. The immediate problem is to manage groundwater so that overdraft is reduced and there is some insurance water to support the village through periodic droughts.

The land area of Amrapur is about 2,000 hectares, of which approximately 1,300 are cultivated. About 700 hectares of this cultivated area are served by about 350 irrigation wells. All wells are equipped with rather uniform pumping power, generally a 5-horsepower pump and rarely a 7.5-horsepower pump. Several wells are capable of virtually continuous pumping for nine months after the monsoons, whereas other wells become exhausted after only one hour of pumping.

The farmers in Amrapur exhibited detailed knowledge of the behavior of their own wells, as well as a somewhat rudimentary understanding of the scope of interdependence among other wells in their immediate vicinity. That is, they seemed to know that pumping activity in particular neighboring wells had an adverse impact on the performance of their own wells. This rough empirical understanding provides a starting point for improved management of groundwater. The amount of water movement among farmers is currently limited. The conveyance of water is facilitated by the general terrain between these wells, but water losses during conveyance are high, thereby reducing the system's efficiency.

Evidence indicates that land values are dramatically responsive to access to groundwater and to the robustness of wells. At the extreme upper edge of the village, near the river, one farmer bought 28 *bighas* of land (2.5 *bighas* equal 1 acre and 6.2 *bighas* equal about 1 hectare in this part of India) without access to water for Rs 4,571 per *bigha*, or about US$1,750 per hectare at the then current exchange rate.[10] After he dug a well, his land was said to be worth twice that amount, or about US$3,500 per hectare. At one of the better wells in the village, land was said to be worth US$5,780 per hectare. This same price was said to prevail at another good well. Land served by one of the best wells in the village—a well that was used as a source of marketed water—was said to have a market value of Rs 20,000

---

10. In 1989 the exchange rate was US$1 to Rs16.2.

per *bigha* (US$7,654 per hectare). Similar land values existed at another champion well.

The important point illustrated by these land values, especially when compared with the values of dry arable land, is the perception of the high marginal value of water. This value can be used to motivate recognition of the extreme opportunity cost, both private and collective, of the current system of water squandering through inefficient conveyance practices and inefficient field irrigation practices.

The high marginal value of water is not reflected in the current price for water sales. That is, while a well can double the value of good farmland, water sales are observed at Rs 2 to Rs 6 per hour. These low prices for access to water suggest that water trades now function simply to over-come temporary—and somewhat small—water shortages in one's own well. A farmer able to sell water may be reluctant to ask too much for fear of needing to buy water sometime soon. The sales do not represent enough water to support a complete crop, but the amount needed to get through a particular dry spell. Hence, prices are lower than one might expect if vil-lagers were imagined to be rational economic actors. However, if we ex-pand our narrow idea of "rationality" within the observed set of the villag-ers' preferences, we can clearly consider this behavior to be quite rational.

If a water pricing scheme were to be introduced in Amrapur, it would need to emphasize the potential benefits to farmers of identifying within the village distinct groundwater management zones containing wells that seem to be linked in terms of recharge and that exhibit pumping interde-pendencies. At present, the known pumping regime of a particular well has a discernible, though currently unknown, effect on the performance of all other wells in the zone. A detailed assessment would establish the na-ture of the reciprocal externalities among wells within a groundwater man-agement zone. The absence of such externalities would demarcate wells in one zone from those in another.

Once these zones had been determined, one could develop groundwa-ter management programs and pricing regimes appropriate for each zone. Such programs would emphasize several aspects, depending upon the char-acteristics of the zone. For instance, if one zone were to have a particularly bounteous well, then developing a system of water trades among the farm-ers in that zone may be possible. The trades could occur in two distinct ways. The first would be for water to move above ground through pipes or ditches from seller to buyer. This method has the obvious advantage that both parties could be certain of the amount of water being sent and re-ceived. It has several disadvantages, however. First, the geographic scope for such trades is constrained by surface terrain. If robust wells happen to be at low elevations, then only a small number of "downstream" farmers would be able to engage in buying water. A second disadvantage is that water losses from open conveyance systems can sometimes be substantial, often approaching 40 percent. Finally, such systems require networks of expensive pipes that need repairs and replacement.

A second way in which water trades could occur is via the groundwater system. That is, if farmers understand the interdependence of all wells in a groundwater management zone, then farmer i could agree not to pump his or her well so that farmer j might have, say, six hours of water that would have otherwise been pumped by farmer i. The advantages of this system are that it avoids investment in pipes, it is less constrained by surface terrain, and it does not entail water losses in conveyance. The obvious requirement is that farmers must understand well interdependence. It also requires some trust among farmers, because the actual movement of water cannot be observed.

The development of a system of water movement within groundwater management zones could facilitate an enhanced cropping system among all farmers within each groundwater zone. Greater budgeting of water would be encouraged by the opportunity to sell unneeded water to someone else within the zone. Equally important, the development of a drought management strategy for each zone would then be possible.

The Case of Husseinabad

Husseinabad encompasses approximately 600 hectares, of which about 500 are cultivated. Approximately 500 wells serve the village, and estimates indicate that somewhat more than half the wells are susceptible to salinity problems from seawater intrusion. The village population is about 2,000 people.

The village overlays a miliolitic limestone aquifer that runs along the coastal plain. The aquifer is in contact with the sea, and this permits the intrusion of saline water as fresh water is withdrawn. Density differences create a stable boundary between the two types of water, but when fresh water is removed from wells nearest the coast the boundary moves inland. A vigorous monsoon can push the boundary somewhat seaward, but active pumping can quickly override this beneficial effect. A weak monsoon can profoundly affect the location of the boundary. Indeed, salinity increased dramatically during the 1987–88 period in response to the failed 1987 monsoon.

The groundwater situation in Husseinabad is very different from that in Amrapur, and a workable and enduring solution will be much more difficult to achieve. First, the boundary of the aquifer is not coincident with the boundary of the village, so the connection between groundwater management actions taken by villagers and tangible results will be difficult to establish. Second, a considerable number of wells have reached an advanced state of salinity and their owners are on the verge of insolvency. Although this might indicate a considerable willingness on their part to cooperate in collective action, many of them will be unable to bring much of a financial contribution to a collective management regime. Third, any effort in Husseinabad to address the salinity problem will require the importation of substantial quantities of fresh water.

A portion of the funds obtained through a water payment scheme could be used to locate fresh water for importation. The durability of this external water supply would be enhanced to the extent that farmers in the village agree to improve their efficiency of water use. The farmers in Husseinabad would need to reach general agreement on the pumping patterns to be followed both individually and collectively. The contribution to the public good would be structured so that each irrigator would be obligated to contribute a small amount to a fund that would be administered by a water management association. The advantage of this payment scheme is that it links the actions of farmers to the status of the aquifer. The water management association would administer the funds with the idea of reinforcing the notion among the farmers that they collectively own the aquifer, and that its long-run viability is a matter under their control. Linking any new capital investments, whether for more check dams or for the supplemental supply of fresh water, to a clear commitment on the part of the farmers would be important. That is, they *must* be willing to undertake both the payment scheme and a program of improved water management before any external assistance should be forthcoming.

Conclusion

I have argued previously (Bromley 1982) that a necessary condition for the efficient and equitable operation of irrigation systems is the establishment of a constitution that binds all farmers together in the management of water and system maintenance. Here, that argument is elaborated in formal terms as a model of the optimal provision of a public good. Although the intervening years have seen great attention devoted to the formal properties of water use and management (for example, Boggess, Lacewell, and Zilberman 1993; Chakravorty, Hochman, and Zilberman 1995; Ostrom and Gardner 1993; Saleth 1994; Saleth, Braden, and Eheart 1991; Shah 1989; Tsur 1991) and the discussion of water pricing is extensive, the literature has devoted insufficient attention to the institutional dimension of irrigation water use. Water pricing and water management must be understood as part of the structure of property regimes in which farmers and water are embedded. Until irrigation systems are comprehended as common property regimes, and until they are organized and managed in such a way that the co-owners of the system (and its annual tranche of water) create incentive-compatible behavioral rules, the advocacy of water pricing will be both inadequate and misplaced.

The examples from Amrapur and Husseinabad suggest that water pricing must be seen as part of a regime in which farmers are induced to contribute to a public good—improved water management—that benefits each of them. The principle of reciprocity requires that all individuals contribute to the public good exactly that amount that they would most prefer every member of the group to make. A particular member's contribution (h_i) must exceed or equal the utility-maximizing level of contribution of all others. It is in i's self-interest to contribute h_i, because this will maximize his or her utility given the contribution of all $N-1$ others in the group. Under this condition, the optimal level of the public good will be provided, and the use of groundwater in Amrapur or Husseinabad will be optimal. Similar logic applies to surface irrigation systems.

References

Baland, Jean-Marie, and Jean-Philippe Platteau. 1996. *Halting Degradation of Natural Resources*. Oxford, U.K.: Clarendon Press.

Boggess, William, Ronald Lacewell, and David Zilberman. 1993. "Economics of Water Use in Agriculture." In Gerald A. Carlson, David Zilberman, and John A. Miranowski, eds., *Agricultural and Environmental Resource Economics*. New York: Oxford University Press.

Bromley, Daniel W. 1982. *Improving Irrigated Agriculture: Institutional Reform and the Small Farmer*. Staff Working Paper no. 531. Washington, D.C.: World Bank.

_____. 1991. *Environment and Economy: Property Rights and Public Policy*. Oxford, U.K.: Blackwell.

Chakravorty, Ujjayant, Eithan Hochman, and David Zilberman. 1995. "A Spatial Model of Optimal Water Conveyance." *Journal of Environmental Economics and Management* 29 (March): 25–41.

Ostrom, Elinor, and Roy Gardner. 1993. "Coping with Asymmetries in the Commons: Self-Governing Irrigation Systems Can Work." *Journal of Economic Perspectives* 7(4): 93–112.

Provencher, Bill. 1995. "Issues in the Conjunctive Use of Surface Water and Groundwater." In Daniel W. Bromley, ed., *Handbook of Environmental Economics*. Oxford, U.K.: Blackwell.

Saleth, R. Maria. 1994. "Groundwater Markets in India: A Legal and Institutional Perspective." *Indian Economic Review* 29(2): 157–76.

Saleth, R. Maria, John B. Braden, and J. Wayland Eheart. 1991. "Bargaining Rules for a Thin Spot Water Market." *Land Economics* 67(3): 326–39.

Shah, Tushaar. 1989. *Efficiency and Equity Impacts of Groundwater Markets: A Review of Issues, Evidence, and Policies.* Anand, India: Institute for Rural Management.

Sugden, Robert. 1984. "Reciprocity: The Supply of Public Goods through Voluntary Contributions." *The Economic Journal* 94 (December): 772–87.

Tsur, Yacov. 1991. "Managing Drainage Problems in a Conjunctive Ground and Surface Water System." In Ariel Dinar and David Zilberman, eds., *The Economics and Management of Water and Drainage in Agriculture.* Boston: Kluwer Academic Publishers.

3

Collective Choice in Water Resource Systems

Gordon C. Rausser

Governments and voluntary organizations throughout much of the world are ill-prepared for the disputes and conflicts that will naturally arise in the management of water resources during the 21st century. From the standpoint of both design and implementation, current water resource institutions are wholly inadequate. Given projected population growth, improper institutions can be expected to foster demand and supply imbalances that could well result in one devastating natural disaster after another (Simon 1998).

Even though active debate exists about worldwide demand and supply regarding water (Kenski 1993; Postel 1996; Rogers 1990), few would argue about the presence of gross inequities in the availability of uncontaminated water across both spatial and temporal dimensions. As studies in World Bank (1992) have noted, diarrheal diseases from unsanitary water kill more than 3 million people per year, most of them children.

Given current institutional frameworks, it is no surprise that inequities and conflicts arise. In water resource systems, negative externalities abound. The finite quantities of resource units extracted by one agent naturally subtracts from the quantity of resource units available to others. In irrigation systems, for example, multiple agents and industries use water simultaneously, and excluding certain potential beneficiaries is costly. Without appropriate institutional and governance structures, appropriations made by any one group or individuals confront the open access problem (Ostrom 1997).

The typical prescription economists offer in the face of demand-supply imbalances is the introduction of water markets (Anderson and Snyder 1997; Howitt 1997). Such institutions have the capacity to rationalize water scarcity, both quantitatively and qualitatively. The potential promotion of efficiency from the creation of market institutions is well documented (Anderson and Snyder 1997; Western Governors' Association Water Efficiency Working Group 1987; Zilberman, MacDougall, and Shah 1994). But market institutions are not a substitute for governmental or voluntary bodies in terms of public trust and fiduciary duty.

The fundamental open access problem and the boundaries of jurisdictions within water resource systems lead to incomplete governance structures. Even where such structures are complete, the benefits and costs of introducing water markets depend on local circumstances. Setting aside equity and public trust concerns, externality costs such as salinity accumulation, groundwater contamination, and other sources of market failure must be weighed by analysts and policymakers against the benefits of stimulating technology adoption, conserving water, and promoting economic efficiency. As many public trust advocates have emphasized, the latter benefits are not achievable unless a well-developed legal and regulatory structure supports water market institutions (Rausser 1992). Such structures are not peculiar to water markets, but their design in this context begs for creativity in institutional and governance structures. The typical aspects of well-articulated and transparent property rights—numerous well-informed buyers and sellers and physical transportability of water—are naive and unhelpful to water administrators and governmental regulators.

Even if we falsely assumed that many of the legal and regulatory conditions for viable and efficient water markets exist, issues of equity, appropriate design of safety nets, and interpretation of public trust remain. A generic market prescription in the face of all these issues is unlikely to be sustainable. The mix of institutions and governance structures that operate effectively in one locality will not necessarily serve the public interest in some other locality. Regardless, the customized mix of market and regulatory institutions requires an examination of collective decisionmaking on the part of all stakeholders who have access to a particular water resource system. The critical first steps in this process involve multilateral bargaining, collective decisionmaking, and negotiating.

What analytical structures can help assess and evaluate processes that must take place to achieve sustainable governance and institutional structures? This chapter presents two analytical frameworks that have been applied to water resource systems. The first is based on the Nash-Harsanyi approach to collective decisionmaking. The second uses the noncooperative model of multilateral bargaining developed by Rausser and Simon (1991). Both analytical frameworks address the specific features of water resource systems, particularly multidimensional issues, spaces, or instruments (such as quotas, prices, options, new infrastructure development, type and level of environmental standards, degree of water transferability, and conjunctive use). Both address multiple stakeholders: agricultural water users, urban water users, environmentalists, low-income water users with varying health risks, and others. Default options and admissible coalitions play critical roles, as stakeholder access to the collective decisionmaking process is one of the determinants of relative political influence and power.

The next section explains the major distinction between the two analytical frameworks. The following sections apply the Nash-Harsanyi collective decisionmaking framework to water resource systems, and the Rausser-Simon multilateral bargaining and negotiation framework to typical water policy negotiations, and they also emphasize the need to integrate a number of modern economic and financial concepts into these analytical frameworks.

Political-Economic Analytical Frameworks

Collective action, whether voluntary or through government intervention, is pervasive in water resource systems for four reasons. First, the technology of water resource utilization involves strong nonconvexities, mostly in the form of indivisibilities and sizable economies of scale. An unregulated market structure is likely to emerge that is noncompetitive. Some form of public regulation designed to minimize potential misallocation of resources and unequal income distribution, while creating a strong safety net, is consequently of societal value. Second, water resource systems are often characterized by strong externalities, such as drawing water from a common aquifer. Some form of collective action is needed to remedy the potential market failure. Third, governments may pursue certain goals, such as increased settlement in arid regions, that require substantial public support as well as water resource development and distribution. Finally, politically powerful groups can benefit from state intervention in the resource system. Such groups are often instrumental in spurring public support for reforms so that they can realize the potential gains.

In most water resource systems, the principal economic and engineering decisions concerning resource management are made collectively. Group choices usually apply to: (a) creating resource development programs, (b) allocating water among users, (c) ensuring water quality, (d) pricing water, (e) creating operational regimes, and (f) formulating environmental protection measures. Obviously, such decisions have far-reaching implications for the distribution of water and are likely to generate considerable conflict among participants. Typically, the water resource political economy operates within a given physical, legal, social, economic, and political environment that imposes constraints and affects choices. Thus, water allocation is, in great measure, circumscribed by existing water rights laws and water availability.

Two political-economic analytical frameworks can be advanced to model collective choice in water resource systems. At their core is a game-theoretical formulation of collective decisionmaking or bargaining. One, the axiomatic approach, suppresses all details of the decisionmaking process and predicts outcomes by identifying conditions that all rational decisionmakers should try to satisfy. These conditions are treated as axioms, from which the outcome is deduced using set-theoretical arguments. Among the various axiomatic approaches, by far the most popular is Nash's solution for a two-person bargaining game (Nash 1950, 1953), which has been generalized to n-person games (Harsanyi 1962b, 1977). The remarkable simplicity of the Nash-Harsanyi approach has facilitated its wide use in both theoretical and empirical work. In particular, its solution can be computed as the point in the bargaining set that maximizes the product of the players' utility gains from cooperation.

For many political-economic problems, the strengths of the basic Nash approach and the axiomatic approach are undeniable. One must, however, be aware of the limitations of the Nash bargaining approach as a tool for studying political-economic and collective decisionmaking processes. If the Nash axioms are violated, an alternative bargaining model (Rausser and Simon 1991) is applicable to a wide range of political-economic problems, especially prescriptive analyses of the underlying collective choice rules (the constitutional space) and institutions that structure the collective decisionmaking process.

The critical axiom in the Nash-Harsanyi analytical framework is the so-called "independence of irrelevant alternatives." This axiom states the following. Suppose that a certain position is the solution to a given bargaining problem. Now delete from the original feasible set one or more alternatives other than either the original solution or the disagreement point. In this case, under the axiom, the solutions to the reduced and to the original problems must coincide. The Rausser-Simon multilateral bargaining model (Rausser and Simon 1991) does not require the independence of irrelevant alternatives axiom. More completely, the Nash-Harsanyi framework generates a unique solution that (a) lies on the Pareto frontier (the Pareto optimality axiom), (b) lies on the 45-degree line if the feasibility set is symmetrical about this line (the symmetry axiom), (c) is invariant to positive linear transformations of the players' utilities (the scale invariance axiom), and (d) is unaffected by the removal of irrelevant alternatives (the independence of irrelevant alternatives axiom).

The Nash-Harsanyi solution can be computed as the point in the feasibility set that maximizes a function equal to the product of the players' utility gains from cooperation, measured relative to the exogenous disagreement point. Nash's central result is to construct a function whose associated maximization map coincides with the solution map implied by his four axioms. A variant of Nash's model that allows for differences in various interests' relative influence on policy decisions is obtained by dropping the symmetry axiom and replacing the Pareto optimality axiom by a requirement that all players gain strictly from cooperation if any player gains (the strong individual rationality axiom). The resulting set of axioms implies a family of solution maps, each of which again coincides with the maximization map of a function equal to the product of the players' utility gains, except that these utility gains are now weighted by a set of nonzero exponents that add up to unity (see Peters 1992 for proof of this result). In any event, the problem either reduces to a simple search over the feasible set for the alternative agreed by all to be the best, because agents share a preference relation, or it reduces to a single-person decision problem, because the ultimate decision is delegated to one agent.

The Rausser and Simon framework represents collective choice as a process by which competing interest groups negotiate a compromise agreement that reflects their relative bargaining strengths. This multilateral bargaining formulation has a fixed, finite number of negotiating rounds. The description of the game includes a set of admissible proposals and a set of admissible coalitions. For example, the set of admissible proposals might consist of an interval $[\underline{x}, \bar{x}]$ representing alternative settings of some policy variable. More generally, the admissible set could be a subset on n-dimensional Euclidean space, representing a package of policy instruments that are being negotiated simultaneously. The set of admissible coalitions typically includes any subgroup of the players that together have the political power to implement a proposal. For example, in a strict majority rule regime any group containing a strict majority of the players would be admissible. Alternatively, if one or more players are given veto power over the negotiations, then any admissible coalition would have to include those players.

The applications of the Rausser and Simon model exploit a key advantage of the framework as a tool for prescriptive policy analysis. Because various constitutional variables—the rules for making rules—must be specified as part of the description of the problem, comparative statics techniques can be applied to obtain insights into the relative merits of alternative constitutional designs. In particular, the modeler must declare who has access and what constitutes an admissible coalition. Thus, one can compare, say, the implications of simple majority rule with those of a two-thirds majority rule.

Nash-Harsanyi Framework

The well-known Nash-Harsanyi collective choice or bargaining models can be represented in reduced form by simple maximization problems. For every bargaining model a solution map assigns to each feasible set (each set of feasible bargaining outcomes) the elements of this set that solve the model.[1] Similarly, for each governance function an analogous maximization map assigns to each feasibility set the element of the set that maximizes the given objective or governance function. For this function to be a valid, reduced-form representation of a bargaining model, there must be a particular objective or governance function—specified independently of the bargaining problems to which it is applied—whose maximization map coincides with the solution map for the original bargaining model. In other words, this requirement is that over a wide range of distinct bargaining problems, that is, distinct feasible sets, the same objective or governance function yields maximums that correspond exactly to the solutions of the underlying bargaining model when applied to those problems. Accordingly, the collective choice problem is transformed into the maximization of a single objective or governance function.

As demonstrated in Rausser and Zusman (forthcoming in 2000), this analytical framework can explicitly incorporate political power into policy formation processes. Moreover, as shown in Zusman and Rausser (1994), the resulting analytical framework can incorporate organizational equilibria and the optimality of collective action.

---

1. More precisely, the map assigns solutions combinations of a feasible set and a so-called "disagreement point" in that set, which represents the bargainers' respective payoffs if they fail to cooperate. It is common practice in bargaining theory, however, to assume that the bargainers have von Neumann-Morgenstern utility functions, which represent their preferences uniquely only up to a positive linear transformation, and to assume also that the solution is independent of the particular utility representations used. By applying suitable positive linear transformations to a bargainer's utility functions, the disagreement point of each feasibility set can be normalized to the origin in utility space. Given this normalization, it is no longer necessary to explicitly distinguish the disagreement point from each feasible set in the domain of what we call the solution map.

Application of this analytical framework to the structure of the political economy of water resources requires modeling the following major components: the physical water resource system, the economic structure, and the political power structure. The equilibrium solution for the hydrological political economy is then derived and compared with the socially optimal solution. The framework can be easily applied to systems involving conjunctive use of groundwater and surface water resources.

The Physical Water Resource Subsystem

The physical water resource subsystem comprises the following components:

1. A central water supply project (CWP) that collects water from a source at one part of the country and delivers it to n districts located throughout the country. The total amount available annually at the northern source is Z_0, of which the CWP collects x_0 ($x_0 < Z_0$). No water distribution losses are incurred. The amount of water the CWP delivers to the ith district is denoted by x_i. Hence, the CWP water balance relationship is

$$(3.1) \qquad \sum_{i=1}^{n} x_i = x_0 \leq Z_0.$$

2. n irrigation districts indexed by i ($i = 1, 2, ..., n$). The amount Z_i of surface water is locally available at no cost at the ith district. The locally available surface water, Z_i, is combined with the water delivered by the CWP and the amount of locally pumped groundwater to be used in irrigation, F_i. Hence, the amount of irrigation water used in the ith region, I_i, is:

$$(3.2) \qquad I_i = Z_i + x_i + F_i,\, i = 1, 2, ..., n.$$

The share of irrigation water percolating below the crop's root zone and into the underground aquifer is k ($0 < k < 1$), and $1 - k$ is the share of irrigation water lost in evapotranspiration; k is assumed to be constant for all districts. Consequently, the annual addition to the amount of underground water caused by the pumping and irrigation activity in district i is G_i, where

$$(3.3) \qquad G_i = k \cdot I_i - F_i = k \cdot (Z_i + x_i) - (1 - k) \cdot F_i.$$

G_i may be negative, implying net water subtraction from the aquifer.

3. An underground aquifer spanning the entire country with perfect water conductivity within the aquifer is assumed, so that the

groundwater level is equal in all districts. The elevation of the groundwater table is proportional to the total amount of water in the aquifer, Q, and may be measured by it. The evolution of ground-water level over time is given by

(3.4) $Q_{t+1} = Q_t + \sum_{i=1}^{n} H_i - \alpha \cdot (Q_t - H)$

where the term $-\alpha \cdot (Q_t - H)$ refers to net water outflow to areas outside the country, α is a positive parameter proportional to water conductivity between the country's aquifer and the adjacent areas, and H is a parameter such that $Q_t - H$ is proportional to the hydro-static head determining the hydraulic flow gradient between the country's aquifer and adjacent groundwater aquifers. When the depth of the water table relative to the soil surface is less than a specified value, water logging occurs and the affected land has to be withdrawn from cultivation. Hence, the amount of cultivatable land, A_i, in each district is a monotone decreasing function of the under-ground water level up to a certain depth. Below the critical level, Q_c, all land is cultivatable. That is, $A_i = A_i(Q)$ where:

$\dfrac{dA_i}{dQ} \equiv A < 0$ for $Q \geq Q_c$ and $A = 0$ for $Q < Q_c$.

The Economic Structure

CWP is assumed to incur two types of cost: a fixed cost denoted by C_0 and a variable cost. The variable cost of delivering x_i units of water to district i, located at a distance of d_i miles from the source, is $\zeta_0 d_i x_i$, where ζ_0 is a constant. The CWP sells water to district i at a price ρ_i. The CWP is a nonprofit, closed-accounting unit. That is, its total cost must be exactly equal to water sales plus the government net subsidy, S. Hence,

(3.5) $C_0 + \zeta_0 \Sigma d_i x_i = \Sigma p_i x_i + S$

where $S < 0$ implies a net tax. The cost of pumping groundwater increases at an increasing rate with the amount pumped and decreases with groundwa-ter level, Q. That is, the pumping cost function in district i is $C_i(F_i, Q)$, where

$$\frac{\partial C_i}{\partial F_i} > 0, \; \frac{\partial C_i}{\partial Q} < 0, \; \frac{\partial^2 C_i}{\partial F_i^2} > 0, \; \frac{\partial^2 C_i}{\partial Q \partial F_i} < 0, \text{ and } \frac{\partial^2 C_i}{\partial Q^2} < 0.$$

The marginal costs of pumping also decrease with the groundwater level. No further costs are incurred in the delivery of imported, locally available, or pumped water to users within the district. The district serves only users located inside the district's boundaries. In the subsequent analysis each district is treated as a single, fully integrated decision unit.[2]

The agricultural production technology in district i is described by the production function

$$f^i = f^i(A_i, I_i, y_i)$$

where y_i denotes the level of other inputs. With an appropriate choice of units of output and of y_i, the given constant prices of output and y_i are normalized to $p_f = p_y = 1$. The production function is assumed to be monotone increasing, twice differentiable, and concave in all inputs. It is further assumed that x_i is not rationed and not constrained by existing water rights, so that the amount of water imported to district i is entirely at the district's discretion. Conditions of certainty prevail so that each district's objective function is identified with the district (aggregate) net income function

$$\Pi_i = f^i(A_i, I_i, y_i) - C_i(F_i, Q) - \rho_i x_i - y_i.$$

Each district selects values of I_i, F_i, x_i, and y_i maximizing Π_i. Let $\Pi_i(\rho_i, Q)$ be the indirect district's net income function, that is,

$$\Pi_i(\rho_i, Q) = \max_{I_i, x_i, F_i, y_i} [f^i(A_i, I_i, y_i) - C_i(F_i, Q) - \rho_i x_i - y_i].$$

As is well known, $\Pi_i(\rho_i, Q)$ is nonincreasing and convex in ρ_i. According to Hotelling's lemma,

$$\frac{\partial \Pi_i}{\partial \rho_i} - x_i(\rho_i, Q) < 0$$

and, by convexity of Π_i (Varian 1984),

$$\frac{\partial^2 \Pi_i}{\partial \rho_i^2} = -\frac{\partial x_i(\rho_i; Q)}{\partial \rho_i} > 0.$$

Hence,

$$(3.6) \qquad \frac{\partial x_i(\rho_i; Q)}{\partial \rho_i} < 0.$$

---

2. In reality, every district consists of many water users, each of whom constitutes an autonomous decision unit. Users in the district are usually served by a local water supply organization that is often incorporated as a nonprofit legal entity. A more realistic analysis should take into account the district's actual organizational structure. The model presented here ignores these complications in the interests of simplicity and brevity.

It is assumed that there are many districts (n is large), each of which is sufficiently small to ignore the effects of its own decisions on the groundwater level. That is, each district regards Q as given. Recall, however, that the district's decision and the resulting net income depend on the level of Q.

How does a change in ρ, holding Q constant, affect the optimal values of the district's decision variables? To answer this question, we first examine how pumping responds to changes in the price of imported water. Because x_i is not restricted in sign (negative values of x_i signify water exports), F_i satisfies the following condition:

$$F_i > 0 \text{ and } \frac{\partial C_i(F_i, Q)}{\partial F_i} = \rho_i \text{ when } \frac{\partial C_i(0, Q)}{\partial F_i} \leq \rho_i$$

and

$$F_i = 0 \text{ when } \frac{\partial C_i(0, Q)}{\partial F_i} > \rho_i.$$

Consequently,

$$(3.7) \qquad \frac{\partial F_i}{\partial \rho_i} = \frac{1}{\partial^2 C_i / \partial F_i^2} > 0 \text{ when } \rho_i \leq \frac{\partial C_i(0, Q)}{\partial F_i}$$

$$\frac{\partial F_i}{\partial \rho_i} = 0 \text{ when } \frac{\partial C_i(0, Q)}{\partial F_i} > \rho_i.$$

The behavior of $x_i(\rho_i, Q)$ is given by equation 3.6. Hence, by equation 3.2,

$$(3.8) \qquad \frac{\partial I_i(\rho_i, Q)}{\partial \rho_i} = \frac{\partial x_i}{\partial \rho_i} + \frac{1}{\partial^2 C_i / \partial F_i^2} < 0$$

and by equations 3.3 and 3.7,

$$(3.9) \qquad \frac{\partial G_i(\rho_i, Q)}{\partial \rho_i} = k\frac{\partial x_i}{\partial \rho_i} - (1-k)\frac{\partial F_i}{\partial \rho_i} < 0.$$

Thus, an increase in the price of imported water unambiguously reduces district i's net addition to groundwater and vice versa.

Consider next a system controlled by prices, for example, the CWP sets water prices $\rho = (\rho_1, \ldots, \rho_n)$ that all districts treat as parametrically given when making their decisions. Obviously, to be feasible, ρ must be chosen to satisfy $\Sigma x_i(\rho_i, Q) \leq Z_0$. A stationary level of groundwater, Q_s, is defined by

$$(3.10) \qquad \Delta Q = \Sigma G_i(\rho_i, Q^s) - \alpha \cdot (Q^s - H) = 0.$$

Hence, $Q^s = Q^s(\rho)$.

The Political Power Structure

There are $n + 2$ players in the specified political economy: n districts, the central water pricing authority, and the government. It has been assumed previously that the CWP sets water prices. However, as water prices have profound effects on the well-being of all other parties, price setting is essentially a political issue to be decided in the political arena in accordance with the participants' political power. In particular, water prices determine S, which legally is a government-controlled instrument. Hence, water prices cannot be decided without the full consent of the government. To understand the power relationships, one must identify the interests of the participating parties and examine their power bases.

THE CENTRAL WATER PRICING AUTHORITY. Organizations such as CWPs are usually established as nonprofit, closed-accounting, legal entities. Unlike the classical capitalistic firm, the CWP does not pursue profits. Its performance is ordinarily judged by the cost-efficiency of its operations. Concern for cost-efficiency may develop into an interest in economic efficiency in general. Accordingly, the CWP policy objective function is specified as

$$(3.11) \quad u_0 = V(\rho, Q) = \sum_i \{f^i[A_i(Q), I_i, y_i] - C_i(F_i, Q) - y_i\} - \zeta_0 \sum_{i=1}^{n} d_i x_i - C_0.$$

However, decisionmakers in the CWP have other, more personal interests as well. They usually seek recognition and sympathy from the other parties and abhor public expressions of dissatisfaction with the CWP or their own personal performances. These individuals may develop aspirations to acquire political office, achieve personal promotion, improve their material well-being, and win interagency rivalries. To advance their interests, they must gain the support of the other parties and avoid being censured. However, this is not a one-sided relationship as the CWP decisionmakers are able to reward and penalize the other parties, primarily through their legal control over water pricing as well as through the loyalty and support of politicians. These relationships are introduced into the model by the devices of strength of power and cost of power functions. The extended objective function of the CWP is then

$$(3.12) \quad U_0 = u_0 + \sum_{i=1}^{n} s_i(c_i^0, \delta_i) + S_{n+1,0}(c_{n+1}^0, \delta_{n+1}^0) - c_0^{n+1}$$

where s_i is the strength of the ith interest group's power over the CWP, $S_{n+1,0}(c_{n+1}^0, \delta_{n+1}^0)$ is the strength of the government's power over the CWP,

c_i^0 is the cost of power to the ith group in influencing the CWP's choices, and δ_i is a strategy indicator variable such that

$$\delta_i = \begin{cases} \alpha_i \text{ when } i \text{ adopts a reward policy toward the CWP} \\ \beta_i \text{ when } i \text{ adopts a penalizing policy toward the CWP} \end{cases}$$

δ_i thus signifies group i's strategy with respect to the CWP. Also, c_{n+1}^0 is the cost of the government's power over the CWP, δ_{n+1}^0 is an indicator variable signifying the strategy adopted by the government toward the CWP, and c_0^{n+1} is the cost to the CWP of influencing the government's choices when the CWP uses means of power other than water prices. Note that the n districts (indexed by $i = 1, 2, 3, \ldots, n$) and the government (indexed by $i = n + 1$) all exert their influences over the CWP's choices.

THE DISTRICT. The objective function of the ith district is identified with its net income, that is,

$$(3.13) \quad u_i = \Pi_i(\rho_i, Q).$$

Recall that whereas the groundwater level, Q, affects the district's net income, each district views Q as an exogenously given collective good or bad. The district ignores the effects of its own decisions on G_i, and thereby on Q. In this respect the district is narrowly rational. As asserted earlier, the individual district can contribute to or detract from the welfare of decisionmakers in the CWP and the government. Districts may provide political rewards by contributing to election funds, making public pronouncements of support, and denouncing political opponents. A district may mobilize goodwill toward decisionmakers in the CWP or the government, support their causes, and assist them in their bureaucratic and political infighting. Alternatively, it may impose political penalties by supporting the opposition and criticizing the performance of incumbent decisionmakers.

But whatever the district does, whether rewarding or penalizing a party, it incurs a certain cost: the cost of power. Hence, the extended policy objective function of the ith district is

$$(3.14) \quad U_i = u_i - c_i^0 - c_i^{n+1}$$

where c_i^0 is the cost to district i of influencing the CWP, and c_i^{n+1} is the cost to district i of influencing the government.

THE GOVERNMENT. Different elements in government ordinarily pursue different and often conflicting goals. The sweeping view of government as a single entity with a well-defined goal is clearly a myth. The literature that deals with political economies often portrays policymakers' interests as exclusively personal: politicians pursue purely selfish goals and political parties support particular policies not because of the perceived intrinsic value of the policy, but to maximize the likelihood of being elected (Rausser and Zusman forthcoming).

I do not subscribe to this cynical view of politics, but presume instead that politicians pursue both selfish and unselfish public interest goals. Specifically, I adopt a rather narrow interpretation of the unselfish goal of government and identify the government's policy objective function with the government's net revenue from the CWP (the negative value of the net subsidy to water users). That is,

$$(3.15) \quad u_{n+1} = -S$$

where S is the water subsidy cost defined by the CWP zero-profit constraint, the tax in equation 3.5 being a negative subsidy. The government thus represents taxpayers or other claimants of the state's financial resources. This interpretation of the government interest by definition identifies the government with those responsible for the state's fiscal policy.[3]

Government decisionmakers also have personal political and economic interests that render them amenable to the influences of interest groups. The government extended objective function may be formulated as follows:

$$(3.16) \quad U_{n+1} = u_{n+1} + \sum_{i=0}^{n} \tilde{S}_i(c_i^{n+1}, \eta_i) - c_{n+1}^0$$

where $\tilde{S}_i$ is the strength of the ith organized group's power over the government; c_i^{n+1} is the cost of power to the ith group over the government; η_i is a strategy indicator variable analogous to δ_i (defined earlier) with $\eta_i = \alpha_i^{n+1}$ if i adopts a reward policy, and $\eta_i = \beta_i^{n+1}$ if i adopts a penalty policy; and c_{n+1}^0 is the cost of power to the government in influencing the CWP. Note that the strength of the CWP's power over the government, $\tilde{S}_0(.,.)$, is incorporated in equation 3.16.

The Hydrological-Political-Economic Equilibrium

In the constructed political-economic model of a water resource system controlled by water prices, the relevant policy instruments are identified

---

3. A broader interpretation of the government's goals may identify them with both V and S. Such a formulation, although not unreasonable, would assign to the CWP a purely passive political role. Alternatively, we could interpret the CWP as "the group interested in overall economic efficiency" and the government as "the group interested in lower net government expenditures."

with the water prices, ρ, and the net subsidy, S. Note that water prices must be nonnegative and must satisfy the CWP's water availability constraint, $\Sigma x_i(\rho_i, Q) \leq Z_0$, with ρ and S interdependent through equation 3.5. Adopting the long-term view, let us focus on the stationary states of the system. The hydrological-political-economic equilibrium water prices are those that maximize the governance function as follows:

$$(3.17) \quad W = u_0 + \sum_{i=1}^{n} b_i u_i + b_{n+1} u_{n+1} = V[\rho, Q^s(\rho)] + \sum_{i=1}^{n} b_i \Pi_i(\rho_i, Q^s) - b_{n+1} S(\rho, Q^s)$$

where $Q^s = Q^s(\rho)$ is the stationary groundwater level, and the narrowly rational individual districts regard Q^s as an exogenously given collective good or bad factor. Assuming an interior solution, the first-order conditions for maximum W with respect to ρ are

$$(3.18) \quad \frac{\partial W}{\partial \rho} = \frac{\partial V}{\partial \rho} + \frac{\partial V}{\partial Q^s} \frac{\partial Q^s}{\partial \rho} + \sum_{i=1}^{n} b_i \frac{\partial Q^s}{\partial \rho} - b_{n+1} \left(\frac{\partial S}{\partial \rho} + \frac{\partial S}{\partial Q^s} \frac{\partial Q^s}{\partial \rho} \right) = 0.$$

Note that in equation 3.18, water districts are assumed to be narrowly rational; that is, they ignore the effect of changes in water price on the stationary groundwater level, that is, $[\Pi_i / Q^s][Q^s / \rho]$ is not included in equation 3.18.

Are equilibrium water prices economically efficient? To answer this question, note that the following two conditions assure efficiency: (a) power is uniformly distributed ($b_i = 1$ for all i), and (b) all individual districts take into account the full effects of their own decisions on the groundwater level (districts' full rationality).

Given the definition of $\Pi_i(\rho_i, Q)$, and substituting equations 3.5, 3.11, 3.13, and 3.15 into equation 3.17, we obtain

$$(3.19) \quad W = 2V[\rho, Q^s(\rho)] = 2 \left\{ \sum_{i=1}^{n} [f^i - C_i - y_i] - \zeta_0 \sum_{i=1}^{n} dx_i - C_0 \right\}$$

so that maximizing W also maximizes V, the net social surplus from the water resource system. When the second condition does not hold, the effects of each district's choices on the groundwater level are fully externalized and the district is narrowly rational. Note also that even if the second condition holds so that no externalities exist, economic efficiency still requires a uniform distribution of power.

The Rausser-Simon Multilateral Bargaining Model

This section introduces an alternative approach to the modeling of political-economic problems based on the framework developed by Rausser and

Simon (1991) and known as the multilateral bargaining model. This model represents politics as a process by which competing interest groups negotiate a compromise agreement that reflects their relative bargaining strengths. Many water policy negotiations are not satisfied by the Nash axioms, especially the "independence of irrelevant alternatives" axiom. As previously noted, the multilateral bargaining analytical framework does not impose this axiom.

The approach considers a sequence of games with finite bargaining horizons and examines the limit points of equilibrium outcomes as the horizon is extended without bounds. These limit points are interpreted as a proxy for the equilibria of a bargaining game in which the number of negotiation rounds is finite, but arbitrarily large.

In a multilateral bargaining game, a finite collection of players meet to select a policy from some collection of possible alternatives. If players fail to reach agreement, a disagreement policy is imposed by default. The specification of a multilateral bargaining problem includes a list of admissible coalitions, which are defined as a subset of the players who can impose a policy decision on the group as a whole. The game has a finite number of negotiating rounds. Prior to each round, a proposer is chosen randomly according to an exogenously specified vector of access probabilities. These probabilities are interpreted as measures of players' relative political effectiveness. Together with the vector of access probabilities, each profile of strategies uniquely identifies an outcome, which is a random variable defined on the set of policies.

There is a simple characterization of the set of equilibrium strategy profiles: in each response round, a player will accept a proposed policy if and only if it generates at least as much utility as that player's reservation utility in that round, that is, the utility the player expects to receive if no agreement is reached and play continues into the following round. In each offer round, a player is faced with a two-part problem. For each admissible coalition, players maximize their utility over the set of policies that provide each coalition member with at least his or her reservation utility in the following round. They then select a utility-maximal policy from among these maximizers.

To demonstrate the use of the multilateral bargaining model, consider the recent water policy negotiations in California. Disputes about water resources in the western United States are well known to anyone familiar with natural resource issues; the contentiousness and intractability of these conflicts is legendary. This is particularly true in California, where a large agriculture industry, a large and rapidly expanding urban population, and a vocal and influential environmental movement have engaged in a constant and increasingly confrontational struggle over water policy issues. Water policy has become a legal and political battleground.

In the early 1990s, however, the three traditionally warring factions began a series of unique negotiations, with representatives meeting on a regular basis to try to reach a consensus on water policy issues. These informal discussions, known popularly as the "three-way negotiations," occurred outside the context of any specific legislative, regulatory, or judicial proceeding, and were not sponsored by or affiliated with any governmental agency. The major issues that arose in the negotiations included the degree to which water would be transferable, the type and level of environmental standards that affected water use, and the development of new infrastructure. Each of these three groups—agricultural water users, urban water users, and environmentalists—has distinct preferences about the three core issues, with each group strongly in favor of one issue, strongly opposed to a second, and generally having a moderate position on the third. This symmetry of issues, players, and preferences makes for a particularly illuminating bargaining problem, because each interest group is a natural ally with different partners on different issues.

Agricultural users consume about 85 percent of the state's developed water supply. They have historically benefited from large subsidies in the form of low water prices and have been relatively free of stringent environmental regulations. Even so, many agricultural producers are facing water constraints that are becoming tighter because of more stringent environmental measures. As a result, agricultural groups strongly oppose increased environmental regulation and strongly support new infrastructure development. Agricultural groups have generally opposed liberal transfer or water marketing policies, fearing that such policies would allow urban water users to "take" water from agriculture. Note, however, that there is considerable heterogeneity among the members of this interest group. A farmer who may profit from policy reforms such as the transition to a system of marketable water rights, for example, may support such reforms.

Urban water users, represented by the water supply districts, are primarily concerned with the availability of affordable water supplies to support continued urban growth. The value of water, measured as willingness to pay, is much higher in urban use than in agriculture, and this group views water markets as the best way to achieve urban water availability. Consequently, urban water user groups are the strongest supporters of unrestricted water markets. They also support new infrastructure development. Although urban water users generally oppose strong environmental regulations regarding water use, the high value of water in urban use tempers this opposition.

Environmental interest groups are primarily concerned with controlling adverse environmental consequences of water use patterns. As such, strong environmental regulations are the primary negotiating objective of this group. Environmentalists strongly oppose new infrastructure development and have mixed positions with respect to water markets. Transferring water from agricultural to urban use may reduce in-stream flows and eliminate many wetlands that serve as wildlife habitat. However, they view water markets as an effective method of meeting increasing urban demands without new infrastructure development, and transferable water rights may allow environmental groups to acquire water for environmental purposes.

Negotiation participants generally agreed that the broad scope of the negotiations helped them make progress. At the outset, the participants agreed that the negotiations would focus on crafting a package that addressed all the major issues, in contrast to most of the past attempts at resolving these issues in which each issue (such as transfers or new infrastructure) was considered individually.

Participants also cited the degree of consensus needed to ratify an agreement as an important factor, but they disagreed about what degree of consensus was appropriate. The negotiations adopted a policy requiring complete consensus to ratify any agreement, but many participants felt that this policy was overly restrictive. Exogenous factors, such as the anticipated disagreement outcome, were also a factor in the negotiations. During the course of the talks, several legal, regulatory, and legislative decisions have altered the status quo of California's water policy, potentially affecting the outcome of the negotiations.

Model Application

To illustrate the experimental technique, two simulations are discussed in detail. With general references to a number of other simulations (Adams, Rausser, and Simon 1996), each investigates the effect of a change in institutional structure on the negotiated outcome. The first simulation concerns the influence of the scope of the negotiations, while the second addresses the implications of heterogeneous interest groups.

Each simulation consists of a family of 25 computational solutions of the bargaining model in which one aspect of the bargaining process—referred to as the target variable—is systematically varied. For example, to investigate the influence of the disagreement policy on the outcome of some negotiations, we would designate the disagreement policy as the target variable. For each of the 25 simulations, the parameters defining the players' utility functions are randomly selected from intervals that are chosen based on prior, but imprecise, knowledge about players' preferences.

In each simulation, we first solve the bargaining model for the initial setting of target variables, summarizing one aspect of the bargaining process. For example, to investigate the influence of the disagreement policy on outcomes, we designate the disagreement policy as a target variable. We then successively increase the value of the target variable, solving the model each time. Thus, each simulation consists of a family of bargaining models, all identical except for the values of the target variable. By systematically comparing the solutions with the games in each family, we can gain insight into the comparative statics effects of the change in the target variable. When observed differences in our results can be traced to differences in one parameter or group of parameters, hypotheses can be formed about causal relationships within the bargaining process. Table 3.1 illustrates how the policy debate is translated into a formal bargaining model. The formal game is limited to three players (agricultural water users, A; urban water users, U; and environmentalists, E) and to three issues (degree of transferability of water rights, degree of environmental protection, and new infrastructure development). Each issue is represented as a dimension of a "policy space" and (without loss of generality) is normalized to the unit interval. A specific proposal or policy is represented as a point in this space, and players have utility functions defined directly in the policy space. These utilities are constant elasticity of substitution functions of the form

$$(3.20) \quad u_i(x) = \left(\sum_{k=1}^{n} \gamma_{i,k} [\theta_i - (x_k - \beta_{i,k})^2]^{\xi_i} \right)^{(1-\rho_i)/\xi_i}$$

where x_k represents the setting of the kth policy variable. The parameter $\beta_{i,k}$ is interpreted as player i's most preferred setting or ideal point for the kth policy variable, while $\gamma_{i,k}$ reflects the relative weight, or importance, that player i attaches to the variable. The substitutability coefficient ξ_i determines the curvature of players' indifference surfaces. Finally, ρ_i is a risk aversion factor. The role of θ_i is to ensure that the term inside the square brackets is always positive.

The first dimension of the policy space represents the degree of new infrastructure development, the second dimension represents the degree of transferability, and the third dimension represents the degree of environmental protection. Environmental groups prefer high levels of environmental protection, while agricultural and urban interests prefer low levels. Thus, the players' ideal points along this dimension, $\beta_{i,3}$, are constrained to be randomly drawn from the (relatively tight) intervals

TABLE 3.1
Range of Parameter Values for Experiment 1

Variable	Agricultural users (A)		Urban users (U)		Environmentalists (E)	
	Lower bound	Upper bound	Lower bound	Upper bound	Lower bound	Upper bound
$\beta_{i,1}$	0.90	1.00	0.90	1.00	0.00	0.10
$\beta_{i,2}$	0.25	0.35	0.90	1.00	0.50	0.60
$\beta_{i,3}$	0.00	0.10	0.00	1.00	0.90	1.00
$\gamma_{i,1}$	0.90	1.00	0.90	1.00	0.75	0.85
$\gamma_{i,2}$	0.25	0.35	0.90	1.00	0.50	0.60
$\gamma_{i,3}$	0.75	0.85	0.25	0.35	0.90	1.00
ξ_i	−6.00	1.00	−6.00	1.00	−6.00	1.00
ρ_i	0.50	0.50	0.50	0.50	0.50	0.50

Source: Author.

of [0.9, 1.0] for the environmental player and [0.0, 0.1] for the urban and agricultural players. Although the most preferred policy setting along this dimension is similar for both the agricultural and the urban interests, the issue is much more important to agricultural interests. Thus, the relative weight that agricultural interests attach to issue $\gamma_{i,3}$ is higher than the weight that urban water users attach to that issue. The intervals for the flexibility, ξ_i, and risk aversion, ρ_i, parameters are equal for all players, reflecting lack of knowledge about the relative or absolute magnitude of these parameters for the different interest groups.

Simulation 1: Varying the Space of Policies under Negotiation

This simulation challenges the rationality of agenda-setting maneuvers. If the issue that one group seeks to exclude from the negotiations is the only issue that another group strongly supports, then a mutually beneficial compromise may be possible only if the issue is placed on the bargaining table. An example from the California water policy negotiations is new infrastructure development. Agricultural and, to a lesser extent, urban groups wished to include infrastructure development in the negotiations, while environmental interests opposed negotiations on this issue. Opposition to all new infrastructure development, however, may be counterproductive for environmental groups. Although environmental groups can block new infrastructure projects, agricultural and urban groups have the power to block many of the water policy goals of the environmental groups. Given this mutual veto over other groups' goals, negotiating a compromise on the issue of infrastructure may be the best strategy for the environmental interests.

The target variable in the simulation is defined to be the range of admissible values that the infrastructure variable (x_1) can take. Initially, x_1 can take any value in the unit interval, representing all possible levels of new infrastructure development. The upper bound on the range of admissible values is then successively reduced by increments of 0.05. Parameter values for each player's utility function are randomly generated from a uniform distribution.

Several conclusions can be drawn from this simulation. At the outset, reducing the upper bound on infrastructure development has no effect on the outcome of negotiations. Once the bound is sufficiently small, a further reduction increases the level of environmental quality and the utility of the environmentalists at the expense of the other two groups. Eventually, however, still further reductions reverse these positive effects, reducing the level of environmental quality and the utility of the environmentalists. The utilities of the other two groups continue to fall.

Table 3.2 presents a full report of the statistical simulations. The first part of this table reports the computed values of the solution vector $[x_1, x_2, x_3]$ for each simulation. The second, fourth, and sixth columns list the numerical values of these variables when the upper bound on infrastructure is 0.5. The third, fifth, and seventh columns report the succession of qualitative changes in each of the variables as the upper bound is reduced by increments of 0.05.[4] For example, in simulation 1, the solution value of $[x_2]$ decreased twice until this bound reached 0.4, then increased four times until the bound reached 0.2, then decreased three more times.

The rest of the table shows the utilities that players derive from the solution vectors. For players A and U, the qualitative changes are listed. Player E's utility first increases as the bound is reduced, then decreases. Because the net effects of these changes are of interest, the table shows (in columns four and six) the utility levels that E obtains when the upper bound on infrastructure is, respectively, 0.5 and 0.05.

Several aspects of these results warrant attention. When the only two options are to include or to exclude the issue of infrastructure investment in the negotiating process, all three groups benefit from its inclusion. When infrastructure is included, the environmental group can concede on that

---

4. To conserve space, table 3.2 reports only the results of the first 10 simulations, and results are reported only for infrastructure bounds of 0.5 or less. Increasing the bounds beyond 0.5 had no effect on the outcome of the negotiations.

TABLE 3.2
Results for Simulation 1
Solution Vectors

Simulation	Infrastructure (1)		Transferability (2)		Environmental protection (3)	
	Initial solution	Sign of change	Initial solution	Sign of change	Initial solution	Sign of change
1	0.4333	---------	0.6455	--++++---	0.6963	---------
2	0.4260	---------	0.6319	--+-++---	0.7226	---------
3	0.4469	---------	0.6275	-+++++---	0.7248	---------
4	0.4186	---------	0.6091	--++++---	0.7058	---------
5	0.4411	---------	0.6436	-+++++---	0.7102	---------
6	0.4184	---------	0.6069	--++++---	0.7065	---------
7	0.4249	---------	0.6351	--+++++--	0.7172	---------
8	0.3947	---------	0.5910	--++++---	0.7376	---------
9	0.4194	---------	0.6507	--++++---	0.7036	---------
10	0.3780	---------	0.5961	--++++---	0.7425	---------

Utility Levels

Simulation	Agricultural users (A) Sign of change	Urban users (U) Sign of change	Environmentalists (E)		
			Initial solution	Sign of change	Final solution
1	---------	---------	99.6652	++++-----	99.5914
2	+--------	---------	99.6336	+++++----	99.5642
3	---------	---------	99.6091	++++-----	99.5234
4	---------	---------	99.6926	+++++----	99.6213
5	+--------	---------	99.6552	+++++----	99.5804
6	+--------	---------	99.6612	++++-----	99.5844
7	+--------	---------	99.6645	+++++----	99.6040
8	+--------	---------	99.6542	-++++----	99.5856
9	---------	---------	99.6854	++++-----	99.6219
10	++-------	---------	99.6510	-++++----	99.5953

Source: Author.

issue in return for concessions by the agricultural group on environmental concerns. When infrastructure is excluded, the policy space does not include any issue that the agricultural group particularly favors, and potential gains from trade are substantially reduced.

Now suppose that the range of admissible infrastructure values is a variable aspect of the negotiating framework. Environmentalists benefit from small reductions in the maximum admissible level of infrastructure development, because these reductions weaken the bargaining (or "threat") positions of the urban and agricultural users. For large reductions, however, the constraint on infrastructure is binding on the environmentalists as well. As bargaining proceeds, the environmentalists will find themselves at a "corner solution": they would prefer to concede along the infrastructure dimension in exchange for more environmental protection, but they are unable to do so because of the exogenously imposed constraint. Gains to trade are sacrificed and all parties are worse off.

Simulation 2: Coalition Breaking and the Degree of Preference Heterogeneity

When negotiations take place among interest groups, each of which represents a diverse constituency, opinions will differ among the members of each negotiating team. For example, the agricultural interest group is actually a conglomeration of subgroups, each of which has a distinct perspective on the water policy debate. Questions immediately arise concerning the relationship between the internal structure of each alliance and its performance within the negotiations. I will test the natural hypothesis that the more homogenous the preferences of the members of an alliance, the more effectively it will perform.

Consider transferability, an issue on which different agricultural interests take widely diverging positions. Agricultural groups as a whole have generally opposed increased transferability of water rights. Identifying those agricultural water users who would benefit most from increased transferability may be a productive strategy for those interest groups favoring more liberal transfer policies.

In this simulation, the agricultural alliance is specified to consist of two subgroups, A and B, each of which is represented by a player in the game. A natural measure of homogeneity is the euclidean distance between each player's ideal point in the policy space. The simulation involves successfully moving A's ideal point farther away from B's.

Four players and two admissible coalitions participate in the simulation. Player E is the environmental interest group, player U is the urban user group, and players A and B are the agricultural users. The two admissible coalitions consist of players E, U, and either player A or player B. That is, implementation of an agreement requires quasi unanimous approval. The utility functions for players A and B are identical except for the locations of their ideal points. The intervals from which parameter values were randomly generated are specified in table 3.3.

We consider the comparative statics effect of increasing the variable $\beta_{B,2}$, which is player B's ideal point along the transferability axis. Note that in all the simulations, the corresponding variable for player A, $\beta_{A,2}$, is held constant and never exceeds $\beta_{B,2}$. The interpretation is that player B stands to gain more from the formation of a market for water transfers.

Two versions of the simulation were considered. The only difference is the relationship between the variables $\beta_{A,1}$ and $\beta_{B,2}$, the two players' ideal points along the infrastructure axis. In version (1) we restrict $\beta_{A,1}$ to slightly greater than $\beta_{B,1}$. In version (2) $\beta_{A,1}$ is slightly less than $\beta_{B,1}$. Either version seems equally plausible as a description of reality. In each case, player B is presumed to represent the subgroup of agricultural users who are potential suppliers within the proposed water market.

In version (1) B's weaker preference for infrastructure might be due to concerns that infrastructure development would increase aggregate water supply and dilute the potential rents to the owners of the existing supply. In version (2), B's greater preference for infrastructure might be due to cost concerns: infrastructure development may reduce the unit cost of transporting water and therefore increase the profitability of selling water.

Intuitively, the distinction between the parameter values in the two versions seems insignificant. Because these two subgroups compete with each other to represent the agricultural interests, differentiating their interests would appear to weaken the bargaining power of each of them, and so shift the negotiated solution in a direction that would benefit the other two groups at the expense of the agricultural alliance. In reality, the two versions yield diametrically opposite results.

In version (1) the effect of increasing $\beta_{B,2}$ is to increase all three policy variables in virtually every element of the sample. The effect on players' utilities is not quite as clear: generally, it decreases the utilities of player A and increases the utilities of players E and U. (For player B, comparisons of utility levels are meaningless, because B's utility function is actually changing as the experiment proceeds.) In version (2) all these effects are reversed: all three policy variables fall as $\beta_{B,2}$ increases, the utility of player A increases, and those of players E and U decrease.

Therefore, if player A prefers less infrastructure than player B, an increase in player B's preference for transferability leads players A and B to act in ways that are increasingly congruent, even though their ideal points are farther apart. As player B's preference for transferability increases, the offers proposed by players A and B move closer together in almost every round of the negotiations. This increased cohesiveness within the agricultural alliance

TABLE 3.3
Parameter Values for Simulation 2

Variable	Agricultural users (A)		Agricultural users (B)		Urban users (U)		Environmentalists (E)	
	Lower bound	Upper bound	Lower bound	Upper bound	Lower bound	Upper bound	Lower bound	Upper bound
$\beta_{i,1}$ (1)	0.90	1.00	0.80	0.90	0.90	1.00	0.00	0.10
$\beta_{i,1}$ (2)	0.70	0.80	0.90	1.00	0.90	1.00	0.00	0.10
$\beta_{1,2}$	0.25	0.25	Target	Variable	0.90	1.00	0.50	0.60
$\beta_{i,3}$	0.00	0.10	0.00	0.10	0.00	0.10	0.90	1.00
$\gamma_{i,1}$	0.90	1.00	0.90	1.00	0.90	1.00	0.75	0.85
$\gamma_{i,2}$	0.25	0.35	0.25	0.35	0.90	1.00	0.50	0.60
$\gamma_{i,3}$	0.75	0.85	0.75	0.85	0.25	0.35	0.90	1.00
ξ_i	-6.00	1.00	-6.00	1.00	-6.00	1.00	-6.00	1.00
ρ_i	0.50	0.50	0.50	0.50	0.50	0.50	0.50	0.50

Note: (1) refers to version (1) setting on $\beta_{i,1}$, and (2) refers to version (2) setting on $\beta_{i,2}$.
Source: Author.

results in changes in the policy variables that benefit both members of the alliance. By contrast, if player A prefers more infrastructure than player B, then an increase in player B's preference for transferability leads the two players to act in ways that are less congruent, resulting in a degradation of the alliance's performance.

The intuition behind this result is that in version (2), for almost every round of negotiations, the offers proposed by players A and B move closer together as $\beta_{B,2}$ increases. Recall that offers are points in the euclidian 3-space, as are players' most preferred points (the vectors β_i). As $\beta_{B,2}$ increases, the most preferred points of players A and B become more distant and their preferences become more dissimilar, yet the optimal negotiation proposals become more similar. In version (1), however, the increase in $\beta_{B,2}$ leads players A and B to act in ways that are increasingly disparate, degrading the performance of both.

The source of this striking disparity becomes readily apparent after inspection of figure 3.1. In almost all rounds of the negotiations, when players A and B make proposals, the participation constraints for players U and E are binding. Each of these constraints is a two-dimensional manifold in R^3, and the intersection of both constraints is thus a one-dimensional manifold. Therefore, players A and B have only one degree of freedom when optimizing subject to U and E's constraints. For a fixed constraint set, let $x_2(x_1)$ and $x_3(x_1)$ denote, respectively, the values of the second variable (transferability) and third variable (environmental quality) once the value of the first variable (infrastructure) is chosen. For the parameter ranges specified for this experiment (see table 3.3), both $\partial x_2(x_1)/\partial x_1$ and $\partial x_3(x_1)/\partial x_1$ are negative.

Figure 3.1 illustrates the projection of a typical constraint manifold onto R^2 (the first and second component of x). Moving southeast along the curve, the suppressed values of x_3 increase. For the relevant interval of x_1, the values of $x_3(\cdot)$ do not exceed the ideal values, $\beta_{A,3}$ and $\beta_{B,3}$, for both types of agricultural users. Thus, both player A and player B, while moving southeast along the curve in each version of the simulation, move closer to their ideal levels for infrastructure and transferability, but farther away from their ideal point for environmental protection.

Consider version (1) of the simulation first. In this case, $\beta_{A,1}$ lies to the right of $\beta_{B,1}$, whereas $\beta_{A,3} \approx \beta_{B,3}$ and, initially, $\beta_{A,2} = \beta_{B,2}$. We have restricted all the other parameters of the two players' utilities to be approximately equal. Thus, at any given point along the curve, the marginal gain to player A from moving southeast along the curve must exceed the marginal gain to player B, while the marginal cost is approximately the same. Hence, at the initial value of $\beta_{B,2}$, player A's

FIGURE 3.1
Optimal Offers and Ideal Points in Simulation 2

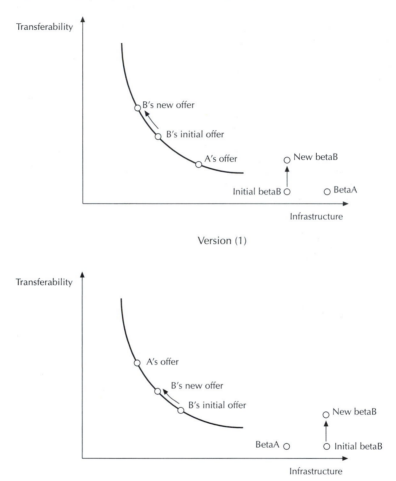

Version (1)

Version (2)

Source: Author.

optimal choice must lie to the southeast of player B's choice. The effect of increasing $\beta_{B,2}$ is to reduce the marginal gain that B obtains from moving southeast along the curve, so that as $\beta_{B,2}$ increases, player B's optimal choice moves to the northwest, farther from player A's optimum, which, of course, is unaffected by the change in $\beta_{B,2}$.

In version (2), everything is the same as in version (1) except that $\beta_{A,1}$ lies to the left of $\beta_{B,1}$. Hence, at the beginning of each simulation, when $\beta_{B,2}$ is set at its initial value, the relative positions of the two players' optima are reversed: player B's choice lies to the southeast of player A's. The effect of increasing $\beta_{B,2}$, however, is the same: player B's optimal choice again moves to the northwest. In this case, however, the optimum moves closer to A's choice, which once again remains constant as B's changes.

This simulation dramatically demonstrates the complexities of multi-issue, multiparty bargaining. Players' behaviors depend on the complex interactions and constraints imposed by both the behaviors of other players and the institutional structure under which negotiations take place. The results of this simulation challenge the intuition that an alliance will fare more poorly in negotiations as the individual interests of the alliance members become more disparate.

Other Simulation Results

Simulations of other aspects of the water policy negotiations were also performed. Without going into a detailed exposition of the simulations, I will briefly review the results. One simulation involved the implications of a change in the disagreement outcome, that is, the policy that would be enforced if no agreement was reached during the negotiation process. Recent legislative and judicial actions have dramatically altered the distribution of rights and responsibilities regarding water use in California. These changes have generally favored the position of environmentalists and urban users relative to agricultural users. As would be expected, this change in the disagreement outcome toward the most preferred point of the environmental interest group benefited the performance of this group in the negotiations. As the disagreement policy becomes more appealing to the environmentalists, they become more able to credibly commit to abandoning the negotiations unless other groups concede.

Another simulation involved changing the access probabilities of various players in the negotiations. An increase in a player's access probability may reflect increased influence by that player on political decision processes. The inclusion of group representatives on state boards governing resource use, or the election of political candidates supportive of group goals, are possible examples of how a group's access probability may increase. Not surprisingly, increasing a group's access probability improves its performance in the negotiations and leads to negotiated positions closer to the group's ideal position. A less obvious result is that increasing the access probability of one player benefits other players who have similar preferences to that player.

A final simulation involved varying the structure of the admissible coalition. This simulation, similar in spirit to the second simulation reported earlier, is also concerned with interest group heterogeneity. If the legal and institutional environment is such that consent from all interest groups, but not all members of all interest groups, is required, then the performance of more heterogeneous coalitions may be expected to diminish. Furthermore, as the percentage of interest group members whose consent is required to reach agreement declines, the detrimental effect of group heterogeneity may be expected to increase.

Broadening the list of admissible coalitions by requiring support from fewer subgroups exacerbates the detrimental effect that preference heterogeneity has on interest group performance. The utility of the excluded subgroups suffers, as does the utility of the included subgroup. In competing for coalition membership, all subgroups modify their negotiation stances to accommodate the views of other interest groups and attract invitation into the ruling coalition. In this competition, all subgroups, including the subgroup eventually included, accept less from the negotiations than they would under a strict majority rule.

Conclusion

To establish institutions that support the rational public trust allocations of water resources, multilateral bargaining, collective decisionmaking, and negotiation processes are necessary first steps. This chapter has outlined two analytical frameworks that can be applied to water resource systems to achieve sustainable governance and institutional structures. The first is based on the Nash-Harsanyi approach and the second uses the noncooperative model of multilateral bargaining developed by Rausser and Simon (1991). Both analytical frameworks admit the specific features of water resource systems. The former framework imposes four fundamental axioms while the latter framework is axiom free. Both frameworks recognize default options or disagreement outcomes and are driven by relative political influence and power.

The traditional features, players, and stakeholders of water resource systems can be expanded to incorporate other fundamental forces. From the standpoint of design, these forces are associated with moral hazard, asymmetric information, communications, and networking. They also include risk management choices facing water regulators, suppliers, and demanders, such as the use of exotic options, derivatives, and conventional financial instruments, including borrowing and alternative credit sources. In the context of implementation, devolution and decentralization and multiple jurisdictional issues can also be integrated into the analytical frameworks presented in this chapter. Here the distinction between stakeholders and their representatives who have access to and are part of the actual negotiation process can be recognized.

Principal agency frameworks and the nonalignment of incentives enrich both the Nash-Harsanyi and the Rausser-Simon collective decision and bargaining frameworks. Ultimately, an insightful investigation of devolution and decentralized decisionmaking requires an examination of formal versus real authority (Aghion and Tirole 1997).

References

Adams, Gregory, Gordon Rausser, and Leo Simon. 1996. "Modeling Multilateral Negotiations: An Application to California Water Policy." *Journal of Economic Behavior & Organization* 30(1): 97–111.

Aghion, Philippe, and Jean Tirole. 1997. "Formal and Real Authority in Organization." *Journal of Political Economy* 105(1): 1–29.

Anderson, Terry L., and Pamela S. Snyder. 1997. *Priming the Invisible Pump*. Washington, D.C.: Cato Institute.

Harsanyi, John C. 1962a. "Measurement of Social Power, Opportunity Cost, and the Theory of Two-Person Bargaining Game." *Behavioral Science* 12(1): 67–80.

_____. 1962b. "Measurement of Social Power in n-Person Cooperative Game." *International Economic Review* 4(2): 194–220.

_____. 1977. *Rational Behavior and Bargaining Equilibrium in Games and Social Situations*. Cambridge, U.K.: Cambridge University Press.

Howitt, Richard. 1997. "Market Based Conflict Resolution." In *Proceedings of the Rosenberg International Forum on Water Policy*. Davis, California: University of California, Water Resources Center.

Kenski, Henry C. 1990. *Saving the Hidden Treasure: The Evolution of Ground Water Policy*. Ames, Iowa: Iowa State University Press.

Nash, John F. 1950. "The Bargaining Problem." *Econometrica* 18(2): 155–162.

_____. 1953. "Two-Person Cooperative Games." *Econometrica* 21(1): 128–40.

Ostrom, Elinor. 1997. "Common-Pool Resources and Institutions: Toward a Revised Theory." In Bruce Gardner and Gordon Rausser, eds., *Handbook of Agricultural Economics*. Amsterdam: Elsevier Science.

Peters, H. J. M. 1992. *Axiomatic Bargaining Game Theory*. Dordrecht, Holland: Kluwer Academic Publishers.

Postel, Sandra. 1996. "Forging a Sustainable Water Strategy." In *State of the World 1996*. Worldwatch Institute Report 1996. New York: W. W. Norton.

Rausser, Gordon C. 1992. "Lessons for Emerging Market Economies in Eastern Europe." In Christopher Clague and Gordon C. Rausser, eds., *The Emergence of Market Economics in Eastern Europe*. Cambridge, Massachusetts: Blackwell Publishers.

Rausser, Gordon C., and Leo K. Simon. 1991. "A Non-Cooperative Model of Collective Decision Making: A Multi-Lateral Bargaining Approach." Working Paper no. 618. University of California Department of Agricultural and Resource Economics, Berkeley.

Rausser, Gordon C., and Pinhas Zusman. Forthcoming. *Political Power and Endogenous Policy Formation.* Cambridge, Massachusetts: Cambridge University Press.

Rogers, Peter. 1993. *America's Water: Federal Roles and Responsibilities.* Cambridge, Massachusetts: MIT Press.

Simon, Paul. 1998. *Tapped Out: The Coming World Crisis in Water and What We Can Do about It.* New York: Welcome Rain.

Varian, Hal R. 1984. *Microeconomic Analysis,* 2nd ed. New York: W. W. Norton.

Western Governors' Association Water Efficiency Working Group. 1987. *Water Efficiency: Opportunities for Action—Report to the Western Governors.* Denver, Colorado.

World Bank. 1992. *World Development Report 1992.* New York: Oxford University Press.

Zilberman, David, Neal MacDougall, and Farhed Shah. 1994. "Changes in Water Allocation Mechanisms for California Agriculture." *Contemporary Economic Policy* 12(1): 122–33.

Zusman, Pinhas, and Gordon C. Rausser. 1994. "Intraorganizational Influence Relations and the Optimality of Collective Action." *Journal of Economic Behavior and Organization* 24(1): 1–17.

4

Governance Rules and Management Decisions in California's Agricultural Water Districts

Richard J. McCann and David Zilberman

An ample literature is available on the efficiency of water use and adoption of conservation technologies in agriculture (Dinar and Zilberman 1991; Green and others 1996). Also, significant evidence indicates that financial incentives, particularly the cost of water, affect water use and management in agriculture. The literature documents that water costs in a state like California vary drastically among regions and within regions, but the reasons for the cost differences have not been extensively investigated. Some of the literature assumes that water providers' behavior as profit maximizing firms, in addition to the effect of conveyance costs, may explain locational differences in water pricing (Chakravorty, Hochman, and Zilberman 1995). Differences in water rights may also lead to water price variation. However, awareness of the importance of public enterprise agencies in water allocation decisions is growing.[1] Looking beyond typical neoclassical assumptions about the theory of the firm may be important to understand how water markets and other management regimes might develop (Holburt, Atwater, and Quinn 1988, p. 45).

The original research was funded by the University of California Water Resources Center. The authors thank Janis Carey, Ariel Dinar, Tony Fisher, Michael Hanemann, Shi-Ling Hsu, Bart McGuire, Gordon Rausser, and participants at the World Bank's Workshop on Political Economy of Water Pricing Implementation for insightful comments, and Dan Osgood for research assistance.

1. Several observers believe that a key impediment to efforts to reform water resource management is the requirement in California law that agricultural water districts must approve any transfer of water rights outside their borders (Holburt, Atwater, and Quinn 1988; Smith and Vaughan 1988; Thompson 1993a,b).

Water districts are the predominant type of organization that provides water to farmers in California and other parts of the western United States. Similar organizations are prevalent elsewhere. These are semigovernmental, nonprofit organizations, and make decisions that are voted on by members. Some districts rely on a popular vote; others use weighted votes that are proportional to assessed land values.

This chapter has two objectives. The first is to derive water pricing rules as functions of alternative voting schemes and analyze the resulting implications of voting rules on technology choice and land use. The second is to test some of these implications using data from California.

The California Water Districts

California law, mostly through 38 types of general district acts, specifies several methods for identifying qualified electors and weighing votes for electing governing boards (Bain, Caves, and Margolis 1966; Goodall, Sullivan, and DeYoung 1978).[2] In addition, more than 100 special district enabling acts were in place as of 1994 (California Department of Water Resources 1994). Members of the governing board may be elected by eligible voters—who may be residents or other property owners of the district—or appointed by the county board of supervisors. In an election, the votes may be counted under a one person, one vote (popular) system, or weighted according to property acreage or assessed value per acre. Whereas the popular vote is predominate in older districts in the Sacramento and east San Joaquin Valleys, the property-weighted scheme is being used increasingly. This latter scheme is especially common in the western and southern areas of the San Joaquin Valley, which is served by newer state and federal water projects and where corporate farms, rather than family-owned farms, are more common (Goodall, Sullivan, and DeYoung 1978). Even older districts have switched to the weighted approach.[3]

A useful institutional perspective is to compare how the operations and financing of water districts reflect the principles of cooperatives (Bain, Caves, and Margolis 1966; Rosen and Sexton 1993). These districts provide service at cost as nonprofit organizations. Benefits are generally distributed in proportion to the use of the managed resource, and returns to equity capital are

---

2. Property qualification, popular vote, appointed boards, and acreage-based voting systems are also used, but not as often.
3. For example, the Glenn-Colusa Irrigation District switched in 1992 and the Richvale Irrigation District switched in 1996.

limited and generally gained through directly related activities, such as sell-ing irrigated crops. Member-users control the district, which meshes with the concept of vertical integration of the water supply with agricultural pro-duction. The cooperative management of input resources has several advan-tages (Sexton 1986). The joint allocation of resources avoids the transaction costs and risks associated with a market type of exchange institution, such as postcontract opportunism by a party (Alston and Gillespie 1989; Williamson 1979, 1983). By extending or avoiding market power, a joint management scheme can encourage the development of asset-specific rela-tionships by removing the risk of breach of contract (Williamson 1983). It also provides a mechanism for avoiding, mitigating, spreading, or sharing risk among members (Thompson and Wilson 1994). The internalization of allocation decisions can avoid government interference in the exchange in-stitution. An example of such interference is the federal reclamation law acre-age limitations (Wahl 1988).

In this chapter we assume that water district board members (and, by implication, line managers) attempt to win a majority of votes by addressing the issues that most affect district members. This is the ba-sis of Peltzman's (1971) median-voter political-economic model.[4] Sev-eral previous studies of agricultural districts have looked at some as-pects of how district decisionmaking processes work (Bain, Caves, and Margolis 1966; Coontz 1989; 1991; Goodall, Sullivan, and DeYoung 1978; Moore 1986). The model in this chapter builds on three political economy models that take different approaches to the question of how district policies are chosen (McDowell and Ugone 1982; Rosen and Sex-ton 1993; Zusman and Rausser 1994). The first two models treat the in-stitutional management selection rules as the focal point of policy deci-sions, and the last one examines the importance of informal political influence. The first and third models put district managers at the center of the decisionmaking process, whereas the second one implies that decisions di-rectly reflect the wishes of the districts' members. The latter two models rely on information about each district's individual members, that is, their farming activities or relative political influence. None of the models as-sume that a district manager maximizes the total net benefits to mem-bers, but rather that coalitions are built by targeting benefits to certain groups within a district.

---

4. The model is informally akin to a Stackelberg-leader game in which the dis-trict managers anticipate actions by individual farmers in setting district policy and in trying to assure the maximum probability that they will be reelected.

Despite their differences, the models rely on a common assumption: Members try to influence district managers to choose management policies that distribute benefits in proportion to political power while maximizing aggregate benefits subject to that constraint. The district's objective, acting as a cooperative, is to maximize net benefits to all members, but the nonprofit constraint means that the district's "rents" must be distributed among its members indirectly, perhaps through changes in water rates or allocations. This distribution is the function of political power within the district, measured in terms of voting share.

This analysis is a snapshot of a dynamic process that actually begins with the formation of a particular district. One could argue that the variety of districts fits with Tiebout's model of local government competition (Kollman, Miller, and Page 1997). The conditions at the outset affect the structure of the political institutions, and those institutions shape the districts' physical characteristics. Water diversion is capital-intensive and can require commitments of up to 40 years, with payments relatively invariant with actual usage. Historically, only a few opportunities have arisen in California to acquire surface water supplies with the initiation or expansion of water projects (the Central Valley Project in the 1940s and 1950s and the State Water Project in the 1960s are two examples), as Bain, Caves, and Margolis (1966) show. These water markets opened for short periods and offered only long-term contracts. While shorter-term water markets are evolving, a district faces significant adjustment and transaction costs in selling or acquiring water supplies that differ from those it chose initially. In addition, the existing political milieu seriously constrains any attempt to increase supply capacity through contracts or construction. This analysis does not account for those initial conditions, but such a historical perspective, along with an examination of the fiscal policies over a period of time, could provide useful insights into how political institutions evolve within economic settings.

Defining the Political Structure of a District

This analysis focuses on the decision and governance rules engendered by the basic political structure of agricultural water districts: voter eligibility and vote weighting. Specifically, it looks at (a) how farmers' decision rules vary under different institutional structures, (b) whether districts differ substantially in how they manage their resources and distribute benefits to their members based on their political structure and governance rules, and (c) whether the distributions of benefits within districts mirror the relative political strength of each member as measured by the formal voting rules.

The analysis reflects the hierarchy of decision making in the California water industry. Farmers make technological choices and resource allocations for growing crops. The district chooses the mix of water rights and storage that meets farmers' demands as a function of investment cost and nature. The projects' water suppliers respond to the districts by delivering water in sufficient quantities and in a reliable manner given political constraints imposed by their respective governments.

Farmers' Choices and Objectives

A farmer proceeds through several decisionmaking stages when selecting crop mix, production levels, investment, and water use. The initial choice is the size of the operation. The decision of how much land to cultivate and irrigate depends on many factors, such as how the land is acquired, available financial resources, which crops are appropriate, past resource use, variation in land quality, and distance to markets. Once this decision is made, a farmer chooses to plant and irrigate on the most fixed asset, land, to the maximum extent possible.

Next, the farmer selects the crops to be grown on this land. This choice drives other factor choices, particularly for water. Most crops require a fairly narrow range of "effective" water application as determined by local evapotranspiration requirements and land quality factors such as permeability, drainage, and nutrient levels (Caswell and Zilberman 1986; Green and others 1996). The amount of effective water, e, is a product of the amount applied, a, and the technical efficiency of the irrigation method, h. The farmer then adjusts either the irrigation technology or the amount of water applied to compensate for changes in the other factor. As a result, the farmer faces a two-stage problem: first to select either the amount of water applied or the irrigation efficiency, then to select the other given conditions that dictate effective water requirements (Caswell, Lichtenberg, and Zilberman 1990).

Although water market opportunities are expanding and environmental regulations are constraining supplies, farmers continue to face long-term choices. Because of this time frame, the amount of water to apply from water district sources appears to be the dominant variable in choosing how to meet effective water requirements, and efficiency is a residual of these choices. Thus, we can leave a choice variable, h, to the second stage. The amount of effective water as a result is based on an expectation about the amount of land under cultivation, the price of water and of irrigation technologies, and the price and availability of other inputs.

Other inputs, x_j, are chosen in different time frames before and within each growing season. To simplify the problem, x represents a composite index of all other inputs. We would expect to see shifts among these inputs with changes in water usage and irrigation investment as well. This variable is included to measure the impact of changes in district policies on nonfarmer district members and residents.

The Water Districts' Infrastructure Investment Decision

Perhaps the most important reason for forming any water district is the provision of a reliable water supply. The issues of overall supply and service quality must be addressed collectively because they have clear common property traits. Adding capacity to a reservoir is likely to improve the supply reliability of everyone within the district if the water rights are effectively correlative (Burness and Quirk 1980). Defining the property rights to this added capacity would undermine the cooperative nature of the district. The district is then searching for the "optimal" choice for these variables based on a set of rules. The choice of the supply capacity, S, directly influences reliability: the greater the storage capacity and transfer capability, the longer the district is able to carry over storage during drought periods.

A district must not only supply water to its customers, but also deliver that water on schedule without large conveyance losses and ensure sufficient quality, for example, low salinity. To this end, the district will have scheduling arrangements and constraints with customers. It may line canals or install pipelines to reduce losses and take measures to ensure that water quality is not degraded during transportation. All these measures have costs beyond simply releasing stored water into district canals. Farmers' costs are affected by these quality factors, such as using laborers to irrigate fields at certain times, managing drainage, and losing yield because of poorer quality water.

Examining Existing Institutions

The water supply and agricultural production institutions as they exist today are bifurcated between control of water rights and control of land rights. The district managers and voters control the water rights, and the farmers control the land property rights. A major issue is how this bifurcation affects the efficiency of the use of these resources, and how the variations in institutional rules affect the different forms of the districts. As a cooperative, the district and the farms are partially integrated, but the exchange of information between the two levels—the district and the farm—is externally manifested through prices and voting, and decisionmaking is decentralized. Farmers use water in amounts and in a manner that balance the benefits of revenues generated against the costs of this and other inputs. The district provides at least a price signal as to the appropriate use of the water. The district managers also respond to farmers' wishes through the electoral process. The responses to signals from both sides are imperfect for a number of reasons, including transaction costs, structure of the tariffs, externally imposed legal requirements, and voting rules for the cooperative. In addition, Arrow's Impossibility Theorem implies that any number of outcomes might occur, including nontransitive social preferences or control of the decisionmaking process by a single key individual. For this reason, the procedural details of the decisionmaking process can greatly influence the outcome (Ordeshook 1986, p. 54).

Choices by District Boards and Managers in Existing District Structures

In water districts, managers choose the levels of investment in water supply infrastructure, and they face per unit costs for transporting that water to members in the district. To meet these expenditures, managers may choose from various instruments, including volumetric and per acre water charges, property taxes, other enterprise activity sales (particularly electric power sales), or sales of water to other entities.

An important constraint is the so-called nonprofit requirement: expenditures and revenues must be in approximate balance. Revenues are often limited to sources directly linked to water use, such as prices, charges, or property taxes, and thus pricing must approximate average, not marginal, costs. Water is not priced to signal the most efficient uses in these cases. The net benefits from the district also may be allocated in any number of ways, some of which distort water use choices by farmers. Finally, water district board members tend to choose policies that allow them to continue to hold office. This means pleasing enough constituents to gain a majority of votes. Policies that increase total district wealth may benefit only a few district members and not generate sufficient political support.

Although board members cannot be certain of winning the support of particular voters, they can affect the likelihood of receiving a positive vote. The board has five variables to consider: the identity of the eligible voters, the well-being of each of those voters, the cost of the district's water supply, the variability and reliability of the supply, and the mode of collecting required revenues. We will focus on the district board's objective function, which is to maximize the number of voters subject to meeting a nonprofit budget constraint.

Consider a cumulative probability density function, γ, that specifies the relationship of individual net benefits for district voters and the likelihood of those voters supporting the incumbent board. This function γ can be interpreted as a single utility function in which the output is a yea or nay vote on the current district management. For our purposes we need only note that γ increases as net benefits increase for members within each interest group.

Farmers' Choices under Existing District Institutions

Under the existing institutional structures, farmers do not see the true marginal cost of their water supply captured in a single price of a facility capacity use link. The nonprofit constraint and the ability to levy taxes unrelated to use leads to a multipart pricing system. These district charges and policies can be modified to attract votes for the district managers. The objective for farmers within a district is to choose the total yield that maximizes net revenues after accounting for costs.

The objective function for a tenant farmer differs from an owner-operator in two ways. First, tenant farmers are more likely to incorporate a risk premium, ρ, on fixed irrigation technology investment because of the nature of tenancy versus ownership (Feder and Feeney 1993; Hartman and Doane 1986). Tenants risk not being able to fully recover their investment costs, because they do not control land use and cannot regain fixed investment in the land value. In other words, their risk of sunk costs in investment can be substantially higher. This effectively increases the apparent cost of upgrading irrigation efficiency if we assume improvements require higher fixed investment (Pindyck 1991). To support these practices, the district would lower the per unit price of water so that higher application rates do not cause higher costs and rely on other revenue sources, such as per acre fees, taxes, or electricity sales.

Second, a property tax has only a secondary effect on land costs for tenants by affecting rents. A portion of the property tax incidence is on landlords. Sharecropping reinforces this tendency, because landlords often must pay the delivered water charge, which comes out of their rent earnings. Thus, tenants do not fully realize the penalty or benefit from changes in this type of tax.

Assessed-Value Weighted-Voting Water Districts

In California, a prevalent form of water district organization is the California water district (Davis 1993). Under its governance rules, only landowners are enfranchised and one vote equals one dollar of assessed value (California Department of Water Resources 1994). By state law, this type of district is restricted to retail service for predominantly agricultural users. Once districts reach a certain threshold of residential and commercial service, they must adopt a popular vote system (Marchini and others 1996).

The choice variables can be separated into two categories. The first category, S, includes those variables that affect districtwide capacity and operations, and must be decided collectively, such as supply capacity and service and delivery quality (timing, flexibility, and conveyance losses). The second category includes those variables that affect the operations of individual farms and do not have direct impacts on other farmers in the district: acreage to be irrigated, L_i; applied water, a_i; and the use of other inputs, x_{ij}, such as labor, fertilizer, and equipment. Farmers see the direct or transparent cost of providing water supplies, as represented by the investment in capacity, $K(S)$, and the variable cost of supply, c.[5] In addition, the cooperative may buy or sell a portion of its supply in the water market at the going price, m. This can be thought of as the outside contract rate for project water acquired during the short windows that opened in the California water market (Bain, Caves, and Margolis 1966). These costs include the opportunity or rental cost, ry of land, L, for applied water, a, irrigation investment $I(h, L)$, pressurization costs associated with more efficient or alternative water irrigation systems, $v(h)$, and other input costs, b.

Imposing a nonprofit constraint on the optimal cooperative district implies that the difference between aggregate marginal costs and average costs accrue to the cooperative members directly through rates, rather than to the district itself. The process becomes a two-stage game in which the farmers first choose their optimal output rules, and the district then establishes the optimal level of supply and electricity generation capacity. We can use these equations to find the preferred levels for district charges on land, l; property taxes, t; and water, w.

The objective function for managers in a district with landowner-enfranchised, assessed-value weighted-voting, and a nonprofit revenue constraint is

(4.1)

$$\max_{L_i, a_i, x_i, S_i} Votes_{AVV} = \sum_{i=1}^{N} \bar{L}_i y_i \gamma(\pi_F)$$

$$\text{s.t.} \quad \sum_{i=1}^{N} (wa_i + l + ty_i) \cdot L_i = K\left(\sum_{i=1}^{N} S_i L_i \right) + \sum_{i=1}^{N} ca_i L_i - \sum_{i=1}^{N} m \cdot (\bar{s}_i - a_i) \cdot L_i$$

---

5. In addition, the cooperative may be supplying a joint product from hydropower generation and covering some of the system capacity costs with the resulting revenues. However, the number of districts with this option is relatively small, and we ignore them for this discussion.

where the enfranchised owner-farmer's profit function is represented as

$$\pi_F = pq(h_i a_i, x_i) \cdot L_i - I(h_i, L_i) - \{[v(h_i) + w] \cdot a_i + l + (r + t) \cdot y_i + bx_i\} \cdot L_i$$

We assume the usual concavity and differentiability properties for the farm production functions, q (Berck and Helfand 1990).[6] We also assume that the usual properties for cross-partials hold between applied water and irrigation efficiency so that we can find the derivative of effective water application on yield. The cost of irrigation technology increases with increased efficiency, a phenomenon commonly seen as farmers move from flood to furrow to sprinkler to drip system (Caswell, Lichtenberg, and Zilberman 1990). The marginal investment costs are also increasing consistent with approaching an ultimate efficiency limit of 100 percent. Pressurization costs go up as well, also at an increasing rate consistent with physics. In the case of land, total investment in farm irrigation increases with size, but at a decreasing rate consistent with economies of scale.

District boards must balance the relative effects of relying on available revenue sources to maintain political support. The scale factor from the Lagrangian multiplier measures the shadow value of how political support varies with changes in these revenue sources. This political support shadow value can be used to evaluate the effect of changing revenue sources compared with the effect on popular vote districts.

An interesting characteristic of the assessed-value voting district is that as the average farm size grows, landowners prefer to see a greater reliance on water sale-based revenues over land-based charges to fund district operations. Storage and conveyance costs generally show economies of scale, at least with respect to the size of the service territory (Bain, Caves, and Margolis 1966). The convexity property requires that marginal costs fall faster with respect to land than to storage. We also know that average water yield must be less than maximum storage. Thus, economies of scale imply that preferred acreage assessment fees, the ad valorem tax rate, or both, decrease as the acreage per farm increases.

Popular Vote Water District

Another common form of agricultural water district organization in California is the irrigation district (Davis 1993). With the formation of the Modesto and Turlock irrigation districts in 1887 under the Wright Act, irrigation

---

6. The model results and associated proofs are fully discussed in McCann and Zilberman (1997).

districts were the first governmental entities formed to serve agricultural customers. Their governance rules rely on universal suffrage and one person, one vote elections (California Department of Water Resources 1994). These voting rules are modeled after those of general government agencies and do not necessarily reflect the goals of economic efficiency.

The objective function for managers in a district with universal franchise, popular-weighted voting, and a nonprofit revenue constraint is shown as

$$\max_{L_i, a_i, x_i, S_i} \; Votes_{PV} = \sum_{i=1}^{N-T} \gamma(\pi_F) + \sum_{i=1}^{T} \gamma(\pi_T) + \sum_{i=1}^{B} \gamma(\pi_B)$$

(4.2)

$$\text{s.t.} \quad \sum_{i=1}^{N}(wa_i + l + ty_i) \cdot L_i + \sum_{j=1}^{B} ty_j \overline{L_i} = K\left(\sum_{i=1}^{N} S_i L_i\right) + \sum_{i=1}^{N} ca_i L_i - \sum_{i=1}^{N} m \cdot (\overline{s}_i - a_i)$$

where the profit functions for the owner-farmer (π_F), tenant farmer (π_T), and input suppliers (that is, laborers, retailers, and others) (π_B) are

$$\pi_F = pq(h_i a_i, x_i) \cdot L_i - I(h_i, L_i) - \{[v(h_i) + w] \cdot a_i + l + (r + t) \cdot y_i + bx_i\} \cdot L_I$$

$$\pi_T = pq(h_i a_i, x_i) \cdot L_i - \rho \cdot I(h_i, L_i) - \{[v(h_i) + w] \cdot a_i + l + r(t) \cdot y_i + bx_i\} \cdot L_I$$

$$\pi_B = \sum_{i=1}^{N} (b - z) \cdot \frac{x_i L_i}{B} - (r + t) \cdot \overline{L}_j$$

In the assessed-value voting district, the value of marginal product for other inputs equals the price of those inputs. However, in the case of the popular vote district, the rule used by the district managers equates the value of marginal product to z, the opportunity cost of the suppliers—not the farmers—in providing the other inputs, x. The ratio of the value of marginal product for x_i for each of the district types is

$$\frac{b}{z} = \frac{\partial q_i / \partial x_{i, AVV}}{\partial q_i / \partial x_{i, PV}} \geq 1$$

because the factors used to produce x would be used elsewhere if they could not command at least their opportunity cost, z. Thus, other inputs are used to a greater degree than in a similarly situated assessed-value weighted-voting district.

Local businesses may prefer two types of outcomes.[7] The first is that crops be grown that require a high level of purchased inputs, such as fertilizer or

---

7. Because farm laborers in California, who are frequently foreign nationals with low incomes, are less likely to vote, labor employment is not considered in this discussion.

equipment. Field crops generate less employment than other crops per acre-foot of water (Mitchell 1993), which might imply that other local inputs such as farm equipment are utilized to a higher degree in production. The second is that business activity remain at a fairly constant or growing level, and that it be of the same nature year to year (Pindyck 1991). This gives businesses a greater assurance that they will recover their investments. To serve both these outcomes, the district will tend to establish pricing structures that do not penalize water use, particularly if the water is for long-established crops. Again, this perspective encourages support for a two-part pricing tariff in which the per water unit charge is relatively small compared with the fixed or property-based portion.

This gives us pricing rule 1: in a popular vote district, the district manager will set rates so that the use of other inputs, x_i, will be equal to or greater than the assessed-valuation weighted-voting district.

Now we compare the political support shadow values between the district forms. Based on assumptions about the property tax incidence on rent, $r(t)$, and assuming that tenants place a risk premium, ρ, on a fixed investment, we can analyze how the addition of tenants influences the district managers' objective functions. However, how district charges affect tenant farmer preferences is indeterminate, because we cannot adequately define the countervailing influences between the magnitude of the risk premium and the property tax incidence. Each of these probably varies significantly and is empirically difficult to measure.

Turning to the businesses and suppliers, pricing rule 2 implies that it adds a strictly positive weight to the popular vote district managers' preference for land-based charges. Assuming that this factor outweighs the indeterminate relationship of the tenant farmers' objective function (which is certainly true for districts with large nonfarm electorates), then support for the land-based charges is higher, and the water use charge lower, for the popular vote districts than for the alternative district forms.

Pricing rule 2 is as follows: in comparison with assessed-value voting districts, district managers in popular vote districts will tend to set land-based charges ($l^{PV} + yt^{PV}$) higher and water charges (w^{PV}) lower because of the electoral influence of tenant farmers and local suppliers and other businesses.

Testing the Political Economy Model of District Management Decisions

From analyzing the theoretical model presented earlier, we developed two hypotheses from pricing rules 1 and 2 on how district managers might respond under different governance rules. The first is whether districts rely to differing degrees on water charges versus land charges based on electoral rules. The second is whether districts tend to choose policies that favor certain types of crops.

In California, the local agencies that provide water delivery services are called special districts. The term refers to a host of districts that provide specialized government services beyond those that counties or cities might offer, such as flood control, mosquito abatement, and waste collection. Special districts that provide services which are charged for directly, such as water utilities or waste collection, are called enterprise districts.

The retail agencies that are the focus of this study are governed by a wide variety of state laws and regulations, contained mostly in the state water code. Many aspects of these districts have been described in other publications (for example, Bain, Caves, and Margolis 1966; Goodall, Sullivan, and DeYoung 1978; Rosen 192b). As with most general and special district governments in California, enterprise water districts generally rely on a universal franchise, one person, one vote system, also known as residential voting. Types of districts that tend to use such a voting system include community services, county water, irrigation, municipal water, public utility, and water conservation. In addition, specified water agencies (Antelope Valley-East Kern and Placer County water agencies) and California water districts in which more than 50 percent of the assessable area is in nonagricultural use often rely on this system of voting.[8] For some irrigation and county water districts, the franchise may be limited to those who own land within the district.[9] Another common method, which reclamation, water storage, and primarily agricultural California water districts use, is to enfranchise landowners, weight their votes by assessed value for the parcel (usually one vote per dollar value), and allow proxy voting in district elections. This type of voting is more common in mutual water companies or corporations in which voting rights and ownership of core assets are linked. The 1927 water conservation districts limit voting to landowners and weight the votes on a per acre basis. County water authorities, which are largely wholesale agencies, have appointed board members selected by the member agencies.[10]

The base data set for the empirical analysis is drawn from a survey of 128 districts conducted by the University of California at Berkeley's Department

---

8. Five California water districts in the data set rely on this type of voting.

9. No districts of this type were included in the data set; however, Glenn-Colusa Irrigation District switched to this system in 1992 after the data had been collected.

10. The San Diego County Water Authority is the only agency in the data set with such characteristics.

of Agricultural and Resources Policy and Economics. The survey methodology and a partial summary of results is included in a department working paper (Zilberman and others 1992), which was followed by an analysis of how the districts altered their behavior during a drought (Zilberman, MacDougall, and Shah 1994). The survey data set relied on three main sources for district-specific information: the Association of California Water Agencies membership list contained information on agricultural and municipal customer usage and rates, the state controller's office had data on special districts' financial transactions for the 1991–92 fiscal year, and the California Department of Water Resources had data on the districts' voting systems (California Department of Water Resources 1994).

The districts in the data set were distributed among 7 regions and 29 of California's 58 counties. Most of the districts and 84 percent of the respondents were located in four regions: the Sacramento and San Joaquin Valleys, the Tulare Lake Basin, and southern California. More than 60 percent were located in the Central Valley. All but 1 of the 42 landowner-enfranchised districts in the data set were located in the 3 Central Valley regions. Because of the widespread urban activity in southern California, landowner-based electoral rules have had difficulty surviving legal and political tests, and none is shown in the data set despite the relatively high proportion of districts located in the region.

Districts with landowner franchise tend to have large farms.[11] One reason for this relationship could be the desire of larger landowners to influence district policies. A second reason may be that the more urbanized districts, which tend to have smaller farm operations, are required to use popular vote electoral rules. A third reason may be simple geography: larger farms tend to be based in the Central Valley where almost all the landowner-enfranchised districts are located.

One way to assess the likely cause of this relationship is to limit the analysis to the most agricultural districts, irrigation and California water districts, and those districts located in the three Central Valley regions and the Inland Empire (Imperial and eastern Riverside counties). Table 4.1 compares the means and correlation coefficients for all districts in the data set to those for irrigation and California water districts located in the Central Valley and Inland Empire. The results differ only

---

11. Average size farm and the acreage irrigated per farm is strongly correlated with an R^2 of 0.932. Because data on irrigated acreage are probably better than data on actual farm size, the irrigated acreage is used as a proxy for farm size.

TABLE 4.1
Correlation Coefficients between Electoral Rules and Average Farm Size for All Districts versus Central Valley and Inland Empire Irrigation and California Water Districts

Variable	Mean value		Correlation with landowner vote	
	All	*Central Valley and Inland Empire*	*All*	*Central Valley and Inland Empire*
Number of sample observations	105	58	105	58
Irrigated farmland (acres)	539.90	668.00	0.38	0.33
Average farm size	815.50	778.10	0.30	0.33

Source: Authors.

slightly, indicating that the relationship between electoral rules and average farm size appears to be invariant with urbanization or location. This relationship appears to be most consistent with the first proposition: large landowners prefer an electoral system in which they can wield greater direct political influence.

Pricing Rule 1: District Manager Biases toward Crop Choices

According to pricing rule 1, if orchard farming requires the use of more local inputs such as equipment, fertilizer, and labor relative to field crops, then district managers will tend to set rates that encourage this crop choice. An indicator of these policies would be a greater preponderance of local-input-intensive crops in these districts. This is consistent with past findings that orchard crops have substantially higher employment rates per acre-foot of water applied than field crops (Mitchell 1993). In addition, a regional economic analysis of the Sacramento Valley found a higher ratio of in-region purchases for the fruit and nuts subsector than for feed grains (Moss and others 1993, appendix C).

Two sets of models distinguish between assessing the entire data set and two district forms dominated by agricultural, irrigation, and California ware districts. While agricultural activities generally dominate both types of districts, California water districts use assessed-value voting, and irrigation districts use the popular vote method.[12] The first set of models evaluates whether electoral rules influence the proportion of orchard crops within a district. The second set evaluates whether electoral rules influence the proportion of field crops within a district. The sample sizes are reduced substantially because of the lack of data on cropping patterns.

Statistical analysis indicates that the proportion of orchard crops is strongly associated with increased irrigation efficiency. The only potentially exogenous variable in the data set positively correlated with efficiency is the proportion of surface water supplies received from the State Water Project (SWP). The resulting ordinary least squares model also includes an intercept dummy for whether the district uses a landowner-enfranchisement rule (AVV). Table 4.2 shows the parameters and test statistics for model 1, all districts, and model 4, irrigation versus California water districts.

Model 1 appears to be significant at the 2.5 percent level, but model 4, which focuses on just the two district forms, does not appear to yield significant results. The parameter estimate for the influence of electoral rules in model

TABLE 4.2
Proportion of Orchard Crops within a District

Variable	Coefficient	Pr>|t|	Degrees of freedom	R^2	F-statistical probability
Model 1:					
All districts			47	0.161	0.023
Constant	0.588	0.000			
AVV	0.308	0.004			
SWP contractor	0.000	0.362			
Model 2:					
California water districts and					
irrigation districts			34	0.045	0.353
Constant	0.414	0.001			
AVV	0.144	0.151			
SWP contractor	0.000	0.339			

Source: Authors.

12. The second model also eliminates those California water districts now using popular voting rules, because their proportion of agricultural water service has fallen below the 50 percent threshold.

1 is consistent with pricing rule 1 and statistically significant at the 1 percent level. Whether the district is an SWP contractor appears to have little influence over whether farmers in the district choose orchard crops.

The second set of models assesses the influence on the choice of crops. Statistical analysis indicates a positive relationship between average farm size and the share of field crops. Given the relatively low revenue and value per acre, this relationship is consistent with economic theory that economies of scale would prevail in these operations. As with the models of district revenue sources, we expect that this scale effect diminishes with the size of the farm, so the natural logarithm of average irrigated acreage, $Log(AIAF)$, is used. The resulting ordinary least squares model also includes an intercept dummy for whether the district uses a landowner-enfranchisement rule (AVV). Table 4.3 shows the parameters and test statistics for model 3, all districts, and model 4, irrigation versus California water districts.

Both models appear to be significant at the 0.01 percent probability level, which probably reflects the inclusion of more than just a dummy variable as a significant explanatory variable. As in model 1, the parameter estimates for the influence of electoral rules are consistent with pricing rule 1 and statistically significant at the 10 percent level in model 3 and 15 percent level for model 4. As expected, farm size positively influences the proportion of district acreage devoted to field crops.

TABLE 4.3
Proportion of Field Crops within a District

Variable	Coefficient	$Pr > |t|$	Degrees of freedom	R^2	F-statistical probability
Model 3:					
All districts			51	0.385	0.000
Constant	−0.162	0.070			
AVV	0.147	0.061			
Log(AIAF)	0.083	0.001			
Model 4:					
California water					
districts and					
irrigation districts			37	0.324	0.000
Constant	−0.113	0.205			
AVV	0.119	0.146			
Log(AIAF)	0.084	0.004			

Source: Authors.

Pricing Rule 2: Relative Reliance on Water Sales Revenues

The first hypothesis tested under pricing rule 2 is whether universal franchise popular vote (PV) districts are less likely to rely on water use charges
than landowner franchise assessed-value-weighted (AVV) districts. Another
way to state this question is do PV districts meet a lower proportion of
their total expenditures with operating revenues than AVV districts? This
assumes a close link between the use of water charges and operating revenues, and between fixed charges and taxes and nonoperating revenues.
Our pricing rule presents a simple test comparing the ratio of water use
and acreage-based charges: the ratio of water use to acreage-based revenues should be greater for AVV districts than for PV districts.

We have assumed in this analysis that water use charges are equivalent
to water sales and water service as defined in the state controller's report.
We can then test equivalently what proportion of total district revenues are
derived from operating revenues as shown in the controller's report.[13] The
resulting dependent variable is the ratio of operating revenues to total expenditures ($Operating\ Revenues_i / Expenditures_i$). Note that this dependent
variable is independent of regional variations in water pricing. A high-cost
district can have the same ratio as a low-cost district. This avoids the problem of having to trace numerous local and institutional factors that create
pricing differentials.[14]

Nevertheless, several other key variables may affect this ratio. The first
is whether the district also delivers wholesale or retail electricity service.
Such a district may be able to cross-subsidize between electric and water
utility service (Chatterjee 1994), and it is likely to be larger than comparable nonelectric districts. Whether a district is also an electric utility (E_i) is
added as a slope dummy to the parameter on district size to account for
economy of scope. The second factor is the economy of scale inherent in
district operations (Bain, Caves, and Margolis 1966). Larger districts are
likely to have lower costs per acre-foot delivered. However, we do not expect a linear relationship because of the law of diminishing returns; rather,
we expect the magnitude of the effect to diminish with increasing district
size. In this case, the natural log of total expenditures, $Log(Size_i)$, is used to
represent economy of district scale. The third is the relative size of farms in

---

13. We have included negative net income as a fixed revenue source equivalent
to draws on nonoperating income.
14. McDowell and Ugone (1982) developed a similar model, but they assessed
the absolute dollar spending on operating expenses and thus had to account for regional disparities across the southwestern United States.

the district. The theoretic model shows that larger farm operations will prefer a greater reliance on water use charges. Again, we do not expect the effect to be linear, and the natural log of average irrigated acreage per farm is used, $Log(AIAF_i)$. A slope dummy is added to assess the effect of larger farm size within landowner franchise, assessed-value weighted-voting districts. Finally, a dummy variable is added to distinguish districts using a landowner-franchised, assessed-value weighted-voting scheme (AVV_i) from those using a universal franchise, popular vote system. Model 5 evaluates pricing rule 2 for most districts with usable data in the sample. Model 6 isolates the effect for two specific district forms: irrigation and California water districts. Table 4.4 presents the model results, estimated using ordinary least squares.[15]

TABLE 4.4
Operating Revenue to Expenditures Ratio Models

Variable	Coefficient	Pr > |t|	Degrees of freedom	R^2	F-statistical probability
Model 5:					
All districts			106	0.103	0.028
Constant	−0.080	0.438			
AVV	1.218	0.002			
Log(Size)	0.072	0.020			
E · Log (Size)	−0.018	0.066			
AVV · Log(AIAF)	0.176	0.003			
Model 6:					
California water districts and irrigation districts			73	0.147	0.027
Constant	−0.447	0.265			
AVV	2.208	0.001			
Log(Size)	0.094	0.030			
E · Log(Size)	0.021	0.081			
AVV · Log(AIAF)	0.283	0.003			

Source: Authors.

15. In addition, a joint null hypothesis is tested for each model that the slope parameters $\beta_4 = \beta_5 = 0$ (Judge and others 1988, p. 434; White 1992, p. 91). For model 1 with 5 parameters and 106 degrees of freedom, the F-statistic probability value equals 0.0097. For model 2 with 5 parameters and 96 degrees of freedom, the F-statistic probability value equals 0.0120.

Both models 5 and 6 support the hypothesis that electoral rules affect district decisions on how to collect revenues. The positive direction of the parameter on AVV is consistent with the hypothesis that landowner-enfranchised districts will tend to rely more on water sales revenues to meet total expenditures: AVV districts rely on about 22 percent more water sales revenues than PV districts. Model 6 indicates that the electoral effect may be stronger in predominantly agricultural districts: California water districts collect about twice the water sales revenues of irrigation districts.

In both models, larger districts tend to rely more on operating revenues. Economies of scope that allow cross-subsidies from electricity operations to water service are evident, but small. The two models give contradictory results, but the effects are not signifiant in either case.

Finally, increasing farm size in landowner-enfranchised districts exerts a depressing effect on the use of water sales revenues in a district, contrary to the model's predictions. However, this may be in part an artifact of the data set being dominated by Central Valley Project contractor districts. Central Valley Project Class 1 contracts tend to reduce the size of farms in a district, consistent with U.S. Bureau of Reclamation rules, but these districts also tend to use landowner-enfranchisement rules. In practice, recorded farm size is not truly reflective, because the farms are often "paper" units that are actually part of a larger management combination. The farms are sized to fit under Bureau of Reclamation rules for eligibility to receive subsidized water. Another possibility is that the economies of scale in the conveyance system are sufficient so that the costs typically allocated to an individual customer are decreasing faster than the desire for large landowners to pay more through water sales than in land-based charges. These latter charges may be allocated in greater proportion to centralized district facilities and operations.

Discussion

The complex institutional relationships within water districts have implications about how these districts allocate resources and respond to administrative and marketplace incentives. The role of district managers may not be to maximize total district wealth, and the electoral rules likely influence their decisions. When relying on a popular vote system, district managers are more likely to be concerned with broader economic development and equity goals. This is manifested through more reliance on land-based revenue sources than on water usage charges.

Each of the districts' management selection procedures gives different incentives to district members and managers. An assessed-value weighted-voting scheme appears more likely than a popular vote system to mimic the prototypical firm in economic modeling because of the closer correlation between the governance process and the distribution of benefits from water use. Agricultural property values reflect the net returns to crops, and to the degree that water application is correlated with land values, the votes would be allocated in proportion to implicit ownership and utilization of the water resource. Water sales outside the district tend to benefit landowners, because the districts' rights are most frequently tied to the land. Thus, we expect property-weighted districts to be more receptive to selling into a water market than districts with other types of governance structures. District "ownership" shares are not necessarily in direct proportion to the value added from water application, as would be the case in a private enterprise in which ownership would be based on output value, not input quantities, because land values reflect other factors such as soil type and relative market location.

Reliance on popular vote rather than property-weighted vote can create a wedge between users versus those defined as members, and benefits may be rebated on a basis different from use. These benefits might extend beyond simply delivering water to reassigning responsibility for water rights, deciding if water sales need approval to protect certain interests within the district, and setting district charges and taxes to achieve economic goals other than efficiency. Equitable distribution of benefits from district operations becomes more important. We might expect that the district managers would attempt to maximize the value of water-related economic activity regardless of its ties to the land. These actions can include maintaining the water resource for tenant farmers who do not hold title to the land, but may have significant fixed investments in their farm, and considering local farm service businesses if they are eligible to vote. Tenant farmers require water to work their land; they are unlikely to receive payment for water sold by the landowner through a district. Local businesses also rely on farming activity, not just income flows to local landholders that might result from water sales. In a popular vote system, the district may choose both to limit outside water sales to maintain farming activity and to price water in a way that maximizes other related economic activity, for example, fertilizer and equipment sales. So, even beyond water management, the district's political form can affect crop choice, water conservation, and individual farmer's decisions on infrastructure investment. Popular vote districts are more likely to be resistant to policies that require more infrastructure investment and to encourage crops that need more local inputs.

The empirical model results highlight the complexity of translating a theoretical model to empirical applications. The overall explanatory power of the various models is not strong, but the parameter estimates of interest are generally significant. If the omitted variables that explain the remaining variation are uncorrelated, then the parameter estimates should be unbiased. The estimation procedure could benefit from both improved data quantity and quality and a more sophisticated econometric approach. The former should be done before the latter, which is why we used ordinary least squares.

Several questions are left unanswered. For example, the choice of crops at the outset may have influenced the selection of district form, and the resulting policies could simply have reflected inertia from this initial decision. Historical records would be necessary to explore this issue. Districts with popular vote systems could still be dominated by agricultural landowners, an issue that could be explored with explicit voter registration data. The empirical estimation would be assisted by supplementing the assessed-value vote dummy with a continuous variable that reflects the proportion of voter registration represented by landowning farmers. This would allow a more refined assessment of how land ownership interests affect district managers' choices. The true farm management unit size in Central Valley Project contractor districts also needs to be identified to better assess the influence of farm size on district managers' decisions. In addition, more data need to be collected on the relative crop shares within districts.

Conclusion

The districts' motives for water management and profit distribution can clearly be quite different than the classic assumption of profit maximization. We can state the hypothesis simply: district managers are likely to distribute benefits in proportion to the political strength of district members rather than in proportion to the members' economic contributions. Our results do not focus on departure from the first-best solution, largely because we are trying to avoid judging the relative merits of one district form over another. In fact, a social welfare function that focuses solely on maximizing total net wealth in a district is an inappropriate model for economists to use. Instead, economists need to understand the political-economic structure of the institution they are studying, and then use the actual objective function in analyzing the outcomes of policy choices.

References

Alston, Lee J., and William Gillespie. 1989. "Resource Coordination and Transaction Costs." *Journal of Economic Behavior and Organization* 11(1): 191–212.

Bain, Joe S., Richard E. Caves, and Julius Margolis. 1966. *Northern California's Water Industry*. Baltimore, Maryland: The Johns Hopkins University Press and Resources for the Future.

Berck, Peter, and Gloria Helfand. 1990. "Reconciling the von Liebig and Differentiable Crop Production Functions." *American Journal of Agricultural Economics* 72(4): 985–96.

Burness, H. Stuart, and James P. Quirk. 1980. "Economic Aspects of Water Rights." *Journal of Environmental Economics and Management* 7(3): 372–88.

California Department of Water Resources. 1994. *General Comparison of Water District Acts*. Bulletin 155–94. Sacramento, California: Resources Agency.

Carlton, Dennis W., and Jeffery M. Perloff. 1990. *Modern Industrial Organization*. New York: Harper Collins.

Caswell, Margriet, Erik Lichtenberg, and David Zilberman. 1990. "The Effects of Pricing Policies on Water Conservation and Drainage." *American Journal of Agricultural Economics* 72(4): 883–90.

Caswell, Margriet F., and David Zilberman. 1986. "The Effects of Well Depth and Land Quality on the Choice of Irrigation Technology." *American Journal of Agricultural Economics* 68(4): 798–811.

Chakravorty, Ujjayant, Eithan Hochman, and David Zilberman. 1995. "A Spatial Model of Optimal Water Conveyance." *Journal of Environmental Economics and Management* 29(March): 25–41.

Chatterjee, Bishu. 1994. "Optimal Provision of Irrigation and Hydropower through Time-Dependent Production in Cooperative Water Supply Organizations." Ph.D. Diss., University of California, Davis.

Coontz, Norman D. 1989. *"Agricultural Drainage Management Organizations in the Drainage Problem Area of the Grasslands Area of the San Joaquin Valley."* U.S. Bureau of Reclamation Contract no. 7-CS-20-05200. Prepared for San Joaquin Valley Drainage Program. Sacramento, California: Ebasco Services.

_____. 1991. "Water Market Reforms for Water Resource Problems: Invisible Hand or Domination in Disguise?" In A. Dinar and D. Zilberman, eds., *The Economics and Management of Water and Drainage in Agriculture*. Boston, Massachusetts: Kluwer Academic Publishers.

Davis, Gray. 1993. *Annual Report of Financial Transactions Concerning Special Districts of California. Fiscal Year 1991–92*. Sacramento, California: Office of the Controller.

Dinar, Ariel, and David Zilberman. 1991. "The Economics of Resource-Conservation, Pollution-Reduction Technology Selection: The Case of Irrigation Water." *Resources and Energy* 13: 323–48.

Feder, Gershon, and David Feeney. 1993. "The Theory of Land Tenure and Property Rights." In K. Hoff, A. Braverman, and J. E. Stiglitz, eds., *The Economics of Rural Organizations: Theory, Practice, and Policy*. New York: Oxford University Press.

Goodall, Merrill R., John D. Sullivan, and Timothy DeYoung. 1978. *California Water: A New Political Economy.* Montclair, New York: Allanheld, Osmum/Universe Books.

Green, Gareth, David Sundig, David Zilberman, and Doug Parker. 1996. "Explaining Irrigation Technology Choices: A Microparameter Approach." *American Journal of Agricultural Economics* 78(4): 1064–72.

Hartman, Raymond S., and Michael J. Doane. 1986. "Household Discount Rates Revisited." *Energy Journal* 7(1): 139–48.

Holburt, Myron B., Richard W. Atwater, and Timothy H. Quinn. 1988. "Water Marketing in Southern California." *American Water Works Association Journal* 80(3): 38–45.

Judge, George G., R. Carter Hill, William E. Griffiths, Helmut Lutkepohl, and Tsoung-Chao Lee. 1988. *Introduction to the Theory and Practice of Econometrics,* 2nd ed. New York: John Wiley & Sons.

Kollman, Ken, John Miller, and Scott E. Page. 1997. "Political Institutions and Sorting in a Tiebout Model." *American Economic Review* 87(5): 977–92.

Marchini, Joseph M., Christopher L. Campbell, James Gaulin, Matthew E. Hoffman, and James G. Van Beek. 1996. Brief for the Association of California Water Agencies as *Amicus Curiae.* Before 95-16951 in U.S. Court of Appeals, Ninth Circuit, March 6. San Francisco, California.

McCann, Richard J., and David Zilberman. 1997. *Political Structure and Management Decisions in California's Agricultural Water Districts.* UCAL-WRC-W-845, Technical Completion Report. Davis, California: University of California Water Resources Center.

McDowell, John M., and Keith R. Ugone. 1982. "The Effect of Institutional Setting on Behavior in Public Enterprises: Irrigation Districts in the Western States." *Arizona State Law Journal* 2(2): 453–96.

Mitchell, David. 1993. *Water Marketing in California: Resolving Third-Party Impact Issues.* San Francisco: The Bay Area Economic Forum and the Metropolitan Water District of Southern California.

Moore, Michael R. 1986. "Economic Aspects of Western Surface Water Allocation." Ph.D. Diss., University of Michigan, Ann Arbor.

Moss, Steven J., David Mitchell, Richard McCann, and Tom Bayh. 1993. *The Economic Impacts of Alternatives to Open-Field Burning of Agricultural Residues.* Contract no. A132-121. Prepared for the California Air Resources Board and California Environmental Protection Agency. San Francisco: Foster Associates.

Ordeshook, Peter C. 1986. *Game Theory and Political Theory.* Cambridge, U.K.: Cambridge University Press.

Peltzman, Samuel. 1971. "Pricing in Public and Private Enterprises: Electric Utilities in the United States." *Journal of Law and Economics* 14(1): 109.

Pindyck, Robert S. 1991. "Irreversibility, Uncertainty, and Investment." *Journal of Economic Literature* 29(3): 1110–48.

Rosen, Michael D. 1992. "Property Rights and Public Choice in Water Districts: An Application to Water Markets." Ph.D. Diss., University of California, Davis.

Rosen, Michael D., and Richard J. Sexton. 1993. "Irrigation Districts and Water Markets: An Application of Cooperative Decision-Making Theory." *Land Economics* 69: 39–53.

Sexton, Richard J. 1986. "The Formation of Cooperatives: A Game-Theoretic Approach with Implications for Cooperative Finance, Decision Making, and Stability." *American Journal of Agricultural Economics* 68(2): 214–25.

Smith, Rodney T., and Roger Vaughan. 1988. "Irrigation Districts: Obstacles to Water Marketing." *American Water Works Association Journal* 80(3): 10.

Thompson, Barton H. 1993a. "The Future of Water Markets: Emerging Institutions, Shifting Paradigms, and Organizations." Paper read at the Conference on Market Approaches to Environmental Protections, December 4, Stanford University, California.

_____. 1993b. "Institutional Perspectives on Water Policy and Markets." *California Law Review* 81(4): 673–762.

Thompson, Gary D., and Paul N. Wilson. 1994. "Common Property as an Institutional Response to Environmental Variability." *Contemporary Economic Policy* 12(3): 10–21.

Wahl, Richard W. 1988. *Markets for Federal Water: Subsidies, Property Rights, and the Bureau of Reclamation.* Washington, D.C.: Resources for the Future.

White, Kenneth J. 1992. *SHAZAM: The Econometrics Computer Program—User's Reference Manual*, version 7.0 ed. New York: McGraw-Hill.

Williamson, Oliver E. 1979. "Transaction Cost Economics: The Governance of Contractual Relations." *Journal of Law and Economics* 22(2): 233–61.

_____. 1983. "Credible Commitments: Using Hostages to Support Exchange." *American Economic Review* 73(2): 519–540.

Zilberman, David, Cherryl Brown, Federico Castillo, Ariel Dinar, Madhu Khanna, and Neal MacDougall. 1992. "Lessons from California's Response to the Drought: On Behavior under Uncertainty." Working Paper. Department of Agricultural and Resource Economics, University of California, Berkeley.

Zilberman, David, Neal MacDougall, and Farhed Shah. 1994. "Changes in Water Allocation Mechanisms for California Agriculture." *Contemporary Economic Policy* 12(2): 122–33.

Zusman, Pinhas, and Gordon Rausser. 1994. "Intraorganizational Influence Relations and the Optimality of Collective Action." *Journal of Economic Behavior and Organization* 24(1): 1–17.

5

Water Regulation via Pricing:

The Role of Implementation Costs and Asymmetric Information

Yacov Tsur

In a typical transaction situation that involves pricing, carried out in a marketplace by an auction or other contractual arrangement, a tangible and observable commodity changes hands from a seller to a buyer, and a payment that equals price times quantity is exchanged in return. The seller initially owns the merchandise (ownership rights) and has full control of it (controllability), and both parties can observe the properties of the transacted good (observability).

Well-defined property rights identify the seller. Controllability ensures that the price will actually be paid when the transaction takes place. Observability is necessary for the agreed on price to represent the preferences of both parties. If any of these conditions are lacking, the transaction becomes more complicated and costly, and is less likely to come about.

Situations that involve a water transaction often lack some of these conditions. Property rights may not be well defined. Even when they are defined, the water may not be in the control of the owner, as the situation generally involves state-owned aquifers that underlie irrigated farmland, stream flows that overlie it, or water that is upstream from the owner. Moreover, when the water is not subject to the seller's control, the seller may not be able to observe the quantity of the purchased water, as is the case when irrigators extract or divert unmetered, state-owned water. This latter pervasive situation introduces the problem of asymmetric information.

This chapter looks at the effects of transaction (or implementation) costs and asymmetric information on water regulation, carried out by means of pricing. It argues that the two are intricately related and discusses implications for water pricing policies.

Existing Methods of Water Pricing

Generally speaking, existing methods of water pricing can be classified into volumetric and nonvolumetric methods (see, for example, Dinar and Subramanian 1997; Tsur and Dinar 1995, 1997). Volumetric methods, such as the single-rate, tiered (multirates), two-part tariff, or market-based prices, rely in one way or another on the volume (quantity) of water used, and hence require a metering water facility. Nonvolumetric methods are based on output or inputs other than water, such as per area pricing based on the cultivated or irrigated area.

Evaluating the performance of the different pricing methods requires a measuring devise—a yardstick. Such a yardstick can be based on efficiency or income distribution or on a combination of the two criteria. Efficiency criteria are concerned with the overall income that can be generated, that is, the size of the pie. Income distribution criteria deal with how a given pie is to be distributed. This chapter considers efficiency criteria only. (Income distribution considerations can be found in Tsur and Dinar 1995 and in the references they cite.)

In the absence of implementation costs, volumetric pricing methods can achieve a first-best allocation—that is, an outcome that maximizes the net benefit that the available water can generate. The maximum benefit that can be attained with input or output pricing is, in general, smaller than the benefit attainable with volumetric pricing. This is because the water charges imposed on other inputs or outputs may distort input-output decisions. Yet such charges are still chosen to maximize a social benefit function, albeit a distorted one. The chapter therefore refers to input-output pricing as second-best efficient (efficient because it maximizes benefit, second-best because the benefit it can achieve falls short of that achieved in volumetric pricing). Per area pricing, being a fixed cost, has a limited effect on input-output decisions and is therefore not considered as an efficient method.

The overall performance of a pricing method, however, must also include implementation costs, which depend on prevailing circumstances. A not uncommon possibility is that the inefficient, per area pricing will outperform an efficient volumetric pricing if the difference in implementation costs between the two outweighs the efficiency difference.

Asymmetric information is another factor that drastically affects the performance of the different pricing methods. In the case of water pricing, asymmetric information often appears in two basic forms: (a) privately observed individual water intakes (unmetered water), and (b) water production technologies that depend on farmer characteristics that are unobserved by the regulator. This chapter discusses how these forms of incomplete information, combined with transaction costs, affect the feasibility and efficiency performance of different water pricing methods. Table 5.1 presents a rough classification of possible combinations of transaction costs and asymmetric information.

The chapter considers each of these cases, discussing water pricing problems associated with the costs and information structures. I will offer solutions when possible. Otherwise, I will suggest additional research.

Case 1: No Transaction Costs and Complete Information

This is a standard textbook situation, to which a standard textbook solution applies. Consider first a single water user. Suppose that the yield (y) response to water (q) can be described by the relation $y = f(q)$, where $f(\cdot)$ is an increasing and strictly concave function (so that more water means more yield, but the additional yield generated by the last unit of water diminishes with water input). Profit-seeking farmers, faced with output and water prices p and w, will choose the water input $q(w)$ that maximizes the profit $pf(q) - wq$ (the profit maximizing water input also depends on output price p, but we suppress this argument for notational convenience). The outcome of this profit maximization exercise is the water derived demand function $q(w) = f'^{-1}(w/p)$ derived from the necessary condition for profit

TABLE 5.1

Classification by Transaction Costs and Asymmetric Information

Transaction costs	Complete information	Unmetered water	Incomplete water-yield function	Unmetered water and incomplete water-yield function
No transaction costs	Case 1	Case 3	Case 5	Case 7
Positive transaction costs	Case 2	Case 4	Case 6	Case 8

Note: The first and second rows correspond to absence and presence of transaction costs, respectively; the columns correspond to information available to the regulator.

Source: Author.

maximization $f'[q(w)] = w/p$. This is the downward sloping curve $pf'(q)$ in figure 5.1 (primes signify derivatives and the superscript $^{-1}$ indicates the inverse function). The corresponding optimal output level is $f[q(w)]$.

With the cost of water supply given by an increasing and convex function $c(q)$, the water planner wishes to set the water price to maximize the social benefit $pf[q(w)] - c[q(w)]$. Note that the water proceeds $wq(w)$ are merely a transfer from the water user to the supplier, and they therefore cancel out of the social benefit calculations, provided that no transaction costs are incurred, that is, a dollar of water proceeds paid by the farmer is equivalent to a dollar received by the regulator. The situation is different in the presence of transaction costs, for instance, when the planner subtracts a certain amount from each dollar of the water proceeds to finance the water pricing operation.

The planner seeks the price that maximizes social benefit, subject to the farmer's derived demand function $q(w) = f'^{-1}(w/p)$. In the absence of transaction costs it is readily verified that the optimal water price w^* is the value of w that solves $w = c'[q(w)] \equiv MC[q(w)]$, which is the marginal cost pricing rule. The optimal output is $y^* = f[q(w^*)]$.

The economic interpretation is simple. The water user will demand water up to the level where the revenue generated by an additional unit of water

FIGURE 5.1
Optimal Pricing for Irrigation Water with One Water User

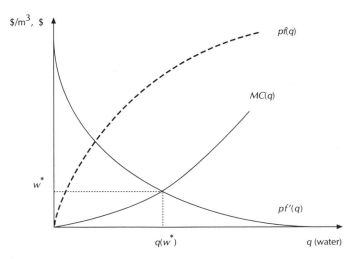

Note: $f(q)$ is the water yield function; $pf(q)$ is the revenue function; $pf'(q)$ is the marginal revenue and the derived demand for water; $MC(q)$ is the marginal cost of water supply; and w^* is the marginal cost price of water at which the demand and supply curves intersect.

Source: Author.

is equal to the price of water. The revenue generated by an additional unit of water simply equals the marginal revenue $pf'(q)$. While generating the revenue $pf'(q)$, an additional water unit inflicts the cost $c'(q) \equiv MC(q)$. Clearly, from society's viewpoint, as long as $pf'(q) > MC(q)$, it pays to supply an additional unit of water, whereas if $pf'(q) < MC(q)$, it pays to reduce the supply by a marginal unit. Thus, the price that maximizes social benefit is the marginal cost price w^*.

No particular difficulty arises with multiple water users, each with an individual derived demand for water $pf_j'(q)$, $j=1, 2, ..., n$. The aggregate derived demand for water is obtained by horizontal summation of the individual demands (figure 5.2), and the marginal cost price is the price at which the aggregate water demand and marginal cost of water supply intersect. In this ideal case, the marginal cost price is first-best in that it maximizes the social benefit (the sum of consumer and producer surpluses).

Case 2: Implementation Costs and Complete Information

Transaction costs associated with water pricing vary across pricing methods and locations. Typically they involve a fixed component, such as installing measuring devices and setting up an administrative structure and

FIGURE 5.2
Optimal Pricing for Irrigation Water with Multiple Water Users

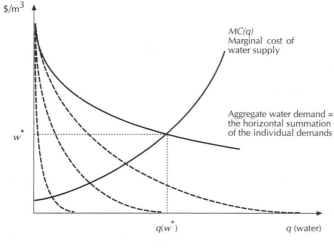

Source: Author.

facilities, and a variable component that increases with the water proceeds, such as monitoring and collection activities. When the latter is proportional to water proceeds, a certain portion of each dollar of water proceeds is used to cover pricing expenses. This transaction costs fraction will be different for each pricing method.

Let us consider volumetric pricing first. The social welfare associated with volumetric pricing when the portion λ^v of the water proceeds is used to cover pricing expenses is given by

$$pf[q(w)] - wq(w) + (1 - \lambda^v)wq(w) - c[q(w)] = pf[q(w)] - \lambda^v wq(w) - c[q(w)]$$

The first two terms on the left represent the profit to water users; the reminder is the profit of the water supplier. The optimal water price $w^*(\lambda^v)$ is now a function of λ^v and in general differs from the marginal cost price w^* obtained in the absence of transaction costs.

The output pricing method admits a different transaction cost structure with a different transaction cost parameter λ^y. Consider the method that charges the fee $wf^{-1}(y)$ for output level y, of which the fraction $\lambda^y wf^{-1}(y)$ is used to cover monitoring and fee collection expenses. Social welfare is then given by

$$py - wf^{-1}(y) + (1 - \lambda^y)wf^{-1}(y) - c[f^{-1}(y)] = py - \lambda^y wf^{-1}(y) - c[f^{-1}(y)].$$

The optimal water fee level $w(\lambda^y)$ is now a function of the transaction cost parameter, and so is the associated social benefit. The difference between volumetric pricing and output pricing is now also due to the difference in transaction costs.

Table 5.2 demonstrates possible effects of implementation costs. It looks at wheat growers deciding on water and nitrogen inputs. Nitrogen is purchased at a fixed price, whereas the price of water is set to maximize net social welfare, conditional on the pricing method used (see Tsur and Dinar 1997). The implementation costs are a fraction of the water proceeds. They will therefore affect the optimal water price level, which generally departs from marginal cost pricing.

The first observation concerns the sensitivity of water prices to implementation costs. In examples 1 to 4 in the table, a simple volumetric pricing method is employed with escalating implementation costs: example 1 entails no implementation costs; example 2 entails a cost of 5 percent (US$0.05 of each dollar of water proceeds are used to cover expenses associated with implementation activities); example 3 entails a cost of 7.5 percent, and example 4 entails a cost of 10 percent. The price of water drops from US$11.52 per acre-inch in example 1 to US$5.57 per acre-inch in

TABLE 5.2
Effects of Transaction Costs

Example	Pricing method	Water price	Water proceeds (US$/acre)	Farmer's profit (US$/acre)	Cost of water (US$/acre-inch)	Social benefit (US$/acre)	Implementation costs as a percentage of water proceeds
1	Volumetric	11.521[a]	355.102	408.710	354.780	409.030	0.000
2	Volumetric	5.569[a]	180.271	596.750	372.590	395.410	0.050
3	Volumetric	2.069[a]	68.837	711.650	383.070	392.260	0.075
4	Volumetric	0.000[a]	0.000	781.050	389.260	391.790	0.100
5	Volumetric with balanced budget	11.510[a]	354.815	409.030	354.810	391.290	0.050
6	Per acre	0.000[b]	0.000	781.050	389.260	391.790	0.000
7	Per acre with balanced budget	389.261[b]	389.261	391.790	389.260	391.790	0.000

a. US$ per acre-inch.
b. US$ per acre.
Source: Tsur and Dinar (1997).

example 2.[1] With 7.5 percent implementation costs, water price is further reduced to $2.07 per acre-inch. When implementation costs are 10 percent or more, the pricing activities are costly enough to render water pricing undesirable. The net benefit with water pricing is smaller than the net benefit when water is free and implementation costs are not incurred.

The second observation emerging from the table is that an inefficient but simple method such as per acre pricing may outperform a potentially efficient but complicated method when implementation costs are accounted for. Examples 4 and 6 yield the same outcome using different methods. In the first, volumetric pricing is employed; in the second, per acre pricing is used. If, however, volumetric pricing entails some fixed cost which has not yet been incurred due, for instance, to the need to install water meters, then it is better to use per acre pricing and avoid the fixed costs and the ensuing implementation costs associated with volumetric pricing.

In examples 1 to 4, we see that higher implementation costs lead to lower water prices. This in turn implies lower proceeds that are insufficient to cover the cost of water delivery.

Often, the water agency is required to have a balanced budget (see McCann and Zilberman, chapter 4 in this volume). Consider the effect on welfare of a balanced budget constraint imposed on volumetric pricing in example 5, which imposes the balanced budget constraint on example 2 (with 5 percent implementation costs). The result is that the farmer's profit is reduced from US$596.75 to US$409.03 per acre, while the social benefit is almost unchanged, decreasing slightly from US$395.41 to US$391.29 per acre.[2] Thus, mandating a balanced budget on the water agency inflicts a heavy toll on farmers. Without this constraint, taxpayers' money would have to finance the water agency's deficits. Given the small effect the balanced budget constraint has on total welfare, the choice of whether to impose it is mostly political, involving the consideration of income distribution between farmers and city dwellers as well as the effects of interest groups.

Examples 6 and 7 consider per acre pricing without and with a balanced budget constraint. When farmers are also required to cover the cost of water delivery, this cost is imposed as a per acre fee in example 7. From society's point of view, the balanced budget constraint makes no difference: the social benefit is the same in both examples. With a balanced budget constraint, the burden of paying for water delivery falls on the user (the farmer). Without this constraint it falls on the wider, taxpayer population.

---

1. 1 acre-inch is equivalent to 12.35 cubic meters.
2. 1 acre is equivalent to 0.4 hectare.

Cases 3 and 4: Unmetered Water

From a global perspective, volumetric pricing of irrigation water is the exception rather than the rule (Bos and Walters 1990), mostly because of a lack of facilities to meter water. Unmetered water implies that the amount of individual water intakes is the farmer's private information. If water users bear the entire cost of water supply, the information asymmetry is harmless, as the farmers themselves will consider the true cost of water in their input-output decisions. Often, however, the cost of water entails external components not directly borne by the farmers. Examples include (a) scarcity rents (temporal externality) that occur when the stock of water is being depleted, (b) extraction cost externality that occurs when current extractions by any farmer make future extractions more expensive to all farmers, or (c) part of the water supply cost being borne by a water agency. These external costs are quite pervasive, occurring, for example, when many users share an aquifer or in large-scale irrigation projects with considerable water conveyance operations.

In such cases, some form of regulation is needed. The problem is setting water prices in a way that induces efficient use without relying on individual water intakes. When the regulator can neither control nor measure the farmer's water intake, volumetric pricing is complicated even in the most favorable circumstance of complete information regarding the production technology.

Obviously, the regulator must base the water price on some observed variable that is related to water input. A natural candidate is the output level y. When output y is observed, it can be used to deduce the water input by inverting the water response relation $y = f(q)$ to obtain $q = f^{-1}(y)$. Then, the water fee rule that requires the farmer to pay the water authority $w^* f^{-1}(y)$ when producing the output y will generate the first-best social benefit $pf(y^*) - c[q(w^*)]$. (Recall that the regulator can calculate w^*, but cannot use it to extract water fees volumetrically when water is unmetered.)[3]

---

3. The farmer will choose the output level to maximize the profit $py - w^* f^{-1}(y)$. The optimal output $y^{\#}$ satisfies the first-order condition $p = w^* f^{-1\prime}(y^{\#})$, or $1/f^{-1\prime}(y^{\#}) = w^*/p$. Using $1/f^{-1\prime}(y) = f'[f^{-1}(y)]$, we obtain $1/f^{-1\prime}(y^{\#}) = f'[f^{-1}(y^{\#})] = w^*/p$. But $f'(q^*) = w^*/p$, hence $f^{-1}(y^{\#}) = f'^{-1}(w^*/p) = q^*$, implying that $y^{\#} = f(q^*) \equiv y^*$—the optimal (first-best) output under the marginal pricing rule. To verify sufficiency, differentiate both sides of $f[f^{-1}(y)] = y$ with respect to y to get $f'[f^{-1}(y)] f^{-1\prime}(y) = 1$ and obtain $f'[f^{-1}(y)] = 1/f^{-1\prime}(y)$. Differentiate twice to get $f''[f^{-1}(y)][f^{-1\prime}(y)]^2 + f'[f^{-1}(y)] f''^{-1}(y) = 0$, so $f''^{-1}(y) = -f''[f^{-1}(y)][f^{-1\prime}(y)]^2/f'[f^{-1}(y)] > 0$, since $f'' < 0$ and $f' > 0$, implying that the sufficient condition for maximum, $-wf''^{-1}(y) < 0$, is satisfied.

This output pricing procedure is demonstrated graphically in figure 5.3. To obtain the water fee associated with output level, say, of y_1, first find the water level q_1 that produces this output by using the yield response function $f(q)$ (the lower-right quadrant of figure 5.3). This can be done when $f(q)$ is known, as is assumed in this case. Next multiply this water level by w^*—the marginal cost price—to get w^*q_1 (the lower-left quadrant of figure 5.3). Again, information regarding the yield function $f(q)$ allows calculating w^*, although it cannot be used to price water volumetrically, because water is unmetered. Finally, transform the water fee w^*q_1 to the vertical axis using the 45° line to obtain the water fee z_1. Repeating this for any output level gives the water fee schedule as a function of output $z(y)$.

In this simple case inducing the farmer to produce the optimal output level y^* is possible.[4] Clearly, a farmer inclined to save water will use the minimal amount of water capable of producing y^*, namely, the optimal level $q^* = f^{-1}(y^*)$. But output pricing alone does not directly induce the farmer to do so because, from the farmer's viewpoint, water is not directly priced. Thus,

FIGURE 5.3
An Output Pricing Example with Water Fee Based on Observable Output

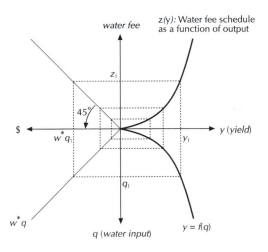

Source: Author.

4. Other output pricing rules yield the same outcome. For example, under the output tax schedule $t(y) = p - be^{-y/y^*}$, with b as an arbitrary normalization coefficient, profit is $[p - t(y)]y = be^{-y/y^*}y$ and the optimal output level is y^*.

if saving water involves some effort or fixed costs that are not accounted for, such as preventing water loss from canals or using a particular irrigation technology, output pricing is unlikely to achieve an efficient outcome.[5]

Now consider case 4: unmetered water, complete knowledge of the water response function, and transaction costs. This case is a bit more involved, but it can be handled in a similar way to case 3. Assume that output is observed, and consider output pricing of the form $wf^{-1}(y)$, where w is a policy choice parameter and f is the (known) output response to water function. That is, at output level y the water user pays $wf^{-1}(y)$ as a water fee. Define $w^*(\lambda)$ to be the solution of

$$\{w(1-\lambda) - c'[f'^{-1}(w/p)]\}f'^{-1}(w/p) = \lambda f'^{-1}(w/p)$$

Then, the water fee schedule $w^*(\lambda)f^{-1}(y)$ is optimal. Figure 5.3 can be used to construct $w^*(\lambda)f^{-1}(y)$ by replacing the marginal cost price w^* with $w^*(\lambda)$ in the lower-left quadrant.

To verify the optimality of $w^*(\lambda)f^{-1}(y)$, note that when charged the water fee $wf^{-1}(y)$, the farmer chooses the output level that maximizes the profit $py - wf^{-1}(y)$. The necessary condition for optimum is $p - wf'^{-1}[y(w)] = 0$, giving $1/f'^{-1}[y(w)] = w/p$. Using $1/f'^{-1}(y) = f'[f^{-1}(y)]$, obtained by writing $f^{-1}[f(q)] = q$, differentiating both sides and rearranging using $q = f^{-1}(y)$, we obtain $f'\{f^{-1}[y(w)]\} = w/p$, hence $y(w) = f[f'^{-1}(w/p)]$. With transaction costs equal to $\lambda wf^{-1}(y)$, the social benefit function is

$$
\begin{aligned}
B(w) &= py(w) - wf^{-1}[y(w)] + (1-\lambda)wf^{-1}[y(w)] - c\{f^{-1}[y(w)]\} \\
&= py(w) - \lambda wf^{-1}[y(w)] - c\{f^{-1}[y(w)]\}
\end{aligned}
$$

which, upon substituting $y(w) = f[f'^{-1}(w/p)]$, is recast as

$$B(w) = pf[f'^{-1}(w/p)] - \lambda wf'^{-1}(w/p) - c[f'^{-1}(w/p)]$$

and $w^*(\lambda)$ is the w-level that maximizes $B(w)$.

Now, suppose that water intake is observed and volumetric pricing is used with the same transaction costs structure as above. The volumetric derived demand for water is $q(w) = f'^{-1}(w/p)$ and the regulator's objective (social benefit) is

$$
\begin{aligned}
B(w) &= pf[q(w)] - wq(w) + (1-\lambda)wq(w) - c[q(w)] \\
&= pf[q(w)] - \lambda wq(w) - c[q(w)]
\end{aligned}
$$

---

5. When additional inputs or outputs are involved, output pricing tends to distort the markets of these outputs or inputs, in which case output pricing can at most achieve a second-best outcome.

which upon substituting $q(w) = f'^{-1}(w/p)$ becomes

$$B(w) = pf[f'^{-1}(w/p)] - \lambda w f'^{-1}(w/p) - c[f'^{-1}(w/p)].$$

However, this is the same objective as under the output pricing above. Therefore, it is maximized when $w = w^*(\lambda)$. It follows that $w^*(\lambda)$ attains the outcome achieved under volumetric pricing with full information, hence it must be optimal.

Indeed, with a known water response function, water input can be deduced from output such that any outcome achieved by volumetric pricing is also attainable via output pricing. Of course, the caveats in relation to output pricing mentioned earlier (no incentive to save water and potential distortions of input-output decisions when more outputs or inputs are involved) apply.

Cases 5 and 6: Observed (Metered) Water Intake with Asymmetric Information Regarding Water Response Function

In the cases of observed water intake with asymmetric information regarding water response function, the water regulator observes the individual water intake, but knows the water response function only up to a type parameter θ (representing such factors as growers' characteristics and soil quality). The yield response to water function $y = f(q, \theta)$ involves the parameter θ, which is the farmer's private information. The regulator's ignorance regarding θ is manifested through a probability distribution for θ defined over a known support. The derived demand for water is $q(w, \theta) = f'^{-1}(w/p, \theta)$, and the marginal cost pricing rule states that the water price should satisfy $w = c'[q(w, \theta)]$. The outcome $w^*(\theta)$ is therefore a function of the privately observed θ. Figure 5.4 depicts derived demand for water functions for three different types of θ. Not knowing which of the θ values prevails, the regulator cannot calculate the true $w^*(\theta)$. The pricing problem now entails finding a quantity-dependent price schedule $w(q)$ that maximizes social benefit.

In the absence of implementation costs (case 5), the price schedule $w(q) = c(q)/q$, which is the average cost of supply, does the job. This is because under the average cost pricing rule, the farmer's profit, $pf(q, \theta) - [c(q)/q]q$, is the same as the social objective, $pf(q, \theta) - c(q)$. The farmer, being fully informed of the true θ while choosing the water input, will adopt the socially optimal water input and output levels. By defining water price as the average cost of supply, the regulator internalizes the

FIGURE 5.4
Derived Demand for Water of Farmer Type θ_1, θ_2, and θ_3

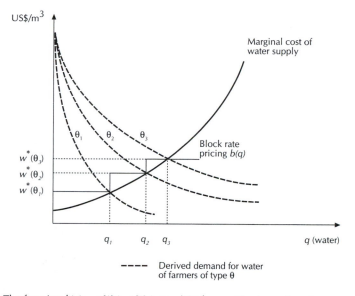

---- Derived demand for water
of farmers of type θ

Note: The function $b(q) = w^*(\theta_1)$, $w^*(\theta_2)$, or $w^*(\theta_3)$ for $q \in [0,q_1]$, $q \in (q_1,q_2]$, or $q > q_2$ is an efficient block rate pricing rule.
Source: Author.

water allocation problem such that the farmer's self-interest coincides with that of the regulator.

Alternatively, if the regulator knows that the true θ can assume one of many possible values, then a block rate pricing rule such as $b(q)$ of figure 5.4 attains the optimal outcome achieved under the full informa-tion (case 1). Indeed, asymmetric information provides a rationale for block rate pricing.

With implementation costs (case 6), the above pricing procedures are no longer optimal, because the transaction costs change the social objec-tive function. Suppose, as above, that a fraction λ of the water proceeds is used to cover pricing expenses. The social benefit now is $pf(q, \theta) - \lambda w(q)q - c(q)$, which depends on the choice of the water price sched-ule $w(q)$. The pricing problem facing the regulator is to specify a price sched-ule $w(q)$ that maximizes $pf(q, \theta) - \lambda w(q)q - c(q)$ at the true θ (unknown to the regulator), subject to individual rationality. Smith and Tsur (1997) ana-lyze this problem in a special case (with constant marginal cost of water supply). A general account is yet to be offered. Nonetheless, their analysis demonstrates the salient relationship between asymmetric information and implementation costs that has been largely overlooked.

Cases 7 and 8: Unmetered Water and Private Water Response Functions

In the cases of unmetered water and private water response functions, the asymmetric information involves both the production technology parameter θ and the water intake q. The regulator may use an observed variable to deduce water input. A natural candidate for this task is output, when it is observed. Smith and Tsur (1997) develop a pricing mechanism based on output for n producers when the production technology of each producer involves private information (unknown to the regulator as well as to the other producers). The outcome of this procedure consists of tax schedules, $t^i(y^i)$, based solely on the observed output of farmer i, $i = 1, 2, \ldots, n$, that induce farmers to produce at the socially optimal level. In the absence of implementation costs, the optimal tax schedules achieve the first-best outcome (the outcome achieved in case 1).

In a numerical example, Smith and Tsur (1997) show the strong effect of transaction costs on the tax schedules and on the ensuing social benefit. They consider a single farmer with a water response function of the form $y = (1 + \theta)q^{0.5}$, where the parameter θ is distributed uniformly over the unit interval [0,1]. The cost of water supply has a private component (for example, the cost of delivering the water from the public canal to the field) borne by the farmer, and a public component (for instance, the cost of water conveyance in the canal) borne by the water agency. The ratio of public to private cost is 1:2 so that two-thirds of the cost is private and one-third is public. The authors then calculate the expected benefit without water pricing at all and with optimal pricing for various levels of implementation costs. The results are presented in table 5.3.

The expected net benefit without water pricing equals 29.17. With water pricing it equals 38.89, 32.02, or 15.05 for implementation costs of 0 percent, 10 percent, or 30 percent, respectively. When water pricing is free of cost, the expected net benefit attains the maximal level of 38.89. When 10 percent of water proceeds are used to cover pricing expenses, the expected benefit drops to 32.02. The 15.05 expected benefit, obtained when 30 percent of the water proceeds are used to cover expenses, is lower than the unregulated benefit of 29.17 (under which no pricing is imposed and no implementation costs are incurred). Hence, at some implementation costs between 10 and 30 percent, pricing water using the output method is counterproductive and should be abandoned.

TABLE 5.3
Expected Benefit under Output Pricing with Privately Observed Water Intake and Production Technology

Category	No regulation	Regulated		
Implementation cost (percentage of water proceeds)	n.a.	0.00	10.00	30.00
Expected benefit (US$)	29.17	38.89	32.02	15.15

n.a. Not applicable.
Source: Smith and Tsur (1997).

Conclusion

For obvious reasons, water markets may provide a partial remedy to regulation, but are unlikely to do away with it. Some form of administrative pricing is likely to remain a principal means of regulation. Yet water pricing is a complicated and costly operation because of the pervasiveness of incomplete ownership rights; lack of control of water intake by users, for example, when irrigation water is unmetered; and incomplete information about water production technologies.

Although the water management literature has given little attention to the roles of asymmetric information and implementation costs, asymmetric information has recently become a central part of regulation theory. It has appeared under the heading of mechanism design or principal-agent theory (Laffont and Tirole 1993), yet few applications to water regulation can be found (see, for example, Loehman and Dinar 1994; Smith and Tsur 1997).

Asymmetric information in water regulation occurs when individual water intakes are known only to the users, or when the water-yield relationship involves parameters that are known to the grower, but not to the regulator. The former, which occurs when irrigation water is unmetered, is ubiquitous; the latter is also pervasive.

In the absence of implementation costs, and with perfect information, efficient pricing is straightforward. Unobserved water intake alone does not pose a real problem, as water input can be deduced from the observed output (or other inputs) and priced indirectly through output. The problem of asymmetric information regarding production technology alone can be overcome by quantity-dependent water price schedules. Implementation costs alone may change the order of efficiency between the different pricing methods, but add no conceptual difficulty otherwise. It is the combination of implementation costs and asymmetric information that requires the use of mechanism design theory to define efficient water allocation and derive efficient price schedules.

This chapter illuminates the role of these two factors in water pricing, beginning with the simple situation of no transaction costs and full information (case 1) through the more realistic situations that involve substantial transaction costs and incomplete information (cases 2–8). A comprehensive account of cases 7–8 is not yet available, although Smith and Tsur's (1997) analysis is a good starting point.

To maintain a sharp focus, this chapter concentrated on water input and abstracted from other inputs that affect crop yield. In actual practice, additional inputs such as fertilizer, machinery, labor, and pesticides would have to be included. The prices of these additional inputs are typically determined outside the irrigation sector. The profit maximizing levels of these inputs can be traced to the water input, and the above analysis can thus be extended to account for additional inputs. Adding inputs would complicate the analysis and magnify the effects of incomplete information and transaction costs, but would not change the qualitative nature of these effects. Another important line of analysis concerns the design and operation of water institutions as a means to mitigate the detrimental effects of transaction costs and asymmetric information.

References

Bos, M. G., and W. Walters. 1990. "Water Charges and Irrigation Efficiencies." *Irrigation and Drainage Systems* 4(3): 267–78.

Dinar, A., and A. Subramanian. 1997. *Water Pricing Experience: An International Perspective*. Technical Paper no. 386. Washington, D.C.: World Bank.

Laffont, J. J., and J. Tirole. 1993. *A Theory of Incentives in Procurement and Regulation*. Cambridge, Massachusetts: MIT Press.

Loehman, E., and A. Dinar. 1994. "Cooperative Solution of Local Externality Problem: A Case of Mechanism Design Applied to Irrigation." *Journal of Environmental Economics and Management* 26: 235–56.

Smith, R. B. W., and Y. Tsur. 1997. "Asymmetric Information and the Pricing of Natural Resouces: Understanding the Case of Unmetered Water." *Land Economics* 73(3): 392–403.

Tsur, Y., and A. Dinar. 1995. "Efficiency and Equity Considerations in Pricing and Allocating Irrigation Water." Policy Research Paper no. 1460. World Bank, Washington, D.C.

_____. 1997. "On the Relative Efficiency of Alternative Methods for Pricing Irrigation Water and Their Implementation." *World Bank Economic Review* 11(2): 243–62.

SECTION B

Empirical Approaches to
the Political Economy
of Water Pricing Reforms

6 (US, Egypt, Kenya)

An Empirical Perspective on Water Pricing Reforms

Steven Renzetti

Q25,
6|5
L95 L98
813

The provision of potable water is one of government's oldest functions, dating back thousands of years. During much of that time, government authorities viewed water demands as beyond their control, and they defined their principal role as an engineering task: how to supply a given quantity of water at minimum cost. In recent years, however, government officials in many countries have become concerned about excessive water use, degraded water quality, and continued inadequate service for many people, especially the very poor. As a result, efforts to reform water resource allocation in a manner that incorporate consumers' preferences and supply constraints into management plans are growing.

Thus, the first motivation of the chapter is the need to understand the structure of water users' preferences as well as the costs of supply. The chapter takes what is known regarding demands and costs, and uses this information to examine the appropriate form for water prices. The second motivation for the chapter stems from the observation that reforms are the result of public policy decisions. As a result, the chapter examines some of the empirical features of the political environment in which water pricing decisions are made.

The Structure of Water Supply Costs

The need to understand the structure of water supply costs is urgent because of

I would like to thank Ariel Dinar, Diane Dupont, Don Tate, and for their comments. Craig Ireland provided valuable research assistance.

increasing pressures on water supply networks in low-income countries, and because of concerns about the management of these networks. Munasinghe (1992) and Biswas (1997) indicate that, for many large urban centers in low-income economies, the unit cost of the next available source of water is two to four times more expensive than the average cost of supply from current sources. Furthermore, evidence indicates that some water supply systems are exacerbating supply externality problems. For example, Munasinghe (1992) demonstrates how the problems of land subsidence in Bangkok and salt water intrusion in Manila are related to the depletion of groundwater by municipal water agencies. These types of externalities imply that the social costs of water supply are rising even faster than the conventional accounting of costs would suggest.

The Cost Structure of Urban Water Supply

Traditionally, public sector agencies or highly regulated private firms have constructed and managed irrigation networks and municipal water supply systems. Much of the justification for this is that these systems were believed by regulators and policymakers to be natural monopolies. A closer examination of the cost structure of these facilities may indicate whether scale economies are indeed ubiquitous and indicate where competition in specific services, for example, maintenance or billing, could potentially increase efficiency and improve service (Easter and Feder 1997).

There are relatively few econometric studies of urban water supply in high-income countries and even fewer for low-income countries. As a result, a number of important questions about the structure of costs, particularly the presence of economies of scale, have yet to be adequately answered. However, a number of studies suggest that increasing returns to scale in water supply systems may not be as prevalent as once thought. This is especially true if the components of the water supply system are separated and particular attention is paid to storage and treatment, distribution and water delivery, and the more service-oriented aspects of water supply.

Kim (1987) estimates a multi-output model of the costs of urban water supply and finds that, whereas commercial service is characterized by economies of scale, residential service exhibits decreasing returns. Recent work by Boisvert and Schmidt (1997) shows that the increasing returns that are found in the storage and collection divisions of small rural water utilities are offset by the decreasing returns found in those utilities' distribution networks.

An important implication of these studies is that improved operational efficiencies are unlikely to come from expanding the scale of water delivery systems. Rather, changing water agencies' structures and operations may be necessary to improve service quality (Galal and Shirley 1995). This could be accomplished by breaking up water monopolies into smaller regional units. Furthermore, these units could be managed by private firms or simply auctioned to private bidders. Rivera (1996, p. 2) concludes that: "Private sector participation in the water and wastewater sector is likely to result in sharply improved managerial practices and higher operating efficiencies." However, Rivera also cautions that these improvements are contingent on an adequate degree of government regulation.

Another set of econometric studies concerns the factors that influence the marginal cost of supply and, thus, may be relevant to the setting of water prices. Boisvert and Schmidt (1997), Renzetti (1992a), and Teeples and Glyer (1987) all find that marginal costs rise with distance (length of the distribution network). This is probably due to the difficulty of maintaining constant pressure and chlorine levels over greater distances. In addition, Munasinghe (1992, table 8.3), Renzetti (1992a), and Russell and Shin (1996) find that marginal costs rise significantly during peak demand periods. For example, Munasinghe reports that marginal costs during peak summer months are double those observed during off-peak periods. These higher marginal costs may be related to higher pumping costs that are, in turn, due to electric power utilities' use of peak load pricing. All these studies are based on utility operations in high-income countries, but there is little reason to expect conditions in low-income countries to be markedly different.

Cost Accounting of Water Costs

A necessary condition for establishing efficient water prices is the complete accounting of the costs of water supply. This exercise raises several challenges. First, translating accounting information into estimates of marginal costs is difficult. This is due, in part, to the indivisibility of capital stocks. Munasinghe (1992, chapter 8) and Russell and Shin (1996) provide excellent treatments of the various methods of approximating marginal costs from accounting data. An important feature of these formulas is that they typically rely on information about the capital requirements of future expansion plans.

Given these difficulties, how can the task of creating marginal cost estimates be simplified for agencies with limited resources? A good example of what can be done is the software developed by Environment Canada (Canadian Water and Wastewater Association 1992). This software requires water utility managers to input accounting information, forecasts of expected water demand growth, and estimates of the capital costs of future water supply sources. Based on the data supplied, the software estimates marginal costs, helping managers to calculate various types of prices.

A separate issue is the consideration of costs when setting water prices. A water agency's reckoning of its own expenditures will usually underestimate the economic costs of supply. In the United States and Canada, for example, urban water agencies sometimes fail to charge depreciation on capital stocks or fail to impute a cost to land holdings. Furthermore, the externalities associated with energy use, reduced water quality, and groundwater withdrawals must be evaluated. For example, Munasinghe (1992) estimates that the long-run marginal cost of supply for Manila would be US$0.13 per cubic meter if the depth of aquifer supplying Manila remains constant. However, the aquifer is falling under current pumping rates, increasing the marginal cost of supply to US$0.142 per cubic meter.

The Structure of Water Demand

Water agencies need to understand the structure of demand to anticipate the impact of water reforms. In addition, officials can use demand information to make decisions about pricing and system design.

Residential Water Demand

Water use is sensitive to economic factors such as prices and incomes in the case of residential water demand and to prices and the level of output in the cases of commercial, industrial, and agricultural water demand. As the recent meta-analysis Espey, Espey, and Shaw (1997) conducted shows, however, there is still uncertainty about the factors that influence the magnitude of price and income-output elasticities. This situation stems, in part, from the prevalence of single-equation models of water demand that fail to place water use in a more general model of consumer preferences.

When modeling the impacts of water price changes, analysts in high-income countries typically have not worried about the impact of the connection charge. This is an important barrier in applying the results of those studies to low-income countries, because households in low-income countries are more likely to choose from among several sources of supply, and those households are sensitive to the relative costs of the alternatives. The World Bank Water Demand Research Team (1993) finds that price elasticities for connection ranged from –0.1 to –0.3 for public taps and from –0.7 to –1.5 for private taps. Singh and others (1993) also find that both the connection fee and the monthly tariff have significant (and negative) influences on the decision to connect to the public water supply. One implication of these findings is that reforms must consider the prices of connection and supply simultaneously. These reforms cannot work under the assumption (commonly made in high-income countries) of a fixed market size.

Another line of research regarding the structure of consumers' preferences indicates that residential water users exhibit significant willingness to pay for improvements. In the context of high-income countries, these improvements are usually modeled as increases in water quality or system reliability. For example, Brox, Kumar, and Stollery (1999) estimate the willingness to pay to upgrade municipally supplied water to provincial water quality standards for a sample of Canadian households. The mean willingness to pay was approximately US$7 per month per household, or 35 percent of the average water bill. In addition, Howe and Smith (1994) find that Colorado residential water users would be willing to pay approximately US$60 per year to halve the probability of a major system failure.

In low-income countries, evidence indicates that households are also willing to pay to connect to reliable public water supplies. This willingness to pay is a complex function of socioeconomic characteristics and other factors (Ashthana 1997; Madanat and Humplick 1993; Mu, Whittington, and Briscoe 1990; Singh and others 1993; World Bank Water Demand Research Team 1993). These studies typically estimate discrete choice models in which households are assumed to choose among supply options such as private piped water, public piped water, water vendors, and private or communal wells. For example, World Bank Water Demand Research Team (1993) estimates that willingness to pay for a private piped connection ranges from 0.5 to 10 percent of household income. Singh and others (1993) also find high levels of willingness to pay for private connections, although this willingness is much stronger when expressed as a monthly tariff as opposed to a connection fee (possibly because of capital market imperfections). Asthana (1997) estimates that rural Indian households' willingness to pay a one-time fee to reduce the travel time needed to acquire safe water is approximately one-half of an unskilled laborer's daily wage.

Industrial and Agricultural Water Demand

Industrial facilities and electrical power plants are usually not the largest users of water, but recent evidence suggests that they may be the fastest growing segment of water demand in some regions (Biswas 1997; Le Moigne and others 1992). The role of water in industrial applications and the production of electrical power has yet to be studied adequately. For example, a 1996–97 report on water use across countries by sector relied on 1987 data for most countries (World Resources Institute 1997). Because of this lack of data, relatively little is known about the specific role that water plays in these technologies, about substitution possibilities between water and other inputs, and about how firms may respond to pricing reforms.

Some information can be gleaned from a small number of studies from high-income countries. Babin, Willis, and Allen (1982) examine water use in the U.S. manufacturing sector and find that intake price elasticities range from 0.0 to –0.801, depending on the manufacturing sector. Furthermore, water is used as complement for capital and a substitute for labor. Renzetti (1992a) estimates water demands for Canadian manufacturing firms and finds that intake elasticities range from –0.155 to –0.588. In all industries, intake and internal water recirculation are substitutes. Furthermore, the largest intake demand elasticities are for those firms that use water predominantly in process-related applications (moving and cleaning raw materials or inclusion in final output) as opposed to using it for heat transfer (cooling or steam production). Dupont and Renzetti (1999) embed water intake and recirculation into an econometric model of Canadian manufacturing, finding that water intake is a substitute for water recirculation, energy, and capital. Furthermore, technological change has been biased in favor of increased water intake, but decreased water recirculation. Renzetti (1993) and Mody (1997) estimate probit models to investigate manufacturing firms' choices in regard to water supply sources. Both find that firms' choices are sensitive to connection fees and volumetric charges, and that publicly supplied firms demonstrate larger price elasticities than self-supplied firms.

Econometric studies that document the role of water in thermoelectric power generation are unavailable. This is an important limitation, because of the large quantities of water used in thermal generating stations and the likelihood that the future demand for electricity may grow rapidly in low-income countries where water is already scarce (Flavin and Lenssen 1994). Stone and Whittington (1984) is an example of the type of analysis that has been done. The authors develop a programming model of the operation of a coal-fired generating station and demonstrate that, despite the small share of costs attributable to water, the plant's technology allows it to respond to increases in the cost of water by reducing water use.

The agriculture sector remains the single largest user of water (World Resources Institute 1997). However, the common absence of metering and volumetric water pricing in this sector means that determining the economic characteristics of the agriculture sector's water use is particularly difficult. Moore, Gollehon, and Carey (1994) use a multi-output econometric model to examine the role of pumping costs (taken as a proxy for the price of water). The authors find that irrigation method, crop choice, and land allocation are all influenced by the price of water, although most elasticities are relatively small. In addition, Caswell (1991) shows that the choices farmers in low-income countries make among alternative types of irrigation technologies depend on land quality, attitudes toward risk, credit market imperfections, and structure of output markets. Thus, these features must be considered if irrigation adoption decisions and the impacts of water pricing reforms are to be modeled. This may be an area in which some of the lessons learned from the extensive analysis of agricultural water use in middle- and high-income countries can be transferred to low-income countries (see Berck, Robinson, and Goldman 1991 and other chapters in that volume).

Pricing Rules

Examples of inefficient water prices can be found in every sector and country (Dinar and Subramanian 1997). Renzetti (1999) examines a sample of Canadian municipal water utilities and finds that marginal costs exceed marginal prices for residential and commercial service by factors of three and two, respectively. In terms of the experience of low-income countries, World Bank (1993, p. 30) concludes that "A recent review of [World] Bank-financed municipal water supply projects found that the price charged for water covered only about 35 percent of the average cost of supply, and charges in many irrigation systems are much less." Furthermore, examples are available of the welfare gains that follow from water pricing reforms. In general, however, there is no agreement on precisely how to reform water prices (see Dalhuisen, de Groot, and Nijkamp 2000). This is because optimal prices depend on the objectives of the water agency as well as on the types of information available to it.

Marginal Cost Pricing

Marginal cost pricing is the indispensable aspect of public sector pricing rules. Despite this, there are few examples of marginal cost pricing being applied in the water sector. Renzetti (1992a) considers the installation of residential water meters and the reform of water pricing in Vancouver, Canada. Munasinghe (1992) conducts a sophisticated analysis of Saõ Paulo's water pricing, in which he measures how far water prices deviate from marginal costs.

Despite these examples, many obstacles stand in the way of implementing marginal cost pricing. These include the difficulty of defining and calculating marginal costs, including the difficult tasks of using historical accounting data, imputing external costs, and apportioning joint costs; the possibility of greater revenue variability under marginal cost pricing; and equity-related concerns. These obstacles have impeded the use of marginal cost pricing by water agencies. For example, the American Water Works Association (1991, p. 50) contends that "the application of the theory [of marginal cost pricing] to water rates lacks considerable practicality."

Feldstein Pricing

Marginal cost pricing is efficient only if the public agency is indifferent to the distribution of welfare in society. In addition, in the face of increasing returns to scale, marginal cost pricing leads to deficits. With respect to the latter problem, a widely accepted solution is to adopt a two-part pricing structure so that a volumetric charge is set at the marginal cost of supply and a connection fee is set to recoup whatever deficit results. However, Feldstein (1972) points out that the connection charge acts like a regressive head tax. If public agencies possess a degree of aversion to income inequality, then such a policy has the potential to lower social welfare. Feldstein derives an optimal two-part pricing rule that allows a public agency to meet a break-even constraint while designing prices that reflect concern for income inequality. Under Feldstein pricing, the volumetric charge rises above marginal cost to lower the needed connection fee. In table 6.1, data from the United States and two developing countries are used to demonstrate that even a weak aversion to income inequality will push prices substantially away from marginal costs. This is because of the significant degree of income inequality in The Arab Republic of Egypt and Kenya and the regressive impacts of the household water connection fee. This simple example suggests that water managers may have to temper their desire to implement marginal cost pricing if the distribution of income in their jurisdictions is very unequal or if they are mandated to consider the distributional consequences of their pricing decisions. An important limitation of the Feldstein model, however, is that it assumes consumers will not respond to the connection fee by changing their supply source. The price implications of relaxing this assumption are examined later.

Nonlinear Prices

Water prices are commonly either increasing or decreasing functions of the level of consumption. Decreasing block rates are often justified by the assertion that higher levels of consumption are cheaper (at the margin) to serve. In contrast, increasing block rate structures are often championed as a way of signaling rising supply costs and encouraging conservation.

TABLE 6.1
Examples of Feldstein Pricing

η[a]	(p/mc) United States	(p/mc) Egypt	(p/mc) Kenya
0.00	1.00	1.00	1.00
0.25	1.13	1.38	1.65
0.50	1.30	2.09	9.70
0.55	1.34	2.33	31.80
0.75	1.53	4.04	< 0.00[b]
1.00	1.82	23.81	< 0.00

Note: The calculations use equation 18 in Feldstein (1972) and the price and income elasticities assumed by Feldstein. Income distribution parameters are calculated from data in World Bank (1996).

a. The parameter η is the elasticity of the social marginal utility of income. Higher values of η are interpreted as reflecting a greater social concern for income inequality. The term (p/mc) measures the socially optimal ratio of price to marginal cost. P is the unit price and mc is marginal cost. Both are measured in the same units (US$ per m³) and, thus, the ratio is dimensionless.

b. Because of the extreme degree of income inequality in Kenya, the equation for the optimal (p/mc) yields negative values at high values of η.

Source: Author.

A substantial literature deals with theoretical models of public utility pricing (Brown and Sibley 1986). One of the results that investigators often find is that the form of efficient nonlinear price schedules is a function of both supply-side and demand-side characteristics. As a result, if the analyst combines information on the structure and distribution of demand with the cost of supply, it is possible to raise welfare by allowing consumers to self-select along the price schedule. This section provides two examples that are particularly relevant to water pricing reforms in low-income countries.

The first example concerns optimal two-part prices. These are similar to Coase two-part prices, except that they allow for nonzero elasticities with respect to the connection fee (Brown and Sibley 1986). Under these prices, the connection fee and constant unit charge for water both deviate from their respective marginal costs, and the magnitude of the deviation is inversely related to the relevant elasticity of demand. For example, if the price elasticity for connections were estimated to be larger than the elasticity for water, this would dictate that connection fees should be set quite close to the marginal cost, while the volumetric charge should deviate by a relatively larger amount from the marginal cost of supply.

The second example of nonlinear prices is optimal nonlinear pricing. This pricing rule extends the analysis by allowing the volumetric charge to be a nonlinear function of quantity. An important result here is that the form of the efficient price schedule is a function of the marginal cost of supply, the elasticity of demand, and the distribution of consumers at every level of consumption. As a result, positively or negatively sloped price schedules are possible. For example, in the case of a utility faced with fixed costs and constant marginal costs of supply and demands that are characterized by elasticities that rise with consumption, efficient price schedules are negatively sloped. This result is an example of second-best Ramsey pricing in which the utility seeks to define a price schedule that minimizes the welfare losses from meeting a break-even constraint. The intuition is that consumers with low quantities also display relatively low demand elasticities. As a result, to minimize the welfare loss from meeting the break-even constraint, the public utility must have marginal price diverge from marginal cost the most for these consumers (because they will respond the least). As the level of consumption rises, so does the demand elasticity. In turn, the gap between marginal price and marginal cost must decrease to avoid the welfare costs arising from large decreases in consumption.

Not surprisingly, a tradeoff is involved in choosing the degree of complexity in a price schedule. More sophisticated schedules may Pareto-dominate simpler ones, but they also require more information on the structure and distribution of demand.

The Impact of Water Pricing Reforms

This section describes the methods and results of studies that have considered the impact of water pricing reforms.

The Welfare Impacts of Water Pricing Reforms

A number of authors have estimated the welfare costs of underpricing water. Renzetti (1992b) estimates that reforming water prices in Vancouver, Canada, will lead to a 4.5 percent increase in social welfare. Russell and Shin (1996) consider the case of the United States city of Phoenix, and they find increases in the consumer surplus from water use ranging from 7.7 to 11.0 percent, depending on the method used to calculate marginal costs.

Note that the welfare gains from reforming water prices in high-income countries almost certainly understate those that are possible in low-income countries. This is because the studies do not emphasize sources of welfare gain relevant to low-income countries, such as reduced pollution, improved health, reduction in illegal connections, and detection of system leakages. A second limitation of these welfare studies is that they are based on the assumption that water demand is separable from other consumer demand. This is because almost all studies of residential water demand have estimated single-equation models and have not examined the role that water plays in more general consumer preferences.

General Equilibrium Effects of Water Price Reforms

Changes in water prices may bring about changes in prices in other sectors in which water accounts for a significant share of production costs, users are unable to find substitutes for the more expensive water, or firms possess some price-setting power in either input or output markets. Thus, households may see changes to electricity and food prices that are brought on by water pricing reforms. These induced price changes and their impacts on firms and households need to be modeled if the impacts of pricing reforms are to be assessed fully.

For example, Renzetti (1992b) considers the reform of water prices in Vancouver, Canada. In that city, moving to marginal cost pricing implies price increases for residential consumers and price decreases for nonresidential customers. A major reason why the proposed price reforms yield a positive net benefit is the assumption that the commercial customers pass on the cost savings associated with lowered water prices in the form of lowered output prices to households.

Sunding and others (1997) examine alternative general equilibrium models used to assess the impacts of government policies aimed at restricting water supplies to California farmers. Although all models show that the impacts on agricultural output of reducing the water supply can be offset by allowing for water trading, the authors also find that there is a tradeoff between the degree of detail used to model farmers' responses and the scope of the models' geographic coverage.

Renzetti and Dupont (1999) consider the introduction of a charge on water withdrawals by all self-supplied water users in the province of Ontario in Canada. Because thermoelectric power generation is by far the largest user of water in the province, the introduction of the charge raises not only water prices, but also electricity prices. In several industries, an increase in the price of electricity has a greater impact on costs than an increase in the unit cost of water because of electricity's larger cost share.

Cross-Subsidization and Relative Price Changes

As indicated earlier, existing water prices rarely bear a close resemblance to the marginal costs of supply. In addition to indicating the inefficiency of water prices, these results imply that the price-marginal cost gap varies across user groups and, as a result, cross-subsidization across user groups is common in water markets.

The significance of this situation is that moving to efficient prices will mean that different user groups will face changes in prices of differing magnitudes, with some prices possibly decreasing (Hall and Hanemann 1996, Le Moigne and others 1992; Renzetti 1992b). This has implications for the issue of whether water agency managers and water users will accept pricing reforms. In the event of significant relative price changes, the efficiency grounds for price reforms may become less important than concerns about the fairness of different user groups facing different price increases.

The Significance of Cost-Income Shares

Some evidence indicates that, throughout much of the world, water is an inferior good. However, the difference between the rich and the poor in the proportion of household income devoted to acquiring water is much larger in low-income countries than in high-income countries. Tate and Lacelle (1995) report that the proportion of income spent on publicly supplied water averages 0.6 percent in Canada, and this proportion falls slowly as household income rises. World Bank (1993) points to instances in which water's cost share in developing countries varies from less than 1 percent for wealthy households to approximately 20 percent for poor urban households.

The share of water in households' (and firms') budgets is important for two primary reasons. First, because water as a commodity is an inferior good, water pricing reforms may raise important equity concerns that need to be addressed. This was illustrated in the Feldstein pricing example. Second, the percentage of money that users spend on water plays a role in determining the impact of water pricing reforms on real living standards.

The Empirical Aspect of Political Issues

In some countries, water pricing reforms are an important political issue. This last section considers two empirical features of the political environment in which water pricing reforms decisions are made.

Transaction Costs

One issue in the reform of water allocation rules in irrigation districts or in situations involving self-supplied firms is the possibility of introducing tradable water use rights. The presence and form of transaction costs is an important determinant of the extent to which markets for these rights will be able to improve water use efficiency. For example, Zilberman, Chakravorty, and Shah (1997) simulate the transition from a water queuing system to a system based on tradable water rights, and they discover that the transition may actually lower aggregate welfare if transaction costs are sufficiently high. This occurs when the potential gains are lost to search and negotiation costs.

Unfortunately, little empirical work has been done to determine the magnitude and form of transaction costs or what factors influence transaction costs. Despite this, an examination of existing permit markets may allow for some general observations.

Clearly many factors play a role in determining transaction costs. Some of these may be specific to a particular case. For example, transaction costs were minimized in the lead reduction program in the United States because of the history of dealings within a particular group: petroleum refineries (Hahn and Hester 1989).

By contrast, some factors should be general enough to apply to most cases. For example, to the extent that government approval is required before a trade may occur, transaction costs will rise. Conversely, to the extent that the government provides information to the market or plays a no-fee brokerage role, transaction costs should fall (Tripp and Dudek 1989).

Stavins (1995) examines the form of the transaction costs function and demonstrates that the relationship between marginal transaction costs and the number of transactions is relevant to the efficiency of the permit market. Unfortunately, little information is available to guide us here. On the one hand, some fixed costs are likely to be associated with transactions (examples might be legal costs and registration fees), and this would suggest declining marginal costs. On the other hand, search costs are more likely to be characterized by rising marginal costs as potential traders search first for those traders who are most willing to trade. Fortunately, a promising area of research is the design of experiments that can examine the factors that influence the form and level of transaction costs and look at how these costs influence the efficiency of trading (Saleth, Braden, and Eheart 1991).

Commitments by Public Agencies

A number of researchers report that many people in low-income countries have grown disenchanted with the failure of water agencies to carry out their mandates (Singh and others 1993; World Bank Water Demand Research Team 1993), treating pronouncements, including those regarding water pricing reforms, with skepticism. As a result, households take defensive measures to protect themselves from the consequences of water agencies' failures. These measures range from installing household storage tanks and cisterns to securing alternative sources of supply.

Thus, the credibility of public agencies can have a major impact on the role of transaction costs in water permit markets. Although this is not something restricted to the behavior of water management agencies, it is worthwhile considering what actions these agencies could take to increase the credibility of their pronouncements. Any increase in the credibility of public agencies pronouncements should lower uncertainty among water users. This may, in turn, improve the workings of water permits markets and increase users' willingness to pay for improved services, as well as to participate in decisionmaking related to water allocations.

Water agency actions that may increase credibility include (a) sharing information about past and current performance, such as financial records, number of personnel devoted to system maintenance, water quality measurements, frequency of service outages, and system pressure readings; (b) including user groups in decisionmaking processes; (c) investing in reputation-building activities, such as sharing facts through media campaigns; and (d) issuing performance bonds. The agency can also pursue institutional reforms, such granting greater autonomy, in an effort to increase its credibility (Galal and Shirley 1995).

Conclusion

I will conclude by stressing five points. First, there is an obvious need for water pricing reforms. The implications of underpricing water are well understood. Economic theory and empirical evidence provide guidance regarding the necessary data collection, cost accounting, and parameter estimation. But more must be learned about the structure and distribution of demand, the structure of the marginal cost of supply, and the magnitude of external costs associated with water supply. Keeping this in mind, we should broaden our perspective beyond concentrating solely on pricing reforms, and also consider water supply reforms in general. This means reconsidering the appropriate mix of public and private provision of water, water agencies' methods of cost accounting, and alternative ways to allow greater user participation in decisionmaking. It may also require integrating decisions regarding the capacity and pricing of water supply and sewage treatment systems (Renzetti 1999).

Second, we must not underestimate consumers' responsiveness to water price changes and their willingness to pay for improved access to reliable water supplies. Many households in low-income countries appear willing to sacrifice a nontrivial share of their incomes to acquire access to safe water.

Third, setting efficient prices requires gathering information about the structure of both supply costs and consumer preferences. By understanding the latter, water agencies will be able to offer price and service menus to consumers that are more efficient than existing prices.

Fourth, although the manner in which reforms are introduced is important, the most efficient approach is unclear. On the one hand, an abrupt introduction may not afford households and firms adequate time to alter their water-related capital stocks. On the other hand, a phased introduction will open the door to opposition based on the distributional consequences of reforms. This may strain the agency's commitment to pricing reforms.

Finally, research that documents the role and value of water in alternative applications in low-income countries is sparse. We need a better understanding of these issues to anticipate the impact of water pricing reforms.

References

American Water Works Association. 1991. *Water Rates Manual*, 4th ed. Denver, Colorado.

Asthana, Anand. 1997. "Where the Water Is Free but the Buckets Are Empty: Demand Analysis of Drinking Water in Rural India." *Open Economies Review* 8(2): 137–49.

Babin, Frank, Cleve Willis, and Peter Allen. 1982. "Estimation of Substitution Possibilities between Water and Other Production Inputs." *American Journal of Agricultural Economics* 64(1): 148–51.

Berck, Peter, Sherman Robinson, and George Goldman. 1991. "The Use of Computable General Equilibrium Models to Assess Water Policies." In Ariel Dinar and David Zilberman, eds., *The Economics and Management of Water and Drainage in Agriculture*. Boston: Kluwer Academic Publishers.

Biswas, Asit K., ed. 1997. "Water Development and Environment." In *Water Resources: Environmental Planning, Management, and Development*. New York: McGraw-Hill.

Boisvert, Richard, and Todd Schmidt. 1997. "Tradeoff between Economies of Size in Treatment and Diseconomies of Distribution for Rural Water Systems." *Agricultural and Resource Economics Review* 27(2): 237–47.

Brown, Stephen, and David Sibley. 1986. *The Theory of Public Utility Pricing*. Cambridge, U.K.: Cambridge University Press.

Brox, James, Ramesh Kumar, and Kenneth Stollery. 1999. "Willingness to Pay for Water-Quality Enhancements: Some Canadian Evidence." Paper presented at the 33rd Annual Meeting of the Canadian Economics Association, May 28–30, Toronto.

Canadian Water and Wastewater Association in cooperation with Environment Canada and the Rawson Academy of Aquatic Science. 1992. *Municipal Water and Wastewater Rate Manual: A New Approach to Rate Setting.* Ottawa.

Caswell, Margriet. 1991. "Irrigation Technology Adoption Designs: Empirical Evidence." In Ariel Dinar and David Zilberman, eds., *The Economics and Management of Water and Drainage in Agriculture.* Boston: Kluwer Academic Publishers.

Dalhuisen, Jasper, Henri L. F. de Groot, and Peter Nijkamp. 2000. "The Economics of Water: A Survey." *International Journal of Development Planning Literature* 15(1): 1–21.

Dinar, Ariel, and Ashok Subramanian, eds. 1997. *Water Pricing Experiences: An International Perspective.* World Bank Technical Paper no. 386. Washington, D.C.: World Bank.

Dupont, Diane, and Steven Renzetti. 1999. "The Role of Water in the Canadian Manufacturing Sector." Paper presented at 33rd Annual Meeting of the Canadian Economics Association, May 28–30, Toronto.

Easter, K. William, and Gershon Feder. 1997. "Water Institutions, Incentives, and Markets." In Douglas Parker and Yacov Tsur, eds., *Decentralization and Coordination of Water Resource Management.* Boston: Kluwer Academic Publishing.

Espey, M., J. Espey, and W. D. Shaw. 1997. "Price Elasticity of Residential Demand for Water: A Meta-Analysis." *Water Resources Research* 33(6): 1369–74.

Feldstein, Martin. 1972. "Equity and Efficiency in Public Sector Pricing: The Optimal Two Part Tariff." *Quarterly Journal of Economics* 86(2): 175–87.

Flavin, Christopher, and Nicholas Lenssen. 1994. "Reshaping the Power Industry." In L. R. Brown, ed., *State of the World.* New York: Norton.

Galal, Ahmed, and Mary Shirley. 1995. *Bureaucrats in Business: The Economics and Politics of Government Ownership.* World Bank Research Report. Oxford, U.K.: Oxford University Press.

Hahn, William, and George Hester. 1989. "Marketable Permits: Lessons from Theory and Practice." *Ecological Law Quarterly* 16(3): 361–406.

Hall, Darwin, and Michael Hanemann. 1996. "Urban Water Rate Design Based on Marginal Cost." In Darwin Hall, ed., *Marginal Cost Rate Design and Wholesale Water Markets, Advances in the Economics of Environmental Resources,* Vol. 1. Greenwich, Connecticut: JAI Press.

Howe, Charles W., and Mark Griffin Smith. 1994. "The Value of Water Supply Reliability in Urban Water Supply Systems." *Journal of Environmental Economics and Management* 26(1): 19–30.

Kim, H. Youn. 1987. "Economies of Scale in Multi-Product Firms: An Empirical Analysis." *Economica* 54(2): 185–206.

Le Moigne, Guy, Shawki Barghouti, Gershon Feder, Lisa Garbus, and X. Mu, eds. 1992. *Country Experiences with Water Resources Management.* Technical Paper no. 175. Washington, D.C.: World Bank.

Madanat, Samer, and Frannie Humplick. 1993. "A Model of Household Choice of Water Supply Systems in Developing Countries." *Water Resources Research* 29(5): 1353–58.

Mody, Jyothsna. 1997. *Industrial Demand for Water in Thailand.* Ph.D. diss., Boston University, Boston.

Moore, Michael, Noel Gollehon, and Marc Carey. 1994. "Multicrop Production Decisions in Western Irrigated Agriculture: The Role of Water Price." *American Journal of Agricultural Economics* 76(4): 859–74.

Mu, Xinming, David Whittington, and John Briscoe. 1990. "Modeling Village Water Demand Behavior: A Discrete Choice Approach." *Water Resources Research* 26(4): 521–29.

Munasinghe, Mohan. 1992. *Water Supply and Environmental Management: Developing World Applications.* Boulder, Colorado: Westview Press.

Renzetti, Steven. 1992a. "Estimating the Structure of Industrial Water Demands: The Case of Canadian Manufacturing." *Land Economics* 68(4): 396–404.

_____. 1992b. "Evaluating the Welfare Effects of Reforming Municipal Water Prices." *Journal of Environmental Economics and Management* 22(2): 147–63.

_____. 1993. "Examining the Differences between Self and Publicly Supplied Firms' Water Demands." *Land Economics* 69(2): 181–188.

_____. 1999. "Municipal Water Supply and Sewage Treatment: Costs, Prices and Distortions." *Canadian Journal of Economics* 32(2): 688–704.

Renzetti, Steven, and Diane Dupont. 1999. "An Assessment of the Impact of a Provincial Water Use Charge." *Canadian Public Policy* 25(2): 1–19.

Rivera, Daniel. 1996. *Private Sector Participation in the Water Supply and Wastewater Sector: Lessons from Six Developing Countries.* Washington, D.C.: World Bank.

Russell, Clifford, and Boo-Shig Shin. 1996 "Public Utility Pricing: Theory and Practical Limitations." In Darwin Hall, ed., *Marginal Cost Rate Design and Wholesale Water Markets, Advances in the Economics of Environmental Resources,* Vol. 1. Greenwich, Connecticut: JAI Press.

Saleth, R. Maria, John Braden, and J. Wayland Eheart. 1991. "Bargaining Rules for a Thin Spot Water Market." *Land Economics* 67(3): 326–39.

Singh, Bhanwar, Radhika Ramasubban, Ramesh Bhatia, John Briscoe, Charles Griffin, and Chongchun Kim. 1993. "Rural Water Supply in Kerala, India: How to Emerge from a Low-Level Equilibrium Trap." *Water Resources Research* 29(7): 1931–42.

Stavins, Robert N. 1995. "Transaction Costs and Tradeable Permits." *Journal of Environmental Economics and Management* 29(2): 133–49.

Stone, John, and Dale Whittington. 1984. "Industrial Water Demands." In Janus Kindler and Clifford Russell, eds., *Modeling Water Demands*. London: Academic Publishers.

Sunding, David, David Zilberman, Neal MacDougall, Richard Howitt, and Ariel Dinar. 1997. "Modeling the Impacts of Reducing Agricultural Water Supplies: Lessons from California's Bay/Delta Problem." In Douglas Parker and Yacov Tsur, eds., *Decentralization and Coordination of Water Resource Management*. Boston: Kluwer Academic Publishers.

Tate, Donald, and David Lacelle. 1995. "Municipal Water Rates in Canada: Current Practices and Prices, 1991." Social Sciences Series no. 30, Water and Habitat Conservation Branch. Ottawa: Environment Canada.

Teeples, Ronald, and David Glyer. 1987. "Cost of Water Delivery Systems: Specification and Ownership Effects." *Review of Economics and Statistics* 69(3): 399–408.

Tripp, J. T., and D. J. Dudek. 1989. "Institutional Guidelines for Designing Successful Transferable Rights Programs." *Yale Journal of Regulation* (6): 369–91.

World Bank. 1993. *Water Resources Management: A World Bank Policy Paper*. Washington, D.C.: World Bank.

_____. 1996. *Development Indicators*. Washington, D.C.

World Bank Water Demand Research Team. 1993. "The Demand for Water in Rural Areas: Determinants and Policy Implications." *The World Bank Research Observer* 8(1): 47–70.

World Resources Institute. 1997. *World Resources: A Guide to the Global Environment*. New York: Oxford University Press.

Zilberman, David, Ujjayant Chakravorty, and Farhed Shah. 1997. "Efficient Management of Water in Agriculture." In Douglas Parker and Yacov Tsur, eds., *Decentralization and Coordination of Water Resource Management*. Boston: Kluwer Academic Publishers.

7

The Win-Win Effect of Joint Water Market and Trade Reform on Interest Groups in Irrigated Agriculture in Morocco

Xinshen Diao and Terry Roe

In her synthesis of the political economy of agricultural pricing policy in developing countries, Krueger (1991) concludes that discrimination against agriculture has generally been pronounced. The more ideologically committed governments are to following industrialization policies that promote import substitution, and the more that agricultural production consists of predominantly exportable commodities, then the more pronounced this discrimination becomes. Whereas direct interventions have tended to discriminate against crops that compete with exports, crops that compete with imports have been protected.

Overall, Krueger concludes that indirect discrimination against agriculture through the trade regime and exchange rate policies has generally been more important than the discrimination caused by direct interventions. Although in recent years many countries have moved in the direction of opening their economies to world markets, reforms remain far from complete (see Diao, Roe, and Yeldan 1999 for a discussion of this point and an analysis of the case in Turkey). Thus, while the magnitude of discrimination against agriculture may have fallen overall, the basic pattern of discrimination remains in place in many countries, with the import competing sectors tending to be protected relative to the export competing sectors, and interventions in other sectors of the economy continuing to discriminate against agriculture as a whole.

This discrimination has deleterious consequences for the efficient allocation of water, particularly in economies where water is relatively scarce and agriculture consumes a relatively large proportion of the mobilized water supply. Clearly, protection of the import competing crops alters the pattern of employment of agricultural and economic resources in those crops' favor. Moreover, in an environment in which irrigation water is priced below its shadow price so that it must be administratively allocated, raising water prices or creating a market for water while leaving trade distortions in place may further implicitly tax the crops that trade policy already discriminates against. In an environment where water allocation must be administered, a reform that removes protection received by producers of the import competing crops may not induce the producers of these formerly protected crops to alter the pattern of water use, even though the use of other resources may fall. This situation can arise when, following trade reform, the new shadow prices of water in the now unprotected crops remain positive, albeit lower than their prior values.

Many of the other effects of trade reform will have indirect, but no less important, benefits for agriculture. They include incentives for households to save a proportion of their increased income for investment, which increases the returns to other primary resources by expanding production possibilities over time. Growth in total exports also provides foreign exchange earnings to import more intermediate inputs at costs lower than would otherwise be possible in the local economy.

Chapter Objectives

The first objective of this chapter is to provide insights into the relative magnitude of the linkages between trade reform and the agriculture sector in the case of an economy where policy reform remains incomplete, and to assess how trade reform might affect the level and pattern of water allocation in irrigated agriculture. The chapter focuses on Morocco for this analysis. It pays particular attention to how a pattern has evolved of failing to do away with discrimination against agriculture as the Moroccan economy approaches a new long-run equilibrium.

The second objective is to ascertain whether reform of Morocco's water pricing regime might also lower the resistance to overall policy reform. Aside from trade reform, the fact that the administered allocation of water in itself results in varying water shadow prices across crops raises the question whether producers of various crops and their associations vary in political influence. Moreover, water pricing and the political economy of water user rights in irrigated agriculture are likely to become even more contentious if trade policy reform is pursued. Because, as in most countries, sector-specific resources are unevenly distributed among Moroccan households, policy reform that alters the flow of rents to sector-specific assets, including water rights, almost always benefits some holders of these rights at the cost to others, even though the economy as a whole typically experiences a net welfare gain.

As already noted, when the water charge price is below water's marginal value product, farmers using irrigation water receive an implicit subsidy. This implicit subsidy is usually higher for protected crops. Such benefits are approximately equivalent to the difference between water's shadow price and the price the government charges. Because policies favoring the import competing sectors have been in place for an extended time, farmers who produce crops protected by the old policies will, at the margin, be made worse off (at least in the short run) as the returns to the resources specific to these crops, including their water quota, fall. Returns to other crop-specific resources may also fall. These include farmers' investment in skills and expertise at growing crops such as sugar beets and sugarcane, land suitable for growing irrigated cereals but not easily shifted in the short run to growing vegetables, and tree crops that typically require several years before the fruit can be profitably harvested. If, in addition to trade reform, the government either redistributed the water quota according to the crop growing plan set out following the trade reform, or raised the water charge price, then the returns to the relatively crop-specific resources of those farmers who grew the formerly protected crops would be further depressed. It is rational for those farmers, and often for the interest groups that represent them, to resist reform and to resist the reallocation of water quotas to the more profitable crops. This source of conflict often becomes a major stumbling block to the entire reform process.

However, political resistance to trade and water pricing reform may be lowered if the decline in returns to the formerly protected crops can be at least partially counterbalanced by some other scheme. Thus, the second goal is to evaluate the potential of a water rights pricing scheme that, through economywide trade reform, can counterbalance these losses while leading to a more efficient allocation of water among crops. The establishment of a water rights market in Morocco could potentially provide such a mechanism. The scheme investigated here is a water rental market in which water user rights can be traded among farmers in the irrigation sector, while the ownership of the user right is based on a farmer's historical prereform allotment of water, or water quota.

An Overview of the Moroccan Case

A semi-arid region in the lower segment of the middle-income category of countries, Morocco continues to protect its import competing sectors through an array of tariff and nontariff barriers despite having made substantial economic reforms since the mid-1980s (Doukkali 1997). In 1994, agriculture accounted for approximately 18.4 percent of gross domestic product and 30 percent of export receipts. It employs about half of the country's active population, and it consumes roughly 85 percent of the country's scarce supplies of mobilized water. Consequently, trade distortions can have negative consequences for the rural sector of the economy, and particularly for the efficient allocation of the country's water resources. The data complied by Doukkali (1997) from various sources suggest that tariff rates of about 50 percent were imposed on imports of wheat and industrial crops, while tariff rates on fruits and vegetables averaged less than 7 percent. In addition, agricultural trade faces various nontariff barriers. The tariff equivalent rate calculated by Doukkali for wheat and livestock ranged from 160 to 270 percent, respectively, of their total import values. Some sectors also received producer price subsidies. The subsidy rates on the producer price for wheat was equivalent to 28 percent of the gross value of wheat produced in 1994 and 3 percent of the gross value of industrial crops.

According to a World Bank study (1986), Morocco enjoys a clear comparative advantage in the production of key irrigated exportables, such as fruits and vegetables. The protected wheat and industrial crops sectors use water intensively relative to the unprotected crops, such as fruits and vegetables, thereby consuming water that could otherwise be allocated to the more profitable crops to further their comparative advantage in world markets. Depending on the country's water allocation policies and water development plans, correcting for these distortions has the benefit, at least in the short run, of potentially reducing the pressure on water resources while leading to a more efficient pattern of water allocation among crops.

Morocco's water development plan entails increasing national water balances by constructing large and medium dams to serve regional demands and to transfer water between basins. Currently, of Morocco's 40 dams, 10 of the largest carry 90 percent of the total volume of water flow. Surface flows account for approximately 75 percent (8.5 billion cubic meters) (World Bank 1995, p. 8) of total mobilized water supplies. As a major consumer of available water resources, the agriculture sector is targeted for technical and institutional reforms aimed at improving water use efficiency (Dinar, Balakrishnam, and Wambia 1998). However, its progress in this direction has been slow.

Nine regional agricultural development authorities under the supervision of the Ministry of Agriculture and Agricultural Development, Rural Engineering Division, are currently responsible for water resource management. The water charge rate to farmers is generally viewed as sufficient only to cover operation and maintenance costs. As the water charge is below the price that marginal users are willing to pay, that is, below the marginal value product of water, the distribution of water must be administered (World Bank 1995, p. 25). When the quota of water that farmers obtain is below the demand for water at the given water that charge rate, then, implicitly, a shadow price for water exists. Depending on the marginal product of water allocated to various crops, this price will vary accordingly, even though the government charges the same price per volumetric of water (Tsur and Dinar 1995). The cost shares of water's contribution to the gross value of outputs produced in the irrigated sector are estimated by Doukkali (1997) to vary from 13 to 37 percent, while water charges administered by government account for only 8 to 24 percent of the gross value of outputs (Ministry of Agriculture and Agricultural Development, Rural Engineering Administration 1997, p. 4). The difference between the shadow price of water and the government's charge accrues as a benefit to the farmer. As the intensity of water use varies by crop, such benefits to farmers growing different crops vary from an estimated 5 to 13 percent of the gross value of the sector's outputs.

Chapter Plan and Principal Findings

The analysis is based on an intertemporal general equilibrium model developed by Diao and Somwaru (forthcoming in 2000), and it draws in many ways on the recent contributions of dynamic computable general equilibrium modeling by Diao, Yeldan, and Roe (1998); Go (1994); Ho (1989); McKibbin (1993); and Mercenier and Sampaïo de Souza (1994). The chapter uses the model to simulate both the short- and long-run transitional dynamic effects of trade reforms and a water user rights market in the context of a whole economy. The model is dynamic in the sense that firms and households make intertemporal optimization decisions (they display forward looking behavior), so that a change in trade policy and water price policy will affect the saving, investment, and capital accumulation activities of the economic agents modeled. The study focuses on agriculture, especially on the irrigated agriculture sector. However, a change in nonagricultural trade policies also affects agriculture through changes in relative prices, allocation of resources, and investment decisions. Hence, the model is built as a general equilibrium model, that is, it includes all economic activities, including the nonagricultural sectors, as well as consumer and government consumption.

The chapter is divided into four sections. The next section presents a brief overview of the intertemporal general equilibrium model and then discusses the data. This is followed by a discussion of the short- and longer-run effects of trade reform alone, with an emphasis on agriculture and the irrigation sector. It finds a strong investment and growth response to reform and a reallocation of resources to the production of fruit and vegetable crops. The shadow price of water rises in some sectors, but it falls in the others. Hence, from a political economy perspective, it is rational for the farmers in a sector in which the water shadow price falls to resist trade reform. The final section analyzes the opportunity provided by trade reform to establish a water user rights market that, at the same time, at least partially compensates those who might otherwise resist both economywide and water policy reforms because of the decline in their real income that reform would cause. Allowing farmers to rent in or out water user rights leads to further economic efficiencies that can be detected even at the national level, while mitigating the postreform decline in income of those producers producing the prereform protected crops.

Methodology and Data

The model is based on intertemporal general equilibrium theory with a multisector specification. For the purpose of the study, the Moroccan economy is aggregated into 20 production sectors, including 6 irrigated agriculture sectors, 6 rainfed agriculture sectors, 4 sectors related to agriculture, and 4 nonagriculture sectors. The agriculture sectors produce 6 commodities (table 7.1).

Firms and Investment

We assume that the representative firm (or farmer) in each sector operates with constant returns to scale technology. For each time period the representative firm chooses the quantities of inputs and level of investment to maximize the value of the firm. Inputs are labor, capital, land, water, and other intermediates, while the investment inputs are forgone final goods produced domestically plus imports. The value added production function is of Cobb-Douglas form, while the intensities of intermediate goods are fixed. Labor and capital are classified as agricultural (including rural services) and nonagricultural. Over time, sectoral capital accumulates while the other factors of production are permitted to reallocate within the agriculture and nonagriculture sectors, but not between sectors. For example, agricultural labor can be reallocated among the various production sectors in agriculture, but migration to the nonagricultural sectors is not permitted, and likewise for urban labor and capital. Land is classified as irrigated and nonirrigated. Irrigation water is initially controlled and distributed by

TABLE 7.1
Sectors and Commodities in the Model

Sector	Commodities
Irrigated soft wheat	Soft wheat
Rainfed soft wheat	Soft wheat
Irrigated hard wheat	Hard wheat
Rainfed hard wheat	Hard wheat
Irrigated other cereal	Other cereal
Rainfed other cereal	Other cereal
Irrigated vegetable and tree fruits	Fruits and vegetables
Rainfed vegetable and tree fruits	Fruits and vegetables
Irrigated industrial crops	Industrial crops
Rainfed industrial crops	Industrial crops
Livestock in irrigated area	Livestock
Livestock in rainfed area	Livestock
Forest	Forest
Food processing industries	Processed foods
Sugar industry	Sugar and sugar products
Rural services	Rural services
Export-oriented manufacturing	Export-oriented manufacturing products
Import-competing manufacturing	Import-competing manufacturing products
Services	Services
Public administration	Services

Source: Authors.

the government, which collects a water charge from farmers in the irrigated sector. Because of data constraints, the analysis omits the use of water by the urban sector.

Firms are presumed to finance investment outlays by retaining profits so that the number of firm equities within the economy remains unchanged. The nonarbitrage condition derived from the first-order condition of the firm's profit maximization implies that

$$wk_{i,t} + \phi_i PI_{i,t} \left(\frac{I_{i,t}}{K_{i,t}} \right)^2 + (1 - \delta_i)q_{i,t} - (1 + r_t)q_{i,t-1} = 0$$

where $wk_{i,t}$ is the sector marginal product of capital; Tobin's $q_{i,t}$ is the shadow price of capital, $K_{i,t}$ is sector capital stock, $PI_{i,t}$ is value per unit of investment goods, $I_{i,t}$ is the quantity of sector physical investment, δ is the physical capital depreciation rate, r_t is the interest rate, and $\phi_i PI_{i,t}(I_{i,t}/K_{i,t})^2$ denotes the installation-adjustment cost per unit of capital.

The output of each sector, except for the rural services and public administration sectors, can be exported abroad or consumed domestically.

Households: Consumption and Saving

Households behave as extended immortal families. They are aggregated into two groups: rural and urban. Rural households own agricultural labor, capital, and land. Urban households own nonagricultural labor and capital. The representative household makes consumption and saving decisions to maximize an intertemporal utility function. The Euler equation derived from the first-order condition of utility maximization implies that the marginal utility across two adjacent periods satisfies the following condition:

$$(7.1) \qquad \frac{u'_{t+1}(1+\rho)^{-1}}{u'_t} = \frac{Ptc_{t+1}(1+r_{t+1})^{-1}}{Ptc_t}$$

where u_t' is the derivative of the instantaneous felicity function, u_t, at time t with respect to the aggregate consumption Q_t, generated from the 13 final goods; ρ is positive and represents the rate of time preference; and Ptc_t is the consumer price index. Equation 7.1 implies that the marginal rate of substitution between consumption at time t and $t + 1$ is equal to the ratio of the consumption price index at time t and $t + 1$. A sequence of aggregate household consumption and savings is determined simultaneously from the equation.

Demand for final goods (including demand by private households, the government, the firms as intermediate inputs, and investment inputs) is satisfied by domestic production and imports, and, with the famous Armington assumption (Armington 1969), domestic goods and imported goods are imperfectly substitutable.

Government Policies

The government intervenes in the economy using a host of instruments: taxes and subsidies, import tariffs, indirect taxes on producers, household taxes and subsidies, producer support price subsidies, and nontariff barriers. The government is also presumed to impose a water charge by the method of volumetric pricing. All policy variables are exogenous.

The Data

Data on sectoral outputs and inputs, household and government consumption, investment, and exports and imports, as well as on levels of various taxes and subsidies, are obtained from a social accounting matrix of Morocco developed by Doukkali (1997). The data represent the Moroccan economy in 1994, including the various levels of interventions mentioned above. Doukkali obtained the data on irrigated areas, water consumption by crops, and other agricultural aspects from the annual reports of regional offices of irrigation to the Department of Rural Engineering, which supervises irrigation; from the department's own estimates; and from other departments of the Ministry of Agriculture. We then compared these estimates with data available from other studies of the irrigation sector conducted by international and national organizations [FAO 1982, 1985, 1986, 1987; World Bank 1995].[1] The share of water charges in the gross value of output was calculated from information provided in Ministry of Agriculture and Agricultural Development, Rural Engineering Administration (1997, p. 4).

The Effects of Trade Reform on the Economy

In this analysis, total reform is presumed, that is, all import tariffs, nontariff barriers, and producer price supports are eliminated. The analysis also abstracts from Morocco's historical growth rates in total factor productivity. As the main purpose of the study is not to focus on trade liberalization, we do not model the process of the reform, for example, by looking at which policy should change first and to what extent.

Trade liberalization will cause adjustments in sector production, capital investment, consumption and savings, and trade. Because the model is dynamic, these adjustments take time, which allows us to estimate both the short- and long-run effects of reforms. During the adjustment process, the demand for water and the shadow price of irrigation water also change. Hence, the political economy of water issues is likely to develop as a result of trade reform. Such effects come not only from changes in producer prices, but also from lowered returns to the water quota common to those sectors at their respective prereform volume. As mentioned earlier, when the water charge price is below the marginal product of water, farmers who use irrigation water receive an implicit subsidy. Such benefits are approximately equivalent to the difference between water's shadow price and the government price. If the government further reduced the water quota for those farmers who grew the crops that were protected before the reform, those farmers would be further hurt by the reform.

---

1. All of these comparisons are done by Doukkali (1997).

To capture the economywide as well as the sector effects of the trade reform, we first fix the water quota allocated to different sectors at the level given by the data, that is, we first ignore the possible effects caused by water quota redistribution on farmers who grow different crops. Although the owners of irrigable land can allocate it to different crops within the sector, they cannot do so instantaneously. Thus, we allow the land allocation across irrigable crops to require time to fully adjust, with about a five-year lag after the trade reforms take place. This assumption is because some resources are sector- or crop-specific, such as land, farmers' investments in skills, and farmers' expertise at growing specific crops. Hence, growers of sugar beets or sugarcane cannot easily switch to growing vegetables or fruits in the short run.

Economywide Effects of Trade Reform: Welfare Gains and Income Growth

The results show a strong economywide growth effect from the removal of the trade distortions and subsidies. Postreform, the country's gross domestic product increases by 2 percent in the short run, rising to 10 percent in the long run (figure 7.1), relative to the status quo.

Social welfare, in the money metric of equivalent variation, rises by 4 percent.[2] Households in rural areas benefit more than those in urban areas, in part because we assume that the government obtains, in lump sum, taxes on urban households to cover the revenue loss from tariffs.[3] The real income for rural households as a group rises by 5 percent in the short run and 14 percent in the long run (table 7.2).

Perhaps more important, the economywide gains from reform mainly accrue from two sources: efficiency gains from the allocation of resources to more profitable activities, and the more rapid accumulation of capital resulting from the more profitable investment alternatives. The growth in the stock of capital not only increases wealth, but it also raises the rental rates of primary resources, such as land, water, and labor.

Interestingly, the urban and rural effects of reform on capital accumulation are not symmetrical (figure 7.2). Urban investment rises sharply almost immediately after the reform takes place, whereas rural investment in the first three years is not sufficient to replace depreciated capital, but subsequently rises in the medium and long term. In the long term, the

---

2. This measure was derived by Mercenier and Yeldan (1997), and it is based on the household's intertemporal utility function.

3. Of course, this assumption has no effect on the allocation of resources.

FIGURE 7.1
Effects of Trade Reform on Total Trade and Gross Domestic Product without a Water Rights Market

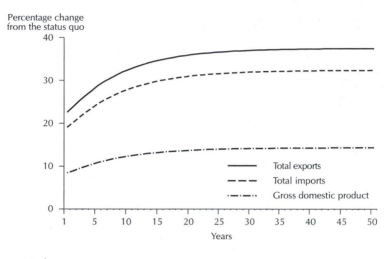

Source: Authors.

growth in investment results in capital stocks that are larger than base stocks by 26 and 12 percent in the urban and rural sectors, respectively.

The major reason for this pattern is that the nonfarm sector is relatively more distorted than the farm sector. Tariffs averaged about 28 percent on nonfarm import competing goods and about 19.5 percent on export competing goods. Tariffs on sugar products and processed food were 54 percent and 23 percent, respectively. The initial decline and then growth in capital stock in the rural sector reflect the effects of the lag in shifting land from the production of the protected crops into the production, primarily, of other cereals, as well as fruits and vegetables. It also reflects, at least initially, the relatively more profitable investment opportunities in the non-farm sector. Of course, these investment opportunities induce households in the short run to forgo some consumption, thus causing a decline in their demand for goods and services.

Agricultural laborers, as well as landowners, generally benefit from reforms. In the long run, the agricultural real wage rate rises by 16 percent, while returns to irrigated land rise by 14 percent and returns to other land rise by 9 percent (table 7.3). However, the increase in the agricultural wage rate is still lower than that of the nonagricultural wage rate (which rises by 25 percent), partly because of the relatively larger increase

TABLE 7.2

Effects of Trade Reform on Welfare and Income, with and without a Water Market

(percentage change from the status quo)

Effect on:	Year 5	Year 10	Year 15	Year 20	Steady state
Without water user rights market					
Rural total income	5.58	7.50	9.57	10.85	12.49
Urban total income (a)	−5.25	−2.26	−0.54	0.42	1.59
Equivalent variation (b)					3.91
With water user rights market					
Rural total income	5.27	8.61	10.84	12.17	13.86
Urban total income (a)	−5.32	−2.31	−0.59	0.37	1.56
Equivalent variation (b)					3.92

a. As government budget is assumed to be balanced at the base level, reduced tariff revenue is covered by household taxes on the urban households, which lowers urban income.

b. Takes into account both transitional effects and steady state (long-term) effects, and gives current effects a higher weight.

Source: Authors.

in the urban capital stock. The widened rural-urban income gap is likely to place further pressures on labor migration out of primary agriculture and into rural nonfarm and urban enterprises. The relative shortage of labor in the nonfarm sector limits the competitiveness of that sector's traded goods in world markets.

Eliminating trade protection stimulates the country's trade, and both imports and exports rise. But the increase in exports exceeds the increase in imports by 4 percentage points in the short run and 8 percentage points in the long run (figure 7.1). The change in sectoral exports and imports is summarized in the "Without water user rights market" panel of table 7.4.

Sectoral Effects of Trade Reform: Some Gain and Some Lose

Trade reform—the elimination of tariff and nontariff barriers and the abolishment of producer price supports—changes the relative prices that producers face. Farmers producing protected crops are made worse off after the reform,

FIGURE 7.2

Change in Capital Stock after Trade Reform without a Water Rights Market

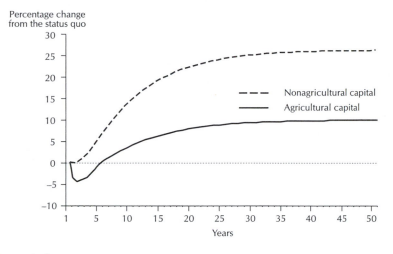

Source: Authors.

as they face lower relative output prices and the gross value of their output falls. Other sectors benefiting from reform compete for the inputs of agricultural labor, capital, and other intermediate inputs, causing the rental rates of many of these inputs to rise. These forces lower the returns to the relatively crop-specific factors of production in the formerly protected sectors. Our simulation results (table 7.3) suggest that in the short and intermediate run, the returns to irrigated land, normalized by the consumer price index, fall for wheat, especially soft wheat, but rise for the other crops. The result is not surprising, as wheat production was highly protected by tariffs and nontariff barriers.

Changes in the returns to land encourage farmers to adjust their cropping patterns. In the simulation, we allow the readjustment of land to occur over a five-year interval. In the real economy, the period of adjustment may be more crop dependent, with some land never being reallocated to other crops. Hence, the simulation should be viewed as providing an upper-bound to land adjustment. From such a best case adjustment, returns to irrigated land rise by 11 percent in the first 10 years and by 15 percent in the long run.

Effects on Sectoral Water Shadow Prices: Some Rise and Some Fall

Given no change in the government's water pricing and distribution policies, reform alters the returns to farmers' water quotas by relatively large and differing magnitudes. The excess demand for water has to be constrained

TABLE 7.3

Effects of Trade Reform on Wage Rates, Returns to Land, and Water Shadow Price, with and without a Water Market

(percentage change from the status quo and deflated by the consumer price index)

Financial impact/crop	Without water user rights market				With water user rights market			
	Year 1	Year 5	Year 10	Steady state	Year 1	Year 5	Year 10	Steady state
Agricultural wage	9.12	8.24	11.56	16.01	9.29	8.49	11.76	16.16
Returns to irrigated land growing:								
Soft wheat	−37.27	−34.75	11.44	14.72	−33.16	−31.64	12.36	15.34
Hard wheat	−1.68	1.40	11.44	14.72	−0.38	2.40	12.36	15.34
Other cereals	9.82	10.95	11.44	14.72	10.36	11.34	12.36	15.34
Fruits and vegetables	20.89	20.34	11.44	14.72	22.07	21.45	12.36	15.34
Industrial crops	5.79	6.38	11.44	14.72	4.28	4.99	12.36	15.34
Other land rents	−1.83	0.53	3.86	8.69	−1.95	0.45	3.79	8.66
Shadow price for water used by:	11.24	11.58	14.93	18.26				
Soft wheat	−37.27	−34.75	−25.36	−22.23	—	—	—	—
Hard wheat	−1.68	1.40	6.44	11.46	—	—	—	—
Other cereals	9.82	10.95	15.79	23.33	—	—	—	—
Fruits and vegetables	20.89	20.34	22.95	25.02	—	—	—	—
Industrial crops	5.79	6.38	6.46	8.00	—	—	—	—
Nonagricultural wage	16.33	19.63	21.76	24.52	16.27	19.57	21.71	24.50

— Not applicable.
Source: Authors.

154

TABLE 7.4
**Effects of Trade Reform on Sectoral Imports and Exports, with and
without a Water Market**
(percentage change from the status quo)

Crop	Year 1	Year 5	Year 10	Year 15	Year 20	Steady state
Without water user rights market						
Exports						
Wheat	24.06	19.10	3.64	1.28	−0.03	−1.67
Other cereals	34.88	29.51	21.56	17.48	15.22	12.46
Industrial crops	36.24	30.98	20.10	15.60	13.15	10.18
Fruits and vegetables	23.95	22.81	22.44	19.08	17.19	14.87
Livestock	26.53	23.06	22.17	22.57	22.78	23.01
Imports						
Wheat	116.66	122.74	131.35	135.86	138.40	141.58
Other cereals	22.33	25.58	30.80	34.03	35.87	38.19
Industrial crops	16.82	18.66	22.93	25.48	26.94	28.77
Fruits and vegetables	0.35	0.44	3.41	5.10	6.07	7.29
Livestock	108.90	113.10	119.53	123.35	125.50	128.20
With water user rights market						
Exports						
Wheat	15.84	11.77	0.54	−1.17	−2.97	−4.56
Other cereals	34.33	29.07	21.41	17.63	15.54	12.94
Industrial crops	32.36	29.07	13.55	9.04	6.58	3.60
Fruits and vegetables	28.47	26.81	26.19	22.52	20.47	17.93
Livestock	25.96	22.67	21.98	22.53	22.87	23.22
Imports						
Wheat	117.18	123.32	131.20	136.34	138.89	142.08
Other cereals	22.34	25.62	30.79	33.96	35.76	38.03
Industrial crops	16.94	18.85	23.31	25.88	27.36	29.20
Fruits and vegetables	0.53	0.67	3.62	5.29	6.25	7.46
Livestock	108.92	113.19	119.62	123.43	125.58	128.28

Source: Authors.

by the government's distribution policy because, as discussed previously,
the water charge rate is lower than the price that the marginal user of water
is willing to pay. Hence, a water shadow price is associated with each water
quota. The difference between the water shadow price and government
charge is equivalent to the rent farmers earn from the water quota. In the

first simulation, trade liberalization causes the shadow price of the water quota for soft wheat production to fall over the entire horizon required to reallocate some land from soft wheat to other crops, and to decline for the case of hard wheat in the short run (bottom panel, table 7.3). In other sectors, the shadow price of water rises with the magnitude of change varying across sectors, ranging from a high of more than 20 percent for vegetables and fruits to a low of less than 10 percent for industrial crops. After the five-year adjustment period, the shadow price of land equilibrates across crops (top panel, table 7.3).

Clearly a close link exists between changes in the sectoral shadow price of water and rates of trade protection. The data show that, prereform, wheat production is highly protected while fruits and vegetables are less protected. When tariff and nontariff trade barriers are removed and producer support price policies are abolished, the country's comparative advantage in the production of fruits and vegetables can be more fully realized. This increases the derived demand for water and the willingness to pay for water in these sectors. However, as producers of irrigated wheat and industrial crops lose their protection, their production falls (top panel, table 7.5). The producers of these commodities also experience a concomitant decline in the returns to the water use rights they held from the government's distribution policy.

Generally speaking, as any policy reform almost always affects somebody's interests negatively, the most difficult task in the reform process is to find a feasible way to compensate the interest groups hurt by the reform, thus reducing their resistance to change. The results from the first simulation have two important implications in this regard. First, farmers producing the prereform protected crops are doubly hurt by a lower output price and a lower water shadow price. Farmers producing the unprotected crops gain, but could gain potentially more if the water quota were redistributed. If after trade reform the government reduces the water quota to farmers of the formerly protected crops in proportion to the production decline of those crops, the farmers are made even worse off, even though water would be allocated more efficiently. In principle, it is individually rational for these producers to resist such reforms. Second, the changes in water shadow prices caused by trade reform create an opportunity to form a water user rights market. In this case, we envision nothing more than giving farmers entitlement to their prereform water user rights, that is, the right to earn the market rents from their historical water quota.

Allowing farmers whose production falls after the reform, to rent out some of their water user rights has two major benefits. First, it reduces the postreform costs faced by farmers whose incomes are hurt by reform, and therefore it may reduce the political resistance to reform. Second, creating

TABLE 7.5
Effects of Trade Reform on Sectoral Outputs of Irrigated Agriculture, with and without a Water Market
(percentage change from the status quo)

Crop	Year 1	Year 5	Year 10	Year 15	Year 20	Steady state
Without water user rights market						
Soft wheat	−17.74	−17.30	−26.17	−25.15	−24.59	−23.89
Hard wheat	−3.06	-2.67	−2.77	−1.50	-0.80	0.08
Other cereals	0.43	0.62	2.54	3.67	4.30	5.10
Industrial crops	−1.02	-0.80	−2.81	−3.12	−3.30	−3.53
Fruits and vegetables	5.22	5.18	7.83	7.34	7.07	6.75
With water user rights market						
Soft wheat	−33.21	−31.91	−30.18	−29.14	−28.57	−27.85
Hard wheat	−7.81	−6.31	−4.03	−2.64	−1.86	−0.89
Other cereals	0.06	0.55	2.68	4.08	4.87	5.85
Industrial crops	−7.59	−7.03	−7.52	−7.89	−8.11	−8.37
Fruits and vegetables	12.27	11.41	10.22	9.54	9.16	8.71

Source: Authors.

a water user rights market should also increase the efficiency of water allocation, yielding benefits to the whole economy by providing incentives for the better husbandry of Morocco's scarce water resources.

The Moroccan government has faced difficulties and encountered delays in its efforts to improve water use efficiency. One reason is that the government's water supply organizations are apparently reluctant to accept more responsibility in developing the country's water resources without any additional compensation (Dinar, Balakrishnam, and Wambia 1998). Also, when the benefits of pricing water below its opportunity cost become embedded in the value of the land or in other factors, it becomes politically difficult for a government to charge and collect water revenues commensurate with either its actual cost or its opportunity cost.

The creation of a water user rights market may not generate revenue for the government in the short term. Nevertheless, the existence of such a market, in which transactions among farmers make explicit the rental price of water, should eventually separate the returns to water from that to the land. This in turn should ease the way for further reforms in water prices, such as the imposition of a water tax to help defray the public costs of water mobilization and distribution. A water user rights market should eventually allow water to be treated as a normal commodity, providing private agents with greater incentives to invest in the maintenance of water sector capital and to better husband this resource.

Win-Win Outcomes from Creating a Water User Rights Market

In the second scenario, in addition to trade reform, farmers within each irrigated sector are allowed to rent in or out their water user rights. The farmers' entitlements to water user rights are assumed to be determined by the water quota allotted them by the government according to the farming practices in the prereform period. The rental price is set at the market clearing shadow price for water and is solved simultaneously with all other endogenous variables in the model. Of course, numerous legal, technical, and practical problems must be addressed when forming a water market, many of which are discussed by Thobanl (1997). While these very real problems are ignored here, the simulation nevertheless provides empirical insights into the relative nature of the possible gains from such a water market pricing scheme.

The results show clearly that allowing farmers to rent their water user rights to others not only increases the efficiency of water use, but also compensates them partially for the loss suffered in the production of prereform protected commodities.

Gains from a Water User Rights Market: Counter Balancing Postreform Losses

The trade in water user rights among farmers in the irrigation perimeter causes some water to be allocated away from crops yielding a relatively low return. Because farmers now pay the full marginal value product of water, the level of total water use can also change. Simulation results show that water consumption increases in two sectors: cereals other than wheat, and fruits and vegetables. Water consumption falls in the other three sectors: soft wheat, hard wheat, and industrial crops (table 7.6) This change in water consumption is consistent with the economy's postreform comparative advantage.

The producers of soft wheat earn income by renting some of their water user rights to producers growing more profitable crops after reform. This causes a decrease in the production of soft wheat (table 7.5), releasing labor and other resources for the more profitable crops. However, even in this open economy, the decline in supply of the formerly protected crops causes the producer prices of these crops to rise (bottom panel, table 7.7). This occurs

TABLE 7.6
Change in Water Consumption by Crops in Irrigated Agriculture after Allowing for Trade in Water User Rights
(percentage change from the status quo)

Crop	Year 1	Year 5	Year 10	Steady state
Soft wheat	−39.21	−37.84	−32.27	−31.51
Hard wheat	−10.44	−8.23	−6.66	-5.19
Other cereals	10.79	−0.22	0.82	3.36
Industrial crops	−6.36	−5.91	−9.34	−10.44
Fruits and vegetables	9.74	8.84	7.88	6.42

Source: Authors.

because domestic wheat is not a perfect substitute for imported varieties. Table 7.7 shows that without a water market, relative to the base period, the posttrade reform producer price of soft wheat falls by more than 20 percent in the short run and more than 5 percent in the medium and long run. The establishment of a water user rights market and the subsequent decline in

TABLE 7.7
Effects of Trade Reform on Producer Prices for Irrigated Agriculture, with and without a Water Market
(percentage change from the status quo)

Crop	Year 1	Year 5	Year 10	Year 15	Year 20	Steady state
Without water user rights market						
Soft wheat	−22.59	−20.96	−6.43	−6.17	−6.03	−5.85
Hard wheat	−4.55	−2.83	0.71	1.22	1.52	1.89
Other cereals	1.68	2.39	4.54	6.12	7.04	8.19
Industrial crops	−2.15	−2.05	−0.74	−0.16	0.17	0.60
Fruits and vegetables	1.15	0.88	0.63	1.34	1.76	2.29
With water user rights market						
Soft wheat	−14.28	−12.96	0.42	0.57	0.66	0.78
Hard wheat	−2.21	−0.96	2.28	2.63	2.83	3.09
Other cereals	2.33	2.74	4.47	5.38	5.92	6.60
Industrial crops	−1.23	−1.22	1.18	1.88	2.30	2.82
Fruits and vegetables	0.06	−0.08	−0.25	0.50	0.94	1.50

Source: Authors.

the production of soft wheat causes the price of soft wheat to fall by less than 1 percent in the first year and then to rise about 1 percent in the long run, relative to the base. The same is true for the prices of industrial crops.

Of course, the decline in domestic supply of soft wheat and industrial crops, and the resulting excess demand for these commodities, is partially offset by imports. This result is shown by the rise in imports of soft wheat and industrial crops in the short and medium run (bottom panel, table 7.4). In the long run, exports exceed the value of imports by the amount required to service the country's foreign debt.

Trade and water market reform still results in a decline in the gross value of the outputs of wheat and industrial crops (table 7.8). The simulation results show that returns to land fall less in the first five years and increase thereafter when a market for water user rights exists (upper right panel, table 7.3). This result indicates that the revenue loss to the growers of wheat and industrial crops is partially compensated for by the increase in the returns to the irrigated land, as well as by revenues earned in renting out water. For the growers of wheat and industrial crops, the major compensation accrues directly from the rental income to the farmer's entitlement to the water user rights.

These values are shown in table 7.9. We use the difference between the two levels of water shadow prices, before and after water right trading is permitted. Put another way, we use the implicit rental value given by the unit gain or loss for each volume of water rented in or out by farmers, and then multiply this value by the traded volume of water to obtain the total gains or losses for each sector. The volume is the sectoral water quota given by the data, minus the same sector's water consumption after water trading is permitted. As some sectors are more aggregated, and hence use

TABLE 7.8

Change in Gross Value of Sectoral Outputs in Irrigated Agriculture after Allowing for Trade in Water User Rights

(percentage change from the status quo)

Crop	Year 1	Year 5	Year 10	Year 15	Year 20	Steady state
Soft wheat	−33.66	−31.83	−29.90	−28.74	−28.09	−27.29
Hard wheat	−6.72	−4.70	−1.84	−0.08	0.92	2.17
Other cereals	2.92	3.70	7.27	9.68	11.07	12.83
Industrial crops	−7.49	−6.88	−6.43	−6.16	−6.00	−5.78
Fruits and vegetables	10.86	9.92	9.94	10.08	10.19	10.34

Source: Authors.

TABLE 7.9
Gains from Water Reallocation by a Water User Right Market
(percentage change from the status quo)

Crop	Year 1	Year 5	Year 10	Steady state
Water shadow price without water user rights market				
Soft wheat	62.73	65.25	74.64	77.77
Hard wheat	98.42	101.40	106.44	111.45
Other cereals	109.82	110.95	115.79	123.33
Industrial crops	105.79	106.38	106.46	108.00
Fruits and vegetables	120.89	120.34	122.95	125.02
Water shadow price with water user rights market	111.24	111.58	114.93	118.26
Sectoral demand for water after water user rights traded				
Soft wheat	60.79	62.16	67.73	68.49
Hard wheat	89.56	91.77	93.34	94.81
Other cereals	99.21	99.78	100.82	103.36
Industrial crops	93.64	94.09	90.66	89.57
Fruits and vegetables	109.74	108.84	107.88	106.42
Direct gains from water user rights market				
Soft wheat	19.02	17.53	13.00	12.75
Hard wheat	1.34	0.84	0.57	0.35
Other cereals	0.01	0.00	0.01	0.17
Industrial crops	0.35	0.31	0.79	1.07
Fruits and vegetables	0.94	0.77	0.63	0.43

Source: Authors.

more water, reporting the absolute value of the gains may be misleading. Thus, the gains and losses from water sales are compared with the returns to water in the base data, prior to trade reform and water marketing. Consider, for example, the following case. Growers of soft wheat gain 19.02 percent from renting their water user rights to others. This implies that, in comparison with the returns they received implicitly from the shadow price of their prereform water quota, they can earn an additional 19 percent of revenue by renting some of their water quota to the growers of other crops.

Three sectors—soft wheat, hard wheat, and industrial crops—rent out water over the entire time period. The bottom panel of table 7.9 shows the rents earned a relatively large gain (13 to 19 percent) for soft wheat growers and a small gain (about 1 percent) for growers of hard wheat and industrial crops. Even though the shadow price of water for some sectors does not fall after reform, growers in these sectors still gain directly from renting in water, that is, from paying the water user right rental fees to the original owners in the wheat and industrial crop sectors. The results show that only the growers of fruits and vegetables rent in water for the entire period, while growers in the cereal sectors rent in some water in the long run as capital accumulation occurs.

Why are the growers of fruits and vegetables willing to pay the rental charges for the additional water? The reason is that the shadow price of water in these sectors is much higher, postreform, than the market clearing price for water if traded (table 7.3). This implies that the growers in these sectors are willing to pay a high rental price for water to earn greater returns to their resources. As the rental rate paid by the growers of fruits and vegetables is lower than the shadow price of the postreform quota, the growers paying the water rental charges still benefit from such trading.

Note from table 7.3 that a water market has positive long-term effects on the rental rates of irrigable lands and on rural wages, because the more efficient use of water increases the marginal product of rural labor employed in the fruit and vegetable sector. This lessens the gap between urban-rural wages, as the urban wage rate remains virtually unchanged after the creation of the water market. Returns to other nonirrigable land fall slightly. The reason is that the irrigated sector becomes more competitive because of the more efficient use of water, and hence competes with the nonirrigated sectors for agricultural labor and capital. However, returns to nonirrigable land are still significantly higher than the corresponding prereform rates. This result suggests that the negative effects of a water market on the nonirrigation sector is quite small, and hence there is less reason for that sector to resist reform.

Thus, creating water rental markets among farmers is, after trade reform, a win-win strategy, as almost all farmers and farm labor benefit and water resources are allocated more efficiently. However, in the real economy the formation of such a market will surely entail transaction costs, which are not taken into account here.

Conclusion

Our intertemporal general equilibrium model finds a strong investment and growth response to trade reform and a reallocation of resources to the production of fruits and vegetables, for which Morocco has a strong comparative advantage. Trade reform causes the shadow price of water to rise for fruits and vegetables relative to the prereform protected crops. The change in returns to sector-specific assets caused by reform is likely to induce interest group conflicts, because reform sets back some farmers of previously protected crops. By contrast, trade reform may create an opportunity to introduce water pricing reforms, because farmers who are worse off after reform can earn income from renting out some of their water to others. In addition, the creation of a water user rights market raises the efficiency of water allocation and therefore benefits the economy as a whole.

As the government water charge rate in Morocco is far below water's real cost and opportunity cost, it is almost impossible politically for the government to charge and collect water revenues commensurate with either the actual marginal cost of water or its opportunity cost. This is particularly true when the benefits of a low water charge have been in existence for so long that the value of water's shadow price becomes embedded in the value of the land or other factors of production. Even though the creation of a water user rights market may not generate revenue for the government in the near term, such a market reveals to all the opportunity cost of water that should, eventually, separate the returns to water from those to land. This, in turn, should spur further reforms, such as imposing a water tax or a property tax on a farmer's water right entitlement, thereby helping to defray government costs. Furthermore, a water user rights market should eventually cause water to be treated like any other good, creating incentives to invest in the water sector and better husband this scarce resource.

References

Armington, P. 1969. "A Theory of Demand for Products Distinguished by Place of Production." *International Monetary Fund Staff Papers*, Vol. 16: 159–176. Washington, D.C.: IMF.

Diao, Xinshen, and Agapi Somwaru. Forthcoming in 2000. "An Inquiry on General Equilibrium Effects of MERCOSUR—An Intertemporal World Model." *Journal of Policy Modeling*.

Diao, Xinshen, Erinc Yeldan, and Terry Roe. 1998. "A Simply Dynamic Applied General Equilibrium Model of a Small Open Economy: Transitional Dynamics and Trade Policy." *Journal of Economic Development* 23(1): 77–101.

Diao, Xinshen, Terry Roe, and Erinc Yeldan. 1999. "How Fiscal Mismanagement May Impede Trade Reform: Lessons from an Intertemporal Multi–Sector General Equilibrium Model for Turkey." *The Developing Economies* XXXVII(1): 59–88.

Dinar, Ariel, Trichur K. Balakrishnam, and Joseph M. Wambia. 1998. "Political Economy and Political Risk of Institutional Reforms in the Water Sector." Policy Research Working Paper no. 1789, World Bank, Washington, D.C.

Doukkali, Mohammed R. 1997. "Economic Analysis of Second Stage of Structural Adjustment in Morocco: Gains from First and Second Best Policy Instrument." Ph.D. diss., University of Minnesota, St. Paul.

FAO (Food and Agriculture Organization). 1982. "Maroc: Projet de Development de la Petite et Moyenne Hydraulique Agricole. Mission de Preparation," Vol. 2. Report no. 21/82 MOR 23. Investment Center, Rome.

_____. 1985. "Maroc: Projet d'Amelioration de la Grande Irrigation. Rapport de Preparation," Vol. 2, Report no. 36/85 MOR 43. Investment Center, Rome.

_____. 1986. "Maroc: Development de la Production Fourragere, Rapport de Synthese." Technical Cooperation Program, FAO Project 124/86 TA-MOR 49 TCP/MOR/4402. Rome.

_____. 1987. "Maroc: Projet de Renovation de l'Irrigation Traditionnelle (PMH II), Rapport de Preparation." Report no. 22/87 MOR 53. Investment Center, Rome.

Go, Delfin S. 1994. "External Shocks, Adjustment Policies, and Investment in a Developing Economy—Illustrations from a Forward–Looking CGE Model of the Philippines." *Journal of Development Economics* 44(2): 229–61.

Ho, Ming Sun. 1989. "The Effects of External Linkages on U.S. Economic Growth: A Dynamic General Equilibrium Analysis." Ph.D. diss., Harvard University, Boston.

Krueger, Anne. 1991. *The Political Economy of Agricultural Pricing Policy*, Vol. 5, *A Synthesis of the Political Economy in Developing Countries*. Baltimore, Maryland: The Johns Hopkins University Press.

McKibbin, Warwick J. 1993. "Integrating Macroeconometric and Multi–Sector Computable General Equilibrium Models." Brookings Discussion Papers in International Economics no. 100. Brookings Institute, Washington, D.C.

Mercenier, Jean, and Maria da C. Sampaïo de Souza. 1994. "Structural Adjustment and Growth in a Highly Indebted Market Economy: Brazil." In Jean Mercenier and T. N. Srinivasan, eds., *Applied General Equilibrium Analysis and Economic Development*. Ann Arbor, Michigan: University of Michigan Press.

Mercenier, Jean, and Erinc Yeldan. 1997. "On Turkey's Trade Policy. Is a Customs Union with EU Enough?" *European Economic Review* 41(3–5): 871–80.

Ministry of Agriculture and Agricultural Development, Rural Engineering Administration. 1997. *Etude de Tariffication de l'Eau d'Irrigation au Maroc: Valorisation de l'Eau en Grande Hydraulique, Royaume du Maroc*. Rabat, Morocco.

Thobanl, Mateen. 1997. "Formal Water Markets: Why, When, and How to Introduce Tradable Water Rights." *The World Bank Research Observer* 12(2): 161–79.

Tsur, Yacor, and Ariel Dinar. 1995. "Efficiency and Equity Considerations in Pricing and Allocating Irrigation Water." Policy Research Working Paper no. 1460. World Bank, Washington, D.C.

World Bank. 1986. *Morocco: Agricultural Prices and Incentives Study.* Report no. 6045-MOR. Washington, D.C.

_____. 1995. *Kingdom of Morocco: Water Sector Review.* Report no. 14750-MOR. Washington, D.C.

8

Assessing Consequences of Political Constraints on Rate Making in Dakar, Senegal:

A Monte Carlo Approach

Alfredo H. Cueva and Donald T. Lauria

In 1993 the World Bank closed its first water supply project for Senegal. Although the project had produced significant improvements in the sector, it did not address institutional reforms needed for sector sustainability. Consequently, the Senegalese government requested additional support from the Bank to launch both the Dakar Water Project and water sector reforms, which respectively address the water system's physical limitations and the sector's institutional problems. Privatization is at the heart of the reform, which was started by creating a public holding company and a private operating company for Dakar. Private management of the water system, including service through connections to the pipe network as well as through public fountains, has reportedly improved operating efficiency, raised water rates, and reduced government subsidies, moving the sector toward financial self-sufficiency. Nevertheless, revenues still fail to cover costs.

Improving the sustainability of water utilities such as Dakar's is a main policy concern for governments and the World Bank (World Bank 1993). Cost recovery and rates are the keys to sector sustainability in developing countries. For the past decade

The authors gratefully acknowledge assistance provided by the Société Nationale des Eaux du Sénégal (SONES), the Société d'Exploitation (SdE), the Direction de la Prévision du Sénégal (DPS), and the World Bank.

Many people facilitated the collection of data that support this research, and the authors would like to thank them all, but the following individuals deserve particular mention: Aladji Dieng and Bara Diakhate (SONES); Mayoro Niang (SdE), Matar Gueye (DPS); and Sylvie Debomy, Annie Savina, and Matar Fall (World Bank).

or so, the World Bank and other international donors have promoted a policy of demand-based planning that relies on the willingness of the direct beneficiaries to cover the entire cost of service. In the case of community water supply, such a policy seems to be defensible on economic grounds, because the social benefits of such systems are primarily private, with only modest spillovers to society at large. In addition to financial self-sufficiency for the utility, rates are frequently aimed at meeting complementary policy goals, such as economic efficiency, distributional equity, poverty alleviation, and health improvement. The main focus of contemporary rate policy, however, is ensuring system viability through financial self-sufficiency. Thus, under the sector reform in Dakar, the water company commissioned a consulting study to recommend water rates that would reach full cost recovery about 2000 and financial equilibrium about 2003. However, the rate consultants faced restrictions because of both explicit and implicit political constraints.

The Political Constraints

The most far-reaching explicit constraint pertained to the use of potable drinking water for irrigation by commercial gardeners. During the mid-1990s, small gardeners were using more than 10 percent of drinking water production for growing flowers that were sold in local markets. Although the gardeners were charged a lower price for water than any other users, their water bills frequently went unpaid. The government commissioned two studies of the situation in 1994. These resulted in an agreement between the gardeners and government officials under which the government would charge an increasing block tariff over the following 10 years, and the average price gardeners paid for water would increase gradually from US$0.20 to US$0.32 per cubic meter (m³) by 1998, and then remain constant until 2004. The gardeners would reduce consumption from 24,000 m³ per day in 1994 to 14,000 m³ per day by 1999, and remain at that level thereafter. This agreement fixed the tariff for the next 10 years, precluding any rate changes.

In addition to this explicit constraint, the rate consultants had to operate under several implicit constraints. For example, in 1993 the government privatized the operation of about 2,600 public fountains in Dakar that about 25 percent of the population uses for water supply. The government charged the concessionaires a price slightly higher than the price in the first block of the household tariff, but it imposed no restrictions on the prices that concessionaires could charge their customers. The consultants were probably not told that the rates charged to concessionaires could not be substantially changed or that restrictions could not be imposed on the maximum prices that concessionaires could charge. However, because these conditions had been negotiated with concessionaires just before the consultants started their work, this limited the scope of the consultants' study.

The objective of this chapter is to describe some of the policy consequences of these constraints. The chapter shows how political barriers jeopardized the objectives of water rate efficiency, equity, health promotion, and affordability. Hundreds of thousands of water system users in Dakar are experiencing privation and high pecuniary costs because of a failure to regulate the concessionaires of about 1,000 public standpipes and to limit the inefficient use of potable water for irrigation by a few thousand farmers. Because financial self-sufficiency of the water sector is a major concern in Dakar, the chapter treats this goal in detail and shows how it was threatened by the imposed policy.

Conventional rate studies, like Dakar's, use deterministic models with measures of central tendency for estimates of consumption, costs, and other relevant variables. Their users typically think such models yield average or median values of revenues and other rate performance indicators, but in practice they provide absolutely no information about risk and uncertainty. If deterministic approaches fail to yield average or median estimates of revenue, which is highly likely if correlations among variables are not explicitly taken into account, then deterministic models can lead to rates that may fail to meet financial self-sufficiency and other planning objectives. Decision analysis employs probabilistic assessments to explicitly take account of risk and uncertainty in decisionmaking. This chapter uses a Monte Carlo simulation (MCS) approach for estimating probabilities that recommended rates will result in financial self-sufficiency of the sector.

The use of MCS for the analysis and design of water rates in developing countries constitutes a new application. Nonetheless, MCS has already informed rate design with reported success in the American cities of Los Angeles and Phoenix (Chesnutt, McSpadden, and Christianson 1996). Our preference for using MCS in analyzing the consequences of the politically constrained recommendations made by the Dakar rate consultants results from an examination of current research that reveals deficiencies in deterministic analytical methods of financial planning and rate design like the one employed in Dakar. For instance, independent studies of 243 Pennsylvania water utilities (Cromwell and others 1997) and 442 Georgia utilities (Jordan, Carlson, and Wilson 1997) reveal that the operation ratio (operating revenue divided by operating costs) should be larger than 1.2 to ensure full cost recovery and system viability. These findings suggest a deficiency in traditional pricing in which an operation ratio of 1.0 is a benchmark for full cost recovery. Although this discrepancy requires further investigation, it is indicative of the risks that underlie rate analysis using conventional deterministic methods.

This chapter is admittedly one-sided, because it focuses only on the negative consequences of the water policy decisions in Senegal. Examining the benefits of those decisions and the pressures behind them is equally important. Unfortunately, we are in no position to do so. Instead, we limit our focus to assessing what lessons can be learned from the Dakar experience.

Water Service and Rates in Dakar

In the greater Dakar area, in 1997 about 201,300 households had private connections to the piped water system. An additional 82,200 households bought water from about 1,200 public standpipe concessionaires, who obtained it from the water company. The total of about 283,500 households that got water from the piped system represented a population of about 2.3 million, because Dakar households average about 8.6 persons. An estimated 20 to 30 percent of households are not served by the piped system in greater Dakar. The water company also sells to commercial gardeners, industry, and government.

The water company submits bills to customers every two months. In 1997 households with private connections faced a rate with three increasing blocks, with the price in the third block about four times that in the first and roughly equal to the long-run marginal cost of water production as estimated by the Bank (about US$1 per m^3). Nearly all of Dakar's 1,200 standpipes had attendants who are concessionaires and who sold water to customers at a price about four times higher than the price they paid to purchase water from the company. Industrial and government customers paid a fixed commodity price (unblocked) that was approximately equal to the Bank's estimate of marginal water production cost. Commercial gardeners also paid a fixed commodity price, but it was the lowest price charged to any of the water customers and only one-fifth of the Bank's estimate of long-run marginal cost.

When the Bank appraised a second water sector loan in 1995, a major objective was to help the water company achieve sustainability through financial self-sufficiency. Other objectives included water affordability, equity, health promotion, and improved service to the poor (World Bank 1995). The project involves improvements to water supply and distribution facilities, including a new source located about 160 kilometers from Dakar, plus 34,000 additional private water connections and 400 new standpipes. The new project engaged an international accounting firm to estimate the amount by which existing prices would have to be raised for revenues to cover costs by a future target date.

Using the best available data, the firm calculated the required increase based on estimates of global sales to different categories of customers (table 8.1) and projections of annual costs under the hypothesis of increased efficiency brought about by the new private administration. No allowance was made for the price elasticity of demand or for the potential effects of households switching from their current water source to an alternative one because of the increased numbers of standpipes and private connections.

The accountants estimated that for 1997, the water company's annual revenues from projected sales would be about US$47.28 million, and the annual cost of water supply would be about US$49.53 million, leaving a projected shortfall of US$2.25 million. The financial goal for 1997 was to reduce the shortfall to US$1.07 million, and the longer-term goal was to achieve financial equilibrium for the water company by 2003. In light of an agreement between the government and commercial gardeners not to raise gardeners' water prices for the next several years, the accountants concluded that an annual across-the-board price increase of 2.23 percent for all

TABLE 8.1
Recommended 1997 Water Rate, Estimated Sales and Estimated Revenue

Customer category	Consumption rate (m³/2 months)	Price (US$/m³)	Sales (million m³/year)	Revenue (million US$/year)
Dakar Water Company				
Private connections	0–20	0.273	19.22	5.25
Private connections	20–100	0.925	13.75	12.72
Private connections	>100	1.062	2.69	2.86
Total: 201,300				
households			35.66	20.83
Standpipe				
concessionaires	>0	0.376	4.79	1.80
Total: residential			40.45	22.63
Commercial gardens	>0	0.187	8.15	1.52
Industry and others	>0	0.929	26.17	24.31
Total: water				
company			74.77	48.46
Standpipe				
concessionaires				
82,200 households	>0	1.500	4.79	7.19

Source: Ernst & Young (1996).

customers except gardeners from 1997 to 2003 would achieve the short- and long-term goals. The resulting rates and breakdown of revenue and sales by customer category for 1997 is shown in table 8.1.

In 1996 the water company retained the writers of this chapter to carry out a willingness-to-pay (WTP) study in the greater Dakar area (Lauria, Cueva, and Kolb 1997). The study sought to estimate the demand for improved water supply by residential households using the contingent valuation method. An important objective was to assess elasticities: how much would consumption by households with connections decrease if prices were raised? Would some households currently using private connections switch to public fountains or other sources? Alternatively, would public fountain users switch to private connections if their own prices were raised (assuming they could get a connection if they wanted one)? In addition to WTP information, the study collected extensive background data on water and sanitation practices, including consumption and expenditures; socioeconomic characteristics such as household size, composition, and income; and preferences of residential customers for improvements. The study surveyed a random sample of about 1,400 households drawn from different areas of the city. Nine different versions of the water questionnaire were used, each containing about 200 questions.

The WTP section of the questionnaire was divided into two parts, one for households without water connections and the other for households with connections. Households without connections were quoted a price for buying water from public fountains and asked whether they would support a plan to improve public fountains if they had to pay for it. Respondents were then given a price for connecting to the network and told that, with a connection, their bimonthly water usage cost would average Y in addition to the connection cost, depending on the quantity they consumed. The survey used split samples to investigate three different prices for Y. Respondents could choose one of three options: improved public fountains, a private connection, or neither.

About 50 percent of the respondents preferred a private connection, 24 percent preferred improved public fountains, and 23 percent preferred no change. A multinomial logit model for predicting the probability of each option was fitted to the data; explanatory variables included household income, owner or renter status, household size, present satisfaction with water service, household location, and water usage cost. All coefficients had the expected signs, and the model correctly predicted about 70 percent of the responses.

Households with water connections were told that their bimonthly water bill would increase by Z within the next year if they continued to use the same amount of water. We used split samples to investigate five different values for Z. The households had the option of continuing their consumption unchanged and therefore paying the increase, or reducing their consumption. About 50 percent of the respondents said they would not reduce consumption. To test the plausibility of reducing consumption, we asked the other 50 percent follow-up questions about their present conservation measures and how they proposed to further reduce their consumption. A binomial logit model was fitted to responses, with income, per capita consumption, household location, and marginal increases in bills as explanatory variables. Coefficients had the expected signs, and the model correctly predicted 62 percent of the responses. The model was used to estimate the price elasticity of demand.

Rate Performance

The most important objectives for Dakar's revised water rate policy included efficiency, equity, health promotion, affordability, and the financial self-sufficiency of the water company. This section examines how the rates proposed by the consultants met these objectives.

Measurable criteria are needed to gauge success in meeting objectives. Prices are efficient if they are set equal to the long-run marginal cost of water production, which in this case has been estimated at about US\$1 per m^3. Hence, price is an indicator of efficiency.

The criteria for equity are equivocal, but many rate analysts adhere to the American Water Works Association (1972) "equity" principle, which recommends charging customers prices that are proportional to the average cost of serving them.

Because the cost of service for different customer categories in Dakar was not available, this chapter assumes that the average cost of service is identical for all utility customers. Thus, the average cost that customers pay for water is the indicator of equity. This implies that if all customer classes were charged a single price equal to the marginal cost of water production, the rate would be not only efficient, but also equitable.

Health promotion applies only to residential customers. For this objective, we selected average per capita water consumption as the criterion. The measure for affordability in this case is the percentage of household income spent on water. Affordability is an issue for all customer classes, not just households, but unfortunately data on the percentage of income or revenue that commercial gardeners, industries, and government agencies in Dakar spend on water are not readily available.

Financial self-sufficiency is widely measured by net revenue, that is, the difference between water company revenues and costs. Table 8.2 summarizes the rate policy objectives and the selected criteria.

TABLE 8.2
Rate Policy Objectives and Criteria

Objective	Criterion
Efficiency	Water price
Equity	Average cost of water
Health	Per capita water consumption
Affordability	Percentage of income spent on water
Financial self-sufficiency	Net revenue

Source: Authors.

The data in table 8.1 provide a basis for estimating all the above criteria except affordability and financial self-sufficiency. Table 8.3 shows the criteria estimates for efficiency, equity, health, and affordability; the affordability data come from the WTP study. Consider the column labeled "Efficiency" for which price is the criterion. The table shows that consumption by households with private connections in the second and third blocks of their rate schedule roughly meets the criterion, as does consumption by government and industry. Hence, nearly 60 percent of the water sold by the utility under

TABLE 8.3
1997 Water Rate Performance Indicators

Customer category	Efficiency price (US$/m³)	Equity average cost (US$/m³)	Health (lcd)	Affordability (percentage of income)
Private connections				
Block 1	0.27	n.a.	n.a.	n.a.
Block 2	0.93	n.a.	n.a.	n.a.
Block 3	1.06	n.a.	n.a.	n.a.
Total private connections	n.a.	0.58	57	4.1
Standpipe concessionaires	0.38	0.38	n.a.	n.a.
Commercial gardens	0.19	0.19	n.a.	n.a.
Industry, government, etc.	0.93	0.93	n.a.	n.a.
Standpipe users	1.50	1.50	20	8.2

n.a. Not applicable
Source: Authors.

the schedule in table 8.1 seems to be efficiently priced, with the rest priced below marginal cost. Public fountain concessionaires charge a price well above the marginal cost of water production.

Based on revenue and sales data in table 8.1, table 8.3 shows average water costs as a measure of equity for the different customer categories. The costs range from a low of US$0.19 per m³ for gardeners to a high of US$1.50 per m³ for public fountain users. As indicated in table 8.3, average cost varies widely among customers, and the rate appears to be quite inequitable, with public fountain users paying an average cost nearly 8 times higher than gardeners and 2.5 times higher than households with private connections. The situation is all the more inequitable considering that public fountain users must carry water to their dwellings whereas others have it delivered to them, and public fountain users face fewer hours of water availability per day than any other customer category. For equitable full cost recovery, all customers should be charged at least US$0.66 per m³, which is the ratio of forecasted cost (US$49.53 million) to total sales (74.77 million m³).

Table 8.3 shows average water consumption (the indicator for health) of 57 liters per capita per day for households with private connections, compared with 20 liters per capita per day for users of public fountains. Without question, households with connections face fewer health risks under this criterion than public fountain users. The last column of table 8.3 shows that households with connections pay, on average, 4.1 percent of their income for water, compared with public fountain users who pay, on average, 8.2 percent of their income. Based on data from the WTP study, the median income of households with connections was about US$180 per month, compared with a median income for standpipe users of about US$94 per month.

The Indicators

Table 8.3 illustrates sharp differences in the water situation for households with private connections compared with those using public fountains. In greater Dakar, about 700,000 public fountain users are subsisting each day on the amount of water equivalent to the quantity used to flush a toilet once or twice. Thus an enormous subsidy clearly goes to commercial gardeners, which is both inefficient and inequitable. Somewhat less clear are the substantial rents being taken by standpipe concessionaires that exploit the poor and would more than cover the water company's financial shortfalls.

The public fountain concessionaires purchase water from the company at an average price of US$0.38 per m³ (higher than the price in the first block of the schedule for households with private connections, but lower than the prices in the subsequent two blocks) and sell it at US$1.50 per m³.

Public fountain concessionaires have virtually no investment costs. The value they add is labor. The nominal rent of US$1.12 (= 1.50–0.38) per m³ is higher than the marginal cost of water production, and higher than the price the water company charges any of its customers. Such a rent would seem to make the standpipe operation a candidate for scrutiny, and possibly for regulation and major rate revision.

Table 8.1 shows that standpipe concessionaires have annual revenues of US$7.19 million and annual costs of US$1.80 million. Thus, the annual rent on the 1,200 public fountains in Dakar is US$5.39 million, or an average of US$4,500 per year per standpipe. About 95 percent of the public fountains operate for no more than about 12 hours per day. Assuming 1,200 attendants can each be employed for, say, US$4 per day, the annual operating cost is about US$1.75 million. Hence, the public fountain concessionaires appear to be earning excess profits on the order of about US$3.6 million per year, which is an average of about US$3,000 per standpipe.

The public fountains in Dakar, for all intents and purposes, constitute spatial monopolies: They are too far apart for users to collect water from more than one or two. Although the standpipe operation in Dakar was privatized in the name of efficiency, in reality it is exploiting the users with virtually no control or regulation by the government. No single standpipe may be making exorbitant profits, but the collective profit is substantial and, if tapped by the water company, would easily meet the financial self-sufficiency goal without any prices being raised. If regulation of standpipe prices were possible, the goal of financial self-sufficiency could even be met with lower prices for the poor who use them. Consider the possibility of the water company charging the concessionaires the same price it charges the government and industry (US$0.929 per m³), which is roughly equal to marginal cost, and hence would be efficient. If the government regulated the selling price to standpipe customers at no more than the present price of US$1.50 per m³, the net income to concessionaires would be more than US$6 per day on average, which is 50 percent higher than the typical wage of an unskilled laborer. The water company, for its part, would get US$4.4 million per year, which would make it financially self-sufficient and more than double its current annual revenue from standpipe concessions of US$1.8 million.

For whatever reasons, officials did not choose to regulate the standpipes. This led to the consultants' recommendation to raise prices across-the-board over six years to meet rate policy goals. The consequence of allowing 1,000 or so concessionaires to reap exorbitant profits is that all water users (except gardeners) will be paying significantly higher water prices before self-sufficiency is attained several years from now.

Another obvious deficiency of the water rate is the price charged to gardeners. The opportunity cost of charging such a minimal price is high. In the WTP study, about 50 percent of the renters and more than 70 percent of the homeowners without private water connections said they were willing to pay the equivalent of US$11 per month to be connected to the piped system. The water company could easily achieve positive net revenue by serving these prospective residential customers using high-cost drinking water for irrigation.

The rate consultants had the task of recommending rate policy that would enable the water company to meet its financial targets in the short and long term. They apparently had to do their work under constraints that required them to exclude the gardeners and make no sweeping changes to public fountain operations. The exact reasons for their selection of a uniform price increase are not entirely clear. Evidently, this alternative simplifies the calculations, but at the cost of keeping the rate structure unchanged. It seems fairly obvious that political decisions had left the across-the-board increase as one of the few remaining options. Without question, the negative consequences of the political constraints on rate policy in Dakar are substantial.

The Financial Self-Sufficiency Objective

The previous section examined the extent to which the water rate met several of the objectives of the Dakar Water Project, but it did not look at the objective of financial self-sufficiency. As indicated at the beginning of this chapter, the rate consultants based their finding that a uniform increase in price would achieve financial goals on (a) gross estimates of global sales to different categories of customers, and (b) detailed projections of annual costs. Such an approach, which is how net revenues are typically forecasted, provides no information on the probability that the proposed rate will achieve its goals. Thus, the remainder of this chapter examines the last, and arguably most important, of the objectives of the Dakar Water Project: what are the chances that the uniform rate increase will generate the intended revenue to cover costs?

We examine this question using the MCS. Although the MCS has been widely used to investigate questions of decisionmaking under uncertainty, it has never been used to test the performance of a proposed rate increase or for rate design in developing countries. An MCS model requires multiple sets of values for its input parameters. Each of these data sets can be thought of as a single record taken from a large sample, which is generated by the researcher. Each of these records contains random values drawn from the probability distributions of the input parameters. Processing each record with a MCS model is defined as a "trial," and processing all the records comprises an MCS. Thus, a stochastic model yields multiple point estimates for its output, and these estimates constitute a frequency distribution that can be analyzed for summary statistics, confidence levels, and hypothesis tests. Table 8.4 lists the input parameters for this analysis.

The basic steps in the MCS approach in this chapter are as follows:

1. Develop a deterministic model for estimating net revenue in Dakar for a single year based on the water customer categories and rates in table 8.1. The model must be capable of forecasting demand and of taking into account residential customers' elasticity and their potential for switching their modes of service, for example, from standpipes to private connections.

2. Estimate the parameters of the model using data from the contingent valuation study (Lauria, Cueva, and Kolb 1997); the financial forecasts of the rate consultants (Ernst & Young 1996); and other sources, including officials from the Société Nacionále des Eaux du Sénégal (The Senegal National Water Society), the Société d`Exploitation (Senegal Water Company), and a nongovernmental organization. To be plausible, the model should produce (under similar assumptions) net revenues similar to those obtained by the consultants who recommended the rate increase for Dakar.

3. Use the "calibrated" deterministic model in hand as a basis for developing a similar MCS model. The two models are essentially identical.

4. Run the deterministic model (using mean values for its parameters) to determine the required increase in the average price that residential customers with private connections would have to pay for revenue to cover 1997 costs, holding prices and revenues for public fountain concessionaires, commercial gardeners, and industries fixed at their proposed levels (recall that the 1996 average cost to private connection users was about US$0.57 per m^3).

5. Make similar runs of the MCS model (using probability distributions for its parameters obtained from the WTP study) to determine the average price that residential customers with private connections would have to pay for mean net revenue to be positive, again holding prices and revenues for public fountain concessionaires, commercial gardeners, and industries fixed at their proposed levels.

From these steps, ascertaining the basic difference between a deterministic approach (such as the one used by the rate consultants or the one presented in next section) and an MCS approach (such as the MCS model in this

TABLE 8.4
Parameters for Rate Models

Parameter description (symbol)	Units	Mean	Median	Probability function
Household income (Hin)	US$/month	194	155	Gamma
Household size (Hsi)	persons/household	8.60	8.00	Empirical histogram
Per capita consumption, private connections (Ico^c)	lcd	71.31	49.46	Lognormal
Per capita consumption, public fountains (Ico^f)	lcd	18.27	16.00	Lognormal
Number of households served (Nhh)	units	283,500	283,500	Uniform
Unaccounted-for-water (υ)	percent	26.50	26.50	Uniform
Total fixed cost (FC)	US$/year (million)	30.10	30.10	Truncated normal
Average variable cost (AVC)	US$/m³	0.22	0.22	Truncated normal
Elasticity of water demand, private connections (ε^c)	n.a.	0.32	0.21	Lognormal
Elasticity of water demand, public fountains (ε^f)	n.a.	0.12	0.10	Lognormal
Billing efficiency (β)	percent/100	0.91	0.91	Triangular
Collection efficiency (γ)	percent/100	0.95	0.95	Triangular
Proportion of households that use public fountains (φf)	n.a.	0.29	0.29	Bernoulli
Probability that household gets a private connection, if not available [Pr(GET_c)]	n.a.	0.08	0.08	Bernoulli
Proportion of households that own their dwellings (φow)	n.a.	0.57	0.57	Bernoulli
Consumption by commercial gardeners (Gco)	m³/month (million)	0.68	0.68	Constant
Consumption by other users (Oco)	m³/month (million)	2.18	2.18	Constant
Revenue not from water sales (OR)	US$/year (million)	7.81	7.81	Constant
Financial cost (FIC)	US$/year (million)	4.02	4.02	Constant

n.a. Not applicable.
Source: Authors.

179

chapter) is possible. The difference is that the former models produce single values for net revenue, whereas the MCS can produce numerous values from which we can estimate the probability that a given price will enable revenues to cover costs.

Deterministic Model for Rate Design

This section introduces the deterministic model for rate design in Dakar, which focuses on residential demand. Both demand and revenue from commercial gardeners, government, and industries are treated as known constants. All households are assumed to use either a private connection or a public fountain (the WTP study in Dakar found that 80 percent of households use a single water source, and 20 percent use two); if feasible, households using public fountains can switch to private connections.

Total water consumption of a household that uses public fountains (Hco^f) is the product of per capita consumption (Ico^f) and household size (Hsi) as follows:

(8.1) $Hco^f = Ico^f \cdot His$.

If P^f is the price that this household pays for its water, then household expenditure for water (Hex^f) is

(8.2) $Hex^f = Hco^f \cdot P^f$.

However, because concessionaires pay a different price (P^f), the effective revenue that this household pays to the water utility (Hre^f) is

(8.3) $Hre^f = Hco^f \cdot p^f$.

The situation is similar for a household with a private connection. Thus, equations 8.1 to 8.3 apply to households with connections simply by replacing the superscript "f" with "c"; however, $P^c = p^c$ for private connection users.

Letting ϕf be the proportion of households served by the utility that get water from public fountains (about 0.29 for Dakar), $(1 - \phi f)$ is the fraction that gets water from private connections. Average household consumption (Hco) is the weighted average of consumption by households using fountains and connections; average household revenue (Hre) is similar, namely,

(8.4) $Hco = -\phi f \cdot Hco^f + (1 - \phi f) \cdot Hco^c$.

(8.5) $Hre = -\phi f \cdot Hre^f + (1 - \phi f) \cdot Hre^c$.

With Nhh total households served by the utility, total residential consumption (Rco) is

(8.6) $Rco = Hco \cdot Nhh.$

Similarly, total revenue paid to the utility by households (Rre) is the product of per household revenue (Hre) and the total number of households (Nhh). However, not all households get a bill from the utility, and not all households that get a bill pay it. Taking account of the utility's billing efficiency (β) and collection efficiency (γ), total revenue paid to the utility from households is

(8.7) $Rre = Hre \cdot Nhh \cdot \beta \cdot \gamma.$

Adding residential consumption (Rco) to consumption by gardeners (Gco) and others (Oco) yields total consumption (Tco)

(8.8) $Tco = Rco + Gco + Oco.$

The total water production (Tpr) required to satisfy this demand taking account of unaccounted-for-water losses (υ) is

(8.9) $Tpr = Tco/(1 - \upsilon).$

The estimated total cost of running the water company (TC) is based on total water production as follows:

(8.10) $Tc = AVC \cdot Tpr + FC + FIC$

where AVC is average variable cost, FC is fixed cost, and FIC is financial cost. FC is treated separately from FIC because in the stochastic model in the next section it is assumed to be uncertain.

Using the prices the utility charges gardeners (p^g) and others (p^o), total revenue received by the utility (Tre) is

(8.11) $Tre = Rre + p^g \cdot Gco + p^o \cdot Oco + OR$

where OR denotes other revenues not related to water sales, such as connection fees and interest on bank accounts. Net revenue (NR) results from subtracting total cost (TC) from total revenue (Tre)

(8.12) $NR = Tre - TC.$

With a rate change, residential (and total) consumption would change because of the price elasticity of demand, which is taken into account by adjusting average per capita consumption. For public fountain users, the following equation applies:

(8.13) $Ico_1^f = Ico_0^f \cdot \left[1 + \varepsilon^f \left(\frac{P_1^f}{P_0^f} - 1 \right) \right]$

where ε^f denotes price elasticity of demand for public fountain users, and P represents prices the household pays for its water. The subscript 0 refers to before a rate change, and 1 refers to after a rate change. Substituting the superscript "c" for "f" in this equation makes it applicable to households with private connections.

Some households may be able to switch from public fountains to private connections. The new proportion of households that would use public fountains (ϕf_1) is

$$(8.14) \quad \phi f_1 = \phi f_0 [1 - Pr(GET\_c) \cdot Pr(YES\_c)]$$

where subscripts 0 and 1 refer to "before" and "after" a rate change, respectively; $Pr(GET\_c)$ is a parameter that represents the probability that a connection becomes available for a household currently without one (the ratio of new available connections to the number of households using public fountains during a given period); and $Pr(YES\_c)$ is the probability that the household decides to switch to a private connection. This can be computed using the following logit model that was estimated from the WTP study:

$$(8.15) \quad Pr(YES\_c) = \frac{202}{248} \{1 + exp[-1.17 + 6.35 \cdot (10^{-1}) \cdot P_1^f + 2.97 \cdot (10^{-2}) \cdot Hex_1^f$$
$$-0.24 \cdot Hco_1^f + 8.15 \cdot (10^{-2}) \cdot Hsi - 3.37 \cdot (10^{-3}) \cdot Hin - 1.10 \cdot \phi ow]\}$$

where Hin is household income, and ϕow denotes the fraction of households that own their dwellings. All coefficients in equation 8.15 were statistically significant at the 10 percent level. Also, except for the coefficient of ϕow, all coefficients in equation 8.15 had the expected signs.

The deterministic model of this section was solved using the mean parameter values from table 8.4 and a set of 100 water prices charged to private connection users, which were randomly selected within the approximate range of US$0.3 to US$1 per m³. Net revenue results are shown by the upper curve in figure 8.1. Note that for net revenue to be nonnegative, the model predicts a required price of US$0.62 per m³, which is essentially identical to the required price obtained by using the approach the rate consultants employed (US$0.614 per m³), thus validating the model in this section. The lower curve in figure 8.1 shows mean net revenue results from the counterpart stochastic model presented in the next section.

Monte Carlo Simulation Model for Rate Design

Recall that equations 8.4 and 8.5 used weighted averages to compute values of household consumption (Hco) and revenue paid to the water utility per household (Hre). The stochastic model does not require weighted averages.

FIGURE 8.1
Net Revenue Obtained with the Deterministic Model versus Mean Net Revenue Obtained with the MCS Model

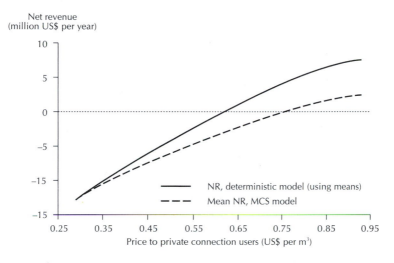

Source: Authors.

It generates a proportion ϕf of trials for households using public fountains and a proportion $(1 - \phi f)$ of trials for households with private connections. Mathematically, this implies using a dichotomous (Bernoulli) random variable that takes the value 1 if a household uses public fountains and 0 if it uses a private connection. By substituting a random variable F~Bernoulli (ϕf) for ϕf in equations 8.4 and 8.5, those equations are adapted for use in the stochastic model. Similarly, equation 8.15 in the stochastic model uses How~Bernoulli (ϕow) instead of ϕow.

The remaining equations of the stochastic model are exactly the same as in the deterministic model. The MCS model in this section was solved using the empirical probability distributions obtained from the WTP study, as shown in table 8.4. We conducted 100 simulations, one for each average price taken from the set of values used with the deterministic model. For 7,500 trials in each simulation, we recorded mean net revenue values, mean standard errors, and the probability that net revenue would equal or exceed zero. We obtained trial values with Latin Hypercube sampling for 1,500 intervals, that is, we divided the probability frequency distribution of each stochastic input into 1,500 parts containing the same probability of occurrence (1/1,500). The trials were then evenly allocated into each interval (7,500/1,500 = 5 per interval) and values were sampled randomly within them. Compared with ordinary random sampling, Latin Hypercube increases accuracy and reduces the number of trials needed to get comparable levels of output accuracy.

The lower curve in figure 8.1 shows mean net revenue results from the stochastic model. The abscissa in figure 8.1 shows prices charged to private connection users, and its ordinate shows values of net revenue for the deterministic model and mean net revenue for the MCS model.

Comparison of Deterministic and MCS Results

Figure 8.1 shows that predictions of net revenue from the deterministic model are generally higher than predictions of mean net revenue from the MCS model. The deterministic model suggests that the 1997 average price of US$0.57 per m^3, which the rate consultants recommended for households with connections, needs to be raised only to US$0.62 per m^3 for revenues to cover costs. The MCS model indicates that the required price needs to be more than 20 percent higher, to US$0.76 per m^3, for expected net revenue to be zero. To test that this chapter's deterministic model yields results comparable to those of the rate consultants' model, we used the same procedure and data that they did to compute the required increase in the 1997 average price for revenues to cover costs. We obtained a result of US$0.621 per m^3, which is identical to the result predicted with our deterministic model.

The MCS model found a probability of just 28 percent that the deterministic approach's price of US$0.62 per m^3 would cover costs. The required price from the MCS model (US$0.76 per m^3) yields a probability of about 42 percent. Thus, even by raising the price to a level that would result in nonnegative expected net revenue, the chance that revenues will cover costs is still less than 50 percent. The risk-neutral price (assumed as the one for which the confidence is 50-50) is about US$0.93 per m^3, which is 50 percent higher than the price indicated by our deterministic model or by the rate consultants. Note that figure 8.2 shows diminishing marginal returns of confidence that net revenue will be nonnegative for prices above US$0.60 per m^3, which is why the risk-neutral price is so high. Thus, the chance that the uniform increase in water prices obtained with the deterministic approach will produce positive net revenues appears to be less than one in three.

The rate consultants had a fairly modest goal: to reduce the 1997 shortfall to US$1.07 million. To reach that goal, figure 8.1 shows that the deterministic model suggests an average price for private connection users of almost US$0.58 per m^3, roughly the same average price the rate consultants recommended. However, for the same goal and user group, the average price suggested by the MCS model is roughly 20

FIGURE 8.2
**Probabilities of Getting Positive Net Revenue for Different Prices
to Private Connections**

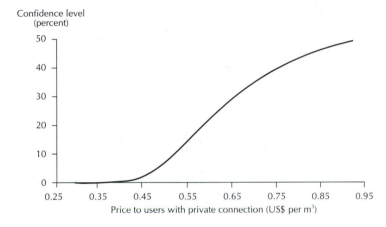

Source: Authors.

percent higher, or US$0.70 per m³. Hence, the prices the rate consult-
ants recommended would seem to have a small chance of meeting the
net revenue goal for 1997.

Some caveats are in order. First, the MCS model treats as stochastic only
residential consumption, which is about 54 percent of total water use in
Dakar. Other customer groups are assumed to consume the same amounts
as in the rate consultant's model. Second, for analyzing full cost recovery,
we impose prices beyond those recommended by the rate consultants only
for households with private connections, which may not be unrealistic given
the political constraints.

Conclusion

The political constraints on rate policy reform in Dakar appear to be
significant obstacles to achieving the water project's objectives. The
policy not to regulate standpipe concessionaires or commercial gardeners basically left the old rate structure intact with all its deficiencies
with respect to efficiency, equity, affordability, service to the poor, and
health. The constraints sharply reduced the available options for rate
making and apparently left the rate consultants with no other alternative for trying to achieve financial self-sufficiency than a uniform price
increase across-the-board.

Of all the rate policy goals, the objective of financial self-sufficiency was the least affected by the political constraints in Dakar. However, raising prices across-the-board may not cover costs as intended because of the use of a deterministic approach to rate design. The government will be making a risky decision if it adopts a price increase that provides only a 28 percent chance that revenues will cover costs. The MCS indicates that the price would have to be more than 20 percent higher for the expected net revenue to be zero and 50 percent higher for being neutral about the chances of getting full cost recovery.

Regulation of the relatively few public fountain concessionaires and gardeners might have achieved the goal of financial self-sufficiency and made a significant advance toward efficiency. Would that have been easier to implement and resulted in less risk for full cost recovery than the selected option of increasing prices across-the-board for hundreds of thousands of customers? This question seems to address the basic tradeoff underlying rate reform in Dakar. Which approach carries greater risk in achieving the goal of financial self-sufficiency: regulating a relatively small number of standpipes and gardeners or raising prices for a large number of customers?

The deterministic approach to rate making in the case of Dakar produced consistently higher predictions of net revenue than the MCS approach. Is that always the case in rate studies or is this result specific to Dakar? The price estimated for full cost recovery with the MCS approach (US$0.76 per m^3) exceeds by about 22 percent the price estimated with the deterministic approach (US$0.62 per m^3). Note that studies conducted by Cromwell and others (1997) and by Jordan, Carlson, and Wilson (1997) in 685 utilities in the United States found that operating revenues needed to exceed operating costs by about 20 percent to ensure full cost recovery and system viability. Whether the similarity between these results and the result of the MCS in this chapter is coincidence should be the subject of future research.

This chapter introduces an application of the MCS to water pricing analysis in developing countries. However, the MCS has already been used to inform rate design in the United States, with reported success (Chesnutt, McSpadden, and Christianson 1996). Applications of the MCS to rate analysis and design are likely to increase in coming years as research continues to reveal deficiencies in deterministic financial analysis and rate design methods.

The Bank and other donors have required contingent valuation studies for many of their water sector projects for more than a decade. Economists have yet to take full advantage of all the information derived from these studies. Our MCS approach to rate design makes fuller use of the data.

The principal rationale for willingness to pay studies is to support demand-based planning, that is, to give the beneficiaries a voice in the planning process. Thus, WTP studies should probably precede rather than follow rate design. Our analysis has the benefit of hindsight. Had the information from the WTP study been available before the imposition of policy constraints on Dakar's water rates, predicting the consequences would have been easier.

References

AWWA (American Water Works Association). 1972. *Water Rates Manual (Manual M1)*. Denver, Colorado.

Chesnutt, Thomas W., Casey McSpadden, and John Christianson. 1996. "Revenue Instability Induced by Conservation Rates." *American Water Works Association Journal* 88(1): 53–63.

Cromwell, John E., Scott J. Rubin, Frederick A. Marrocco, and Mark E. Leevan. 1997. "Business Planning for Small System Capacity Development." *American Water Works Association Journal* 89(1): 47–57.

Ernst & Young. 1996. "Mise à Jour du Modèle Avec les Données Auditées au 31/12/95: Projections 1995–2021." A report to the Senegal National Water Society, the government of Senegal, and the World Bank, unpublished. Paris.

Jordan, Jeffrey L., Christopher N. Carlson, and James R. Wilson. 1997. "Financial Indicators Measure Fiscal Health." *American Water Works Association Journal* 89(8): 34–40.

Lauria, Donald T., Alfredo H. Cueva, and Anthony A. Kolb. 1997. "Final Report on Willingness to Pay for Improved Water and Sanitation in Dakar, Senegal." A report to the Senegal National Water Society, the government of Senegal, and the World Bank, unpublished. Chapel Hill, North Carolina.

World Bank. 1993. *Water Resources Management*. Washington, D.C.: World Bank.

_____. 1995. "Staff Appraisal Report: Republic of Senegal, Water Sector Project." Report no. 14008-SE. World Bank, Western Africa Department, Infrastructure Operations Division, Washington, D.C.

9

(U$/

Public Choice and Water Rate Design

Darwin C. Hall

In the 1970s, electric utilities made the transition from embedded cost rate design to marginal cost rate design (Hall and Hanemann 1996). Embedded cost rate design is an attempt to allocate historical (sunk) capital costs and operating costs to present-day consumers. Embedded cost rate design has many variants, and it is not a well-defined, single-rate design. Developed by engineers and accountants, it is endorsed by the American Water Works Association (1991). However, it violates the theorems in economics that joint costs cannot be allocated (Hall 1973; Lau 1978). Marginal cost rate design is based on the marginal cost of additional water, not the sunk costs of constructing the existing water collection and distribution system.

Prior to the 1990s, Tucson, Arizona, was the only city that had ever adopted marginal cost rates for water. This occurred after the two-year drought of 1976–77. One year after the adoption of those rates, the entire city council was voted out of office because of the water rates.

After the six-year drought of 1986–91, Los Angeles Mayor Tom Bradley appointed the Mayor's Blue Ribbon Committee on Water Rates (BRC).[1] Committee members were told that Tucson illustrated the political unfeasibility of marginal cost rates for water. In the end, however, the committee recommended marginal cost water rates (BRC 1992), and the city council passed an ordinance adopting the recommendations,

---

1. The author was appointed by Bradley and later retained as a member of the reconstituted committee.

including unique innovations that could make marginal cost rates politically acceptable elsewhere. After some residents protested the rates, the new mayor, Richard Riordan, reconvened a reconstituted committee. The committee recommended refinements to the rate design (BRC 1994) that increased the economic efficiency of the rates and their perceived fairness, and the city council passed a second ordinance adopting the recommendations. Why did this happen? Were other outcomes possible, or more likely? And if other outcomes were more likely, what was different about the process or circumstances for Los Angeles?

The process that determined the outcome of the rate reform began with the education of all the members of the BRC about the basics of standard microeconomic analysis of rate design for natural monopoly. This is discussed in the second section of this chapter, which is drawn partly from Hall (1996) and to a lesser extent from Hall and Hanemann (1996).

The third section, which is drawn partly from Hall and Hanemann (1996), describes the subsequent process and political intrigue, including the formative decisions of the BRC. The committee went through a process to learn about designing rates, estimating marginal cost rates, and considering alternative rate designs based on marginal costs. It also created a technical advisory subcommittee that included experts from the University of California at Berkeley. Each of the two-rate designs (BRC 1992, 1994) that the city council enacted contain innovative features, sequentially increasing economic efficiency, and the perceived fairness and equity arising from marginal cost rates.

The fourth section uses public choice models to explain why the committee chose a marginal cost rate design over an embedded cost design. A Peltzman-type model (similar to one found in Viscusi, Vernon, and Harrington 1995, pp. 331–33) explains why an earlier blue ribbon committee in 1977 did not recommend switching from embedded cost rate design to marginal cost rate design. The model also explains how a city council, such as the one in Tuscon, could be voted out of office for implementing marginal cost rates. The Becker model (Viscusi, Vernon, and Harrington 1995, pp. 333–37) is consistent with a switch to a marginal cost rate design during a drought. Both models predict that Los Angeles would change back to embedded cost rate design after the drought ended, yet that did not happen. Why not? The Peltzman and Becker approaches do not explain how a government can innovate and become better.

The last section speculates about the beneficial policy changes that remain unexplained by the public choice models, based partly on my experience of serving on the committee.

Rate Design for Natural Monopoly

A natural monopoly is defined as a firm with a declining long-run average cost curve over the range of output relevant to market demand, as shown in figure 9.1. The curve is declining prior to investment. Once investment is made, the capital costs are sunk, and in the short run they are called fixed costs. Natural monopolies typically have high fixed costs and low variable costs.

In a competitive industry, the market clearing price equates demand and supply, and the profit maximizing firm produces at the output where price equals short-run marginal cost. In long-run equilibrium, the price is just sufficient to cover variable costs and replacement of capital. It is not higher or lower, so there are no incentives for expansion or contraction (hence, equilibrium). This occurs at the output with the minimum long-run average cost. At that output, there is equality among all the following: price, long-run marginal cost, long-run average cost, short-run marginal cost, and short-run average cost. For a natural monopoly, if the market clearing price were set equal to the long-run marginal cost, total revenue would be lower than total cost by the rectangle in figure 9.1. In the long run, such a firm would go out of business.

FIGURE 9.1
Determining Rates for a Natural Monopoly

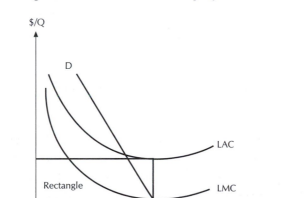

Source: Author.

FIGURE 9.2
Embedded Cost Design: Commodity Charge

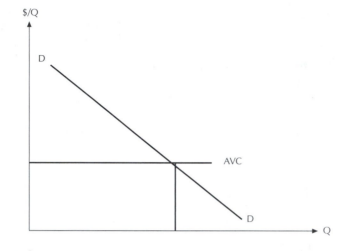

Source: Author.

Embedded Cost Rate Design

One solution for the price-regulated monopoly is a two-part tariff: a fixed charge to collect revenue equal to the fixed cost, and a commodity charge that equals the average variable cost of the monopolist. Then total revenue equals total cost for any output below or equal to the system maximum, defined as the lower of the available water or the system capacity for water conveyance and treatment facilities. For example, in figure 9.2 the average variable cost is constant. If a fixed charge is levied such that the fixed charge multiplied by the number of customers equals the fixed costs of the monopoly, then the commodity charge can be set equal to the average variable cost, and total revenue will equal total cost. This solution is a simplified representation of the principle of embedded cost rate design. Note the stability of net revenue: for any output equal to or below the system maximum, net revenue equals zero.

If the short-run marginal cost of procuring more water rises with output, then the average variable cost also rises. With embedded cost rates, the commodity charge and the demand curve determine the quantity consumed. A shift in demand will cause an increase in the quantity consumed. A higher quantity means that the average variable cost will no longer equal the commodity charge in the rate design, but the rate cannot be changed until after the next rate approval process and enactment of a new rate ordinance. The solution to this problem is typically to have a rate ordinance that includes an adjustment process. The commodity charge is increased or decreased to match total variable cost with the portion of revenue collected from the commodity charge. Again, for output below the system maximum the net revenue is stable at zero.

If demand grows beyond system capacity, or if there is a drought that curtails the available water supply below the quantity demanded at the regulated price, then a water shortage occurs. In the short run, embedded cost rate design has no solution to this problem, and water use must be curtailed with mandatory or voluntary conservation. In the long run, the solution based on embedded cost rate design is to procure additional sources of water, to expand system capacity, or to do both. This requires expensive capital additions. Prior to the capital expansion, the long-run marginal cost is higher than the historical long-run average cost, but this does not mean that, at existing output, the theoretical long-run average cost curve is rising. If the entire water system were to be designed from scratch, nothing like the existing capital structure would be built. The long-run average cost curve of the hypothetically efficient new system may be falling well beyond the range of output that defines the current system maximum. We still have a natural monopoly, but we also have a putty-clay problem with the existing actual system.

To clarify the concept of putty-clay, distinguish between the theoretical long-run average cost curve of a hypothetical water system designed from scratch and the long-run average cost curve of the existing system. For the actual system, just prior to an investment in additional water sources or additional delivery capacity, the long-run average cost curve is given by the average variable cost curve for output less than the system maximum, because the fixed costs of the existing system are sunk. For greater output, the long-run average cost curve may be falling, as shown in figure 9.3, but figure 9.3 is only relevant until the new capacity is added. Once that occurs, those costs are also sunk.

Embedded cost rate design is considerably more complicated than as explained earlier. All the fixed costs are not simply collected through a fixed charge—such as a customer charge—in the rate design. The fixed costs are apportioned among customer classes based on principles that engineers, accountants, and lawyers have come to believe are somehow fair. For example, their reasoning may go like this. The residential customers are the ones who have landscaping that must be watered in the summer, causing seasonal variation in demand. Therefore, the residential customers "caused" the system to be designed to deliver more water in the summer. A system designed to serve a seasonally uniform demand would

FIGURE 9.3
Incremental Cost with Lumpy Investment

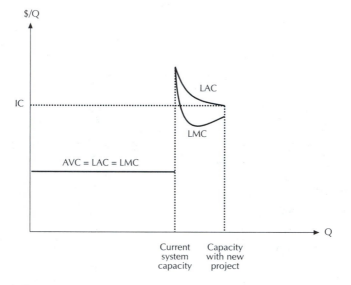

Source: Author.

cost less. The difference in capital costs between the existing system and a hypothetically designed system with uniform demand should be included in the rates residential customers pay.

A second example of their reasoning might be that the theoretical long-run cost curve is falling for a hypothetical water system designed from scratch. Therefore, large industrial and commercial customers should face a declining block commodity charge that will lower their average cost of buying water.

A third example concerns the size of the customer's connection to the water main. This represents potential water use at the maximum rate that the pipe could provide, which by specious reasoning could be considered a latent demand. The rest of the system must be designed to serve the latent demand. Consequently, the rate design should include a fixed charge to pay for the increase in the system capacity that was "caused" by the latent demand. This fixed charge—called a demand charge—could vary with the size of the pipe connection to the system. Such a demand charge has nothing to do with what economists refer to as demand.

As these three examples illustrate, embedded cost rate design allocates joint costs in ways that economists consider arbitrary.

Marginal Cost Rate Design

In a competitive market, demand and supply determine price, and the price equals marginal cost. Abstracting for a moment from externality and public good aspects of water, marginal cost rate design results in economic efficiency. Economic efficiency occurs when the marginal value to consumers equals the marginal cost of production, and no other quantity of water can increase the net value to society. If the water rate equals the marginal cost, consumers will not buy more water than the amount for which the price equals the marginal value in use. The water seller will not be able to sell more water than the amount for which the additional cost equals the price.

The calculation of the marginal cost entails a number of unresolved theoretical aspects (Hall 1996). Water supply sources are individual, resulting in lumpy cost curves with discontinuities. Demand is shifting over time. Customers can invest in water conservation, and the optimal price signal must provide the incentive for that investment when it is less expensive than new supply. This is part of the debate about short-run versus long-run marginal cost as the appropriate basis for rate design. With shifting cost curves over time, the actual system marginal cost differs from the optimal system marginal cost. The combination of heterogeneous technology and periodic demand results in an optimal mix of production technologies, and cost varies with time-of-use. System reliability is another complication. Water supply options have varying externalities. Each of these problems, modeled separately, results in a complex marginal cost calculus, but these problems have not been addressed simultaneously.

In the southwestern United States, many historic factors in water utility cost and demand relationships have changed—circumstances not unlike those the electric utilities faced about 25 years ago. Demand is growing, but the costs of increasing water supply are rapidly rising, as shown in figure 9.3. The long-run marginal cost of additional supply can be approximated as the incremental cost of building and operating at capacity the next most expensive water reclamation project. The incremental cost is actually the long-run average cost of the next project added to the system, indicated in figure 9.3.

The marginal cost calculation is somewhat complicated by issues of transmission, water treatment, distribution, and storage. Storage costs can be used to calculate seasonally differentiated marginal costs (Hall 1996). The simplest way to approximate the marginal cost is to calculate the incremental cost (IC), as shown in figure 9.3.

The simplest marginal cost rate design would be to have only a commodity charge, and to set that charge equal to the marginal cost (MC). To visualize this, imagine replacing the average variable cost with the marginal cost in figure 9.2, with the rectangle showing the revenue that would be collected. If that amount of revenue is greater than the historical total cost, a solution is an increasing block rate design. The initial block commodity charge is applicable to an initial amount of water per billing period, and the tail block commodity charge is applicable to all water purchased above the initial amount. The total bill that a customer with demand given by D would pay is shown by the two rectangles in figure 9.4.

For many water utilities, the incremental cost of water is higher than the water rates because the historical costs are lower than the incremental cost. Today many utilities have increasing block rate designs, but those rate designs are not necessarily based on marginal cost. To be considered a marginal cost rate design, the tail block rate must equal the marginal cost. If the marginal cost is approximated by the incremental cost, then the rate design should correspond to incremental cost, as the tail block rate in figure 9.4 corresponds to the incremental cost in figure 9.3.

The Blue Ribbon Committee Process and Political Intrigue

Prior to the creation of the BRC, rates steadily increased, because costs rose while demand grew. Demand grew not only in Los Angeles, but also in

FIGURE 9.4
Long-Run Marginal Cost Design: Increasing Block Rate

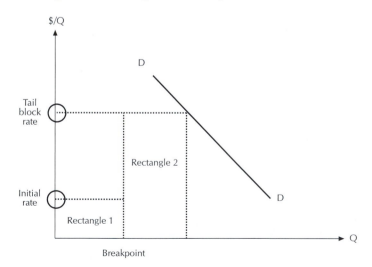

Source: Author.

other cities and states in the southwestern United States that competed for the same water for agricultural, environmental, and urban uses. The residential Los Angeles rate design included seasonally differentiated flat commodity charges, with demand and customer charges, for a four-part tariff. By 1991 the differential between the summer and winter commodity charges was about 25 percent.

By April 1991, the customary end of the rainy season in California, water agencies braced for the fifth year of a drought with severe disruption of the state's water system, and urban users in southern California faced cuts in their water supply. The Los Angeles Department of Water and Power (DWP) called for a voluntary 15 percent reduction in water use. Citizens responded eagerly, and water use fell by more than 20 percent. So did water revenues, which created a severe financial problem. The DWP had to ask for a rate increase. This created a political furor, because those who had conserved water at the behest of the DWP would be penalized by a rate increase. Responding to this furor, Mayor Bradley appointed the BRC to reform the rates.

Although it took a drought that was unprecedented in the 20th century to spur the creation of the BRC, rate reform could increase economic efficiency, with potential savings that could benefit everyone. The environmental costs of water are now reflected in restrictions on the amounts DWP takes from Mono Lake (Wegge, Hanemann, and Loomis 1996) and from the Sacramento Valley (Fisher, Hanemann, and Keeler 1991). Growing demand in Arizona, Colorado, and Nevada has restricted the share of Colorado River water available to the Metropolitan Water District of southern California (MWD). MWD is the wholesale water agency that buys water from the State Water Project and takes water from the Colorado River. MWD then sells the water to other water agencies throughout southern California, including DWP. MWD forecasts that its wholesale rates will rise rapidly, shifting the DWP cost curves. The marginal cost to the DWP is from reclamation projects in increasing order of cost, and eventually from desalination. These marginal costs rise rapidly. The difference between the low historic average cost rates and the marginal cost represents potential savings to ratepayers from rate reform. Marginal cost rate design could increase economic efficiency, while reducing growth in consumption and slowing the addition of capacity and the frequency of increases in water rates.

Phase I: Switching Paradigms from Embedded Cost to Marginal Cost Rate Design

The BRC had 16 members representing all geographic areas and major constituencies in one of the most racially and ethnically diverse cities in the

United States. This diversity is part of a landscape that defines city politics, exacerbating divisions, but also creating opportunities for alliances on all significant issues, including the DWP rate design. Of the committee's 16 members, 15 were civic leaders with substantially divergent interests and no special knowledge of utilities, water, or rate design. The 16th was the author, an economist who, decades earlier, had been employed by the California Energy Commission (working on electricity rate design) and then by the state's Department of Water Resources.

The BRC was given one year and well over US$100,000 to hire its own consultants; learn about rate design, water utilities, and specific aspects of the DWP; and recommend changes to the water rates. All the appointed public members were disinterested, with no income from or financial stake in the water industry. They shared another characteristic: an interest in making government work more efficiently.

The BRC conducted extensive investigations and issued a report (BRC 1992) in June that recommended a series of changes that would create a two-tier, increasing block rate structure based on marginal cost. In December 1992 the city council adopted this proposal with minor modifications, and it went into effect in February 1993. This outcome was a surprise.

Formative decisions led to this outcome. The first was a vote by the BRC to confine voting to the 16 public members, although the BRC meetings were attended by DWP staff, DWP consultants, and staff from city departments, as well as aides to city council members and the mayor's office. All could voice opinions, and the votes were cast with a show of hands.

The second formative decision was to extend the time for potential consultants to respond to the request for proposals. This second decision averted a predestined outcome. The executives of the DWP had sent the request for proposals to serve as the consultant to the BRC to standard water engineering firms. Any of the major water engineering firms would have steered the process toward embedded cost rate design, the standard set by the American Water Works Association (1991). None included economists. As a result of the time extension imposed by the BRC, the applicants included two firms with economists. The one the BRC selected had an economist as a subcontractor. At first, the (subcontractor) economist's role was minor, explaining the option of marginal cost rate design. The majority of the consulting services were devoted to embedded cost rate design. It took four more months before the members of the BRC established control over the relative contribution by the economist subcontractor and focused on the critical question of whether to propose rates based on embedded cost principles or on marginal cost.

After two more months of investigation and debate, the BRC decided in favor of designing rates based on the principle of marginal cost, and it allocated the remaining time and consulting resources to calculate the marginal cost and to consider alternative rate designs based on those costs. The BRC formed a technical advisory subcommittee, including faculty from the University of California at Berkeley, to work with both the BRC's consultants and the DWP's consultants. The subcommittee was charged with resolving critical differences between the two consulting firms about the correct calculation of the marginal cost and the design of rates based on it. This part of the process was critical. The literature contains many misleading arguments regarding technical aspects of the "correct" calculation of marginal cost.

As a preview to the discussion that follows, the rate design recommended by the BRC has innovative features, partially summarized in tables 9.1 and 9.2. Table 9.1 shows that, in normal years, the tail block rate is set to the marginal cost, which varies between the winter and summer. The initial block rate is set so that revenue, the sum of the two rectangles in figure 9.4, equals total cost. The breakpoint was selected by balancing economic efficiency gains and losses with the BRC's perceptions of what would be politically feasible. Table 9.2 shows the rate design for droughts of differing severity. The tail block rate is set to equate the quantity demanded with the available water. The breakpoint is reduced by an amount that increases with the severity of the drought to emphasize the price signal. As explained later, the initial block rate is adjusted to equate revenues and costs.

TABLE 9.1
Normal Year Water Rates

Customer class	Low block (US$)	Breakpoint	High block (US$)
Residential			
Single family	1.71	21 billing units (175% of median)	2.92 summer 2.27 winter
Multifamily	1.71	125% of winter average	2.92 summer 1.71 winter
Commercial/ industrial	1.78	125% of winter average	2.92 summer 1.78 winter

Note: A billing unit equals 748 gallons or 100 cubic feet. One acre-foot equals 435 billing units.
Source: BRC (1992).

TABLE 9.2
Shortage Year Water Rates

Shortages	Low block (US$)	Breakpoint	High block (US$)
10% shortage			
Residential			
Single family	1.71	19 billing units	3.70
Multifamily	1.71	115% of winter average	3.70
Commercial/			
industrial	1.78	115% of winter average	3.70
15% shortage			
Residential			
Single family	1.71	18 billing units	4.44
Multifamily	1.71	115% of winter average	4.44
Commercial/			
industrial	1.78	115% of winter average	4.44
20% shortage			
Residential			
Single family	1.71	17 billing units	5.18
Multifamily	1.71	110% of winter average	5.18
Commercial/			
industrial	1.78	110% of winter average	5.18
25% shortage			
Residential			
Single family	1.71	16 billing units	6.05
Multifamily	1.71	110% of winter average	6.05
Commercial/			
industrial	1.78	110% of winter average	6.05

Note: A billing unit equals 748 gallons or 100 cubic feet. One acre-foot equals 435 billing units.
Source: BRC (1992).

For a period of several months, the BRC held regular meetings, working through numerical exercises, to learn the basics of rate design. The BRC was influenced by the argument that a shift to a marginal cost rate design would be a Pareto superior move, that is, creating a surplus that could be shared among the citizens. The environmental benefits from the expected reduction in water use also helped sway the committee. In addition, the issue of fairness proved to be influential. The existing rate structure had customer and demand charges, both of which resulted in higher average bills for low-income residents relative to high-income residents who used more water, typically for landscaping.[2]

The BRC faced the serious problem of the political acceptability of a marginal cost rate design, given the potential losers of the change in rate design. The DWP management, large commercial and industrial customers, and large residential users all could be adversely affected. Obtaining support, or at least avoiding opposition, from large commercial and industrial customers was particularly important. The DWP management favored an embedded cost rate design, which benefits large customers, and it had the ability to help its large customers oppose a marginal cost rate design.

A publicly owned monopoly's bond ratings depend on revenue being sufficient to cover costs adequately. Revenue shortfalls lead to requests to approve rate increases. However, excess revenue can be a political liability to the utility management, who then request approval of rate decreases. Maintaining the embedded cost rate design would have the advantage, from the DWP's perspective, of resulting in revenue that more closely tracked costs, given growing water demand, as long as system capacity could be expanded fast enough to prevent shortages. From the perspective of DWP management, embedded-cost rate design avoids the rate approval process and associated political instability.

BRC members argued in response that embedded cost rate design results in political instability. Mandatory curtailment and public appeals for conservation during the drought caused the political furor noted earlier, whereby customers faced a rate increase because they had voluntarily saved 20 percent during a year when water supply dropped 15 percent. The BRC contended that marginal cost-based rates could be established to clear the market during years of shortages, as shown in table 9.2, avoiding that political instability.

The BRC also suggested that it persuade the DWP management with its recommendation that marginal cost-based rates include a provision in the rate ordinance for adjusting the initial block rate to match revenue with cost, avoiding the need to repeatedly return to the city council for changes in the rate ordinance. The rate adjustment process in the municipal ordinance for normal and shortage years became a key feature of the rate proposal that made the marginal cost rate design politically palatable from the DWP's perspective.

---

2. See the previous section on rate design. The demand charge is based on the diameter of the pipe that connects the customer to the system and has nothing to do with the economic definition of demand—a schedule of quantities and prices.

Another innovative feature that made marginal cost rate design politically feasible was the distinction between cost allocation among customer classes and the principle of setting the tail block rate equal to the marginal cost. By making this distinction, the BRC could design rates that were revenue neutral between customer classes. By allowing variation among customer classes of the amount of water to which the initial block rate is applicable, the revenue collected from each customer class could be varied to any preselected amount. In short, it is possible to construct a rate approval process in which the political forces involved could determine the relative contribution to revenue collection from competing customer classes, while still setting the tail block rate equal to the marginal cost to achieve economic efficiency. The BRC recommended that costs be allocated among customer classes using a simple average cost calculation. Commercial and industrial customers were assuaged by this decision, but they were concerned about one remaining issue.

A unique feature of the rate design applies only to commercial and industrial customers. These customers have a great variation in water use. This heterogeneous demand means that an increasing block rate design could potentially cause extreme variation in the average rate paid by large users in this customer class compared with the average rate paid by smaller users in this class. Solutions to this problem could include setting up subclasses according to the size of the pipe connection, the number of connections to the water main, or both. The BRC approach was to set the breakpoint for increasing block summertime rates for each customer at 25 percent more than the amount of water of that customer's previous winter use, as shown in table 9.1. The winter rates were simple average cost rates.

Finally, there is the matter of heterogeneity of residential customer demand. With variation among residential water users, some customers are represented by the demand curve in figure 9.4, but low-income customers may have a demand curve significantly to the left of the one shown—a curve that crosses the horizontal dotted line depicting the initial block rate. Those customers would not have the economically efficient price signal.

Residential customers are the voters who elect the city council, and the city council must approve the rate ordinance. To attain the greatest economic efficiency, the ideal rate design would set the breakpoint as close to zero as possible, taking into account the revenue constraint. In figure 9.4, the breakpoint can be moved to the left, keeping the area under the two rectangles constant, but the initial block rate has to be lowered. At the lowest possible breakpoint, the initial block rate is zero, where the area in rectangle 2 gives just enough revenue to cover total cost. The farther to the left the breakpoint is moved, the higher the percentage of customers who buy at least some water at the marginal cost.

The political feasibility of a rate design depends on the fraction of voters who experience an increase in their water bills. As long as customers buy only a few units of water at the tail block rate, their total bill will be equal to or less than the bill based on the existing rate design. By shifting the breakpoint to the right, a larger percentage of voters have lower water bills. There is a tradeoff between economic efficiency and political feasibility. The BRC concluded that if the breakpoint were set at 175 percent of the median annual use (see table 9.1), all four city districts would give the plan overwhelming political support. Water bills would fall for 75.3 percent of all city customers, with 92.4, 87.5, 76.7, and 66.1 percent of the customers within each of the four districts receiving lower bills. (Hall and Hanemann 1996). On a political note, the BRC failed to account for the the city council's desire to make at least some token change to the rate design to put its stamp on it. Moreover, the council had the incentive to select political feasibility at the cost of economic efficiency. In the rate ordinance that passed, the city council increased the breakpoint to 200 percent of the median annual use.

Phase II: Keeping the Marginal Cost Paradigm, Improving Efficiency and Fairness

After decades in office, Mayor Bradley decided not to run for another term. The Republican candidate, Richard Riordan, defeated the Democratic candidate whom Bradley had endorsed. Riordan took office in July 1993.

July and August were somewhat cool months by local standards, but September was a relatively warm month and many customers found their water bills rising as their usage entered the higher block range. This was especially true for residents of the San Fernando Valley, a warmer part of the DWP service area and a bastion of support for Riordan. In response to citizen protests, Riordan reconstituted and reconvened the BRC, adding three members from the San Fernando Valley. Riordan's BRC held hearings throughout the city and conducted further analyses. The Northridge earthquake in January 1994, which damaged part of the DWP distribution system, delayed the committee's work. In August 1994 the new BRC issued a report (BRC 1994) recommending refinements to the rate design, but retaining the two-tier, increasing block rates. In March 1995 the city council adopted this proposal with some minor changes, and it went into effect in April 1995, reaffirming marginal cost rates for Los Angeles.

This result was also a surprise. Voters from the San Fernando Valley were lobbying for a flat, historical average cost rate design. The reconstituted BRC had lost several significant original members, and the newly appointed members from the San Fernando Valley supported an average cost rate design. One of the valley city council members who voted for the original rate ordinance lost the election to a vocal detractor of the new rate design. Moreover, the mayor's office, in concert with city council members from the valley, was scheduling a series of BRC hearings packed with angry valley residents, some of whom made death threats and others of whom threatened lawsuits.

The Northridge earthquake turned out to be important to the outcome, because the BRC needed time. Given enough time, veteran commission members could work with and educate the new members, as well as the staff of the new mayor. It could convince them that a more efficient rate design produces gains that can be shared geographically if all sides work together to refine the rates. Building the needed mutual respect and trust regarding others' motives takes time, as well as a willingness to listen to all sides, a forum for the exchange of dispassionate reason, and monetary disinterest in the outcome.

The key to achieving greater efficiency with increasing block rates is to partition the residential customers into subgroups, each of which has more homogeneous usage patterns than the group as a whole. Setting the breakpoint for each subgroup closer to the subgroup's median water use is politically feasible. With subgroups, those consuming in the tail block have fewer units charged at the tail block rate, compared with the previous increasing block rate design without subgroups. Thus, the percentage of customers who share in the benefits of increased economic efficiency is larger, because the average rate each customer actually pays is closer to the rate averaged across all residential customers. Moreover, with subgroups an increasing number of customers consume a quantity within the tail block. More customers face the marginal cost incentive. By creating subgroups, each with a different breakpoint, the BRC designed rates that were both more efficient and fair.

The BRC divided residential customers into four lot sizes and three temperature zones (table 9.3). The lot sizes and temperature zones were based on the following criteria: homogeneity of use, historical lot size zoning patterns, temperature zones, and administrative practicality.

Because each subclass is more homogeneous, the breakpoint recommended by the BRC in 1994 was 120 percent of the subclass median. Compare this to the 1992 recommendation in which all residential customers were treated as one customer class. After the city council modification in 1993, the breakpoint was 200 percent of the median use. The 1994 refinement increased the number of customers actually facing the marginal cost incentive to conserve.

TABLE 9.3
1994 BRC Recommended Temperature and Lot Size Breakpoints

Lot size (sq. ft.)	Summer average daily high	Number of billing units charged at low initial block rate	
		Winter	Summer
<7,500	<75º	13	16
	75–85º	13	17
	>85º	13	17
7,500–10,999	<75º	16	23
	75–85º	16	25
	>85º	16	26
11,000–17,499	<75º	23	36
	75–85º	24	39
	>85º	24	40
>17,499	<75º	29	45
	75–85º	30	48
	>85º	30	49
1993 rate design breakpoint			
All lots	All temperatures	22	28

Note: A billing unit equals 748 gallons or 100 cubic feet. One acre-foot equals 435 billing units.
Source: BRC (1994).

A bill impact analysis compares the 1993 rate design with the design pro-posed by the BRC in 1994. More than 12 percent of the valley customers saw a decrease in their bills greater than 6 percent. These were the same customers who had received the largest bill increases because of the 1993 rate design. The refinements in the 1995 rate design ameliorated the impact of marginal cost rates on a politically significant customer class, thereby more equitably shar-ing the benefits of increased economic efficiency from marginal cost pricing.

The DWP Board of Commissioners altered the 1994 BRC recommenda-tions by adding another category for extremely large lots to reduce bills paid by that group, and increased the breakpoint allocation for higher tempera-ture zones. This adjustment by the commissioners was primarily for the ben-efit of customers in the hotter San Fernando Valley, and also for upper-middle-income and upper-income customers with lot sizes larger than one acre. The commissioners' proposal enjoyed the support of council mem-bers from the valley, but they needed additional votes to pass the ordinance.

On average, lower-income families are larger. For family size, the BRC recommended that the initial block be augmented as household size increases from 6 to 13 people. This increased the breakpoint by an extra 2 billing units per person each month for household sizes of 7 to 8 people, 1.5 billing units per person for households with 9 to 10 people, and 1 billing unit per person for households with 11 to 13 people. Customers could apply for initial block rate adjustments based on household size.

The city council required a further adjustment to benefit lower-income residents. Customers in densely populated zones automatically received an augmentation to the initial block for indoor use by large families. Using the 1990 census, the BRC identified zip code zones in which 10 percent or more of water customers were eligible for a large household adjustment (BRC 1994). All customers in those zones were granted a conditional classification of eight people per household until verified by a change in service (that is, until they moved). An estimated 16 percent of the customers in those zones benefited from the adjustment. These customers do little landscaping.

Adding the variables of lot size, temperature zones, and population density to define the breakpoint can more evenly distribute the benefits from rate reform among all the customers. The finer partitioning of the residential customer class into subclasses improved the economic efficiency of increasing block rates by lowering the breakpoint for more customers, and also enabled the benefits of rate reform to be more equitably allocated. Winners could compensate a greater number of losers. Moreover, the two-tiered design allowed politicians to focus on where the breakpoint would occur, giving them something to change without destroying the signal for economic efficiency. Marginal cost rate design can meet the political test of compensating losers.

Public Choice Models

Public choice models can help explain the selection of embedded cost rate design and the subsequent switch to a marginal cost rate design. A Peltzman-type model is consistent with the long-time use of embedded cost rate design. The Becker model is consistent with the switch to a marginal cost rate design during a drought.

A Peltzman-Type Model

This section explains why embedded cost rate design dominates the water industry, and why Los Angeles chose it prior to switching to marginal cost rate design.

The American Water Works Association has a manual on embedded cost rate design. The rate design has been captured by the industry. Viscusi, Vernon, and Harrington (1995, pp. 327–33) attribute the theory of capture to Stigler (1971), formalized by Peltzman (1976). The theory is modeled as a tradeoff between industry profit and monopoly prices. The constraint shows how industry profit varies with price. The objective function is depicted as a set of iso-political support curves, with support for politicians rising with industry profit and falling with an increase in monopoly price. This model cannot be applied directly to municipal utilities.

Municipal utilities are not allowed to make a profit. Management wants to avoid the rate approval process, so it desires a rate design that achieves political stability (not revenue stability, as the American Water Works Association rate manual states). Political stability requires that revenues vary directly with costs so that net revenue is stable and equal to zero. Embedded cost rate design achieves political stability as long as water supply and system capacity are sufficient to meet the quantity demanded at the given rates. This means that with growing demand, municipal water agencies strive to increase system capacity even if the marginal cost of new supply is extraordinarily high. It also means that municipal water agencies are willing to support water conservation subsidies.

In the Peltzman-type model presented here, commercial and industrial customers, along with water utility management, can control the rate design process. For this Peltzman-type model, divide water customers into two groups: residential customers who vote and commercial and industrial customers who provide campaign contributions. Assume that demand is homogeneous within each group. Each group would like to have a low average water price in the rate design. A declining block rate design results in low average water prices for commercial and industrial customers and high average water prices for residential customers. Variants of embedded cost rate design alter the extent to which the design has declining block commodity charges, and the size of the fixed (demand and customer) charges relative to the commodity charges. Each rate design variant implies a particular combination of average water prices for each customer group.

Define a politically efficient rate design as one in which lowering the average water price for one group is not possible without increasing the average water price for the other group. Then the variants of alternative politically efficient rate designs that generate zero net revenue are convex to the origin, as shown in figure 9.5. As we move from the lower right to the upper left of the iso-net-revenue curve, the rate design changes from declining block rates with high fixed charges, to flatter average cost rate designs, to increasing block rate designs. This curve represents the

FIGURE 9.5
Peltzman-Type Model

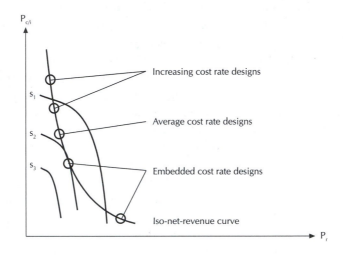

Source: Author.

constraint that defines the rate designs from which one will be chosen that maximizes the political support function.

Next, define the political support function, $S = s(P_r, P_{cfi})$, as a monotonically decreasing function in the average price of residential customers (P_r) and in the average price of commercial and industrial customers (P_{cfi}). The family of iso-support curves, shown in figure 9.5, is concave to the origin, and the level of political support increases as one moves toward the origin. The shape of the political support function is determined by the political strength of the commercial and industrial customers relative to the political strength of the residential customers. Because the free rider effect is greater for the relatively unorganized, larger group of residential customers, the management of the water utility can work with the smaller group of commercial and industrial customers to influence the outcome in favor of an embedded cost rate design.

This model explains the capture of the rate design process. It also could explain how a city council, such as in Tuscon, could be voted out of office for implementing marginal cost rates, if one assumes two groups of residential customers: high water use customers with greater political strength and low water use customers with less political organization. This model leaves unexplained the shift from embedded cost rates to marginal cost rates in Los Angeles, a topic covered in the next section.

FIGURE 9.6
Becker-Type Model

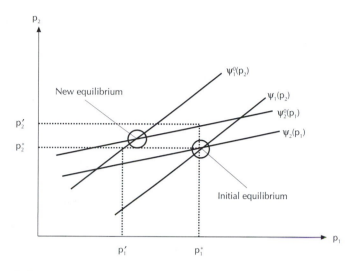

Source: Author.

The Becker Model Applied to Marginal Cost Rate Design

Viscusi, Vernon, and Harrington (1995, pp. 333–37) present the Becker (1983) model as shown in figure 9.6. The model focuses on competition between interest groups. Group 1 gets a wealth transfer equal to $T = I(p_1, p_2)$, where I is the influence function that increases with p_1, the political pressure of group 1, and decreases with p_2, the political pressure of group 2. The loss to group 2 is $(1 + x) \cdot T$, where $x \geq 0$, and xT is the welfare loss; $x > 0$ means more wealth is lost than transferred. In this model, government regulation results in a transfer.

In the Becker model, aggregate pressure is determined by the intersection of two curves, shown in figure 9.6. The equilibrium is determined by relative pressure. Each group tries to select the optimal level of pressure given the amount chosen by the competing group. The optimal pressure of group 1 depends on the pressure of group 2—$\psi_1(p_2)$, group 1's best response function. The function shows that the more pressure group 2 applies, the larger the optimal amount of pressure from group 1, upward sloping. The political equilibrium is the pair of pressures where neither group has any incentive to change the level of pressure, denoted as $(p_1{}^*, p_2{}^*)$ with an asterisk in figure 9.6—a Nash equilibrium. Note the free rider problem is now relative to the competing group. Note also that both groups are better off without as much competition, that is, there is a negative sum game of wasting resources on political pressure.

In the standard application of the Becker model, a testable hypothesis is that the larger x is, the less likely the regulation and wealth transfer, because the payoff is smaller relative to the loss. A rise in x shifts up $\psi_2(p_1)$ and shifts in $\psi_1(p_2)$. At the new equilibrium, the influence function is lower than the initial equilibrium, and regulatory activity is reduced. Hence, market failure with the potential for lower deadweight loss, or even a gain (x is negative), leads to a greater chance of regulation.

The application of this model to rate design is as follows. To avoid political instability from a water shortage, with embedded cost rate design and growing water demand, management of the water utility builds increasingly expensive sources of water, creating ever-increasing economic inefficiency over time. A drought accentuates the losses from inefficient rate design. In figure 9.6, group 1 is the larger water user group and group 2 is the smaller water user group.

Prior to the drought, the smaller water users were subsidizing the larger users. A drought increases the efficiency gains from marginal cost rate design. Conversely, a drought increases the efficiency losses from the subsidy. For any given level of subsidy received by large users, the large users are willing to exert pressure, say p_1^*. Given p_1^*, the optimal pressure for group 2 prior to the drought is p_2^*. During a drought, if group 1 were to continue pressure p_1^* to receive the same level of subsidy, group 2 would have to incur higher losses. Consequently, the optimal pressure in response by group 2 increases to p_2', denoted by an upward shift in the function from $\psi_2(p_1)$ to $\psi_2^0(p_1)$. If group 2 were to continue at pressure p_2^* during the drought, consistent with it paying the same subsidy, group 1 would receive less because of the drought, and would therefore be willing to apply less pressure, p_1', denoted by a leftward shift in the function from $\psi_1(p_2)$ to $\psi_1^0(p_2)$. The new equilibrium is a reduction in political pressure from large users (group 1) and an increase in political pressure from small users (group 2). Recall the amount of the subsidy is $I(p_1, p_2)$, where I is the influence function, which increases with p_1, the political pressure of group 1, and decreases with p_2, the political pressure of group 2. Hence, a drought reduces the subsidy by increasing the likelihood of marginal cost rate design.

Conclusion

The Peltzman-type model is consistent with Los Angeles originally having embedded cost rate design, and the Becker model is consistent with the switch to marginal cost rate design. Both models would predict that Los

Angeles would change back to embedded cost rate design after the drought ended, yet that did not happen. Why not? One could claim that the BRC's innovations in rate design made the Becker model consistent with retaining the marginal cost rate design. That is, the BRC's refinements to the rate design caused the same shifts in the Becker influence functions as a drought. However, this merely begs the questions. Why did the BRC bother to spend months of time educating itself about rate design in the first place? How did the members of the BRC learn to trust each other's motives and to accept compromises that would harm the interest groups from whom they were chosen, in order to benefit the city as a whole?

The new terminology that accompanies models of public choice includes the word stakeholders, which means interest groups. Once we accept the basic construct of these models, we buy into the idea that the relative strengths of competing interests will determine the course of the future. In this context the only way to solve a problem is to get the stakeholders to negotiate a mutually acceptable outcome, which usually involves a subsidy from the general public.

An alternative exists to accepting the notion that the solution to social conflict should come from the involved interest groups. The process of selecting a blue ribbon committee exemplifies this alternative. The example outlined here required resources and time for disinterested, public-spirited citizens to learn enough to make educated choices. It also is a process that is only invoked infrequently. This leaves us with the question: why infrequently?

References

American Water Works Association. 1991. *Water Rates*, 4th ed. Denver, Colorado.

Becker, Gary S. 1983. "A Theory of Competition among Pressure Groups for Political Influence." *Quarterly Journal of Economics* 98: 371–400.

BRC (Mayor's Blue Ribbon Committee on Water Rates). 1992. *Assuring Our Future Water Supply: A Consensus Approach to Water Rates*. Los Angeles.

_____. 1994. *Recommendations for Revisions to Water Rates*. Los Angeles.

Fisher, Anthony C., W. Michael Hanemann, and Andrew G. Keeler. 1991. "Integrating Fishery and Water Resource Management: A Biological Model of a California Salmon Fishery." *Journal of Environmental Economics and Management* 20(3): 234–61.

Hall, Darwin C. 1996. "Calculating Marginal Cost for Water Rates." In Darwin C. Hall, ed., *Advances in the Economics of Environmental Resources: Marginal Cost Rate Design and Wholesale Water Markets*, Vol. 1. Greenwich, Connecticut: JAI Press.

Hall, Darwin C., and W. Michael Hanemann. 1996, "Urban Water Rate Design Based on Marginal Cost." In Darwin C. Hall, ed., *Advances in the Economics of Environmental Resources: Marginal Cost Rate Design and Wholesale Water Markets*, Vol. 1. Greenwich, Connecticut: JAI Press.

Hall, Robert. 1973. "The Specification of Technology with Several Kinds of Output." *Journal of Political Economy* 81(4): 879–92.

Lau, Lawrence. 1978. "Applications of Profit Functions." In Melvyn Fuss and Daniel McFadden, eds., *Production and Economics: A Dual Approach to Theory and Applications*, Vol. 1. New York: North-Holland.

Peltzman, Sam. 1976. "Toward a More General Theory of Regulation." *Journal of Law and Economics* 19(2): 211–40.

Stigler, George J. 1971. "The Theory of Economic Regulation." *Bell Journal of Economics and Management* 2(1): 3–21.

Viscusi, W. Kip, John M. Vernon, and Joseph E. Harrington, Jr. 1995. *Economics of Regulation and Antitrust*, 2nd ed. Cambridge, Massachusetts: MIT Press.

Wegge, Thomas C., W. Michael Hanemann, and John Loomis. 1996. "Comparing Benefits and Costs of Water Resource Allocation Policies for California's Mono Basin." In Darwin C. Hall, ed., *Advances in the Economics of Environmental Resources: Marginal Cost Rate Design and Wholesale Water Markets*, Vol. 1. Greenwich, Connecticut: JAI Press.

SECTION C

Political Economy of Urban Water
Pricing Implementation

10

The Political Economy of Water Tariff Design in Developing Countries:

Increasing Block Tariffs versus Uniform Price with Rebate

John J. Boland and Dale Whittington

Increasing block tariffs (IBTs) are now the tariff structure of choice in developing countries. Multilateral donors, international financial and engineering consultants, and water sector professionals working in developing countries commonly presume that IBT structures are the most appropriate way to determine water users' monthly bills. Most recent water tariff studies (Asian Development Bank 1993) for developing countries propose IBT structures.

IBTs, like other block-type tariffs, set two or more prices for water, with each price applying to consumption within a defined block. Prices rise in each successive block. Some tariff structures have as many as 10 blocks, each with a different price. Developing countries typically apply IBTs so that the first block price is below cost (however cost may be defined). Designers of IBTs tend to pay much attention to the size and price of the first block.

Despite the widespread consensus that IBTs are good policy, this type of tariff deserves more careful examination. Even at first glance, the consensus appears somewhat curious because, although IBT structures were first designed in industrial countries to assist poor households by providing revenue-neutral cross-subsidies, only a small minority of water companies in countries like the United States now use them.[1] Differences in water

---

The authors are grateful for substantive contributions as well as careful review of earlier versions of this chapter by Jennifer Davis, Ariel Dinar, Harvey A. Garn, Sumila Gulyani, W. Michael Hanemann, Julie Hewitt, Kristin Komives, Donald T. Lauria, and Xun Wu.

1. Ernst and Young's surveys (1990, 1992) found that 18 percent and 16 percent, respectively, of a nonrandom sample of U.S. water utilities used

and sanitation conditions may help explain the fact that IBTs are increasingly popular in developing countries while playing a minor role in industrial countries, but this explanation is not obvious. In many cities in developing countries, most poor households do not have private metered connections to the water distribution system, and thus IBTs do not help them.

This chapter critically examines the use of IBTs in developing countries. The following section reviews the common arguments made to justify IBTs and looks at how selected cities are currently using IBTs. The third section discusses the objectives and considerations involved in water tariff design to provide a basis for judging the appropriateness of IBTs. The fourth section examines five IBT problems and limitations that the literature has not sufficiently addressed, namely:

1. The inability of water utilities to limit the size of the initial block for residential users because of political and other pressures
2. The difficulty of providing most users with the proper economic incentives without significantly distorting incentives to other users
3. The difficulty of raising revenues to meet a financial cost-recovery target without significantly departing from marginal cost pricing because of limited knowledge about household demand
4. The lack of transparency in the rate structure and the difficulty of administering the tariffs
5. The difficulty of preventing households with metered connections from supplying unconnected neighbors or vendors.

The fifth section compares a simple IBT structure with a tariff based on a uniform volumetric price coupled with a lump sum rebate. It illustrates the important advantages of the latter. Finally, the chapter offers some general observations about academic and political support for IBTs.

Background

A tariff structure is a set of procedural rules that determine the service conditions and charges for various categories of water users. A water user's monthly bill may be based on two components: the volume of water consumed and a set of factors other than water use. Conceptually, one of

---

an increasing block design for at least some customers. A larger ($n = 827$), but also non-random survey by the American Water Works Association recorded 22 percent of water utilities using some form of IBT (AWWA 1998). In the last decade some large utilities in metropolitan areas have abandoned IBTs (East Bay Municipal Utility District, California, and the city of Phoenix, Arizona) while others adopted them (city of Los Angeles).

these components could be zero and the other could solely determine the water bill. For example, a water bill could be based entirely on the value of the property on which the connection to a municipal distribution network is located, rather than on the level of consumption. Alternatively, the bill could be determined by multiplying the volume of water used in a billing period by a per unit price, meaning that factors other than consumption would be zero. In contrast, a two-part tariff would incorporate both components, perhaps by combining a fixed monthly charge with a per unit charge based on consumption.

An IBT structure is based on the volumetric component. It may or may not be combined with a nonuse component. A water user in a particular category, such as residential, is charged a relatively low per unit price for consumption up to a specified amount. This amount defines the end of the initial or first block. A user who extracts more water faces a higher per unit price for this additional consumption until reaching the end of the second block, and then a still higher price until reaching the top block in the increasing block structure. The user can typically extract as much water as desired in this top block, but for each additional unit of water used, the bill increases by an amount equal to the highest price in the rate structure. Figure 10.1 illustrates actual IBT structures for residential customers in six Asian cities.

To design an IBT structure, officials must set three parameters for each category of water use: the number of blocks, the volume of water use in each block, and the per unit prices for each block.[2] The municipality of La Paz, Bolivia, adopted an IBT in 1997 that typifies the type of tariff many developing countries employ (table 10.1). First, residential users face large price differentials between blocks. In La Paz, the price in the most expensive block is more than five times the price in the least expensive block. Second, tariff designers generally focus on household water users, which means that the residential category contains more blocks than the commercial or industrial categories. La Paz has four blocks for residential connections, two for commercial connections, and one for industrial connections. Third, the prices charged for industrial and commercial water use are much higher than those charged for typical levels of residential water use.

The use of such IBTs is widespread. In a survey of urban water utilities in Asia, the Asian Development Bank (1993) found that the majority of

2. Utilities tend to place residential, commercial, and industrial users in separate categories. Some take the additional step of creating several categories of residential user based on housing type or neighborhood characteristics.

FIGURE 10.1
Six Examples of Increasing Block Tariff Designs

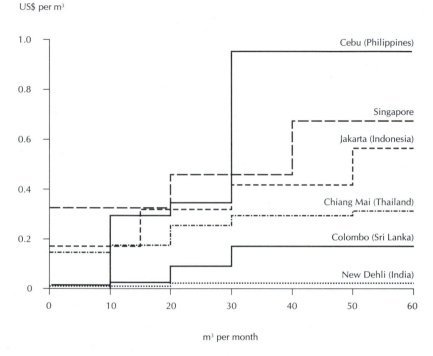

US$ per m³

Source: Asian Development Bank (1993).

utilities in their sample (20 out of 32) used an IBT structure.[3] The global trend toward privatization in the municipal water sector has not decreased the popularity of IBTs, even though profit-seeking purveyors would seem to have strong reasons to prefer other structures. In bidding documents and requests for proposals, governments often require private concessionaires to use an IBT.

Water utility officials and other experts tend to make several arguments in support of IBT structures. First, some of them claim that IBTs promote equity by forcing wealthy households to cross-subsidize the water usage of poor households. The argument (which assumes that all households have private metered connections) is that wealthy households use more water than poor

---

3. Of the 12 utilities that did not use an IBT, 8 used constant volumetric charges. The others received payment through a property tax.

TABLE 10.1
**Example of an Increasing Block Tariff Structure, Aguas del Illimani,
La Paz, Bolivia**

Volumetric charge (US$ per m³)	Domestic water connections (m³)	Commercial water connections (m³)	Industrial water connections (m³)
0.22	1 to 30	n.a.	n.a.
0.44	31 to 150	n.a.	n.a.
0.66	151 to 300	1–20	n.a.
1.19	301 and above	21 and above	1 and above

n.a. Not applicable.
Source: Komives (1998).

households, because water is a normal good and use increases with income. For example, high-income households consume more water in part because they may have gardens to tend, cars to wash, and appliances that use water. Because a greater percentage of their water use occurs in the higher blocks, they pay a higher average price for water. This means the poor can obtain enough water for essential needs at a low price in the initial block.

Second, IBT advocates contend that charging industrial and commercial customers a higher rate than most residential customers also promotes equity. The rate structure enables the water utility to cross-subsidize poor residential customers with revenues from large industrial firms.

Third, they argue that IBTs can promote water conservation and sustainable water use. That is because the price in the highest block can be made punitively high, and thus discourage wasteful water use.

Fourth, some water utility experts argue that IBTs are needed to implement marginal cost pricing principles. Their rationale, assuming rising marginal costs of municipal water supply, is that setting the price of water in the most expensive block at marginal cost accomplishes marginal cost pricing (Hall and Hanemann 1996). A more elaborate version of this argument is that an IBT is an optimal means of second-best pricing, that is, pursuing an economic efficiency objective subject to a cost-recovery constraint (Porter 1996). A variant of this fourth rationale is the claim that an IBT is needed to match a presumed rising marginal cost curve. It is argued that because marginal costs are expected to rise with total water use, prices should rise accordingly with individual household use. Officials have used this justification for some multiblock designs, especially those with a relatively large number of blocks.

A fifth rationale focuses on the issue of public health externalities (see, for example, Vincent and others 1997, p. 242). The argument is that one household's consumption of potable water confers positive externalities on other households by reducing the risks of communicable diseases throughout the community. The existence of such positive externalities would argue for a subsidized price of water to "internalize" this external-ity. The flip side of the argument, however, is that high water prices (due perhaps to marginal cost or cost-recovery pricing) would reduce house-hold water use and thus decrease these positive public health externalities.

Design of Water Tariffs

Officials create water tariffs in various ways. Sometimes they simply in-herit an existing tariff. If the tariff has not been controversial, and if no outside lending agency is pressing for change, they may choose to make minimal changes in the existing structure. In other cases, a national legisla-tive formula may determine the tariff (as in Ukraine), and a national agency may regulate it (as in Colombia). These constraints reflect a social concern about the fairness of water tariffs, but officials rarely revise them to ac-count for changing circumstances or rising costs. In these cases, individual water suppliers may have little opportunity to consider the broader issues of tariff design, at least in the short run.

When such constraints are not a factor, water agencies must from time to time consider the proper design for the tariff. The process is often com-plex and can involve outside consulting firms, lending institutions, po-litical leaders, various stakeholders from the user population, and some-times local and national legislatures. The conflicting objectives and considerations of the various parties cause much of the complexity.

Objectives

A water tariff is a powerful and versatile management tool. Officials can use it to promote a number of objectives, although they often must make tradeoffs between objectives, such as efficiency and equity. This section describes the more common objectives, but note that not all par-ties to a tariff design effort embrace all objectives. Furthermore, some parties may define the objectives differently.

REVENUE SUFFICIENCY. From the water supplier's point of view, the main purpose of the tariff is cost recovery. Before beginning their design, offi-cials must decide how much revenue the tariff should recover. Thus the aim of tariff design is to achieve a particular revenue target. In fact, the revenue goal may be more important than any other single objective in price-setting decisions.

ECONOMIC EFFICIENCY. An efficient tariff will create incentives to ensure, for a fixed water supply cost, that users obtain the largest possible aggregate benefits. In other words, for a given level of aggregate benefits from water use, the supply cost should be minimized. Generations of economists have insisted on the importance of this objective, and noted that it can be achieved by setting all prices equal to their relevant marginal costs.

EQUITY AND FAIRNESS. The terms equity and fairness are often used interchangeably, but they have different meanings. Equity requires that equals be treated equally and unequals be treated unequally. In public utility tariff design, this usually means that users pay amounts proportionate to the costs they impose on the utility. Equity is thus a quantifiable proposition, subject to precise definition and verification. Fairness, by contrast, is wholly subjective. Each participant in a tariff design process may have a different notion of the meaning of fairness. One person may think it is fair to set a high price for industrial water use; another may object to such a scheme. One person may think that charging all customers the same price is fair (even when, because of cost-of-service differences, this is not necessarily equitable), whereas another may believe that fairness requires subsidies to some customers. A marginal cost-based tariff should be equitable, but it is not necessarily fair.

INCOME REDISTRIBUTION. Although income redistribution may be considered part of the fairness objective, officials frequently list it separately. Briefly, officials widely assume that utility tariffs in developing countries should be used to redistribute income among groups of customers. IBTs, as usually applied, set a price below average revenue for the first block, with one or more prices above average revenue in the higher blocks. This causes large water users (who pay more than average revenue) to subsidize small users (who pay less). Similarly, if industrial water prices are set above the cost of supply and also above residential prices, it is commonly assumed that income is redistributed from firms to individuals.

RESOURCE CONSERVATION. Officials often seek to use water tariffs to discourage excessive uses of water, thus promoting sustainable use. An IBT design may assume that large water users are the most likely group to consume excessive quantities, and confront them with higher prices to discourage futher use. This approach, of course, rests on the belief that only large users waste water. It also assumes that these users are aware of the significance of the various thresholds of the tariff design and can respond accordingly.

Considerations

Other factors bear on tariff design, although they may be less fundamental and long lasting than the objectives listed earlier. This section refers to these as considerations to emphasize their lesser importance, but keep in mind that the following considerations still play a role when officials weigh alternative tariff structures:

PUBLIC ACCEPTABILITY. A successful tariff design is one that is not controversial. It should not become a focus of public criticism of the water supply agency.

POLITICAL ACCEPTABILITY. A tariff design that is objectionable to political leaders will lose political support, possibly causing politicians to interfere in the operations of the water agency.

SIMPLICITY AND TRANSPARENCY. A tariff design should be easy to explain and understand. Most users should know the price they are paying for water.

NET REVENUE STABILITY. When weather or economic conditions affect water consumption, revenue and cost should change by approximately equal amounts. Otherwise, cyclical changes will result in net revenue volatility, creating cash flow and financing difficulties for the agency.

EASE OF IMPLEMENTATION. The tariff should be easy to implement. It should not run into significant barriers because of legal issues, administrative complexities, information requirements, or billing procedures.

Pro-IBT Arguments Revisited

A previous section listed six commonly stated arguments in favor of IBTs. Let us now examine whether these claims meet the conventional objectives and considerations of tariff design.

First, consider the argument that IBTs promote equity by creating desirable cross-subsidies. Cross-subsidies reflect notions of fairness, not equity, and thus spark conflicting opinions. However, even when the direction of the subsidy (from rich to poor households) is relatively uncontroversial, keeping the limitations of this tariff characteristic in mind is important. The maximum possible subsidy is small: the largest first block subsidy shown in Figure 10.1 is US$2.96 per month, and most are much smaller.[4] In addition, it is blockwise regressive. This means that a household must use the entire first block of water to receive the full subsidy. As a household reduces its water use, its receives a smaller subsidy.

Next, consider the point that IBTs cause firms to subsidize individuals. Because separate tariffs are commonly used for separate classes of users, there is no need to employ an IBT to set industrial prices above residential prices. Furthermore, the desirability of creating such subsidies is questionable. This practice conflicts with the objectives of economic efficiency and equity, and it also applies the highest prices to those customers who are, in many cases, the most likely to exit the system. This may place residential customers at a disadvantage in the long run because, as large users elect to exit, the water agency loses economies of scale in water intake, treatment, transmission, and distribution.

What about the argument that IBTs discourage excessive use? Presumably, "excessive" refers to water used in a way that fails to provide a benefit commensurate with the resource cost of delivering it. But if the price is set equal to marginal cost, each user is required to pay the full cost of replacing each unit of water used. Economic theory holds that this is sufficient incentive to discourage wasteful use, and a higher price merely creates inefficiency.

This brings us to the issue of whether IBTs are consistent with marginal cost pricing. Economic efficiency is promoted when prices reflect the marginal costs of the services provided. Under IBTs, different customers pay different prices for the same service: the delivery of water. At most, one of these prices equals marginal cost. But a large number of customers probably face different prices, either higher or lower. In contrast, marginal cost pricing imposes a single price for all users with similar cost accountability (such as residential users), although that price may vary according to time of use or location.[5]

---

4. The first block for the city of Cebu in the Philippines has a zero price and a size of 10 cubic meters per month. If the second block price (US$0.296 per cubic meter) applied to this use, the cost of the first block would be US$2.96. At the other extreme, the first block subsidy for Delhi is US$0.24.

5. It is, of course, possible for different residential users to impose different costs on the water system. An example is a service area in hilly terrain, where customers at different elevations may impose widely different pumping costs.

Those who say that IBTs are needed to match the rising marginal cost of supply appear to be mistaken about the nature of costs and prices. Even assuming that marginal costs do rise with increased aggregate use (they may remain constant or decline, as well), they do not rise perceptibly with any individual household's use. The role of the tariff is to charge a price equal to the cost of increased consumption. There is only one such price at any given time. If all users increase water consumption over time, and marginal costs rise over time as a result, then the marginal cost price must also eventually rise—for all users and for all use. A block-type tariff does not capture this relationship.

Finally, consider the argument that IBTs promote public health. The implicit assumptions behind the public health externalities argument are that (a) the unconnected households are more likely to connect to a piped distribution system if an IBT is in effect, (b) the level of household water use among the lowest-income families will be greater in the presence of an IBT than for other tariff designs, and (c) the resulting increase in water use is significant with respect to public health externalities.

The literature contains no empirical evidence to support any of these three assumptions. Certainly water use increases dramatically when a household switches from a source outside the home, such as a handpump or well, to a connection to a piped distribution system (White, Bradley, and White 1972). Daily use may increase from 20 liters per capita to 100 liters or more. Even though the evidence is mixed, one may plausibly assume that this increase in water use generally confers some health benefits on the household (provided that it does not simultaneously create negative health externalities associated with wastewater disposal). But little evidence indicates that this increased water consumption confers health benefits on the wider community (Esrey 1996; Esrey and others 1989). Furthermore, there is no evidence that households are more likely to connect to a piped distribution system if an IBT is in effect. Households base their connection decisions more on the connection charge than on volumetric charges (Singh and others 1993).

The argument in support of IBT health benefits is even more tenuous. IBT advocates claim that significant, positive public health externalities result when households that already have private, metered connections increase their water consumption in response to lower water prices in the first block of the IBT. This argument suggests that positive public health externalities occur when residents increase their daily per capita consumption from, say, 100 to 120 liters, or from 75 to 85 liters. But no evidence exists that such changes in water use result in either private health benefits to the household or in positive public health externalities, nor is there any reason to expect such results.

Limitations of IBTs in Practice

The usual rationale for employing an IBT design, therefore, is either in-complete (for cross-subsidies) or faulty. However, examining issues that arise in the actual application of IBTs may be more important. This section discusses five such issues.

Setting the Initial Block

One can imagine an IBT structure that minimizes the conceptual problems mentioned previously. It would be a two-step tariff in which the first block price is set below marginal cost and the second block price is equal to marginal cost. The size of the first block is set so that relatively few users terminate their consumption in it. The regressivity of the subsidy would not be an issue: nearly all users would face the marginal cost price, and cross-subsidies would be limited to those low-income users who are generally considered to need them. However, water utilities find it difficult to limit the size of the initial block for residential users because of political pressure. Most influential residents, after all, want to keep the size of the initial block as large as possible to keep their water prices low.

To successfully target the poor (assuming that all households have private, metered connections), the designer of an IBT must set the water volume in the initial block equal to a household's essential water needs. How much water does a low-income household need? Internationally cited standards for basic water needs are usually in the range of 25–30 liters per capita per day (Gleick 1996; United Nations 1993; WHO 1997). For a household of five, this amounts to 4–5 cubic meters (m^3) per month per household.

The IBT structures in most cities give households with private connections much more water than this at the lowest price. For example, of the 17 water utilities in the Asian Development Bank's data set that used increasing block structures and for which information was available on the size of the initial block, only two had a first block of 4–5 m^3 per month or less (table 10.2).[6] Most of the others had initial blocks of 15 m^3 per month or more.

These data support the common observation that politicians and senior civil servants cannot easily restrict the size of the initial block of an IBT, because a large initial block directly benefits all residents with private

---

6. The two cities with initial blocks of 4–5 m^3 or less were Nuku'alofa (Kingdom of Tonga) and Vientiane (Laos).

TABLE 10.2
First Block Size for Utilities Employing an Increasing Block Tariff Structure

First block size (m³)	Number of utilities	Percent of utilities
4	1	5.9
5	1	5.9
10	6	35.3
15	4	23.5
20	4	23.5
30	1	5.9
Total	17	100.0

Source: Asian Development Bank (1993).

connections, not just the poor. Because middle- and upper-income households in many cities have the majority of private, metered connections, they often receive the vast majority of water sold at the subsidized price. The amount of revenue a water company loses as a result of an increase in the size of the initial block costs is generally not known. It is easy to assume that industrial and commercial users will simply make up for any resulting budget shortfall.

Moreover, the amount of water a household needs for essential purposes is open to debate. Because IBTs do not adjust the size of the initial block for the number of members of a household, one could argue that a volume of 4–5 m³ per month does not meet the essential needs of a household with 10 members. The political reality of most tariff-setting procedures means that stakeholders or consultants participating in the process rarely pay attention to the adverse financial and economic efficiency consequences of expanding the size of this initial block.

The same political realities make it difficult to restrict the size of the middle blocks as well. For example, the IBT for La Paz, Bolivia, shown in table 10.1 permits a household to take 300 m³ per month before paying the highest price in the block structure. For a household with five members, this translates into 10 m³ per day, or 2 m³ per person per day—80 times the basic needs estimate of 25 liters per capita per day. These data suggest that, in practice, at least some IBTs are not performing as their advocates had anticipated.

Mismatch between Price and Marginal Cost

Figure 10.2 illustrates the difficulty of using an IBT to give users the proper economic incentives. The figure shows a cumulative probability

FIGURE 10.2
Residential Water Distribution for a Developing Country

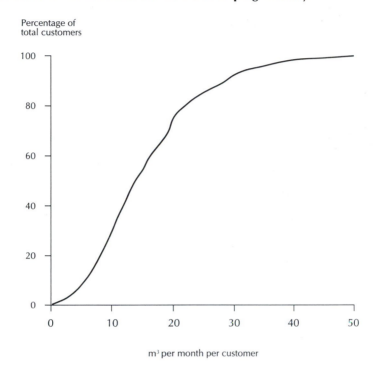

Source: Authors.

density function for household water use in Soe, Indonesia, truncated at 50 m³ per month.[7] Suppose the strategy is to design a two-step IBT, with the second block price equal to marginal cost. To preserve the proper economic incentives, all or nearly all users must terminate their consumption in the second block. Figure 10.2 indicates that this goal requires a very small first block, certainly not more than 5 m³ per month. But, as previously noted, political and consumer pressures make it difficult to set such a small first block. More typical block sizes in the range of 10–20 m³ per month would result in 30–75 percent of households paying the artificially low first block price. This problem is exacerbated by multiblock designs in which the price closest to marginal cost may be at the third, fourth, or fifth block.

---

7. Because no measured use data were available below 10 m³ per month, the lower tail of the distribution is extrapolated for illustrative purposes.

Revenue Sufficiency versus Economic Efficiency

All tariffs, even those designed to address other objectives, have a revenue recovery function. The most basic design criterion is that the tariff produces a particular stream of revenue, ranging from the full long-run cost of operations to a more modest partial share of variable operating costs. Designing an IBT to produce a specified revenue stream leads to two significant difficulties: (a) utilities typically lack the information about user demand needed to predict the revenue that any particular IBT will produce, and (b) compromises between revenue collection and economic efficiency objectives may distort other functions of the tariff.

Forecasting the revenue that an IBT will produce, even approximately, requires knowledge of the probability distribution of water use under the former tariff (similar to the situation in figure 10.2, but for all customer classes). It also requires some way to estimate the price elasticity of customers at different points in that distribution. This information is almost never available for cities in developing countries. What may be available instead is a water use estimate for each customer class and a plausible estimate of overall price elasticity for the class. This information is sufficient to forecast the revenue that a single price tariff produces, but can lead to large errors in the case of multiple blocks.

The second issue pertains to the often cited claim of a conflict between revenue sufficiency and economic efficiency. It is usually argued that, where marginal cost pricing produces too much or too little revenue, prices can be adjusted in a way that meets the revenue constraint while minimizing the inevitable loss of economic efficiency. This type of adjustment is often called Ramsey pricing (Ramsey 1927). Some authors, such as Porter (1996), have further claimed that IBTs can achieve an optimum balance between the two objectives. Porter cites his mathematical appendix as proving that, where additional revenue must be raised, a two-block IBT can achieve an optimal departure from marginal cost pricing.

Porter's conclusion seems counterintuitive in light of the usual assumption that larger water users (such as upper-income households) have a higher price elasticity of demand. A common characterization of Ramsey pricing is that it assigns the highest prices to the least elastic users, which in the case of residential water use would be the small users, presumably the poorer households. This would contradict an IBT's price structure. However, a closer inspection of Porter's derivation shows that his assumed linear demand curves actually make the demands of the poor more elastic than the rich, which is highly unlikely. Thus, his conclusions about the optimality of IBTs are unfounded.

However, a more fundamental problem exists with both the Porter and the Ramsey approaches. Both assume that all revenue must be recovered from the volumetric charge. This is not true for public utility services (Ramsey's work has more often been applied to agricultural commodities). Rather, one may levy a fixed charge, which in principle could be either positive or negative, as a means of adjusting revenue recovery. This option renders the optimal departure from marginal cost literature moot, as this chapter will demonstrate.

Simplicity, Transparency, and Implementation

IBTs have achieved some degree of public and political acceptability, perhaps because officials have applied them so routinely, but they are certainly not simple or transparent. With a typical IBT, it is impossible for all but the most analytical and determined users to deduce the average or marginal price that they actually pay for water. The kind of price signal that most customers rely on (the change in a total bill that results from a conscious change in water usage) becomes misleading and confusing when the resulting water use moves from one block to another. This is an important point, because customers cannot respond as expected when they cannot detect a coherent price signal.

The use of IBTs may also affect perceptions of fairness. When a tariff cannot be easily understood, it can incorporate unwarranted advantages for favored users. Complex tariffs may create customer relations problems, making it difficult for water agency representatives to explain bills to users. IBTs are difficult to implement. Also, because of the nature of the assumptions embodied in block size and block prices, a conscientious water agency would need to revisit the design details at intervals in the future. In contrast, a tariff with a single volumetric price is simple, transparent, equitable, robust, and easy to implement. It sends understandable and consistent price signals.

Shared Connection

Some literature (Whittington 1992) has noted an additional—and serious—problem with IBTs. IBT structures can only work as their proponents advocate if each household (rich and poor) has a private, metered water connection. Yet many cities in developing countries do not meet this condition. Private, metered water connections are often available only to upper- and middle-income households; the poor must obtain water from shared connections, neighbors with private connections, water vendors, or other sources. If several households share a metered connection and an IBT is in effect, water use by the group quickly exceeds the volume in the initial block, pushing water use into the higher priced blocks. To the extent that households sharing water connections are more likely to be poor than households with private connections, the IBT will have precisely the opposite effect from its intent: the poor will pay higher average prices for water than the rich.

This problem is exacerbated when households with private, metered connections sell water to neighbors without connections or to vendors who resell the water to unconnected households. If a household sells water to more than a few neighbors or vendors, the water volume billed through its metered connection will be pushed into a high priced block. This household faces the same situation as households with a shared connection: the more water sold, the higher the average price. In this case, a higher-income household with a metered connection can capture the benefits of the first block price, while charging neighbors or water vendors a price that will recover the highest per unit charge in the IBT plus some markup for the inconvenience of selling water. Once again, the poor pay more than the rich.

A water company can address this IBT limitation by increasing the amount of water sold at the first block price to account for the number of households sharing a private, metered connection, but this type of manipulation is time-consuming and subject to corruption. It requires the utility to fine-tune household billing in a way that is often impractical, and conflicts with the goal of having a water tariff that is transparent and easy to administer.

A Practical Alternative: Uniform Price with Rebate

If the marginal cost of supplying water exceeds the average cost, perhaps because of the increasing opportunity cost of raw water, then setting a price equal to marginal cost results in excess revenues for the water utility. In this case, an important political goal in tariff design is achieving economic efficiency without collecting too much revenue. IBTs would appear to accomplish this, because the marginal cost is assessed only on the last units of water consumed by users in the highest blocks. However, a tariff in which a household's water bill is based on (a) a volumetric charge set equal to marginal cost, and (b) a fixed monthly rebate (negative fixed charge) can also result in lower revenues while fully preserving marginal cost pricing.[8] This alternative, the uniform price with rebate (UPR) structure, offers important advantages over an IBT.

---

8. The same option, with many of the same advantages, applies where marginal cost is less than average cost. In this case, a uniform volumetric price plus a fixed monthly charge (instead of a rebate) can be used to cover the potential deficit while preserving marginal cost pricing.

Consider a situation in which the marginal cost of water supply is US$1 per m³. Table 10.3 compares monthly water bills under two alternative tariff designs. The first is an IBT with two blocks: a charge of US$0.50 per m³ for the first 15 m³ and US$1 per m³ for quantities above 15 m³. The second is a UPR tariff consisting of a single volumetric charge, set equal to the marginal cost, coupled with a monthly rebate of US$6.69. To avoid zero or negative bills, both tariffs incorporate a minimum monthly charge of US$2.50. The amount of the UPR rebate is set so that the two tariffs produce the same total revenue when applied to a water use distribution similar to that shown in figure 10.2. An analysis of the bills and the water use incentives illustrates the differences between the tariffs.

With either tariff design, the presence of a minimum charge causes households to face a zero price for water at very low levels of use—below 5 m³ per month for the IBT and below 9 m³ for the UPR.[9] However, under the IBT, households do not face the full marginal cost of water supply until they use 15 m³ per month or more. The UPR tariff, by

TABLE 10.3
Comparison of an IBT with a UPR Marginal Cost-Based Tariff

Monthly water use (m³/household)	UPR structure[a]	IBT structure[b]
0	2.50	2.50
5	2.50	2.50
10	3.31	5.00
15	8.31	7.50
20	13.31	12.50
25	18.31	17.50
30	23.31	22.50
35	28.31	27.50
40	33.31	32.50
45	38.31	37.50

a. Water bill = US$1.00 per m³ minus US$6.69 rebate, US$2.50 monthly minimum charge.
b. Water bill = US$0.50 per m³ for the first 15 cubic meters; US$1.00 per m³ for use over 15 m³, US$2.50 monthly minimum charge.
Source: Authors.

---

9. One reviewer noted that, despite the claim of a uniform price, the hypothetical UPR tariff is also, in a sense, an IBT. Price rises from 0 to US$1 at 9 m³ per month. This is the necessary consequence of introducing a minimum bill, and the point applies to any tariff design that has a minimum bill.

contrast, charges all customers using more than 9 m³ the full marginal
cost of water—US$1 per m³. Yet, for small users, the UPR tariff often
produces smaller total bills. This is illustrated by an incidence analysis,
depicted in figure 10.3. Again, based on the water use distribution of
figure 10.2, the 48 percent of households with lower water use pay a bill
under the UPR tariff that is equal to or smaller than the alternative IBT
bill. The 52 percent of households with higher water use pay a larger
bill under the UPR tariff, although the monthly differences are never
more than US$0.81.

In this simple example, about 10 percent of all households would receive the same bill under either structure; about 38 percent, including most
poor households, would receive a lower bill under the UPR tariff; and the
remaining 52 percent would receive a higher bill under the UPR tariff. The
full marginal cost price would be billed to 75 percent of all households
under the UPR tariff, but only 46 percent of the households under the IBT.

FIGURE 10.3
Comparison of Incidence for IBT and UPR Designs

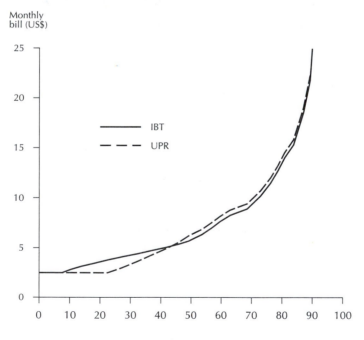

Source: Authors.

Considering the objectives of economic efficiency and income redistribution, the UPR tariff is superior for all customers who use more than 9 m³ (those who pay more than the minimum bill). Determining which design is preferable for customers below that level requires a careful examination of the circumstances of very low water use.

It is worth examining households that consume 5–9 m³ per month (about 15 percent of all households in this example). Here the comparison is between a zero price for water (UPR tariff) and a low first block price (US$0.50 for the IBT). One expects household water demand at such low levels to be very inelastic with respect to price. Given that the practical necessity of a minimum bill prevents either tariff from charging the full marginal cost to these customers, the presence of a zero price for the UPR tariff is unlikely to induce water use behavior that is significantly more inefficient than under the IBT.[10]

The numbers in table 10.3 are hypothetical. Real-world conditions, which could vary widely, would drive design decisions such as the size of the rebate in the UPR structure, the number and size of the blocks, the price charged at each block of the IBT structure, and any minimum charge. Actual IBTs are typically more inefficient than the one proposed here; they are likely to have more blocks and larger differences between prices. Conversely, more efficient UPR tariffs are possible. The example in this chapter uses a nontargeted subsidy, one that flows to all users regardless of need. One can make the subsidy larger by confining it to low-income households and increasing the fraction of total water use that is billed at the marginal cost. This would improve both the tariff's income transfer and its economic efficiency characteristics. Reliable identification of low-income households is problematic, of course, but where the institutional capacity to do so is available, existing social agencies may be able to administer the subsidy. This is happening in Chile.

For most variants in these two tariff structures, comparisons will produce the same general conclusions. Both structures return excess revenues to households and can potentially distort incentives to use water efficiently. However, because of the nature of household water demand at low levels of use, the UPR tariff has a smaller probability of inducing economic inefficiency and is more effective at transferring income. Furthermore, the UPR tariff is simple,

---

10. Politicians might seek to change the size of the UPR tariff rebate, as they have with the first block in the IBT. But the UPR tariff has the advantage of transparency. Subsidy increases resulting from political intervention would be fully visible to those larger, wealthier users who must provide that subsidy.

transparent, easy to implement, arguably fair, and equitable in most circumstances. It requires less data for design and revenue estimation. Altogether, we believe it is a superior tariff to the widely promoted IBT.

Conclusion

This chapter shows that IBTs introduce inefficiency, inequity, complexity, lack of transparency, instability, and forecasting difficulties. As reviewed here, every claimed advantage of an IBT can be achieved with a simpler and more efficient tariff design—a UPR—that does not use blocking.

If IBTs have so many problems, why are they so popular? There are two possible explanations: either policymakers intentionally do not take into account all the consequences of their actions, or academics do not have tools to take into account the consequences of their advice to policymakers. When governments adopt policies that differ from those advocated by scholars, academia's traditional explanation is that politicians and policymakers are ignorant of the indirect effects of their actions. We believe that, to the contrary, policymakers generally have carefully considered political and other reasons for favoring one policy over another, and that it is typically the academics who do not take into account the political economy aspects in their policy advice. In the preceding discussion we noted political reasons (such as lack of transparency and the resulting ability of a water utility to deliver cheap water to middle- and upper-income groups while appearing to serve the poor) for policymakers to prefer IBTs over other water tariff structures.

However, in this instance we do not feel that the political economy argument provides an adequate explanation for the widespread popularity of IBTs. Based on our professional experience in the water sector, we are forced to return to what is usually an overly simplistic answer. It is our opinion that many water sector professionals really ignore the indirect consequences and hidden costs of IBTs, particularly their often adverse effects on poor households.

References

Asian Development Bank. 1993. *Water Utilities Handbook: Asian and Pacific Region*. Manila, Philippines.

AWWA (American Water Works Association). 1998. "Water: Stats: The Water Utility Database, 1996 Survey." Denver, Colorado: American Water Works Association, http://www.awwa.org/h2ostats/h2ostats.htm.

Ernst and Young. 1990. *1990 National Water and Wastewater Rate Survey*. Charlotte, North Carolina.

_____. 1992. *1992 National Water and Wastewater Rate Survey*. Charlotte, North Carolina.

Esrey, Steven. 1996. "Water, Waste, and Well-Being: A Multicountry Study." *American Journal of Epidemiology* 43(6): 608–23.

Esrey, Steven, Clive Shiff, Leslie Roberts, and James Potash. 1989. *Health Benefits for Improvements in Water Supply and Sanitation: Survey and Analysis of the Literature on Selected Diseases.* Water and Sanitation for Health Project Technical Report no. 66. Washington, D.C.: U.S. Agency for International Development.

Gleick, P. H. 1996. "Basic Water Requirements for Human Activities: Meeting Human Needs." *Water International* 21(2): 83–92.

Hall, Darwin C., and W. Michael Hanemann. 1996. "Urban Water Rate Design Based on Marginal Cost." In Darwin C. Hall, ed., *Advances in the Economics of Environmental Resources: Marginal Cost Rate Design and Wholesale Water Markets,* Vol. 1. Greenwich, Connecticut: JAI Press.

Komives, Kristin. 1998. "Designing Pro-Poor Water and Sewer Concessions: Early Lessons from Bolivia." Policy Research Working Paper no. 2243. World Bank, Private Participation in Infrastructure, Private Sector Development Division, Washington, D.C.

Porter, Richard C. 1996. *The Economics of Water and Waste: A Case Study of Jakarta, Indonesia.* Aldershot, U.K.: Avebury Publishing.

Ramsey, F. 1927. "A Contribution to the Theory of Taxation." *Economic Journal* 37: 47–61.

Singh, Bhanwar, Radhika Ramasubban, Ramesh Bhatia, John Briscoe, Charles Griffin, and C. Kim. 1993. "Rural Water Supply in Kerala, India: How to Emerge from a Low-Level Equilibrium Trap." *Water Resources Research* 29(7): 1931–42.

United Nations. 1993. *Agenda 21: The United Nations Programme of Action from Rio.* New York.

Vincent, Jeffrey R., Rozali Mohamed Ali, and Associates. 1997. *Environment and Development in a Resource-Rich Economy: Malaysia under the New Economic Policy.* Cambridge, Massachusetts: Harvard Institute for International Development, and Kuala Lumpur, Malaysia: Institute of Strategic and International Studies.

White, Gilbert, David Bradley, and Anne White. 1972. *Drawers of Water: Domestic Water Use in East Africa.* Chicago: University of Chicago Press.

Whittington, Dale. 1992. "Possible Adverse Effects of Increasing Block Water Tariffs in Developing Countries." *Economic Development and Cultural Change* 41(1): 75–87.

WHO (World Health Organization). 1997. *Health and Environment in Sustainable Development: Five Years After the Earth Summit.* Geneva.

11

A Political Economy Analysis of Water Pricing in Honduras's Capital, Tegucigalpa

Jon Strand

This chapter discusses some aspects of water pricing policy in Tegucigalpa, the capital of Honduras. Honduras is a small, poor country in Central America with about 6 million people and a gross domestic product per capita of about US$1,000. Almost 1 million people live in the Tegucigalpa area. Although Honduras is relatively rich in resources and blessed with plentiful rainfall, its water sector management is problematic, leading to inefficiencies and inequities in water availability.

The nation's inadequate water pricing policy is a key failing. The government charges households that have access to piped water only about 20 percent of long-run marginal water costs, even though this has a number of adverse and interrelated consequences. First, the policy may adversely affect distribution, because low-income households with no access to piped potable water pay a higher actual price for water than households with such access that belong to higher-income groups. Second, cheap water prices encourage those with easy access to use water excessively. Third, the water utility does not receive enough revenues to improve and maintain the water system, resulting in high water losses, poor service for those served, and reduced incentives to extend water to additional

Much of the work in this chapter is based on a project for the Inter-American Development Bank, "Economic and Ecologic Studies of Parque Nacional La Tigra" (Strand 1998). All views presented here are those of the author and not the Inter-American Development Bank. The author thanks Astrid Mathiassen, World Bank reviewers, and participants at the World Bank-sponsored Workshop on Political Economy of Water Pricing Implementation for helpful comments on a previous version.

groups of households. Note that the real water price has been cut in half over the past 20 years, which appears to be a result of institutional incentives to keep water prices low.

This chapter discusses these issues and suggests ways to improve the current system. It first studies water supply and demand in Tegucigalpa, both at present levels and as projected through 2010, and looks at the implications of the prevailing low water prices.[1] It then studies the political and economic consequences of low water prices, including incentives to supply water, water user behavior, and overall allocation. Finally, it conducts a stakeholder analysis, analyzing how various economic and political players have differing incentives to maintain or change water prices and differing abilities to influence water policy in practice. It identifies three types of actors: those external to the country, those in the Honduran government, and those in the country but not in the government.

The chapter concludes with a discussion of necessary conditions for successful pricing reform. Pressure by the World Bank and the Inter-American Development Bank (IADB), coupled with political support from major domestic voter groups, appears to be critical for reform. Price increases must not be too rapid, and they must be accompanied by improvements in service for most households that already have some type of service. Higher marginal water prices should be accompanied by less expensive inframarginal consumption, thus limiting the increasing household expenditures on water and making it easier to garner initial support for price reform. At present, most residents are unhappy with the water situation but are skeptical about reform. Residents with water service, who are in the majority and are politically strong, are afraid that a reform will simply lead to higher water prices without significant service improvements.

Water Supply, Demand, and Pricing: The Current Situation in Tegucigalpa

The government's Servicio Autónomo Nacional de Acueductos y Alcantarillados (SANAA), or National Water Service, runs the public water system in Tegucigalpa. Almost all the city's water comes from three sources: Los Laureles and Concepción, which are reservoirs, and La Tigra National Park. The national park is a valuable rain forest preserve that is severely threatened by deforestation, which may drastically reduce its value, both as a water source and as a natural preserve. The city's total water

---

1. This section is based largely on Strand (1998).

supply in 1995 and 1996 (which were normal years) was about 53 million cubic meters (m^3) per year, of which about 27 percent was lost in the distribution system, implying a net annual water consumption of 39 million m^3. Almost half the water came from Concepción, more than 30 percent from Los Laureles, and about 20 percent from the national park (Salgado 1996; SANAA 1997). However, current supply capacity is higher, because the government could improve its management of aqueducts and collection lines, reducing the rate of system loss to as low as 20 percent. A reasonable estimate of net supply capacity in normal precipitation years is 59 million m^3. The national park supplies about 32 percent of that total.

The long-run marginal cost of supplying additional water from new sources is estimated at US$0.40 per m^3. Allowing for a loss rate of 20 percent, this implies that the long-run marginal cost of net supply reaching consumers is US$0.50 per m^3, or about L 6.25 (at an exchange rate of US$1 = L 12.5).

Water Demand

Table 11.1 shows 1995 water use in Tegucigalpa by three main user groups: domestic households with access to piped water, commercial and government users, and households with no water supply. An estimated 58 percent of Tegucigalpa's population have a legal piped water connection to SANAA's system, and 22 percent are supplied either by private networks or illicitly from SANAA's system (these figures are controversial; see Walker and others 1999).

The rest of the public does not have household connections. Its consumption must come from public taps, private wells, or water that is purchased from water vendors. This group consumes a relatively small amount of water, possibly less than 1 million m^3 per year. Thus the 80 percent of the population with connections consumes almost all the residential water. The consumption rate per household is quite large. The average SANAA household consumes 350–400 m^3 per year. In comparison, the equivalent figure for Oslo, Norway, is about 200 m^3 per year. Even accounting for the hotter climate, the high figure in Tegucigalpa indicates the potential for water conservation, provided that water is appropriately priced and metered.

Finding information on water consumption by residents who are supplied illegally or privately is difficult. However, those residents probably consume far less than the regular SANAA clients, both because service is generally inferior (with low water pressure and unreliable supply) and because these households generally are in lower-income groups, which implies less water demand and less investment in private water pumping and storage. The per household consumption of these residents has been estimated at 100–200 m^3 per year. That is much higher than the consumption of

TABLE 11.1
Water Demand in Tegucigalpa by Main User Groups, 1995

User type	Number of users	Consumption, SANAA (million m³)	Average consumption (m³)	Average price (L/m³)
Domestic households, SANAA connection	75,000	26.2	350–400	1.47
Commercial and government	4,350	8.8	2,023	4.06
Domestic households, other connections	25,000–30,000	3.0	100–200 (est.)	6–12
Domestic households, no connections	20,000–25,000	0.7	45	26
Total	n.a.	38.7	n.a.	2.04

n.a. Not applicable.
Source: SANAA (1995).

households with no domestic supply at all, which Walker and others (1999) estimate at approximately 45 m^3 per year. This latter group pays very high average prices for its water: L 26 per m^3 in 1994.[2] Those with illicit and private connections are likely to face lower average water prices than those without connections, but higher than those with SANAA connections. A tentative assessment of their average price is L 6 to L 12 per m^3.[3]

Note that I am discussing realized demand and not necessarily what residents ideally wish to consume. As Walker and Ordoñez (1995) document, water service is substandard for all groups of consumers, because pressure is low and water is available only for part of the day. When asked what public services are most in need of improvement, about 40 percent of all households put water supply first, way ahead of any other service (the closely related issue of sewage disposal was in distant second place, at about 10 percent). Water service is far poorer in such marginal areas as the sections of the city located at higher elevations, where pressure is particularly low and regular SANAA customers generally get only 3–6 hours of service per day. In wealthier areas, households typically enjoy better pressure and 9–12 hours of service per day. This means that a true equilibrium in the current water market requires higher water prices than those currently prevailing. People with no service, including those served by public wells, known as *llaves publicos*, live almost exclusively in the marginal quarters (*barrios marginales*). Nearly 50 percent of households in these *barrios* have no service, whereas less than 5 percent in wealthier neighborhoods lack service. All households that report spending more than 5 percent of their income on water live in the marginal *barrios*. On average, *barrio* residents with no service spend 7.2 percent of their household income on water, and those with service spend 1.9 percent. In contrast, households in wealthier areas spend, on average, only about 1 percent of their income on water.

Table 11.2 illustrates the water tariff structure for various SANAA customers in Tegucigalpa. The first figure in each line gives the total (lump sum) tariff for consumption up to 20 m^3. The following figures represent average prices per m^3 when consumption exceeds this minimum level. Most

---

2. Although this seems extreme, it is far from unique. Many countries have water provision systems with similar real price variations. Nigeria is an example, as reported in Whittington, Lauria, and Mu (1991).

3. It might appear that those with illicit connections face a zero water price, as they do not pay for their actual SANAA supply. These households, however, are likely to buy a substantial amount of their water in the private market, as their tap service is usually poor. Accordingly, my price estimate for this group corresponds to the average price across all supply sources.

TABLE 11.2
Marginal Water Prices for Various SANAA Customers in Tegucigalpa,
1996–97
(L/m³)

Consumer type	Water consumption block (m³)					
	20 or less	21–30	31–40	41–50	51–60	61 or higher
Household	0.14	1.00	1.20	1.70	1.85	3.95
Commercial	46.80	2.55	2.75	2.95	3.25	4.70
Industry	MC	MC	MC	175.50	3.90	4.70
Government	C	C	C	0.52	2.35	3.90

MC Minimum charge of L 175.50 for consumption of 50 m³ per month.
C Charge of L 0.52m³ for the first 50 m³ per month.
Note: Because the figures are average prices for all consumption, marginal water prices are very high at the borders of the different consumption blocks. For example, the increase in the water charge from 40 to 41 m³ is L 20 per m³.
Source: SANAA (1995).

of these households pay relatively low prices, for example, those that consume 31–40 m³ per month pay L 1.20 (about US$0.10) per m³. This is only about 20 percent of the long-run marginal cost, which is about L 6.25 per m³. For commercial and industry users (and for very large household users) the prices are closer to the long-run marginal cost.

About 865,000 people lived in the Tegucigalpa area in 1995, with the population expected to increase by 5 percent per year to about 1.8 million in 2010. Consider two scenarios for the development of new legal water connections to keep up with population growth. In the pessimistic scenario, the present 61 percent rate of coverage is kept constant. The number of people with legal water connections increases from 530,000 at present to 1.1 million in 2010. In the optimistic scenario, the coverage rate increases to 85 percent, which is the current coverage rate in San Pedro Sula, Honduras's second-largest city. As a result, the number of people with connections increases to more than 1.5 million in 2010.

Table 11.3 shows total water demand and supply in Tegucigalpa under these two scenarios, with constant water prices, current realized demand per household for given type of service, and supply from existing sources. It assumes that commercial demand (which includes government and industrial demand) also increases at a 5 percent annual rate. If coverage rates are constant, water demand in Tegucigalpa increases at 5 percent per year in proportion to the increase in population, approximately doubling by 2010 to nearly 80 million m³ per year. But with coverage increasing to 85 percent, overall water demand jumps to more than 100 million m³ per year.

TABLE 11.3
Projected Water Demand and Supply in Tegucigalpa for Different
Coverage Rates in 2010
(million m³ per year)

Year	Household demand	Commercial demand	Total demand	Supply, existing sources
1996	30.5	9.3	39.8	40.0
2010, 61% coverage	60.4	18.5	78.2	58.6
2010, 85% coverage	83.2	18.5	101.7	58.6

Source: Author's estimates, based on Strand (1998).

This means that, at present prices, the discrepancy between demand and supply would widen by 2010 to about 59 million m.³ per year.

Thus, in both cases demand will considerably outstrip supply, given current prices and no new water sources. Barring more cuts in daily water supply, this situation must be dealt with by increased supply or reduced demand.

Market Clearing Water Prices in Tegucigalpa, 1997–2010

An efficient allocation of water generally requires that all water users face prices that reflect the scarcity value of water in the system. With no new sources, such scarcity prices will equalize demand and supply. When this scarcity price equals or exceeds the long-run marginal cost of bringing new water into the system (L 6.25 per m³), new sources should be added to keep the market clearing price at this level. Thus the price should be at least as high as the current price, but no higher than L 6.25 per m³. The government should add new capacity only when the clearing price exceeds this level.

Although the price charged to commercial users is approximately 65 percent of the long-run marginal cost, the price charged to most households is only 20–25 percent of the long-run marginal cost. Because household demand represents about 80 percent of total demand (in both scenarios described earlier), concentrating the discussion of efficient water pricing on household water prices is relevant.[4]

---

4. The situation in Tegucigalpa is far from unusual. The 1992 *World Development Report* (World Bank 1992) concludes that households in many developing countries pay only about 20 percent of total water costs at the margin. Dinar and Subramanian (1997) also review a number of studies and conclude that there is a strong tendency for household water prices to be significantly below the long-run marginal cost.

A crucial issue is the response of household water demand to increases in water prices.[5] In table 11.1, households with tap water have an average demand of about 33 m^3 per month and pay slightly more than L 1 per m^3, whereas households without tap water consume only about 3.7 m^3 per month and pay about L 26 per m^3. If we assume that the demand functions for these two groups are otherwise identical, this yields two points on a common demand function. Assuming such a common demand function and that it is either linear or log-linear, the average water demand of households with piped water connections drops to 28 m^3 per month in the linear case, and to 10 m^3 per month in the log-linear case, when the price increases to L 6.25 per m^3. Possibly, the correct relationship in this range is more nearly linear (Strand 1998).

Now assume that the level of service among the group of households with access to piped water remains constant, and the water price is capped at L 6.25 (as new sources of water are added). Let us consider four demand scenarios, corresponding to constant and increasing coverage rates, and assume linear demand versus demand midway between linear and log-linear. The fastest increase in the clearing price then occurs under the combination of increasing coverage rates and a linear demand response, which reaches the long-run marginal cost by 1999. The slowest increase comes under the opposite combination—constant coverage rates and the intermediate demand response alternative. In this case, the clearing price reaches L 4 per m^3 in 2010, and the long-run marginal cost is thus not reached. In the two remaining cases, the long-run marginal cost is reached in 2002 and 2006, respectively. Arguably, linear demand is the more realistic alternative, which implies that the clearing price is likely to reach the long-run marginal cost within only a few years. Strengthening the argument for a rapid increase in the clearing price, households with piped connections that are currently facing low pressure and other restrictions have expressed a willingness to pay an average of about L 50 per month for improved service.

Implications of Low Water Prices in Tegucigalpa

This section discusses the consequences of low water prices in Tegucigalpa from a political economy perspective. Ideally, it would analyze the underlying causes of inefficiencies, including economic, political, and social conditions. In addition, to pave the way for more efficient management regimes, it would

---

5. See Humplick, Kudat, and Madanat (1993) for an approach for deriving water demand responses that focuses on supply quality rather than on prices.

also examine the relevant institutional constraints, although these should not necessarily be viewed as insurmountable hurdles, after all, radical institutional changes are often needed for successful reform. However, a full treatment of such complex issues would involve the analysis of incentive and information economics, as well as political-economic analysis.[6] In particular, the issue of how the apparently institutional roadblocks to progress depend on informational and incentive constraints is a complicated, but potentially fruitful, area for investigation. Many, perhaps most, problems with regulation of the Tegucigalpa water system can probably be traced to informational and incentive problems, mainly of the moral hazard type. For a general discussion of moral hazard and incentive problems, see Kreps (1990) and Laffont (1994); for the broader issue of public-sector regulation under informational constraints, see Laffont and Tirole (1993).[7]

Discussion of SANAA's Administration of the Tegucigalpa Water System

In recent years, SANAA has failed to make significant improvements to the Tegucigalpa water system. Piped water coverage to households has remained in the 50–60 percent range since the 1970s. Most households face limited hours of service and low pressure, and more than half the water may be lost in the distribution system and to illegal connections and unregistered use by SANAA consumers.

SANAA's cost structure is also inefficient. Walker and others (1999) conclude that the agency employs about three times more workers than necessary. This is partly because of explicit and implicit agreements between SANAA and unions that prohibit workers from performing multiple tasks. A lack of explicit performance criteria has led to the retention of a heavily bureaucratized and multilayered central management structure. Moreover,

---

6. For general discussions of problems with institutional reform in developing countries, see Israel (1987) and White (1990). In this particular context, for emphasis on regulatory, theoretical, and political-economic issues, see Savedoff and Spiller (1999), especially the introduction in chapter 1 and the case studies for Argentina and Chile describing the successful implementation of reform.

7. Laffont and Tirole argue that virtually all institutional and political economy problems can be traced to agency problems of the moral hazard or adverse selection type. Such agency problems arise in several types of relationships: between the public and politicians, between politicians and national government bureaucrats, between such bureaucrats and the agency providing the service, and between the agency and subcontractors. Although not necessarily adopting such an extreme position here, I clearly recognize that informational constraints play a great role in these relationships.

strong SANAA unions translate tariff increases into roughly equivalent increases in salaries. The agency as a whole (and the Tegucigalpa system in particular) has been running a continuous deficit over the last 15 years, even though the national government subsidizes SANAA's investment, electricity, and chemicals costs. Put simply, SANAA is not financially responsible.

Historical Water Prices in Tegucigalpa

Table 11.4 shows average real water prices for households and other users from 1978 to 1997. Clearly, real household water prices fell during this period. In 1995 the government tried to increase water prices in response to decreased SANAA revenues, but the new prices (depicted in the table as the 1997 prices, which correspond to the tariff rates in table 11.2 above) are still only little more than half the 1978 level. For commercial and industrial users, prices are relatively higher and are closer to the 1978 level.

SANAA has no direct control over its prices. Instead, the National Utility Board (CNSSP) sets them. Officially, the main argument for low household water prices is that water is a basic necessity and should be made affordable. This could be valid if all households had access to piped water. In practice, the argument has less merit. We have already seen that about 20 percent of all households in Tegucigalpa have no access to piped water and that another 20–30 percent are served by systems other than SANAA. Generally, those with no service are likely to be at the bottom of the income scale, and their water prices are 20–30 times higher than those of SANAA customers. This implies that low SANAA water prices make the overall income distribution less equitable, not more.

TABLE 11.4
Development of Real Prices of Water in Tegucigalpa, Selected Years, 1978–97
(L/m^3,1978 prices)

Type of user	1978	1983	1990	1995	1997
Household	0.38	0.32	0.25	0.15	0.21
Other[a]	0.50	0.41	0.37	0.21	0.45
Total	0.42	0.35	0.29	0.17	0.29

a. A weighted average of commercial, industrial, and government prices.
Source: SANAA (1995).

Political and Economic Consequences of Low Water Prices

The low water prices have numerous effects on the city's water supply and the behavior of consumers and institutions. In addition, they have allocational, macroeconomic, and social consequences.

LOCAL WATER SUPPLY IN TEGUCIGALPA. The low prices mean low revenues for SANAA. As noted earlier, SANAA is not able to cover even its variable costs through water tariffs. Consequently, the agency has minimized its activities, except those required directly by law, but not cut its staff. As a result, the water sector in Honduras causes a drain on public funds that amounts to about 1–2 percent of gross domestic product.

Low water prices reduce SANAA's incentive to extend coverage to new consumer groups. Almost all the people without service live in marginal *barrios*, many on the Tegucigalpa hillsides where installing connections and supply water is expensive. SANAA would lose money by extending service to these households, especially because it does not receive special funding for such service extensions. If SANAA consumers paid higher water prices, this would facilitate expansion and result in significant social gains. In fact, the potential net welfare gains from extending service to more households in Tegucigalpa may be several times more than total current SANAA revenues (Walker and others 1999).

SANAA also has few incentives to collect water bills as a result of the low prices. In Tegucigalpa, many households (20–30 percent) in any given year avoid paying their water bills entirely without being prosecuted. This is likely to lead to a social equilibrium in which avoiding payments is common and socially acceptable. For similar reasons, SANAA has few incentives to ensure that water connections are legal and to stop the theft of water from the system through illicit connections. Perhaps 20 percent or more of Tegucigalpa's population have illicit connections, but so far nothing has been done by the authorities to investigate this.

Today, barely more than half of SANAA's residential customers have water meters. Installing and reading water meters is costly and may not be profitable given the low prices. Low reading of meters is also likely to be widespread, according to private informed sources, although no figures are available. Given the low water prices and lack of financial responsibility, SANAA may have little incentive to investigate low readings.

The low water prices also discourage maintenance, improvements in the distribution system, and customer service. This issue has at least three aspects. First, low revenues limit the amount of maintenance SANAA can perform. Second, good maintenance is less profitable for SANAA because of the low prices. Third, the low prices may make it harder for residents to complain about inferior service. In fact, residents may be more accepting of the service because of the price.

The system discourages the government from improving water output from existing sources. This has consequences for La Tigra National Park. SANAA has little incentive to care for the park, because revenue from park water is low. The agency performs minimal maintenance on the water flow systems from the national park, and it does nothing whatsoever for general park protection. The legally designated caretaker for the park, Fundación Amitigra (Friends of La Tigra), helps to protect the park, but it lacks the financial resources to do so effectively. As Strand (1998) argues, the only practical way to provide secure financing of Fundación Amitigra operations is through a surcharge on the park's water. At current water prices, the political will does not exist to enact such a surcharge. An increase in the average household water price to, say, L 3 per m³ would make it easier to provide financing for park protection out of water revenues, and such an increase may be politically feasible (a required charge for park protection is about L 0.5 per m³).

The low prices mean little incentive exists for expanding existing water sources or opening up new ones. At current water prices, expansion projects appear economically inefficient and prohibitively expensive. The local and national water administration cannot afford them without large external subsidies to the Honduran water sector.

Private Agent Behavior. Low prices cause consumers who are not severely affected by low pressure and other restrictions to use water inefficiently. If water prices were increased to the long-run marginal cost, average household demand would drop by perhaps one-third (from 350 m³ to 200–250 m³ per year). Water consumption higher than this level is inefficient, because the social value of the water is lower than the cost of supply.

Low water prices tend to cause poor service, such as weak pressure and irregular supply. Consumers can respond rationally by installing private cisterns that are filled when running water is available and tapped at other times of the day. Such investments waste social resources when the alternative is fulltime water supply.

The lack of regular service to many households creates a number of incentive effects in the private water market. Residents extract and illegally resell water from the SANAA system. Allocation is particularly inefficient for households with no piped water service. Trucks bring water directly to consumers by trucks and sell it "by the bucket" at high prices. This is a costly way to supply water, and is thus a direct social waste.

OTHER OVERALL ECONOMIC AND SOCIAL CONSEQUENCES. As previously noted, low water prices have immediate income distribution consequences. Because households with regular SANAA connections and good service generally have higher incomes than those without, income distribution effects tend to be adverse, possibly grossly so. Walker and others (1999) indicate that the poorest groups of households with no regular service may spend as much as 10–15 percent of their gross household income on water, and still obtain little of it. However, those with connections constitute the majority of the population, and an overwhelming majority of people who vote or control other political resources. Table 11.2 demonstrates that the current pricing system still has a certain income leveling effect, as households with very high consumption (presumably the richest) pay relatively high water prices.

The main macroeconomic consequence of low water prices is the implication for public sector deficits. As previously noted, the water sector in Honduras costs the government the equivalent of about 1–2 percent of the country's gross domestic product. This contributes to a higher government debt burden, with serious long-run consequences. The International Monetary Fund has suspended Honduras for long periods for failing to fulfill government deficit targets. A large water sector deficit makes it more difficult for the government to fulfill its targets. Such a situation creates an uncertain climate for potential foreign investors, and recent direct foreign investment in Honduras has been small.

Strategic interactions with international lending and donor institutions, in particular the World Bank and the IADB, may affect water prices in Tegucigalpa. Currently these banks finance most major water sector investments in Honduras, largely on a concessional basis. The large deficits run up by the water sector in Honduras (and especially in Tegucigalpa) make the apparent need for such financing more visible. Under the current pricing structure, domestic financing of large new water projects appears unlikely. The rational short-run response of international institutions may be to bail out the Honduran government, because the apparent alternative is no action at all. Such bailouts make it less advantageous for the government to raise water prices and thereby make room for greater domestic financing. In game theory terms, viewing the Honduran government as a Stackelberg leader (by setting water prices) in the game against the international institutions (which decide on water sector financing), the Honduran approach of keeping water prices low, and thereby attracting bank financing, may constitute a subgame perfect equilibrium in the sequential game. In such a game, follower behavior by the banks distorts domestic incentives in the direction of setting low water prices, with all the resulting inefficiencies discussed previously. To create an efficient water situation, the World Bank and the IADB may need to take the lead, perhaps by making future loans contingent on a Honduran water pricing reform.

Water sector reform may have additional benefits. Tegucigalpa's municipal government has been reluctant to take over the water system, apparently out of concern that this would burden local government budgets (and, perhaps, also out of concern that it could be blamed for ongoing system problems). A different pricing regime might change its position.

The public health problems that are caused by a lack of access to running water are well known. Groups without running water suffer from higher rates of infectious diseases and infant mortality. Price reform is needed for Honduras to extend portable water service to such groups.

Water prices and coverage also affect migration. Currently, thousands of settlers arrive annually at the outskirts of Tegucigalpa, largely in the marginal *barrios*. Low water coverage discourages migration into the city, because most new settlers are forced to settle in sections of the city with expensive and poor quality water. Access to inexpensive, piped water would have the opposite effect on migration. Reforming the water system could have mixed effects on migration. If the dominant result of reform is higher coverage, that could increase migration. Many city officials and residents may consider that undesirable. But the overall effects of migration can be complex (Ray 1998). Arguably, greater urbanization could be an efficient mechanism for raising average living standards in a country such as Honduras. It costs the government less to provide basic services, such as transportation, sanitation, electricity, water service, telephone connections, and even television broadcasting, in urban areas than in the countryside. Furthermore, labor productivity is generally higher.

SOME FAVORABLE EFFECTS OF LOW WATER PRICES. This section has focused on the negative effects of low water prices, but low prices may have positive effects by limiting water administration corruption and the amount of money spent unnecessarily on infrastructure. In Tegucigalpa, significantly greater water revenues could create room for greater water administration waste in the form of higher salaries, overstaffing, and excessive spending on buildings and equipment. Higher water rates and more extensive metering of water might also create greater incentives for meter readers to accept bribes for underreporting water consumption. If the water administration ran a surplus instead of a deficit, higher authorities may fail to scrutinize its budget and expenses as thoroughly, potentially increasing the opportunities for water sector management corruption.

There may, however, be countervailing forces. The government would have greater incentives to monitor revenue flows if water sector revenues contributed more to the government's overall finances. Also, higher prices could create pressure to transfer the water system to a more efficient municipal or private organization. On balance, then, the net effect is ambiguous.

Equilibrium Water Prices and Service in a Political Economy Perspective

Let us consider factors that affect the setting of water prices in Tegucigalpa and the political possibilities for changing the current price regime. This section starts with a discussion of the price-setting mechanism as it has functioned for the last 10 years. It then conducts a stakeholder analysis, looking at the basic interests of important political and economic actors. Finally, the section weighs the practical possibilities for raising water prices in Tegucigalpa and for changing the organizational structure of the water sector.

The Determination of Water Prices in Tegucigalpa

As previously noted, a national utility board, the CNSSP, has set water prices in Tegucigalpa since its establishment in 1991. The CNSSP was created as part of Honduras's first structural adjustment program, when the World Bank and the IADB proposed that an independent agency regulate several public services. The statute for the CNSSP to set water prices directly conflicted with other legislation giving municipal operators the right to set local water tariffs. In practice, the CNSSP has confined itself to setting the SANAA tariff.

A basic premise for the creation of the CNSSP was that tariffs should be based on "the real economic cost of providing services to each category of consumers" (Article 1 in Decree 85-91). Although formally autonomous, in practice the CNSSP is linked to the Transport Ministry and has few independent economic resources at its disposal. As Walker and others (1999, p. 10) note, this board has, at best, served as "a body for the political negotiation of public service tariffs, rather than as a technical body dedicated to the independent determination of the costs of the service and equitable mechanisms for their recovery." In practice, the CNSSP's performance may have been even worse, because prices may have been set largely on the basis of the political interests of the board members and their constituencies, subject only to tacit approval from the national government, with little direct pressure from other groups or bodies. As a result, the board has set the water price as low as is politically possible. In an inflationary environment, a straightforward way of attaining such a goal has been to keep the nominal water price constant and let the real value of water deteriorate correspondingly.

Putting all the blame for falling water prices on the CNSSP—which is, after all, appointed by the government and influenced by a number of economic and political players—is, of course, too simple. The issue of water pricing is deeply integrated into the larger issue of possible water sector reform in Honduras. The question arises as to why the country has not already enacted a water sector reform.

In retrospect, one may question the wisdom of pushing for the establishment of a national pricing board. It probably would have been better for the World Bank and the IADB to have recommended the establishment of a technical commission, which could have relied on outside expertise and consultants to determine the correct real economic costs of water provision, and thus the appropriate water prices. The banks may have feared that a technical commission would be politically unacceptable and hoped that an independent board would be able to set prices according to the stipulated principles. Obviously, the board has failed to do so.

An Analysis of Stakeholders' Incentives

Table 11.5 presents a stakeholder analysis of the various major political and economic actors, and it describes their interests in water pricing reform and their ability to force policy changes. These actors fall into three basic types: external (1–4 in the table), internal political and administrative (5–10), and other internal (11–17).

Both the World Bank and the IADB strongly favor sectoral reform. They have potential leverage, because they may withhold both approved and potential future funding until Honduras begins the reform process. Other foreign actors, such as bilateral donors and lenders and international firms, also tend to favor reform, but they have less direct influence on the policies of the Honduran government.

Within the government, interests seem more diverse. Few officials in the national government support general sector reform, and SANAA is strongly against it. One national government agency that has come out in favor of reform is the Economic Cabinet, which is responsible for overall policies such as general resource allocation and budget balance. Cabinet members realize that World Bank and International Monetary Fund funding and support will be easier to obtain with reform than without it. On the more specific issue of water price increases, SANAA has naturally

TABLE 11.5
Stakeholder Analysis of Incentives to Promote Water Pricing Reform in Tegucigalpa

Player/group	Issue of interest	Current position	Resources available
World Bank	Promotes sectoral reform	Strong support	Basic loan financing US$30 million structural adjustment financing
Inter-American Development Bank	Promotes sectoral reform	Strong support	Investment loans to sector; US$35 million structural adjustment financing
International firms	Possible management, concession, and consultancy contracts	Support	Possible technical assistance to assist reform
Bilateral lenders	Provision of financial assistance	Varied positions	Financial resources, technical assistance
SANAA	Remaining in power of water administration	Strong opposition to general reform, favors price increases	Technical and informational capacity, tacit support from government
Honduran president	Responsible for domestic issues and relationship with international lenders	No apparent interest in issue	Executive power, but cannot directly block congressional decisions
Honduran economic cabinet	Balance of payments improvments, infrastructure efficiency	Leaning toward support	Ability to influence president
Honduran ministries	Responsible for sectoral development	No declared positions	Various political and adminstrative influences
CNSSP	Existing tariff regulation	Strongly opposed	Ability to question proposals, influence with president

(table continues on following page)

Table 11.5 continues

Player/group	Issue of interest	Current position	Resources available
Honduran congress	Overall legislation and resource use	No declared position	Legislative power could block reform
Municipality	May take over administration from SANAA	Disinterested	Lobbying power, could block reform
SANAA union	May lose jobs, suffer corruption	Strong opposition	Lobbying power
Fundación Amitigra	Caretaker for national park	Strong support	Small financial and political resources
Public users of SANAA system	May face higher water prices, but get improved service	No clear public opinion, but skeptical	Political/voting power
Households without access to SANAA system	Need better service	No expressed opinion	Small
Domestic private industry	Fear increased tariffs, but contract opportunities	No expressed opinion	Lobbying power
Political parties	Popularity gains/losses	No clear opinion	Influence on Congress

Note: This table, with few modifications, is adapted from Walker and others (1999), who make a similar analysis of incentives for general water sector reform in Honduras.
Sources: Author; Walker and others (1999).

come out in favor, and so has the Economic Cabinet. Other political actors are either resisting price increases or are silent on the issue. At the local level, the city government of Tegucigalpa is, as previously noted, skeptical about the possibility of taking over the local water system.

Among other domestic actors, households with access to water are reluctant to accept either reform or price increases. We may roughly distinguish between households with relatively high income and generally good service (virtually all of which are served by SANAA), and households with lower income and poor service (including a number of regular SANAA customers and many of the illicit and private non-SANAA consumers). Both groups fear that an independently run and less strictly controlled water administration may impose higher prices without improving service. Members of the former group already have good water service and may think they have little to gain from water sector reform. They would face the possibility of a doubling or tripling of water prices without a guarantee of service improvements. This group may be small, but it is important. It comprises most vocal and politically resourceful individuals, including all politicians and top bureaucrats. The second group is much larger and could have more to gain from water sector reform, because there is more room for service improvement. But they may also lose more by water price increases, because they currently face lower water prices than do high-income groups and are less tolerant of given price increases. Thus, uncertainty about service improvements could make this group—at least, those who are regular SANAA clients—even more negative toward water price reform. Low-income households with non-SANAA service should be more positive, because some of them already pay water prices well in excess of the long-run marginal cost.

Households currently without water access stand to gain the most from reform. This group is large (at least about 20 percent of the population, and perhaps more) but unorganized. Many are illiterate or have recently migrated to Tegucigalpa. This group has little political clout, because it has few active voters.

Overall, most potential voters, and virtually all politically vocal and resourceful individuals, have access to low-cost piped water. This implies that water price increases are politically unpopular. Therefore, a proposal for water sector reform is unlikely to win support from the president, Congress, or political parties.

Conclusion

At present, little organized effort exists to challenge the Tegucigalpa water sector's pricing and administrative regime. The World Bank and the IADB can play a key role, but they have not yet pushed strongly for pricing and sectoral reform—perhaps because of the absence of broad domestic support for such reform.[8]

However, more direct pressure by the World Bank and other institutions seems to be needed if reform is to take place. The institutions must,

---

8. The banks also must be very careful when treading into politically sensitive territory in which their policies clash strongly with those of the borrowing countries' political leadership. Kreuger (1998) points out that some of the failures of World Bank projects have exposed the Bank to attack by various critics, including countries that receive funding from it.

however, be careful in applying such pressure. The stakeholder analysis in this chapter shows that a key to favorable policy change is winning the support of several important domestic political actors. The implementation of reform requires broad public agreement. Such consensus must be built within population groups with access to piped water, because they are economically and politically dominant.

To be politically feasible, a water sector price reform must be introduced gradually, and it must be accompanied by noticeable service improvements to compensate households for price increases. The government could give guarantees on a year-to-year basis, linking water price increases to prespecified service improvements. The water company should install meters in the households affected by price increases. This would allow for the implementation of efficient marginal pricing without corresponding large increases in household water expenditures, at least initially. Officials could set prices for inframarginal consumption units lower than marginal ones, thereby generating some of the benefits of reform (in particular, reducing public overuse of water and increasing the marginal value of water for the water administration) without creating great public resistance to the reform. Water administration revenues would then increase less rapidly, avoiding some of the problems associated with falling revenues that were noted previously. Given that the consequences of reform are positive for the average consumer, reform advocates should, over time, be able to build a political consensus for gradually increasing water prices. It is paramount that they inform and convince the public about the positive relationship between increasing water prices and better service. The successful case of Chile, where similar reform has already been implemented, could serve as a useful example (Morandé and Doña 1999).

The exact political mechanism by which a popular consensus in favor of increased water prices can be translated into political action, however, remains a complex question. As stated previously, the World Bank and the IADB probably should be far more involved in this process.

References

Dinar, Ariel, and Ashok Subramanian. 1997. *Water Pricing Experiences—An International Perspective*. Technical Paper no. 386. Washington, D.C.: World Bank.

Humplick, Frannie, Ayse Kudat, and Samer Madanat. 1993. *Modeling Household Responses to Water Supply: A Service Quality Approach*. Transportation, Water, and Urban Development Department Working Paper no. 4. World Bank, Washington, D.C.

Israel, Arturo. 1987. *Institutional Development: Incentives to Performance*. Baltimore, Maryland: The Johns Hopkins University Press.

Kreps, David M. 1990. *A Course in Microeconomic Theory*. Princeton, New Jersey: Princeton University Press.

Kreuger, Anne O. 1998. "Whither the World Bank and the IMF?" *Journal of Economic Literature* 36(4): 1983–2020.

Laffont, Jean-Jacques. 1994. *The Economics of Uncertainty and Information*. Cambridge, Massachusetts: MIT Press.

Laffont, Jean-Jacques, and Jean Tirole. 1993. *A Theory of Incentives in Procurement and Regulation*. Cambridge, Massachusetts: MIT Press.

Morandé, Felipe, and Juan E. Doña. 1999. "Governance and Regulation in Chile: Fragmentation of the Public Water Sector." In W. Savedoff and P. Spiller, eds., *Spilled Water: Institutional Commitment in the Provision of Water Services*. Washington, D.C.: Inter-American Development Bank.

Ray, Debraj. 1998. *Development Economics*. Princeton, New Jersey: Princeton University Press.

Salgado, Artica, and Leslie Jeaneth. 1996. "Valoricación economica del agua para uso urbano, proveniente del Parque Nacional la Tigra, Tegucigalpa, Honduras." Masters thesis, Centro Agronómico Tropical de Investigación Enseñanza, Turrialba, Costa Rica.

SANAA (Servicio Autónomo Nacional de Acueductos y Alcantarillados or National Water Service). 1995. *Situacion del sistema de agua potable y saneamiento*. Document no. ST-005/95. Tegucigalpa.

_____. 1997. *Informe anual 1996*. Division metropolitana, departemento de operacion (Metropolitan Division, Operations Department). Tegucigalpa.

Savedoff, William, and Pablo Spiller. 1999. *Spilled Water: Institutional Commitment in the Provision of Water Services*. Washington, D.C.: Inter-American Development Bank.

Strand, Jon. 1998. "Economic and Ecologic Analyses of Parque National La Tigra." Consultancy report, prepared for the Inter-American Development Bank. Oslo, Norway.

Walker, Ian, and Fidel Ordoñez. 1995. "Encuesta de usuarios de agua en Honduras." Consultancy report, ESA Consultants. Tegucigalpa.

Walker, Ian, Max Velásquez, Fidel Ordoñez, and Florencia Rodriguez. 1999. "Regulation, Organization, and Incentives: The Political Economy of Potable Water Services. Case Study: Honduras." In William Savedoff and Pablo Spiller, eds., *Spilled Water: Institutional Commitment in the Provision of Water Services*. Washington, D.C.: Inter-American Development Bank.

White, Louise G. 1990. *Implementing Policy Reforms in LDCs*. London: Lynne Rienner Publishers.

Whittington, Dale, Donald T. Lauria, and Xinming Mu. 1991. "A Study of Water Vending and Willingness to Pay for Water in Onitsha, Nigeria." *World Development* 19(2/3): 179–98.

World Bank. 1992. *World Development Report 1992: Development and the Environment*. New York: Oxford University Press.

12

An [US]
Investigation
into the
Reasons Why
Water Utilities
Choose
Particular
Residential
Rate
Structures

Julie A. Hewitt

The price of water is usually administratively determined rather than being the result of a *tâtonnement* process, such as conducted by the Walrasian auctioneer. Although a significant academic and policy literature suggests that market prices are preferable to administrative rates, this chapter looks at whether the focus on market pricing has obscured the fact that not all administered water rates are created equal. Some administered rates more closely approximate market processes than others. The following analysis asks why utilities choose market mimicking rates. It focuses on residential water rates, because residential customers are more homogeneous across utilities than agricultural, commercial, or industrial customers.

The next section presents background information on residential water rate structures. It focuses on the United States, but also includes some details about Latin America. The third section provides a broad overview of the academic literature on residential water rates and raises the question of why a utility would ever choose increasing block rates. The fourth section provides a theoretical answer based on the theory of price discrimination, and the subsequent section offers empirical evidence in support of this answer. The conclusion summarizes the findings and describes directions for further research.

Residential Water Rate Structures

The American Water Works Association (AWWA) has published a manual on water rates since 1954. Although every edition has suggested that rate making be based on cost-of-service principles, the latest edition (AWWA 1991) notes several alternative rate structures that utilities increasingly employ. Two of these structures have market mimicking potential: increasing block tariff (IBT) and seasonal (or peak) rates.

The IBT structure is a series of marginal prices that increase in steps as consumption rises. The seasonal rate is a type of peak/off-peak structure in which the peak period is a season, usually summer, the high point of irrigation. In both cases, as demand shifts far enough to the right of the quantity-price space during peak usage, the result is that water is scarcer and the price paid for the marginal unit of water is higher. In the case of IBTs, this occurs only for some households, whereas in the seasonal rate case, this occurs for all households and in aggregate. These rate structures have more potential than uniform or decreasing block (DB) rates to mimic a *tâtonnement* process in response to an increase in demand. With the latter rates, an increase in demand produces no change or a decrease in price, as if supply were either perfectly price elastic, or even negatively sloped. Although the academic literature lends some support for the notion that IBT and seasonal rates are more efficient than uniform and DB rates, academics have never systematically studied the residential water rate structure as an endogenous choice.

The AWWA-Recommended Rate Methodology

Before considering rate making, we should look at the AWWA-recommended rate methodology (AWWA 1991). AWWA's method starts with determining utility revenue requirements (that is, projected costs or budget) for the rate period. This total is then allocated to broad cost components, such as the number of customers or accounts; the base, or average load; and the costs of extra capacity, or peak load. Next, utility officials allocate these cost components to customer classes, such as residential, commercial, and industrial, via unit costs (economists' average costs) to determine the total revenue to be recovered from each customer class. Finally, they design rates to recover these costs as nearly as possible.

One might be tempted to object to this methodology on the basis that it is average cost pricing, rather than the theoretically defensible marginal cost pricing. However, several points should be noted. First, the result is historically-based average cost pricing only if the "projected" period is backward looking. Second, when forward looking, the AWWA's rate methodology seems similar to the normal cost pricing behavior of manufacturing firms that can carry inventories of their final product and, hence, can choose prices, production, and storage over time to maximize profits (Philips 1983). That is, although this methodology may resemble average cost pricing, one can justify normal cost pricing as profit maximizing price discrimination, in which discounted marginal costs of production through time equal discounted marginal revenue of sales, and sales can occur from production or inventory.

Returning to the question at hand: What type of rate structure does the AWWA's cost-of-service methodology produce? The utility first sets the service charge based on costs associated with customers, such as metering and billing, regardless of volumetric charges. Next, the utility sets the volumetric charges based on the base load and extra capacity. For the volumetric charges, the AWWA manual recommends a single-rate structure applied to all customer classes. If the utility cannot categorize customers into classes such as residential, commercial, and industrial, which have different consumption patterns and, therefore, different cost burdens, then it should establish a uniform volumetric rate. In this case, the overall rate is a two-part tariff.

If the utility can distinguish between customer classes, AWWA recommends using a block rate designed to charge different marginal rates to the different classes. To determine the block boundaries, measure account usage per billing period on the horizontal axis and probability on the vertical axis of the quantity-price space, and place a probability distribution function (pdf) for each customer class on the graph. For a fairly typical utility, the residential class will be the leftmost pdf, followed by the commercial class and, finally, the industrial class. Although the central tendency of each pdf will be distinct, the tails of the distributions will likely overlap somewhat. The quantities at which the pdfs cross define the block change points for the block rate structure.[1] The marginal rate associated with each consumption range is the sum of base load unit cost (constant across all classes) and the extra capacity associated with the customer class most represented in that consumption range. The marginal rates decline with consumption if the customer classes place successively lower burdens on system capacity above the base, producing a DB rate with a service charge. Unless larger customers' extra capacity costs are greater than those of smaller customers—that is, more of their consumption occurs during peak periods—the AWWA methodology does not lead to a market mimicking rate.[2]

---

1. Choosing the block change points in this way minimizes the amount of consumption that one class is billed at the rate designed for another class.

2. The AWWA manual presents a parallel methodology, which is similar except that the cost components are customer, commodity (total volume), and demand (maximum rate). Unlike base costs, commodity costs do not include the capital costs of average load. Demand costs include the full capital costs of meeting peak demand, whereas extra capacity costs include peak demand less average demand. If customers' contributions to peak and average loads are proportional, the two methods will result in similar rates. Without additional information, predicting which method is more likely to lead to market mimicking rates is difficult.

Descriptive Statistics on Rate Structures

Let us take a look at descriptive statistics regarding rate structures in the United States. Prior to the invention of meter technology in the early 1900s, water utilities charged a flat rate or fixed charge per billing period, regardless of consumption. They adopted volumetric rates with the advent of metering technology. The AWWA-recommended single schedule designed to segment customer classes remained the predominant rate until relatively recently, when utilities increasingly adopted uniform and IBTs, as well as customer class-based rates. In recent years, with the adoption of more types of rate structures, analysts have begun collecting data on the use of the different structures.

In a 1994 biannual survey of water utilities in more than 100 of the largest U.S. cities, Ernst & Young (1994) report that 38 percent use DB rates, 37 percent use uniform rates, 22 percent use IBTs, and fewer than 3 percent use seasonal rates.[3] On a regional basis, IBTs are most popular in the West and South, where they are used by 32 percent and 30 percent of the utilities surveyed, respectively. In contrast, 11 percent of Midwestern and 8 percent of Northeastern utilities use IBTs. In every region, the percentage of utilities employing DB rates fell from 1986 to 1994. The use of DB rates dropped from 30 to 4 percent in the West (the largest relative change), from 54 to 36 percent in the South, and from 76 to 71 percent in the Midwest. Except in the Midwest, there is a clear trend away from using DB rates, and a weaker trend toward IBTs. (The 1986 survey covered only 82 cities, of which just three reported using IBTs).

The most comprehensive survey of water utilities in the United States is the Community Water Systems Survey, conducted periodically by the U.S. Environmental Protection Agency (1997). For its 1995 water systems survey, the agency questioned 3,700 community water systems out of nearly 50,000 water utilities in the United States, receiving responses from 54 percent. Of those responding, 49 percent reported using uniform rates, 16 percent reported using DB rates, 11 percent reported using IBTs, and fewer than 1 percent reported using seasonal rates. Taken together, the Ernst & Young and Environmental Protection Agency surveys suggest that larger utilities are more inclined than smaller utilities to adopt IBTs.

---

3. In reality, most rate structures classified as uniform are really two-part tariffs (a uniform rate combined with a fixed charge). Although distinguishing between these two-rate structures is critical in econometric analysis and revenue prediction, the industry typically uses the term uniform to mean two-part tariffs. Nearly all utilities employ fixed charges.

I conducted a brief review of Central and South American water agencies as part of a separate research project; the results are somewhat useful in describing whether developing country rate structures differ greatly from those in the United States. Although this review is an ongoing work, clearly many Latin American countries employ IBTs. For example, La Paz, Bolivia; Mexico City; the urban areas of Belize; the Canton Quito and Esmeralda regions of Ecuador; and all of Uruguay use IBTs. The IBT structures in these areas use anywhere from 3 to 13 blocks. In this connection, we need to keep in mind that in developing countries, international lending authorities may influence rates for the infrastructure projects that they finance, whereas U.S. utilities generally face little direct external rate making pressure.

These statistics show that IBTs are neither uncommon nor predominant, and they are much more common than seasonal rates. Thus, it would be fruitful to understand why certain utilities voluntarily choose IBT or seasonal rates; whether such rates are efficient; and what effect, if any, lenders' policies have on their use. The next section provides a broad overview of the academic literature, suggesting a set of conflicting assumptions that lead one to wonder why a utility would voluntarily choose these types of rates.

Overview of the Literature

The economics literature on residential water demand has focused rather narrowly on the price elasticity of demand. The appropriateness of water rate structures has become an issue in some communities only as demand growth has outstripped supply. Whether water rate increases induce conservation depends on the price elasticity of demand.

Over the last 20 years or so, water utilities began to use rates other than the AWWA-recommended rates noted previously. In an article published just as utilities were becoming more likely to eschew such rates, Willig (1978) demonstrates that one could always find a DB schedule that was Pareto superior to a uniform rate. No literature followed regarding the optimality results of IBTs, although utilities continued switching to IBTs.

Many utility managers thought that residential water demand was fairly price inelastic, and economists had difficulty demonstrating otherwise until recently. This difficulty stemmed from the focus on data collected from systems that used IBTs, and the confounding effect that quantity has on price with an IBT. As consumption rises over a certain threshold, marginal price rises also, according to an IBT schedule, although marginal willingness to pay decreases as we move along a demand function. Unless care is taken to account for the rate schedule effect in estimating a demand curve, the combination of these two opposing effects may result in an estimated price coefficient that is insignificantly different from zero. Until a solution was found for separating the rate schedule effect from the demand curve (Hewitt and Hanemann 1995), the reasons that utilities chose certain rate structures did not appear to be an economics issue. Hewitt and Hanemann (1995) demonstrate that water demand can be responsive to price, although their price elasticity estimate—an elastic summer demand for water—may not be widely applicable outside the Texas community of their study. Their results imply that a switch to IBTs, or a rate increase (regardless of whether the structure is IBT), or both, can induce water conservation.

Many authors have presumed that summer demand is more elastic than winter demand, and hence that IBT and seasonal rates induce conservation. This presumption, although not critical to the outcome of these studies, is nonetheless troubling in view of water utilities' voluntary adoption of these rate structures. A theoretical underpinning of industrial organization is that profit maximizing firms charge higher prices to customers with more inelastic demands (for example, Perloff 1999, pp. 485–86).

The fact that utilities continue to voluntarily switch to market mimicking rates is puzzling, in light of the theory of price discrimination and the presumption that summer demand is more elastic than winter demand.

Price Discrimination and Rate Structure

Consider a more in-depth model of residential water demand that demonstrates that price discrimination is the rationale for IBTs. Pigou (1932) identifies three degrees of price discrimination according to the firm's ability to distinguish customer classes. First-degree is perfect price discrimination. Second-degree is the type embodied by block rates, meaning that customers face the same rate schedule, but self-select the portion containing their marginal willingness to pay. Third-degree is the type in which customers are grouped according to some observable, discrete characteristic that implies the rate the utility should charge them. Pigou (1932, pp. 280–81) suggests that first-degree discrimination was unlikely, because it requires bargaining separately with each customer, and he summarily dismisses second-degree price discrimination. Thus, he focused on the third-degree type.[4]

---

4. Some water utilities practice third-degree price discrimination. This discrimination takes the form of different rates or rate schedules for groups that differ according to such factors as geographic location. These rate differences are not precisely equal to cost-of-service differentials.

One feature of the IBTs of second-degree price discrimination is that they contribute to equity by allowing low- and fixed-income households to pay lower rates for water than other households. Under IBTs, these households must consume less to obtain a lower rate, which is likely to be the case when income and water demand are highly correlated. How might a utility use equity as a means of arriving at an IBT as its optimal rate structure? Economists have long argued that utilities should use marginal cost pricing for efficiency. However, charging the marginal cost for all units will lead to a deficit or surplus, as average costs are either above or below marginal cost. The usual remedy is a lump sum tax or subsidy. Writing in 1895, Wicksell (1994, p. 104) was apparently the first to suggest that the lump sum need not be collected as a part of general taxes, but could be tied to consumption.

Tying the lump sum to consumption to improve equity can lead to an IBT, regardless of whether the lump sum is required to make up a deficit or disburse a surplus. Even if the starting point is a uniform rate set at a constant marginal cost—with a premium paid for consumption units above some threshold to make up a deficit, or a subsidy given below a threshold to disburse a surplus—some consumption units are sold at a price other than the marginal cost. Unless demand is completely unresponsive to price or income, an equitable IBT in the face of constant marginal cost distorts consumption somewhat. However, rate makers might be interested in making the tradeoff of efficiency for equity.

Though water analysts often mention equity as an advantage of IBTs, one might question whether it alone is sufficient to warrant the adoption of IBTs, or simply is consistent with other reasons for adopting IBTs. The possibility that utility managers are not concerned with efficiency because utilities are usually not organized as for-profit firms argues that equity alone is a sufficient reason. However, even though managers might state that efficiency is not a motivation, there is reason to doubt this: any rents earned from supplying water services efficiently would accrue to managers in the form of nonmonetary benefits. Furthermore, the equity argument for IBTs does not explain why it would be of greater concern in the western and southern regions of the United States, where utilities choose IBTs more frequently. Further probing of the theory of price discrimination therefore seems to be warranted.

As suggested above, households are relatively homogenous across utilities, at least with respect to other utility customer classes. Still, households are surely heterogeneous, at least in one broad respect: the amount of water used outdoors. Thus, we can break down household demand for water into indoor uses and outdoor uses. Assume that households have similar indoor demands, but that their outdoor demands vary, perhaps dramatically. Suppose that outdoor demands range anywhere from zero (at all prices) to a downward sloping demand with quantities significant relative to indoor demand, depending on the size of the household's lot and its tastes in greenery. The household's total demand for water is the horizontal sum of these demands, producing a range of total demands that vary from indoor only to indoor plus the largest outdoor demand. Again, if faced with an IBT or seasonal rate, the households with the greater outdoor demand are also the households with the greater total demand, and the ones most likely to pay the higher marginal rates.

If the utility is to engage in profitable price discrimination, managers face the central difficulty of determining the elasticity of demand of various household types. If households could be placed into one of several outdoor water demand classes (observationally equivalent to total demand classes if indoor usage is truly the same for all households), then the utility could employ third-degree price discrimination, using perhaps a set of two-part tariffs differing in entry fee, marginal price, or both. However, if indoor demands are not truly the same for all households, the utility can never really be certain which households have the greater outdoor demands, unless separate indoor and outdoor meters are employed. Leland and Meyer (1976) hypothesize that second-degree price discrimination occurs when the monopolist cannot directly observe a meaningful characteristic by which to segment customers, instead using block rates to induce households to reveal the information that the utility otherwise lacks (see also Tsur, chapter 5 in this volume).

Are indoor and outdoor uses really unobservable? In previous studies recognizing different demand motivations for indoor and outdoor usage, authors have commonly assumed that indoor demand is stable through the year and outdoor demand occurs only in the summer (Howe and Linaweaver 1967). If so, one can reasonably equate indoor demand to winter demand and subtract indoor demand from summer demand to derive outdoor demand. The measurement error introduced by this breakdown is a function of the variability of indoor demand during the year. Indoor water use surely depends on the number of people at home, as well as on the utilization rate of appliances that use water.[5] Thus, utilities face difficulty in using third-degree price discrimination to effectively discriminate

---

5. For instance, households may take vacations at different times of the year, and individuals' bathing, showering, and laundry patterns may vary throughout the year. Finally, the number of household members in residence may vary seasonally.

between low- and high-demand households. Note that seasonal rates are a form of third-degree price discrimination in which billing periods of a household's water consumption are distinguished; however, for this type of price discrimination to be profitable, it must be true that summer demand is less elastic than winter demand for all households, not just some households. That this condition does not hold for all households is a possible explanation for the low use of seasonal rates.

A utility will, of course, voluntarily adopt second-degree price discriminatory rates in the form of IBTs only if that is in its best interest. To demonstrate that such rates are in the utility's best interest, we must make an assumption about the marginal cost of supplying households. A convenient assumption is that the marginal cost of water is constant. Analysts often argue that IBTs are appropriate precisely because marginal costs differ (that is, that the marginal cost of outdoor, peak period, or extra capacity consumption is higher than the marginal cost of indoor, off-peak, or base capacity consumption), but this argument is weakened by the utility's inability to determine how water is used. Even if one argued that capacity costs differ for the two types of demand, the utility without separate indoor and outdoor meters can charge only an average marginal price, which by definition would be constant. If marginal costs are indeed increasing, the following argument is strengthened.

Figure 12.1 shows the demand functions of two types of households, where $D_A < D_B$. These functions represent the total water demand of each household. A marginal revenue function is associated with each demand function, and marginal cost is constant. If the water utility could classify households into demand classes for third-degree price discrimination, the optimal prices would be found by noting the intersection of marginal cost and the marginal revenue functions. These determine the profit maximizing quantities to deliver to households in each customer class, with the profit maximizing price determined by the demand curves.[6] Note that the profit maximizing marginal prices rise with quantity consumed, or $P_A < P_B$ while $Q_A < Q_B$.

Given that the utility cannot observe the demand type of a particular household, but knows that it is one of these types, the values, P_A, P_B, and Q_A, become parameters defining the rate schedule, with Q denoting the household's choice of water consumption. The utility will present all households with the following volumetric rate structure for household bills:

---

6. To simplify this, the monthly service charge is ignored, but it could be added without loss of generality.

FIGURE 12.1
Utility's Construction of an IBT rate

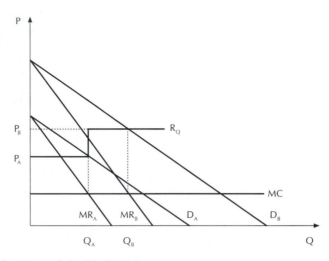

Note: All terms are defined in the text.
Source: Author.

$$R(Q) = \begin{cases} P_A Q \text{ if } 0 < Q \le Q_A \\ P_A Q_A + P_B \cdot (Q - Q_A) \text{ if } Q_A < Q \end{cases}$$

where $R(Q)$ is the monetary value of the bill associated with the consumption of Q.

Differentiating $R(Q)$ (the monetary value of the bill associated with consumption of Q) with respect to Q results in an IBT structure, shown as the step function, R_Q, in figure 12.1. Note that each household will choose the same consumption level (Q_A or Q_B) under either second- or third-degree price discrimination, assuming negligible income effects.

If the utility has a zero-profit constraint, such that it can neither incur a loss nor earn a profit, it can alter the block threshold (say to Q_A'), and the monthly service charge to produce lump-sum effects that achieve the zero profit condition. If the utility can do this so such that $Q_A < Q_A' < Q_B$, then consumption behavior is unchanged at the margin.

Of course, this example results in a rate with two blocks that is driven by the use of two distinct residential demand functions in figure 12.1. More generally, let household demand vary from D_A to D_B with some household characteristic denoted by the parameter, φ. The optimal price schedule depends on the distribution of φ. If household demand varies continuously and monotonically with φ, the optimal nonuniform price is a continuous function of quantity. Although the characteristics that lead to an IBT structure are not easily summarized, discontinuities in the φ distribution or a nonmonotonic relationship between φ and demand functions lead to IBTs (Brown and Sibley 1986; Goldman, Leland, and Sibley 1984).

Although figure 12.1 demonstrates a utility's construction of an IBT, we turn now to the question of which household's demand is more elastic: A or B.[7] Let the vertical intercept (or reservation price) for D_A be A and for D_B be B, where $A < B$. The price elasticity of demand for D_A households is $-(A + MC)/(A - MC)$, whereas the price elasticity of demand for D_B households is $-(B + MC)/(B - MC)$. Both elasticities are greater than one in absolute value, with D_A being the more elastic. Thus, the higher marginal price is indeed charged on units of demand that are less elastic, as is always the case in price discrimination.

This demonstrates that an IBT can be profitable, but does it also imply that summer demand is less elastic than winter demand? The answer is not readily apparent. To begin with, note that D_A and D_B are demands for a single household, not aggregated household demand. The most elastic portion of a linear demand is the upper left segment. The more a household consumes, moving along its demand curve, the less elastic is its demand. Of course, demand may take other forms; however, the fact that utilities voluntarily choose IBTs tells us that the households in their service areas with greater demand have more inelastic demand, other things being constant. By contrast, it is difficult to reconcile the notion of a less elastic summer outdoor demand with the rule of thumb that the demand for luxury goods is more elastic than the demand for necessities.

To summarize the discussion of figure 12.1, sufficient conditions for a utility to choose an IBT structure are that the utility know there are different classes of households according to demand (although it cannot distinguish these classes), and that households with greater demand also have more inelastic demand (guaranteed in figure 12.1 by $A < B$). Despite AWWA's emphasis on cost-of-service based rates, marginal cost differences are not necessary to justify IBTs.

Factors Influencing the Choice of IBTs

To return to the question of which utilities will choose IBTs, let φ (from above) be a parameter that indexes outdoor demands. This is a useful interpretation

---

7. The figure contains linear demands for ease of exposition, and the following elasticity discussion is based on linear demands. These results are not restricted to linear demands; however, a categorization of demand forms for which results are similar is beyond the scope of this chapter.

of φ if heterogeneous total demands are more likely to be driven by household variations in outdoor demands than by variations in indoor demands. Furthermore, as φ increases, a household's total demand shifts outward, and there is a monotonic relationship between φ and demand. Thus, we need only concern ourselves with the distribution of φ and factors affecting its distribution, which might lead to discontinuities in water rates.

What factors influence the shape of the distribution of φ? Clearly, weather affects φ. As lawn and garden watering is a significant outdoor use of water, consider the effect weather has on watering. The water needs of various species of plants are characterized by the plants' potential evapotranspiration, which is a complicated function of average daily temperature, wind speed, humidity, and sunshine. A portion of potential evapotranspiration may be met by rainfall. Plants thrive when the amount of water applied is equal to potential evapotranspiration less rainfall. Plants in areas with periodic rainfall throughout the summer need less watering than plants in areas with longer, sunnier, and hotter growing seasons or in areas without consistent rainfall (other factors being constant). Thus, the probability distributions of weather variables affect the distribution of φ, possibly causing multiple modes in the φ distribution, if not actual discontinuities.

A second factor affecting the φ distribution is the heterogeneity of households with respect to landscaped areas requiring watering. That is, households in one utility's service area may have similar lot sizes and vegetation, whereas those in another utility's area may be more variable. Utility service areas in arid regions are likely to have a broader distribution of plant species (some with native vegetation, others with more water-intensive vegetation) than utilities in more humid areas. Other factors being constant, utilities with larger service areas are likely to have a greater diversity of plant species. They are also likely to have greater variety in household lot sizes. Each of these factors contributes to the probability that the φ distribution has several modes (or peaks), or is descrete, both of which lead to the use of IBTs.

Factors Mitigating the Use of IBTs

Recently, the utility management literature has noted the potential of IBTs to cause utility revenue to be more variable (Chesnutt, McSpadden, and Christianson 1996). This may occur if a greater percentage of a utility's revenue is due to consumption of units of water at the margin where prices are highest. (Note, however, that in choosing the block thresholds, the utility can affect its level of revenue variability.) These results may have significant implications for the financial health of water utilities. Thus, utilities that are more concerned with financial effects will be less likely, other things being constant, to employ IBTs.

What characterizes utilities that are more likely to be concerned with financial health? Many municipalities in the United States borrow funds through the bond market to finance infrastructure projects. To maintain high-quality bond ratings, and thereby keep interest payments lower, these utilities must generate revenue for capital expenses (that is, the amount of revenue that exceeds operating and maintenance expenditures) equivalent to at least 125 percent of the annual principal and interest obligations of the issued bonds. This constraint, often explicitly stated in the bond prospectus, provides utilities with a strong incentive to avoid risking reductions in revenue.[8]

Utilities that borrow to finance capital spending will thus be more interested in rates that generate minimum, stable, and predictable revenue. To reliably predict revenue under a uniform rate or two-part tariff, the utility need predict only total consumption and number of customers. But to reliably predict revenue under a block rate, the utility must predict how many units are sold at each marginal price.[9] This, of course, requires an understanding of why different households consume different quantities of water. However, we have seen that a utility cannot observe an individual household's various uses of water. Small utilities are less likely to have staff to undertake such an exercise, and will therefore be especially uncertain of the distribution of revenue under IBTs compared with the distribution under uniform or DB rates.

Empirical Evidence Supporting the Price Discrimination Rationale

As noted previously, areas with longer, sunnier, hotter, and drier growing seasons are more likely to have φ distributions that cause utilities to choose IBTs. In a regional sense, this is apparent from the Ernst & Young (1994) survey results described earlier. The western and southern regions of the United States, which are generally the longer, sunnier, hotter, and drier areas, have the highest adoption rates for IBTs.

---

8. Of course, utilities could mitigate the risk of variable revenue through the use of a revenue stabilization fund (AWWA 1992). However, the extent to which utilities avail themselves of this option is unclear.

9. A utility will clearly have some information on its units sold at each price when such rates are already in place. See Hirshleifer, DeHaven, and Milliman (1960) on the unacceptability of a trial-and-error rate setting process.

To test this hypothesis at the utility level, one has to combine the Ernst & Young data with National Weather Service (U.S. National Oceanic and Atmospheric Administration 1994) data by city. Means of the weather variables were calculated for the subsets of observations employing and not employing IBTs. Table 12.1 shows the results, which are consistent with regional level results. The service areas of utilities employing IBTs have, on average, sunnier, warmer, and drier weather and longer growing seasons. Each of these factors contributes to higher plant evapotranspiration rates. However, these differences are not statistically significant. This is likely due to the small number of observations, the possible selectivity bias of considering only utilities in large cities, the variability of weather, and weather being just one factor affecting utilities' choice of rate structure. A more complete model is necessary, one based on more data than are available in the Ernst & Young study.

The more complete model of utility behavior explains the discrete dependent variable measuring rate structure. The dependent variable employed here denotes one of three rate structures: uniform, DB, or IBT. Although the focus of the discussion has mainly been on IBTs, the model also distinguishes between DB and uniform rates because the AWWA-recommended methodology and revenue variability effects favor the choice of DB rates. The model employs the U.S. Environmental Protection Agency's

TABLE 12.1
Weather Data, Utilities with and without IBTs

Weather conditions	Not employing IBT	Employing IBT
Sunny days	101.33	113.21
Partly cloudy days	107.70	112.00
Cloudy days	156.24	139.79
Average daily temperature (F°)	56.77	62.38
Cooling degree days	1,383.52	2,072.52
Heating degree days	4,352.67	2,999.83
Average daily maximum temperature	66.73	72.22
Average daily minimum temperature	46.77	52.51
Precipitation (inches)	37.71	36.02
Percentage of sunshine	59.24	62.58
Rainy days	113.40	101.90
Number of observations	98	29

Source: Author.

1995 Community Water System Survey, which collected operating and financial information on approximately 2,000 water utilities in the United States. Several conditions should be noted. First, the analysis includes only public and private utilities, not ancillary systems (systems in which the supply of water is ancillary to the primary business, such as a mobile home park). Second, it includes only water utilities that meter residential service, because it focuses on whether volumetric charges vary with consumption. Third, only utilities reporting uniform, DB, or IBTs are considered, not utilities employing seasonal rates. Although seasonal rates are also market mimicking, their use is insufficient to model effectively. Finally, it includes only utilities that report a single water rate structure for residential customers. Relatively few utilities report a mixture of rates, and their rate structures are highly variable. This analysis is thus simplified without loss of generality by narrowing the criteria.

I further restrict the analysis to utilities responding to questions about their water sources, customers, number of operations employees, percentage of capital expenditures financed by debt, and bond ratings. This resulted in 1,021 usable observations. The coefficient sets estimated are for IBT and DB rates, relative to uniform rates.

DB rates are the opposite of IBTs in terms of revenue variability. Thus, those independent variables that increase revenue variability (or its importance in utility decisionmaking) will increase the probability of a utility adopting DB rates and decrease its probability of adopting IBTs, resulting in opposite signs on the coefficients of these variables. Independent variables not directly affecting revenue variability may or may not have opposite signs. Table 12.2 displays the results. The first row for each independent variable shows its effect on the probability of choosing DB rates, and the second row shows its effect on the probability of choosing IBTs.

Privately owned water utilities are more likely to adopt DB rates and less likely to adopt IBTs, although the IBT effect is not significant. Utilities that serve larger populations are more likely to adopt IBTs and less likely to adopt DB rates, although neither effect is significant. The insignificance may well be due to the next variable also approximating the effects of size of utility. The number of operations personnel has a significant and positive impact on the adoption of both DB rates and IBTs, relative to uniform rates. This is consistent with the conclusion that both types of block rates are somewhat more difficult to administer than uniform rates.

The next set of variables shows the relative importance of three sources of water supply: purchased, surface, and groundwater. Groundwater is excluded from the estimation. The percentage of water that the utility purchases is not very significant in explaining rate structure, although it has a

TABLE 12.2
Logit Results Explaining Rate Structure

Variable	Logit estimate	Standard error	T-value
Constant	−1.27744	0.1595	−8.01
	−1.42256	0.1784	−7.98
Private	0.33910	0.1628	2.08
	−0.14198	0.2054	−0.69
Population served	−0.00475	0.0055	−0.86
	0.00105	0.0040	0.26
Operations employees	0.02997	0.0149	2.01
	0.03755	0.0150	2.50
Percent purchased water	0.21560	0.1838	1.17
	0.07433	0.2139	0.35
Percent surface water	0.52482	0.1991	2.64
	−0.42291	0.2640	−1.60
Debt ÷ capital expenditures	0.55712	0.5859	0.95
	−0.05091	0.7365	−0.07
Bond rating	0.16640	0.0547	3.04
	0.20513	0.0618	3.32

Note: First row for each variable is DB coefficient; second row is IBT coefficient. Both are relative to uniform rate.
Source: Author.

greater impact on the choice of DB rates. The percentage of water that the utility supplies to its customers from surface storage is significant, and it has a positive impact on the use of DB rates and a negative impact on the use of IBTs. Note that surface water storage typically implies greater infrastructure expenditures than either purchased water or groundwater. Thus, utilities with greater infrastructure costs, other things being equal, are less likely to adopt IBT and more likely to adopt DB rates. This is consistent with the notion that greater infrastructure costs generally imply financing greater sums, and thus a greater concern with revenue variability. The next variable shows the percentage of capital expenditures financed by debt. This variable is not significant, although the direction of effect is similar to the previous set of variables.

Finally, the model includes a variable denoting bond rating. The intent here is to control for the financial health of the water utilities. This variable is highly significant and a positive influence on the adoption of both DB rates and IBTs. This suggests that financially sound utilities are more likely to adopt either block rate relative to uniform rates. Care should be taken in interpreting this coefficient, because utility behavior with respect to rate setting may have a feedback effect on their bond rating. However, these coefficients suggest that the bond rating process does not induce utilities to favor DB rates over IBTs.

These results have the following implications for public policy. First, private utilities are more likely to eschew market-oriented rates, perhaps because they have no recourse to raising revenue via taxes. This suggests that regulatory oversight of private utilities is justified, particularly in light of the trend toward privatization of water services.

Second, smaller water utilities are less likely to adopt market-oriented rates, which suggests that it may be possible to increase efficiency by implementing national programs to help smaller utilities design market-oriented rates. Finally, high infrastructure costs and debt financing of these costs discourage the use of market-oriented rates. This implies that the imposition of IBTs in return for financing by lending agencies is sound policy. Although beyond the scope of this chapter, the results indicate the need for public involvement in capacity building of small water utilities. Such involvement can take the form of training, credit provision, and information support and regulatory oversight.

An unfortunate constraint of the Community Water System Survey data is that the utilities are not identified by name or location, so that the analysis cannot simultaneously control for weather. Hence, one cannot use these data to estimate a model that captures both utility viewpoints (price discrimination and revenue stability) regarding the adoption of IBTs. This tempers the usefulness of these results. Fortunately, a data set will soon be available for estimating a model with both weather and revenue effects. It is the "water:\stats" data of the AWWA 1996 survey of approximately 1,000 utilities in the United States and Canada (AWWA 1998).

Conclusion

Analyzing the reasons that water utilities choose rate structures is important, because different rate structures vary in their market orientation and affect economic efficiency. IBTs raise marginal prices for households that increase their demand and make water relatively more scarce. Utilities are more likely to voluntarily adopt this market mimicking rate structure if they are located in climates characterized by some combination of hot, dry, sunny, and lengthy growing season. By contrast, utilities that are concerned with keeping the variability of revenue low to be certain of meeting all their debt obligations are less likely to adopt the market mimicking IBTs. Smaller utilities are also less likely to adopt them, because they lack the human capital to develop, track, and administer these rates.

These results demonstrate how water utilities may be expected to choose different rate structures in the absence of government regulations or lending agency constraints. They indicate a possible justification for establishing regulatory oversight over water utility rate setting. They also indicate that politicians and members of the public may be justified in raising questions about rate structures during the privatization of utilities and the granting of concessions to water suppliers. Although the empirical analysis focuses on the United States, the results pertain to utilities of various sizes and in many climates that generally are not subject to rate regulation.

References

AWWA (American Water Works Association). 1991. *Water Rates, Manual M1,* 4th ed. Denver, Colorado.

_____. 1992. *Alternative Rates, Manual M34.* Denver, Colorado.

_____. 1998. "Water:\Stats: The Water Utility Database, 1996 Survey." Denver, Colorado: American Water Works Association, http://www.awwa.org/ h20stats/h20stats.htm.

Brown, Stephen J., and David S. Sibley. 1986. *The Theory of Public Utility Pricing.* Cambridge, U.K.: Cambridge University Press.

Chesnutt, Thomas W., Casey McSpadden, and John Christianson. 1996. "Revenue Instability Induced by Conservation Rates." *Journal of the American Water Works Association* 88(1): 52–63.

Ernst & Young. 1994. *Ernst & Young 1994 National Water and Wastewater Rate Survey.* Washington, D.C.

Goldman, M. Barry, Hayne E. Leland, and David S. Sibley. 1984. "Optimal Nonuniform Prices." *Review of Economic Studies* 51(2): 305–19.

Hewitt, Julie A., and W. Michael Hanemann. 1995. "A Discrete/Continuous Choice Approach to Residential Water Demand under Block Rate Pricing." *Land Economics* 71(2): 173–92.

Hirshleifer, Jack, James C. DeHaven, and Jerome W. Milliman. 1960. *Water Supply: Economics, Technology, and Policy.* Chicago: University of Chicago Press.

Howe, Charles W., and F. P. Linaweaver, Jr. 1967. "The Impact of Price on Residential Water Demand and Its Relation to System Design and Price Structure." *Water Resources Research* 3(1): 13–32.

Leland, Hayne E., and Robert A. Meyer. 1976. "Monopoly Pricing Structures with Imperfect Discrimination." *Bell Journal of Economics* 7(2): 449–62.

Perloff, Jeffrey M. 1999. *Microeconomics.* Reading, Massachusetts: Addison-Wesley.

Philips, Louis. 1983. *The Economics of Price Discrimination*. Cambridge, U.K.: Cambridge University Press.

Pigou, A. C. 1932. *The Economics of Welfare*, 4th ed. London: Macmillan Publishing.

U.S. Environmental Protection Agency. 1997. *Community Water System Survey*, Vol. 2, *Detailed Survey Result Tables and Methodology Report*. EPA 815-R-001b. Office of Water: Washington, D.C.

U.S. National Oceanic and Atmospheric Administration. 1994. *U.S. Divisional and Station Climatic Data and Normals*, Vol. 1. TD-9640. Washington, D.C.

Wicksell, Knut. 1994. "A New Principle of Just Taxation." In Richard A. Musgrave and Alan T. Peacock, eds., *Classics in the Theory of Public Finance*. New York: St. Martin's Press.

Willig, Robert D. 1978. "Pareto-Superior Nonlinear Outlay Schedules." *Bell Journal of Economics* 9(1): 56–69.

13

The Distributive Effects of Water Price Reform on Households in the Flanders Region of Belgium

Peter Van Humbeeck

Households in the Flanders region in Belgium every year pay a fee for drinking water and a fee for wastewater. Residents pay the wastewater charge to the Flemish government, which uses it to finance environmental programs (Van Humbeeck 1997). They pay the drinking water fee to 1 of 24 private water companies in Flanders, which use the money to pay for drinking water production and distribution.

A social correction, in the form of a pricing formula to help low-income and large families pay for wastewater, has always accompanied the wastewater charge. In 1997, however, the government replaced this approach with a tax exemption for certain underprivileged groups. Moreover, the reform created a new formula to calculate the drinking water fee. Households with water connections now receive 15 cubic meters (m^3) of drinking water per person per year for free.

Government officials assumed that this reform would help the targeted families more than the previous social correction. However, it has never conducted a thorough study comparing the social welfare effects of the former and present approaches.

This chapter analyzes the social welfare effects of the reform.[1] It first provides some background on the social compensation policies of the Flemish government with respect to the wastewater charge and explains the need for an empirical analysis. The next part describes the method used to analyze the distributive effects of the reform, and it discusses the analysis outcome and conclusions. Finally, it discusses the policy impact of the analysis.

---

1. It is based on a report published by the Social and Economic Council of Flanders (SERV 1997).

Social Compensation Policies and the Wastewater Charge

To determine the wastewater charge, the government calculates a household's pollution load with a pollution conversion coefficient.[2] The basic tax formula looks like this:

(13.1) $H = T \cdot OC \cdot Q$

where H is the tax amount that is due; T is the flat tax rate (BF 600 in 1991–95, BF 900 in 1996–99); OC is the conversion coefficient that is applied for domestic wastewater effluents (0.025); and Q is the water consumption expressed in m^3.[3]

The government, however, has always amended this basic formula with a social correction. In 1991 it exempted the first 30 m^3 of water consumed per household from charges. This was applied to all households. The reasoning was that low-income households would consume less, and thus the exemption would proportionately benefit them the most. Furthermore, it reduced the charges by BF 250 per child for couples with three or more children, starting with the third child. In other words, it calculated the 1991 charge by applying the following formula:

(13.2) $H = T \cdot OC \cdot (Q - 30) - 250 \cdot (k - 2)$

where k is the number of children (for $k > 2$).

Because of administrative difficulties with implementing these measures, the government introduced a different social compensation scheme in 1992. It multiplied the charge by a social compensation factor, K_s, that varied from 0.20 to 0.95, depending on the volume of water consumption. Hence, until 1996 it calculated the tax amount as follows:

(13.3) $H = T \cdot OC \cdot Q \cdot K_s$

where K_s depends on the volume of water consumed, $K_s = K_s(Q)$, as table 13.1 demonstrates.

---

2. The conversion coefficient expresses the quantitative relationship between a certain parameter that can easily be measured—which, in the case of domestic wastewater, is the annual water consumption—and the pollution resulting from this activity.

3. At present, BF1 = ECU 0.0246 = US$0.027; ECU 1 = BF 40.650; US1 = BF 36.75. The government linked the rates for the wastewater charges to the index of consumption prices beginning in 1994. The real rate in 1998 was BF 991. The water consumption in this formula is based on the invoice of the water company, the household size (for households using water from a private water collection system such as groundwater or rainwater), or both variables.

It was soon realized that this scheme also did not work well. Despite the increasing block rate, the lowest-income groups paid substantially more taxes than higher-income groups as a percentage of total income. Moreover, the plan placed a proportionately heavier burden on larger households (Decoster and Van Dongen 1994; SERV 1993; Van Humbeeck 1994). Several alternatives were proposed, but the government hestitated to change the formula.

Finally, the government abolished the K_s factors in 1997. Instead, it introduced a tax exemption for certain underprivileged groups: elderly taxpayers who receive the minimum state pension, low-income residents who receive welfare money, and disabled residents who receive a government allowance. For nonexempt households it used a formula corresponding with equation 13.1 to calculate the wastewater charge. To compensate for the abolition of the K_s factors in the wastewater charge, the government passed a new regulation: beginning in 1997, the water companies had to supply all household customers with 15 m³ of drinking water per person per year free of charge.

The Need for an Empirical Analysis

When the new scheme was introduced, the Flemish minister for the environment compared it with the previous system. Based on an analysis of a given family size with a low, average, or high water consumption (see table 13.2), the minister concluded that (Vlaams Parlement 1996, p. 19):

> Logically it has…to be assumed that the price for the additional tap water will rise substantially as a consequence of the obligation to supply minimum quantities of tap water free of charge. The free supply of the first 15 m³ per person, combined with an increased marginal water price will result in the rational water consumers actually having to pay less for their tap water. Since it has already been established that water consumption is increasing with the family income, it can be assumed that the effect of the free supply will yield the desired social correction.

TABLE 13.1
Social Compensation Factor K_s as a Function of Water Consumption

Q (m)³	0–50	51–100	101–150	151–200	201–300	301–400	401–500
K_s	0.20	0.40	0.60	0.70	0.85	0.90	0.95

Note: Q and K_s are defined in the text.
Source: Vlaams Parlement (1992).

TABLE 13.2
Comparison of the Former and Current Pricing Structures

Number of family members	20 m³/person		30 m³/person		40 m³/person		60 m³/person	
	BF 40/m³ (a)	BF 59/m³ (b)	BF 40/m³ (a)	BF 59/m³ (b)	BF 40/m³ (a)	BF 59/m³ (b)	BF 40/m³ (a)	BF 59/m³ (b)
1	800	295	1,200	885	1,600	1,475	2,400	2,655
2	1,600	590	2,400	1,770	3,200	2,950	4,800	5,310
3	2,400	885	3,600	2,655	4,800	4,425	7,200	7,965
4	3,200	1,180	4,800	3,540	6,400	5,900	9,600	10,620
5	4,000	1,475	6,000	4,425	8,000	7,375	12,000	13,275

Amount due for an annual water consumption of: (column group heading)

a. Regulation without free water supply.
b. Regulation with 15 m3 of free water supply per year per person.
Note: Payment figures do not include subscription fee.
Source: Vlaams Parlement (1996).

Both hypotheses are confirmed by later data. From 1996 to 1998, almost every company increased marginal water prices from 22 percent to as much as 122 percent. In Flanders, the marginal tariff (including the value added tax, and weighted with respect to the number of inhabitants per municipality) rose an average of 50 percent, from approximately BF 40 to BF 60 per m³. Moreover, the Belgian National Institute of Statistics reported that average water consumption per family increased with family income and size (NIS 1997; see also Janssens, Van Mol, and D'hont 1996; SERV 1993). But do these findings indeed mean that the reform has a desirable social effect?

The literature clearly stresses the danger of extrapolating broad trends from certain categories of families as was pointed out by several studies (Decoster and Van Dongen 1994; Decoster, Proost, and Schokkaert 1992). For example, probably few families of five with an average consumption of 20 m³ per person really exist in Flanders. This information can therefore be misleading if used in an analysis, as government studies have done (see table 13.2). Moreover, these family-type analyses may yield only limited information. For example, they may not examine possible adaptations in a family's behavior, such as more rational water consumption, and they also may fail to explain impacts on income distribution.

Methodology

Instead of using a partial and intuitive approach, the distributive effects were calculated for a large number of existing families, starting with a representative cross-section of the Flemish population. The results were extrapolated for subgroups of the whole population. The basic data stem from the 1995–96 family budget survey of the Belgian National Institute of Statistics.[4] This survey allowed the establishment of a relationship between water consumption and several family characteristics, including income and family size.

---

4. A family budget survey is a statistical investigation into the size and composition of family incomes and expenses. The most recent Belgian National Institute of Statistics survey, conducted from June 1995 to May 1996, had results for 2,724 families, including 1,231 in Flanders. Limitations of the available data forced us to make some adaptations to improve the reliability of the sample survey. We concluded that some of the hypotheses we used can lead to an overestimation of the distributive effects, and others to an underestimation, but the conclusions do not need to be adjusted. For a full description of these problems and hypotheses, see SERV (1997).

Assessment of Distributive Effects

An analysis of a measure's social impact or distributive effects usually distinguishes between two parameters. The first parameter is vertical equity. Vertical redistribution implies a change in the income structure: purchasing power is transferred from higher-income to lower-income households, or vice versa. The second parameter is horizontal equity. This reflects income transfers based on differences in living conditions, and can involve the transfer of purchasing power from the healthy to the sick, the employed to the unemployed, the childless to people with children, and so on.

This chapter focuses only on the vertical distributive effects of the reform. The analysis divided the population into income deciles, each of which included exactly 10 percent of the total Flemish population and studied the effects for each decile.[5] The first decile contained the poorest 10 percent of the Flemish population, and the tenth decile contained the richest 10 percent. We calculated the purchasing power effects of the former and current water pricing structure in absolute and relative terms. In relative terms, they are expressed in per mills of spending and income. (For the analysis of the horizontal effects, see SERV 1997).

Assessment of Policy Measures

An assessment of policy reform measures requires three steps: (a) assessing the reference situation prior to the introduction of the policy measures, (b) assessing the situation after the introduction of the policy measures, and (c) analyzing the changes in the situation (for further methodological considerations, see Harrison 1994).

THE REFERENCE SITUATION. In the reference situation, the government continues to apply the K_s factors. There exists neither a wastewater charge exemption for the underprivileged population groups nor a free supply of 15 m^3 of drinking water per person. Water consumption, income, family size, geographic location, and drinking water tariff are kept at their 1996 levels, but the wastewater tariff is raised to its 1998 level.

---

5. We used data on individual families in the family budget survey for all calculations. Using the extrapolation coefficients, we converted these statistics into averages per decile or per family category. This method yields more correct results than an analysis using calculations based on average values per decile or per family category.

THE NEW SITUATION. The situation after the reform is characterized by (a) the abolishment of the K_s factors in the wastewater charge, (b) the introduction of a wastewater charge exemption for underprivileged population groups, and (c) the free supply of 15 m^3 of drinking water per person. An important variable, however, is the change in water consumption as a result of the higher drinking water tariffs.[6]

Price changes give rise to two effects: income and substitution. In an income effect, the total purchasing power changes. If the price increases, a family can no longer buy the same goods and services with the same nominal income as before. If it decreases, a family saves part of its income after buying the same goods and services. In a substitution effect, relative prices change. The original goods and services have become more (or less) expensive, and a family replaces them with other products and services. Usually, an income increase leads to increased consumption of the product, whereas a relative product price increase leads to decreased consumption. The impact of these effects is traditionally represented by elasticities.

Our analysis does not take the income effect into account. It is almost negligible because of the limited influence of the price changes on the portion of income that is spent on water (on average less than 0.1 percent) in combination with the low-income elasticity of drinking water and the short-term perspective of the analysis (Janssens, Val Mol, and D'hont 1996; SERV 1993).

The relative price effect is more important. The marginal drinking water tariffs increase considerably almost everywhere. Under the hypothesis of a fixed level of water consumption, the drinking water invoice for some families will be much higher in the new situation, that is, the average price is increasing. Moreover, water consumption is price sensitive. Data used for Flanders show that higher water prices appear to correspond with considerably reduced water consumption.

However, this is a long-term effect in which consumers adapt over several years to the price structure. In the short term, the price elasticity of the demand for tap water is rather small, as various studies (Janssens, Van Mol, and D'hont 1996; SERV 1993) have demonstrated. This means that the immediate effect of the price increases on water consumption should not be overestimated.

---

6. Policymakers and analysts expected that the introduction of the free supply of 15 m^3 of drinking water per person would lead to more rational water consumption, but this was not quantified. Moreover, other factors can also change water consumption (Janssens, Van Mol, and D'hont 1996). Here the other factors are kept constant.

This chapter's analysis uses three values for the price elasticity of household demand for drinking water: –0.05 for consumption that is less than 30 m^3, –0.3 for consumption from 30 m^3 to 120 m^3, and –0.4 for consumption that is more than 120 m^3. This indicates that minor quantities of water are a necessity (for drinking and cooking). The price elasticity is higher for other types of water consumption, such as laundry, personal hygiene, and toilet flushing, and higher still for yet other types of consumption, such as washing cars or filling swimming pools. These elasticities applied only when prices increased. In other words, a price decrease does not yield a consumption increase in our model. In addition, the sensitivity analysis calculated some additional higher and lower values for the price elasticity.[7]

A last remark regarding the analysis: the family budget survey does not provide sufficiently detailed information on the origins of family incomes to allow for a straightforward assessment of the social impact of the wastewater charge exemption.[8] This assessment is therefore inevitably rather rough. The government estimated that nearly 150,000 families in Flanders are eligible for the exemption. Assuming that all these families belong to the lowest-income decile, it is possible to calculate a new average tax for this decile that takes the exemption into account, using the average tax amount that is calculated for the remaining families in this decile. This permits assessing the average nominal effects, the vertical distributive effects, and the influence of the exemption.

ANALYSIS OF THE CHANGES. In the last step in the analysis, the reference situation was compared with the current situation. By analyzing vertical and horizontal distributive effects of both situations, one can determine the winners and the losers.

Results

Tables 13.3 and 13.4 show the results of that analysis.

---

7. The results of this sensitivity analysis are not presented in this chapter. The sensitivity analysis has shown that even a sharp decrease in drinking water consumption (price elasticity $E = -1$) does not change our general conclusions. For more information see SERV (1997).

8. This number is based on the applications for exemption that were sent to the Flemish government.

TABLE 13.3
Vertical Distribution Effects: Reference and Current Situations

Decile	Tax (BF)	Water (BF)	Total (BF)	Tax/ income[a]	Tax/ spending[b]	Total/ income[c]	Total/ spending[d]
(Reference situation)							
1	848	2,811	3,660	1.82	1.65	8.03	7.34
2	953	3,208	4,161	1.49	1.64	6.48	7.15
3	1,088	3,377	4,465	1.37	1.38	5.60	5.86
4	1,415	4,061	5,476	1.53	1.69	5.93	6.56
5	1,630	4,475	6,105	1.54	1.69	5.79	6.41
6	2,112	5,052	7,164	1.76	2.21	5.97	7.39
7	1,936	4,850	6,786	1.43	1.68	5.01	5.86
8	2,067	5,305	7,372	1.34	1.61	4.78	5.79
9	2,361	6,123	8,485	1.31	1.61	4.71	5.85
10	2,201	5,432	7,633	0.87	1.36	3.08	4.71
(Current situation)							
1	1,423	3,339	4,762	3.11	2.89	10.54	9.76
2	1,641	3,513	5,154	2.54	2.80	8.02	8.86
3	1,832	3,716	5,547	2.29	2.38	6.96	7.35
4	2,266	4,327	6,593	2.45	2.71	7.13	7.89
5	2,506	4,557	7,063	2.38	2.65	6.71	7.43
6	2,963	5,190	8,153	2.47	3.04	6.79	8.43
7	2,885	5,073	7,958	2.13	2.49	5.87	6.83

(table continues on following page)

Table 13.3 continues

Decile	Tax (BF)	Water (BF)	Total (BF)	Tax/income[a]	Tax/spending[b]	Total/income[c]	Total/spending[d]
8	3,074	5,125	8,198	1.99	2.42	5.31	6.46
9	3,324	5,965	9,289	1.84	2.31	5.15	6.40
10	3,100	5,190	8,290	1.25	1.92	3.35	5.14

a. Tax/income is the annual amount a household pays for the wastewater tax divided by the annual income of the household, multiplied by 1,000.

b. Tax/spending is the annual amount a household pays for the wastewater tax divided by the annual spending of the household, multiplied by 1,000. (Annual spending = annual income − savings + spending).

c. Total/income is the annual amount a household pays for the wastewater tax plus the drinking water supply (total expenditures for water services), divided by the annual income of the household, multiplied by 1,000.

d. Total/spending is the annual amount a household pays for the wastewater tax plus the drinking water supply (total expenditures for water services), divided by the annual spending of the household, multiplied by 1,000 (annual spending = annual income − savings + spending).

Source: Author.

TABLE 13.4
Comparison of Vertical Distributive Effects: Reference and Current Situations

Decile	Tax 1996 (with K_s)	Tax 1998 (E <> 0)	Percentage increase	Water 1996	Water 1998 (E <> 0)	Percentage increase	Total 1996	Total 1998 (E <> 0)	Percentage increase
Average	1,661	2,501	51	4,469	4,599	3	6,131	7,101	16
1	848	1,423	68	2,811	3,339	19	3,660	4,762	30
2	953	1,641	72	3,208	3,513	10	4,161	5,154	24
3	1,088	1,832	68	3,377	3,716	10	4,465	5,547	24
4	1,415	2,266	60	4,061	4,327	7	5,476	6,593	20
5	1,630	2,506	54	4,475	4,557	2	6,105	7,063	16
6	2,112	2,963	40	5,052	5,190	3	7,164	8,153	14
7	1,936	2,885	49	4,850	5,073	5	6,786	7,958	17
8	2,067	3,074	49	5,305	5,125	–3	7,372	8,198	11
9	2,361	3,324	41	6,123	5,965	–3	8,485	9,289	9
10	2,201	3,100	41	5,432	5,190	–4	7,633	8,290	9

Note: E <> means that various elasticities were used for each decile along with the consumption of water. See text for further explanation.
Source: Author.

Wastewater Charge

The government implemented two measures relating to the wastewater charge. First, it abolished the so-call K_s factors. Then it introduced a
tax exemption for certain categories of social income.

The calculations confirm earlier findings (Decoster and Van Dongen 1994;
SERV 1993). The K_s factors (equation 13.3) had a certain leveling impact on the
regressivity of the wastewater charge without a social correction (equation
13.1). The abolition of the K_s factors thus leaves poorer families relatively worse
off. In nominal terms, all families are worse off. Everybody pays more than
before (more than 50 percent on average, as figure 13.1 illustrates). This can be
explained easily by the abolition of the K_s factors. These were formerly all
below the level of 1 and were lowest for households with little water consumption, which are statistically also the lowest-income groups.

The exemption for families in certain social categories, however, improves the score of the new tax regulation. It has an obvious positive effect
on the vertical level. For the families that do not receive any exemption,
the nominal purchasing power effects still increase considerably. As a result,

Figure 13.1
Relative Vertical Distributive Effects: Wasterwater Charge

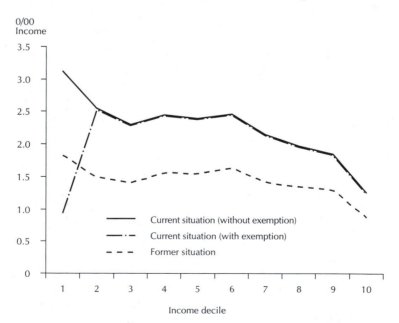

Note: 0/00 income defined in text.
Source: Author.

the expenses continue to weigh rather heavily on the families in the lowest income groups that are not entitled to an exemption.

The government had indeed predicted these adverse effects. The question is whether the free supply of 15 m³ of drinking water per person is adequate compensation, as the government assumed.

Drinking Water Reform

The drinking water reform has generated quite different results. Prior to reform, drinking water expenses were regressively distributed over the various deciles. Families in the lowest two deciles spent an especially high proportion of their income on water.

The new drinking water price structure increased the average family spending for drinking water. If the water consumption volume remains constant compared with the reference situation, the short-term effect is that the budget increase is 13 percent. But if water consumption decreases because of the tariffs, the average family increase is 3 percent.

On average, the increase is highest for poor families. Overall, the lower-income deciles pay more than in the reference scenario whereas the highest deciles pay slightly less. Therefore, the relative position of the poorer families is deteriorating. The regressivity of drinking water prices is greater than it had been prior to the reform (see figure 13.2). This holds true for both constant and decreased water consumption.

The fact that the reform is imposing additional administrative costs on the water distribution companies is partly responsible for the drinking water cost increases. The relationship between water consumption, household size, and family income also helps to explain the regressive impact of the reform. Because the largest families in Flanders have higher incomes, at least statistically, the free supply of 15 m³ of water per person distributes more to the wealthy.[9]

Note that these results rely on averages, and that there are winners as well as losers in each decile. In the lowest decile for example, 87 percent of the families pay more than before and 13 percent pay less. In the highest decile, 47 percent come out losers and 53 percent come out winners.

Total Expenses

A comparison of the total wastewater and drinking water expenses in the reference and current situation shows that Flemish households, on

---

9. The situation can obviously be quite different in other countries, as Renzetti explains in chapter 6 of this book.

FIGURE 13.2
Relative Vertical Distributive Effects: Drinking Water Expenses

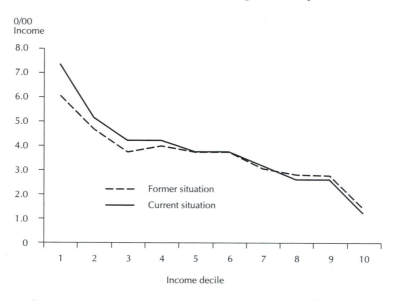

Note: 0/00 income defined in text.
Source: Author.

average, pay more after the reform. On average, total wastewater and drinking water expenses per family increase approximately BF 1,600 if water consumption does not decrease in the short term, and BF 1,000 if it does decrease.

Moreover, in both cases, the relative welfare of the poorer families deteriorates. On average, the poorer families are mainly confronted with the highest increase in expenses. Consequently, the situation has become more regressive (see figure 13.3). Even the systems without K_s factors and without a free supply of drinking water yield better results on the vertical level than does the current scheme.

The tax exemption fails to change this conclusion. The wastewater charge exemption cannot sufficiently compensate for the regressivity of the drinking water expenses. Only families in the lowest-income category are, on average, relatively less worse off.

Although the analysis confirms that water consumption increases with family income, the government's hypothesis that water costs will therefore decrease for low-income households is erroneous. To the contrary, after the reform the poor seem to be relatively worse off than the rich.

FIGURE 13.3
Relative Vertical Distributive Effects: Total Wastewater and Water Expenses

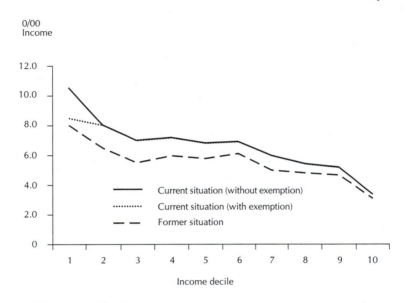

Note: 0/00 income defined in text.
Source: Author.

Conclusion

The Social and Economic Council of Flanders published the results of this study at the end of 1997. Although the Flemish government discussed the results, it did not revamp the reform. This may be due to several reasons.

First, the minister who proposed the reform had to deal with protests in Parliament and the press at the time the Social and Economic Council published the results. It would probably be politically suicidal for the minister to admit to the adverse effects of the reform.

Second, the Flemish government is comfortable with the reform, partly because the new policy has helped increase receipts from the wastewater charge from BF 3.6 billion to more than BF 5 billion, providing additional money for the government's environmental programs. Some policy analysts, academicians, and politicians believe this was the government's real objective in reforming the water price structure.

Third, industry is, on the whole, pleased with the reform. That is because households now pay a larger part of their share of wastewater treatment costs, and they are no longer subsidized to a large extent by industry.

Fourth, environmental protection groups are generally content with the reform, because the increased marginal drinking water prices are expected to lower household water consumption.

Fifth, the water companies tend to oppose changes in rate structures. This means that, whereas they had resisted the reform initially, they oppose additional changes now that the new scheme has been implemented.

Finally, the labor unions are concerned with equity, but they have little support from the other key players and interest groups in their demand for effective social protection.

In our opinion, the most important lesson we can learn from Flanders is that reforms should be carefully prepared *before* they are implemented. The reason is that reforms are often difficult to implement, but once they have been implemented, they are even harder to modify.

References

Decoster, André, and Hilde Van Dongen. 1994. "Verdelingseffecten van Milieuheffingen." In Aviel Verbruggen, ed., *Milieu-en natuurrapport Vlaanderen 1994*. Mechelen, Belgium. Flemish Society for the Environment.

Decoster, André, Stef Proost, and Erik Schokkaert. 1992. "Hervorming van Indirecte Belastingen: Winnaars en Verliezers." *Leuvense Economische Standpunten* (63).

Harrison, David M. 1994. *The Distributive Effects of Economic Instruments for Environmental Policy*. Paris: Organisation for Economic Co-operation and Development.

Janssens, Ilse, M. Van Mol, and Didier D'hont. 1996. "Watervoorziening." In Aviel Verbruggen, ed., *Milieu-en natuurrapport Vlaanderen 1996*. Mechelen, Belgium: Flemish Society for the Environment.

NIS (Nationaal Insituut voor de Statistiek, or National Institute of Statistics). 1997. *Gezinsbudgetetenquête 1995–96*. Brussels.

SERV (Sociaal-Economische Raad van Vlaanderen, or Social and Economic Council of Flanders). 1993. *Advies over de Sociale Correctie met betrekking tot de Heffing op de Verontreiniging van de Oppervlaktewateren*. Brussels.

_____. 1997. *The Distributive Effects of the New System for the Wastewater Charge and Drinking Water Tariffs*. Brussels.

Van Humbeeck, Peter. 1994. "Naar een nieuwe sociale correctie van de Vlaamse afvalwaterheffing." *Water* 13(74): 3–9.

_____. 1997. "Environmental Taxation in Flanders." *Environmental Taxation and Accounting* 1(4): 52–61.

Vlaams Parlement. 1992. *Decreet houdende diverse bepalingen tot begeleiding van de begroting 1992*. Brussels: Belgisch Stoatsblad.

_____. 1996. *Decreet houdende bepalingen tot begeleiding van de begroting 1997. Stuk 1996–97, 428/18.* Brussels: Belgisch Stoatsblad.

PART 2

Country Case

Studies

14

The Political Economy of Water Price Reform in Australia

Warren Musgrave

Australian officials are comprehensively reforming water policy in general and water prices in particular. This reflects their concerns about the consequences of past policies, as well as fundamental shifts in the way that Australians view economic, environmental, and social imperatives. Prior to reform, officials set water prices below the cost of supply and did not link them to use. Cross-subsidies were common. Reform has led to, among other things, an increase in levels of cost recovery, the removal of many cross-subsidies, and the development of water markets.

Australia is a federation of six states and two territories. Under its constitution, the states are responsible for the land and water within their boundaries. The federal, or commonwealth, government has the authority, however, to considerably influence resource policy, principally through the power of the purse strings: it collects most of the taxes and distributes general revenue money to the states.

This chapter reviews the pressures for reform. It then presents two case studies. The first is a pioneering exercise in urban water price reform that Hunter Water Board undertook. The second is the Independent Pricing and Regulatory Tribunal's

The helpful comments and advice of officers of the New South Wales Department of Land and Water Conservation and of the New South Wales Independent Pricing and Regulatory Tribunal are acknowledged, particularly Bob Burford, Jim Cox, Robert Marsh, Colin Reid, and Pamela Stark. Andrew Amos of the Hunter Water Corporation was a valuable source of advice and assistance, particularly with regard to the Newcastle case study.

determination of bulk water prices in the state of New South Wales. The chapter also discusses the general relationship of water reform to microeconomic reform and summarizes the progress Australian states and territories are making in implementing water price reform.

Pressures for Reform

After Europeans started to settle Australia in 1788, land ownership became increasingly concentrated. Beginning in about 1860, the government sponsored rural development measures. This included settlements of smallholder irrigators on either state-owned land or on large private holdings acquired by the government (Campbell and Dumsday 1990). Such activity reflected a widespread desire to develop the infant nation and pursue equity objectives through the redistribution of land.

In the 1960s, the attitudes underpinning these policies started to dissipate. This was prompted by fundamental changes in economic influences, including a decline in the importance of agriculture in the economy. Officials also recognized that they could pursue the goals of equity and redistribution more effectively through policies other than the redistribution of land and other natural resources. Furthermore, the century-old support of denser settlement was becoming inappropriate, because changes in agricultural technology favored increasing farm size (Campbell and Dumsday 1990). In the case of water, as discussed later, the development ethic based on increasing extraction increasingly came under question.

Economic policy also faced fundamental change. When the six Australian colonies created a federation in 1901, they adopted a national policy of protection aimed at encouraging immigration and creating manufacturing employment. This represented a way that the wealth created by the export-based rural sector could be redistributed to the urban sector. As Australia has always been a predominantly urban nation, this policy also served to reduce dependence on land development for income redistribution. The ability to sustain such a policy relied, however, on maintaining the strength of the resource-based export sector.

However, the nation suffered a chronic decline in its terms of trade, which resulted in erosion of the export sector's ability to sustain this policy in a politically tolerable manner. For more than a half-century, this trend was offset or concealed by the adoption of technological advances, the disruptions caused by two world wars, a series of commodity booms, and the country's major mineral discoveries. By the 1980s, however, it had become clear that the 1901 policy could no longer be sustained. The resulting pressures for reform prompted the formation of powerful political coalitions able to overcome the resistance of those who might be hurt by change (Kelly 1992). These coalitions made irrigation reform a high priority.

Pressures for Reform of the Irrigation Industry

As a result of highly variable precipitation, the absence of extensive snow packs, and high rates of summer evaporation, Australia needs to store relatively large amounts of water for irrigation. Irrigation projects in such circumstances are expensive, and pioneering attempts by the private sector to develop irrigation systems in the late 1800s ran into financial difficulties. As a result, state-supported irrigation development became the norm, and stirred little controversy for more than 60 years. In the 1960s, however, agricultural economists (Campbell 1964; Davidson 1969) and then other groups began questioning both the justification of past development and the desirability of future investment.

The initial criticism, coming from economists, focused on the inefficient nature of irrigation development. This was because governments set water prices below the short-run marginal cost of supply and, in the long run, the returns did not justify the investment in irrigation. Other critics soon joined in, questioning irrigation systems on equity, fiscal and, eventually, environmental grounds. The critics who focused on equity and fiscal issues strengthened the arguments of economists by drawing attention to the burden that irrigation costs placed on taxpayers. The increasingly influential environmental movement raised concerns about the adverse impact of irrigation on waterlogging (which occurs when the water table rises close to the surface), land salinization, and riverine degradation.

The government also had concerns about water shortages, public sector fiscal health, and, to a lesser extent, resource degradation.[1] In a seminal paper, Watson and Rose (1980) identified the government's concerns and referred to Australia as having a mature water economy. By this, they meant that water supply costs were increasing incrementally and water users faced greater interdependence. Although the paper was not a statement of government policy, it appeared at a time when the political tide had definitely turned against the developers. Momentum for reform picked up throughout the 1980s, and by the 1990s at least some states had adopted reforms that could be described as comprehensive.

---

1. Langford, Forster, and Malcolm (1999) refer to the influence of unsustainable public sector debt on irrigation reform in Victoria. Arguably, this may be the reason that Victoria moved to the forefront of water reform.

This chapter does not review the totality of Australian water policy reform. Instead, it focuses on significant innovations, such as measuring the entitlements in volumetric terms instead of as fixed per hectare units and permitting their transfer. Both innovations were necessary to develop markets in irrigation water. These markets, although suffering from a number of imperfections (Musgrave 1996), have generated prices that probably better represent the scarcity value of water than the cost-recovery prices charged for bulk water after price reform.[2]

Prior to 1990, most states indicated that they would raise prices to recover most, if not all, the costs of supply, with some states setting a goal of recovering all operating and maintenance costs. But they made variable progress, approving mostly minor and gradual price increases. Victoria made the most progress, and it was able to report that the deficit from the operation of irrigation systems dropped by 80 percent from 1984 to 1994. It also abolished the central water authority, transferring responsibility for bulk water supply to a number of regional, statutory authorities, which were required to operate according to commercial principles. (For a comprehensive review of irrigation in Victoria, see Langford, Forster, and Malcolm 1999.)

Pressure for Reform of the Urban Sector

Urban water prices generated less controversy than irrigation prices. Water quality and reliability generally were satisfactory; and pricing policies favored the politically potent residential sector. As a result of cross-subsidies from the commercial and industrial sectors, residential customers faced prices well below the cost of delivery. All major metropolitan water authorities had sufficient revenue to cover their operation and maintenance costs, and service debts, while paying a return on capital (Industry Commission 1992). While flawed in the eyes of the economic purist, urban water price policy did not face significant dissent until relatively recently.

---

2. Permanent transfers in a number of New South Wales valleys are reported to have occurred recently at prices between US$0.276 and US$0.780 per cubic meter ($A 1 = US$0.65). In annualized terms, these prices are considerably higher than any likely cost-recovery price. For example, the New South Wales Independent Pricing and Regulatory Tribunal (IPART) estimates a cost-recovery price per cubic meter on the Murray River of about US$0.00325, which is equivalent to a capitalized value of about US$0.046 at a 7 percent discount rate. An equivalent capitalized value on the Border Rivers in the northern part of the state is US$0.086 (New South Wales Independent Pricing and Regulatory Tribunal 1998).

The water systems typically achieved cross-subsidization by basing fees on property values, with the result that owners of expensive property paid more and therefore subsidized those owning less expensive property. Although this meant that households with more expensive land subsidized less expensive land, by far the most substantial subsidies were from the commercial sector to households in general. The Industry Commission (1992) reported that in 1990–91, the average household paid US$0.51 per cubic meter of water, whereas the average business paid US$7.82.

The concerns expressed from time to time about urban water prices were similar to those raised about irrigated water prices. Critics said the system failed to encourage efficient allocation of water and caused inequities. In addition, after 1980, some analysts raised concerns about the financial condition of the water utilities.

In a number of cases, these concerns were exacerbated by the prospect of metropolitan areas imposing demands on catchments that were valued either by environmentalists because they were relatively pristine, or by rural residents because they were regarded as part of the rural "preserve." At the other end of the urban water system, concerns about wastewater disposal, particularly in Sydney, also spurred pressure for reform. In Sydney, reports of the poor state of the infrastructure and the large investments needed to protect water quality and public health helped generate support for price increases.

The first water utility to break from traditional practice in the face of such pressures was the Hunter District Water Board in New South Wales.

The Hunter District Reforms

The Hunter District Water Board supplied Newcastle, the second-largest city in New South Wales. In the 1970s, the board (which would become a state-owned corporation, the Hunter Water Corporation, in 1990) considered constructing a new dam to satisfy projected demand growth. But the expansion, if undertaken, would have severely strained the board's finances. Furthermore, the proposed location of the project was in a politically sensitive area where voters strongly opposed the dam.

In 1982, the board resolved the dilemma by reforming its tariff structure, thereby simultaneously reducing demand and increasing revenue.[3]

---

3. Although a dominant issue, price reform was just part of a package of initiatives. These initiatives and the overall reform process are described in Lloyd, Troy, and Schreiner (1992).

As a result, the board was able to postpone construction of the new storage project, perhaps for several decades, while gaining increased financial security. Figures 14.1 and 14.2 illustrate the reform's impact on total consumption and average household use.

Prior to this reform, the board used a tariff structure that was common in Australian cities. Users paid a flat fee, based on the value of their property, for a base or free allowance of water. The free allowance was generous, with the result that the cost to most consumers at the marginal unit of water consumed was zero. Consumers who exceeded the base allowance paid a volumetric charge.

The reform abolished the base allowance and introduced a two-part tariff consisting of a fixed charge and a per unit charge. (In a related move, the board also introduced a volumetric charge for sewerage services.) The board modified the fixed charge, which was still based on land value, to reflect the intention that it should cover only fixed costs.

The Hunger reforms were largely the initiative of Dr. John Paterson, president of the board from 1982 to 1984. The responsible minister in the state government, following the board's recommendation, approved the reforms. This

FIGURE 14.1
Total Water Use in the Hunter Region

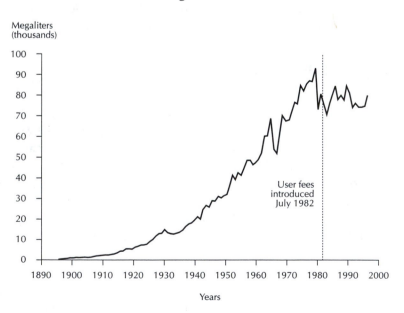

Source: Sydney Water Corporation and Hunter Water Corporation (1998).

FIGURE 14.2
Average Household Use in the Hunter Region 1978–97

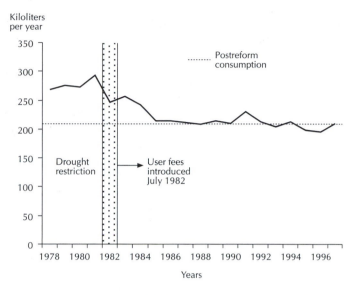

Source: Sydney Water Corporation and Hunter Water Corporation (1998).

spurred strong opposition by some members of the community who alleged that the board was merely concerned about increasing its revenue. To overcome this opposition, the board conducted an extensive public relations campaign emphasizing that the reforms would reduce consumption, relieve the need for more storage capacity, reduce maintenance costs, and lower charges for many customers (Lloyd, Troy, and Schreiner 1992, pp. 286–87).

The reforms were refined for several years after their introduction. In particular, the board phased out the property value basis for charges for all customers. By 1998, the reformed tariff structure consisted of five components:

1. A small fixed charge for water service access
2. A significant water usage charge with a two-tiered structure, which maintained a clear price signal for demand management
3. A moderate fixed service charge for sewer service access
4. An imputed volumetric charge for sewer usage, based on a discharge factor implied by water usage
5. An environmental improvement charge that helped fund a backlog sewerage scheme called the Hunter Sewerage Project (Sydney Water Corporation and Hunter Water Corporation 1998, p. 38).

The reforms had an immediate and dramatic impact. The resulting favorable publicity did much to promote the cause of microeconomic reform generally, and of urban water price reform in particular. Several years after the board's initial adoption of reforms in 1982, its example helped spur similar reforms by most urban water authorities.

In New South Wales, the Government Pricing Tribunal played an important role in furthering urban water reform. It is also playing a significant part in reforming rural bulk water prices, which is proceeding more sluggishly. Although the tribunal is not unique among Australian state agencies, it is a significant and successful price regulator, which makes it worthy of attention. The next section discusses the tribunal's experience with bulk water prices.

The New South Wales Independent Pricing and Regulatory Tribunal

New South Wales established the Government Pricing Tribunal in 1992, renaming it the Independent Pricing and Regulatory Tribunal (IPART) in 1996. The tribunal determines the maximum prices that government monopolies can charge. Commercial proprietary matters aside, the tribunal's proceedings are open to the public. All submissions are on the public record, as are transcripts of hearings. Although the tribunal does not rely on rules of evidence, it has earned a reputation for being honest, balanced, and independent, and for serving the public interest. Government monopolies cannot charge prices that exceed the tribunal's determinations, although they can charge prices that are lower than the determinations.

Other Australian jurisdictions (except the Northern Territory) have competition or price regulators, and some have emulated New South Wales in determining bulk and urban retail water prices through an open and independent process. The state of South Australia appointed a competition commissioner to investigate water prices in 1997. The government, however, did not accept the commissioner's recommendations. Western Australia has a water service regulator who provides advice on water prices to the minister for water resources. Tasmania has a regulator, the Government Prices Oversight Commission, and its recommendations for maximum prices of the three major regional water authorities were accepted by the government in 1999. The Australian Capital Territory Independent Pricing and Regulatory Commission sets prices for the Australian Capital Territory Electricity and Water Authority. In Victoria, a plan to have the Office of the Regulator General set water prices was put on hold in late 1995 because of a number of government concerns. In Queensland, no water prices have been referred to the Queensland Competition Authority for determination. Local authorities in that state have been required, however, to conform with Council of Australian Government (COAG) principles (detailed later in this chapter) in setting water prices (Australian Competition and Consumer Commission 1997, p. 22).

Bulk Water Price Reform in New South Wales

In November 1995, IPART began determining prices for the bulk water services that the Department of Land and Water Conservation (DLWC) provides. The services typically help extractive users, such as irrigation companies or towns, who distribute the water to individual users. The tribunal identified three DLWC services: (a) ensuring sustainable use and water quality, (b) supplying extractive users through river systems and artificial channels, and (c) enforcing user standards and license conditions (IPART 1996, p. iii).

Identifying the DLWC functions that provided these services, and the costs of those functions, proved difficult. The department had a number of functions relating to a variety of resources. Even when IPART could identify the functions relating to bulk water services, it faced a daunting task in calculating their costs and in classifying them as regulation, resource management, or standard setting, particularly when a function contributed to the delivery of more than one service. Moreover, IPART often had to calculate economic costs for data that were organized according to accounting conventions, not economic theory.

The tribunal also faced a contentious task in assigning the costs of functions that delivered more than one service. It employed the basic principle that such costs should be paid for by those who benefit from the service in proportion to the benefit received, with the government paying for the cost of public benefits. The difficulty, of course, was identifying all benefits, costs, and beneficiaries. Identifying resource management costs and benefits, many of which were intangible, proved particularly difficult. In the end, the determination of cost shares had an inescapably arbitrary element that, given the tribunal's transparent process, has sparked continued debate.

To date, IPART has made three price determinations, first for the 1996–97 irrigation season, then for the 1997–98 season, and finally for the 1998–99 and 1999–2000 seasons. In the 1996–97 determination, the tribunal found reasons to make significant reform. It concluded, however, that the available data were so inadequate that it could do no more than freeze prices and call for better data. At the same time, it released an interim report laying out the principles guiding its inquiry and summarizing the work that was still needed to produce essential data (IPART 1996).

Although the interim report fell short of fixing the data situation entirely, it generated enough of a response—particularly by the DLWC—to enable the tribunal to both increase prices and change their structure. IPART took this action in its 1997–98 determination, even though it said the DLWC was "unable to provide full detail of the actual costs incurred, including key performance standards and efficiency targets" (IPART 1997, p. i). The tribunal also had to resolve the issue of cost sharing. It created two-part tariffs to recover recorded actual known costs plus half of a renewals annuity to finance future capital and maintenance expenditure. Despite the uncertainties involved and the magnitude of the price increase for some users, IPART was persuaded that "the revenues resulting from the proposed new prices will not result in over recovery of the users' share of efficient costs" (IPART 1997, p. i).

By 1998, the amount of data on benefits, efficiency, and cost shares had increased to such an extent that the tribunal set prices for two seasons ahead. It also increased prices further and imposed some additional restructuring. It assumed that the DLWC could achieve efficiency gains of 20 percent over the following two years. Even then, a revenue shortfall of US$5.8 million was expected in the 1999–2000 season. At present, IPART needs further improvements in cost information, in addition to progress in DLWC institutional reforms, before setting a longer-term price path.

Figure 14.3 illustrates the expected progress in cost recovery, as well as the divergence between cost estimates by IPART and the DLWC. The tribunal explains this divergence as reflecting (a) the tribunal's assumptions about the DLWC efficiency gains, (b) the DLWC's assumptions about certain policy administration costs, (c) the cost revisions that occurred after the DLWC submission to the tribunal, (d) the differing opinions regarding the appropriate sharing of joint costs, and (e) the DLWC's inclusion of a rate of return on existing investments.

On this last issue, IPART made a number of arguments against charging a rate of return on existing investments. These included the low opportunity cost of the infrastructure involved, the industry history of not charging such a rate, and doubts about the capacity of some irrigators to pay. The department and the tribunal agreed, however, that new investments should earn a positive rate of return.

Although it would be inaccurate to say that the price determinations of IPART did not generate any objections, the adverse responses were not sufficient to deter the government from accepting them. No doubt the prospect of competition policy payments, discussed later in this chapter,

FIGURE 14.3
Progress to Cost Recovery of New South Wales Bulk Water Service, 1996/97–2000/01

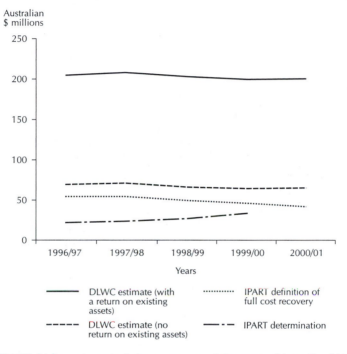

Note: DLWC's higher estimate includes a return on existing assets of Australian $130 million (6 percent return on replacement cost). DLWC estimates assume DLWC's proposed cost sharing ratios, and growth in costs of 2.8 percent in 1997–98 and 1998–99, offset by efficiency targets of 2.1 percent per year. IPART full cost recovery assumes IPART's cost sharing ratios, efficiency targets of 20 percent over three years (10 percent in 1998–99) for water delivery and resource management costs (Australian $40.3 million at 2000–01) and efficiency targets of 30 percent over three years (20 percent in 1998–99 for licensing costs (Australian $3.3 million at 2000–01).
Source: Independent Pricing and Regulatory Tribunal (1998).

encouraged government officials to accept the tribunal's price increases. Furthermore, significant groups rallied behind the reforms, including environmentalists, who believed that the elasticities of bulk water demand were such that rising prices would lead to declining consumption and so leave more water for the rivers (IPART 1996). Note that environmentalists played a major role in promoting both rural and urban reforms.

Opposition to the price increases came, not surprisingly, from the extractive users, predominately the irrigators. Although normally politically effective, the extractive users could not overcome the force of the tribunal's arguments, which were reinforced by the transparency of the process and IPART's careful consultation with the stakeholders, including environmentalists, government agencies, and irrigation interests. The extractors' clout also was undercut by some users who told the tribunal that they were prepared to pay the accurately determined costs of efficient and necessary services (IPART 1997). The IPART determinations undoubtedly moved the system toward accurate cost assessment.

The Council of Australian Governments and Microeconomic Reform of the Water Industry

COAG, which was established in 1992, has developed an explicit water policy reform agenda. COAG consists of the commonwealth prime minister, the state premiers, the territory chief ministers, and the president of the Australian Local Government Association. It puts together major polices for the future of the Australian federation and is an important instrument of cooperative federalism. In 1993 it concluded that significant economic and environmental benefits could be achieved by further water reform (Working Group on Water Resources Policy Secretariat 1995). This reinforced a report by the Industry Commission (1992) that reached similar conclusions.

In response, COAG established the Working Group on Water Resource Policy to develop a framework for water industry reform. The group's recommendations (Working Group on Water Resource Policy 1995) were adopted, almost without change, by COAG. The COAG strategic framework was incorporated into the national competition policy. As a result, competition payments helped spur state action on water reform. In turn, the breadth of the COAG framework has facilitated the pursuit of the national competition policy objectives with regard to water. The framework is important for its provisions on ecological sustainability and for generating community awareness and education. As a result, it is attractive to the environmental movement while raising the probability of general public understanding and support.

The strategic framework, which COAG adopted in 1995, includes a number of significant water system reforms. First, it calls for pricing reform based on the principles of consumption-based pricing, full cost recovery, and the removal of cross-subsidies. Remaining subsidies should become transparent. Second, states and territories should implement comprehensive systems of water allocations or entitlements, including allocations for the environment as a legitimate user. Water property rights are separated from land titles, so entitlements could be transferred between land titleholders. Third, by 1998, government should achieve structural separation of the roles of water service provision from water resource management, standard setting and from regulatory enforcement. Fourth, water systems should adopt two-part tariffs for urban water when such an approach is cost-effective. They should also introduce arrangements for trading in water allocations or entitlements. Fifth, by 2001, rural water charges should reflect full cost recovery with transparent subsidies. Whenever practicable, the charges should achieve positive real rates of return on the written-down replacement costs of assets. Sixth, any future investment in new irrigation projects or extensions to existing projects should be undertaken only after an appraisal indicates that the proposal is economically viable and ecologically sustainable.

Because of the far-reaching nature of the proposals, the council agreed to a five- to eight-year implementation period. Furthermore, the first tranche of competition payments in 1997 was not made conditional on progress in water reform.

The Water Reform Task Force

In February 1994, the council established a water reform task force to assist states and territories with the COAG reforms. The task force consisted of senior federal and state water agency officials, and it was chaired by an independent businessperson. It has promoted a uniform approach to reform, established milestones to help states and territories comply with the framework, assisted in clarifying issues, and provided guidance on controversial matters. In 1998 a high-level steering group on water, consisting of the heads of the relevant agencies in each jurisdiction, replaced the task force.

During its existence, the task force reported on progress in implementing reforms, as well as on such difficulties as cost recovery in the rural sector. It made a significant contribution to the contentious issue of how to value assets in the water industry if government business enterprises are to meet the COAG requirements for full cost recovery. Although the scope of this chapter does not permit a comprehensive discussion of these issues, note that debate focused on thorny issues, such as how to measure asset consumption, establish suitable rates of return, and take account of externalities in establishing full economic cost. The task force wrestled with the conundrum of how to escape the circular relationship of asset values, rates of return, and prices that is inherent in the cost-recovery situation for regulated monopoly service providers.

The task force also developed pricing guidelines, which were accepted for use at the national level. These guidelines define upper and lower boundaries for cost recovery. To be regarded as viable, water businesses at a minimum must recover operational, maintenance, and administrative costs;

externalities; taxes or their equivalent (excluding income tax); interest cost on debt; and dividends (if any), as well as make provisions for asset maintenance and replacement. At a maximum, and to avoid monopoly rents, water businesses must not recover more than operational, maintenance, and administrative costs; externalities; taxes or their equivalent; provisions for cost-of-asset consumption; and the weighted average cost of capital. Dividends are to be set at a level that reflects commercial realities and simulates a competitive market outcome. The guidelines also recommend the use of the optimized deprival value method of asset valuation, full transparency in the treatment of dividend payments and community service obligations, and the use of a renewals annuity to ensure provision is made for future infrastructure investment.

The guidelines note that the final determination of full cost recovery is at the discretion of the appropriate state or territory body. The New South Wales government has taken an approach under which existing assets are valued by discounting expected future cash flows, and the cost of future investment is incurred annually as a renewals annuity (Sydney Water Corporation and Hunter Water Corporation 1998, pp. 12–21). IPART has adopted a more flexible approach in the case of bulk water.

Competition Reform in Australia

As part of a program of microeconomic reform, Australian officials have developed a national competition policy legislative package. It consists of national legislation and complementary intergovernmental agreements. The National Competition Council, one of the organizations established to administer the policy, has advisory and research functions and makes recommendations about access to essential infrastructure facilities. The council reviews state compliance with national competition policy and makes recommendations to the commonwealth treasurer regarding national grants to compliant states.

The National Competition Policy and Related Reforms Agreement sets out the mechanism for the commonwealth to provide financial assistance to the states that implement the agreed-on reforms and determines which states are eligible. This mechanism enables the commonwealth to use its financial muscle to induce the states to support the policy. There are three tranches of competition payments; the last one is due in July 2001. Failure by a state to meet significant elements of the policy reform agenda would render it ineligible for scheduled payments. In total, the commonwealth will allocate US$10 billion to the states between the 1997–98 and the 2005–06 fiscal years. The National Competition Council determines state eligibility for the payments.

The water reform task force, the COAG framework, and the national competition policy have proven to be important tools in achieving water reform in a consistent way across jurisdictions. By setting principles, targets, and incentives, and allowing the states to determine the best course of implementation within a highly consultative framework, officials have developed a noncoercive process. This is enabling the commonwealth government to spur reform despite the diversity and complexity of the Australian federation.

Progress with Reform

In July 1999, the National Competition Council issued its second tranche assessment of progress with regard to the water reform framework. As there was agreement that payment of the first tranche would not be conditional on progress with water reform, this was the first scorecard produced by the National Competition Policy. Previously, a variety of sources has produced a number of progress reports. Overall, the reform process is incomplete and assessment of the effects is only partial. Table 14.1 provides an overview of water price reform across the nation through 1997.

By 1998, all but one of the states and territories were able to claim progress in meeting COAG objectives for urban water price reform (Stark 1998). In addition, all but one of the nation's major urban water authorities had introduced two-part tariffs, consisting of an access price plus a usage price, with no base allowance (Furmage 1998).

A consistent theme, however, was a reluctance on the part of state and territorial officials to apply full cost-recovery principles to small local authorities because of limitations on the capacity of the small communities to pay.[4] In such circumstances, the COAG framework would seem to call for full and transparent identification of the resulting subsidies.

The relatively slower rate of reform of rural bulk water prices could reflect a number of other influences, including the political strength of the irrigation lobby and the extent to which it influences bulk water supply agencies. In addition, determining the costs of supply has proven difficult.[5]

---

4. Furmage (1998) points out that local governments generally do not directly receive competition payments, a policy that does not encourage local officials to implement reforms. Queensland, however, has agreed to pass on a share of its competition payments to local governments to encourage them to participate in reforms.

5. Stark (1998) concludes her review of progress through mid-1998 with the observation that much remains to be done, especially when it comes to understanding what constitutes full cost recovery and appropriate cost sharing in rural water services.

TABLE 14.1
Jurisdictional Progress in implementing Water Price Reform in Australia, 1997

Type of reform	New South Wales	Victoria	Queensland	Western Australia	South Australia	Tasmania	Australian Capital Territory	Northern Territory
Urban water (1998)								
Two-part tariff	✓	✓	✓	✓	✓	✓	✓	✓
Full cost recovery	□	✓	✗	□	□	□	□	✓
Reduction/elimination of cross-subsidies	✗	□	✗	✗	✓	✗	□	✓
Remaining subsidies made transparent	✗	□	✗	□	✓	✗	□	✓
Positive rate of return	✓	✓	□	□	✓	✗	✓	✓
Rural water (2001)								
Consumption-based pricing	□	□	□	□	□	□	n.a.	□
Full cost recovery	□	□	✗	□	□	□	n.a.	□
Reduction/elimination of cross-subsidies	□	✓	□	□	□	✗	n.a.	□
Remaining subsidies made transparent	□	✓	✗	✓	✓	✗	n.a.	✓
Rate of return	□	✓	✗	✗	□	✗	n.a.	□
Sinking fund	□	✓	✗	✗	□	✗	n.a.	□

n.a. Not applicable.
✓ Implemented.
□ Implementing.
✗ Little or no progress.
Source: Productivity Commission (1999).

314

Furthermore, even where political support for reform exists, officials took a cautious approach because of concerns about the possible impact of price increases on farms and rural communities. This concern was reasonable, given that the gap between actual and cost-recovery prices was greater for rural than urban water. This, in turn, reflected the poor condition of rural water infrastructure. The infrastructure, in many cases, represented investment decisions that, in retrospect, should not have been made.

The Productivity Commission (1999), in discussing the rate of rural water reform, refers to a number of stakeholder concerns. These concerns include the imposition of a rate-of-return requirement on water infrastructure and the establishment of sinking funds, in addition to depreciation charges. The commission points to the efficiency and equity arguments to emphasize the need for rates of return that reflect the opportunity cost of investment capital, efficient depreciation charges that cover maintenance requirements of assets, and sinking fund charges that cover expected asset refurbishment and replacement costs. It recognizes, however, the equity arguments involved in the choice between sinking fund and borrowing to fund asset replacement, as well as the question of whether existing users should be asked to fund the costs caused by past government neglect.

The incomplete nature of the reform process, and the time needed for reforms to have an impact means that, the Hunter experience aside, the effects of water price reform in Australia are not yet very obvious. However, the Productivity Commission has collected some revealing information. It reports that between 1991–92 and 1996–97, real prices for household and commercial water services fell in New South Wales and Victoria, but rose in other jurisdictions. The removal of cross-subsidies led to a 40 percent price decline for commercial users in Sydney and Melbourne in 1997. By contrast, the potentially adverse effects of reform in some towns in rural areas had to be ameliorated by the provision of explicit community service obligations.[6]

Little specific information on the impact of rural bulk water price reform is available. However, there are reports of significant price increases in some areas and associated shifts from low-value to high-value crops as a result.

In its June 1999 review, the National Competition Council reported substantial progress on the implementation of the COAG framework, although it identified issues regarding certain aspects of the agreed-on framework

---

6. The commission defines a community service obligation as arising when a government requires an enterprise to carry out activities relating to outputs or inputs that it would not do voluntarily except for higher prices. The commonwealth government has agreed that the nature of such obligations should be explicit and public.

in a number of states (National Competition Council 1999a). It reported price reform as contributing to an 18 percent reduction in water prices to Victorians, a 20 percent decline in water use in Brisbane, and a nearly 50 percent decline in real water costs for businesses in Western Australia between 1992–93 and 1997–98 (National Competition Council 1999b). In its 1999 annual report, the council cited reports that Australian commercial water users now receive the third cheapest bills of 15 major Western countries and that water businesses are returning increased dividends to governments (National Competition Council 1999a).

The review found that Australian Capital Territory (which has no irrigation) and Victoria have largely met their reform obligations. So too has the Murray-Darling Basin Commission, the intergovernmental body that is the wholesale supplier of water along the interstate Murray River. Of the remaining jurisdictions, New South Wales and Western Australia have made substantial progress, but they still need to reform property rights and water trading. The council assessed South Australia as complying with most of its second tranche commitments, although a number of pricing issues are outstanding. The others (Queensland, the Northern Territory, and Tasmania) were reported to have significant outstanding issues, including urban price reform. In a number of instances, the council is continuing its assessment prior to finalizing its recommendations concerning payment of second tranche funds. It has recommended suspending 25 percent of Queensland's payments for 1999–2000 pending resolution of concerns over a number of new rural schemes.

Amid ongoing consideration of property rights reform, officials are gaining an improved understanding of measures that promote both efficient markets and ecological sustainability. This appears to have led to slower progress with such reform than officials had hoped when the agreements were signed in 1994. In 2001, the council will also review rural water pricing for the first time. In recognition of the complexities of implementing water rights and trading, implementation of reforms has been extended for three years to 2001. More rigorous specification of commitments and implementation paths has accompanied this action (National Competition Council 1999a).

Conclusion

The political economy of water price reform in Australia is instructive in a number of respects. First, it confirms that successful reform requires the backing of an effective political coalition. Second, it demonstrates the difficulty of cost identification, measurement, and sharing, particularly in the rural sector. Third, it provides potential solutions to some of these problems. Fourth, it indicates that a consultative, incentive-based, and transparent process can propel reform in a federation.

Of the two case studies, Hunter illustrates the potentially dramatic positive impact of reform, and the value of a focused program of communication with the community to combat opposition. IPART provides an illustration of overcoming obstacles by applying reform principles in a rigorous, yet publicly defensible, way. It also demonstrates the value of a price-determining body, independent of government, that applies such principles in a transparent, consultative, and pragmatic way.

The COAG framework and the national competition policy have been important components of the reform process. To be sure, pressure for reform of bulk water prices had built before the creation of the framework and the policy, and reformers had already made considerable progress in both bulk and urban water matters. However, the framework and the policy helped codify principles, promote consistency across the nation, provide incentives, and contribute to debate on contentious matters, once again in a consultative and transparent fashion.

The reform process is not complete, and many of its costs and benefits have yet to manifest themselves. However, reformers have made considerable achievements, particularly in the urban sector. The social costs of reform are greater in the rural sector, and the forces opposed to it are stronger. Indeed, the opposition appears to be gaining strength, as evidenced recently by apparent electorate fatigue with reform. Despite this, there is good reason to expect the COAG targets to be met, at least in New South Wales and Victoria, and in the Australian Capital Territory, the Northern Territory, and South Australia. The outcome in Queensland, Western Australia, and Tasmania will be awaited with interest. In the event those states do not meet their deadlines, some compromise may be reached between them and the commonwealth, which could be approved by the other conforming jurisdictions.

References

Australian Competition and Consumer Council. 1997. *Public Utility Regulators Forum*, no. 1. Melbourne.

Campbell, K. O. 1964. "An Assessment of the Case for Irrigation Development in Australia." In *Water Resource Use and Management*. Melbourne: Melbourne University Press.

Campbell K. O., and R. G. Dumsday. 1990. "Land Policy." In D. B. Williams, ed., *Agriculture in the Australian Economy*, 3rd ed. Sydney: Sydney University Press.

Davidson, B. R. 1969. *Australia Wet or Dry.* Melbourne: Melbourne University Press.

Furmage, B. 1998. "Towards an Efficient and Sustainable Water Industry: National Competition Policy and Water Reform." Paper presented at the annual conference of the Victoria Branch of the Economic Society of Australia and New Zealand, July 2, Melbourne.

IPART (Independent Pricing and Regulatory Tribunal of New South Wales). 1996. *Bulk Water Prices: An Interim Report.* Sydney.

_____. 1997. *Bulk Water Prices from July 1997.* Sydney.

_____. 1998. *Bulk Water Prices for 1998/99 and 1999/00.* Sydney.

Industry Commission. 1992. *Water Resources and Waste Water Disposal.* Report no. 26. Canberra: Australian Government Publishing Service.

Kelly, P. 1992. *The End of Certainty: The Story of the 1980s.* Sydney: Allen and Unwin.

Langford, K. J., C. L. Forster, and D. M. Malcolm. 1999. *Towards a Financially Sustainable Irrigation System: Lessons from the State of Victoria, Australia, 1984–1994.* Technical Paper no. 413. Washington, D.C.: World Bank.

Lloyd, C., P. Troy, and S. Schreiner. 1992. *For the Public Health: The Hunter District Water Board 1892–1992.* Melbourne: Longman Cheshire.

Musgrave, W. F. 1996. "The Irrigation Industry in the Murray Darling Basin and Aspects of Its Reform." In J. J. Pigram, ed., *Security and Sustainability in a Mature Water Economy: A Global Perspective.* Armidale, Australia: University of New England, Centre for Water Policy Research.

National Competition Council. 1999a. *Annual Report.* Canberra: Australian Government Printing Service.

_____. 1999b. *Second Tranche Assessment of State and Territory Progress with Implementing National Competition Policy and Related Reform,* Vols. 1, 2, and 3. Canberra: Australian Government Printing Service.

Productivity Commission. 1999. "Impact of Competition Policy Reforms on Rural and Regional Australia." Draft report. Canberra.

Stark, P. 1998. "National Progress in Meeting Key Elements of the COAG Water Reform Agenda." *Australian Water* (June): 23–24.

Sydney Water Corporation and Hunter Water Corporation. 1998. *COAG Stocktake Report: Metropolitan Urban Water Service Providers Compliance with the COAG Strategic Framework for Water Reform 1994.* Sydney and Newcastle.

Watson, W., and R. Rose. 1980. "Irrigation Issues for the Eighties: Focusing on Efficiency and Equity in the Management of Agricultural Water Supplies." Paper presented at the annual conference of the Australian Agricultural Economics Society, Feb. 12–14, Adelaide, Australia.

Working Group on Water Resources Policy Secretariat. 1995. "The Council of Australian Governments' Strategic Framework for Water Resource Policy." In *Focus on Policy Developments and Options for Irrigation in the Lower Murray-Darling Basin*. Proceedings of an Irrigation Policy Workshop. Armidale and Canberra, Australia: Centre for Water Policy Research and the Australian Bureau of Agricultural and Resource Economics.

15

The Political Process Behind the Implementation of Bulk Water Pricing in Brazil

Luiz Gabriel T. de Azevedo and Musa Asad

Following recent congressional approval of a sweeping federal water law, Brazil is on the verge of implementing wide-ranging water sector reforms, including the introduction of bulk water pricing.[1] This chapter reviews the political process behind the development of a national water resources management system and draws lessons from recent analytical work and practice in Brazil. It then offers recommendations for the development of both water pricing and allocation policies to facilitate the introduction of bulk water pricing in Brazil.

Note the distinction between the price of water as a resource and the price of providing the resource to users. Although Brazil has a long record of legislation, policies, and procedures for pricing the latter, which is secondary retail distribution, it has yet to establish methods for pricing the former, which is bulk or wholesale water supply. Obviously, different levels of service are involved in the supply of water. Whereas most pricing discussions focus on retail water supply and distribution, this chapter deals only with the wholesale aspects of water pricing. (For more on the distinction between retail and bulk water pricing, see Asad and others 1999).

Regarding bulk water, Brazil faces two issues. The first is how to finance the construction and maintenance of the required infrastructure. Officials need to decide who should pay for projects such as multiple-use reservoirs and conveyance structures, as well as for collecting bulk water from its

---

1. An English language version of the law (Law 9,433, signed January 1997) is available on the web at the Brazilian Water Resources Association homepage http://www.abrh.org.

natural source and transporting it to the intermediate water service company. How much are consumers willing and able to pay for this part of the overall water supply service? The second issue is how to use pricing to achieve more efficient allocation and use of water. If, for instance, a system provided free bulk water to industrial plants, irrigation districts, and municipal water utilities, there would be no indication of how to allocate the resource based on its highest valued use. That is, one could not decide, based on economic efficiency, whether to allocate water mainly for agricultural, domestic, or industrial use.

Moreover, without adequate pricing, consumers have no signal indicating the value of water, and therefore no incentive to use the resource efficiently. Similarly, low prices cause maintenance problems. If water service companies are involved in providing bulk water (many utilities operate their own reservoirs and bulk water distribution systems) but cannot recover the costs from their final customers, the systems will deteriorate. Such deterioration can be seen worldwide, particularly in developing countries. Finally, water companies have little incentive to reduce water pollution if the cost of maintaining clean water is not incorporated into prices. As a result, water supplies could become increasingly unsafe.

Some economists have argued that the ideal theoretical solution for bulk water pricing is to establish economic efficiency as the main objective and set prices according to full cost-recovery criteria. Attaining this ideal, however, is generally not practical because of political realities and the complexities of administering water systems and disseminating information. Ignoring such issues, or leaving relevant stakeholders out of the reform process, could significantly hinder the momentum behind Brazil's efforts to implement bulk water pricing.

The following sections present the history and current situation of water pricing in Brazil. The final section makes recommendations for Brazil to sustain its pricing reform efforts.

Geographic and Institutional Background

Brazil has a surface area of 8.5 million square kilometers and a population of approximately 160 million people. The country is characterized by significant geographic, hydrologic, cultural, and economic regional diversities that affect the value of water as a resource. The Amazon Basin accounts for 202,000 cubic meters per second of average annual water flow, out of 251,000 cubic meters per second for the entire country (Azevedo and Simpson 1995). However, a significant portion of the territory, including the Northeast and the São Francisco River Basin, has a semi-arid climate that limits socioeconomic development. The south and southeast encompass more developed and humid areas, with large industrial and urban centers, intensive water use, and severe pollution problems. In these more developed regions, poor water scarcity is related to the quality of water.

Brazil can be divided into several geographic regions (Azevedo and Simpson 1995) with different water characteristics:

1. The Amazon Basin (located in the north and west-central parts of the country) accounts for 80 percent of the total fresh water and 63 percent of the land area, but only 5 percent of the population.
2. The Southeast contains 60 percent of the population, but just 10 percent of the land area and 12 percent of the fresh water.
3. The Northeast, which is facing the most critical water shortages, contains 35 percent of the population, with 13 percent of the land area and just 4 percent of the country's fresh water.

Both legally and culturally, Brazilians perceive water as a public good that belongs to the national or state governments. Based on the 1988 constitution, the federal government is responsible for developing a national water resources management system, although authority over the country's waters is divided between Brasília and the 26 states. Waters under national control, or federal waters, are defined as those that flow through more than one state or that serve as boundaries between states or between Brazil and its neighbors. State waters are defined as those existing solely within the territory of a single state.

In the past decade, water resources managers have become more concerned about severe problems related to excessive water use, pollution, and ecosystem degradation. The constitutional provision for a national water resources management system has presented the opportunity to implement institutional and legal frameworks for integrated, comprehensive water resources management. Shortly after the adoption of the 1988 constitution, states began to implement management systems for their waters. The federal government moved more slowly in formulating a proposal to deal with federal waters, and Congress took six years before approving the new national water law. Although these developments appeared to be slow, poorly coordinated, and decentralized, the process did lead to significant education about national water resources systems in other countries. The differing state approaches also enabled the federal government to develop a national law that incorporated common elements of state laws. In other words, the reform successfully combined top-down and bottom-up political processes.

Historical Background and Legal Framework

The legal foundation for water resources management in Brazil dates back to 1850. Portugal, still under Spanish rule, subscribed to the *Ordenação Filipinas* (Filipinas Ordinance), broad-based legislation that regulated a range of issues in the Spanish territories, including the use of water resources. The issue of water was important even then because of the scarcity of water in the Iberian peninsula, which included Portugal and Spain. The law laid the foundation for public water rights and allocations on a sectoral, rather than comprehensive, basis.

The next significant development took place 80 years later. Following the 1930s revolution, the government's Legislative Commission created a special subcommission to work on the development of a national water code. This work led to the adoption of the 1934 Water Code, the first significant legislation to regulate water resources management. Although the code aimed mainly to promote significant hydroelectric development and a subsequent industrial boom, it was a step in the direction of a comprehensive national water resources management system. Such a system came about 50 years later with the approval of the 1988 constitution and, more recently, the current water law that goes even further in promoting a national integrated water resources management system (see Kelman 1997).

In 1988, the Brazilian Congress stipulated in the new constitution that the federal government was responsible for implementing a national water resources management system, which included planning and regulating the use, preservation, and restoration of the country's water resources. The new constitution also stipulated that the federal government and the states were jointly responsible for legislation regarding forests, fisheries, environmental protection, soil conservation, and pollution control.

In 1991, the president sent to Congress the first official draft law dealing with the national water resources policy. About the same time, the state of São Paulo approved its Water Resources Management Act, the first state water law in the country. In 1992 the Northeastern state of Ceará approved its own system. During the following three years, five other states approved water laws. At the same time that states were developing water laws, bulk water pricing issues stirred heated debate and became major political issues. At first, many groups feared that bulk water pricing would increase production costs and seriously hurt Brazilian agriculture, potentially leading to higher food prices nationwide. Officials seeking technical guidance turned to the Brazilian Water Resources Association, which consists of water managers, academicians, policymakers, and others. In addition, the officials turned to universities and received assistance from the World Bank. As a result, important political groups realized that bulk water pricing was necessary to improve water system infrastructure and increase water use efficiency. It became clear that bulk water pricing constituted an essential tool for sound water resources management.

Shortsighted political opponents feared that increasing water costs and prices would antagonize voters. In addition, many well-established political groups worried that implementing transparent and participatory water management systems would cost them power over water resources allocation. This was particularly the case in the arid Northeast, where the "drought industry" (which promoted heavy investment expenditures) had long supported local political leaders. In the Southern and Southeastern regions, the industrial sector and other user groups who benefited from subsidized or free water fanned political opposition.

A few leading politicians, however, battled back. Their primary reform goals were (a) cutting unnecessary water subsidies; (b) providing adequate operation and maintenance funds for federal and state hydraulic infrastructure; and (c) imposing sound technical and economic criteria for the construction of new, and perhaps unnecessary, projects. Other major reform motivations included increasing the efficient use of water, reducing environmental impacts, and improving services to the poor.

In 1995 the government of President Fernando Henrique Cardoso created the Secretariat of Water Resources (SRH) within the Ministry of Water Resources, Environment, and Legal Amazon. The creation of the SRH came at a high political cost as it significantly shifted the long-time balance of power in water resources. For about three decades, from the 1960s to the 1980s, the electrical sector had dominated water resources management in Brazil, emphasizing hydropower generation as the priority use of water. The creation of the SRH not only shifted power from the electrical sector, but it also threatened to reduce or eliminate the sector's mandate to collect millions of dollars through tariffs for multipurpose water resources projects. The resulting power struggle between the newly created and still vulnerable SRH and the well-established and competent electrical sector dominated the SRH's agenda during the initial two years of its existence, significantly affecting the secretariat's ability to effectively implement the national water resources management system.

In 1996 and 1997, the privatization of the electrical sector and the creation of a national energy regulatory agency diverted the electrical sector's focus. This enabled the president to win congressional approval of the water law that empowered the SRH to collect bulk water fees from federal watersheds.

The House and Senate passed the National Water Resources Management Act in the latter part of 1996. President Cardoso signed it on January 8, 1997, some six years after Congress had received the original proposal. The original principles of decentralization, integrated management, river basin management (as opposed to the management of water according to political and administrative boundaries), and the economic value of water remained the law's main guidelines.

Current Practices in Brazil

In general, Brazil does not charge bulk water fees for irrigation or water supply. In the hydroelectric subsector, power companies pay a royalty fee, based on a percentage of the revenues they collect, to the states and municipalities where their hydroelectric facilities are located (see, for example, Seroa da Motta 1998). Urban water users pay for the treatment and distribution of water and the collection of sewage, and farmers in public irrigation projects pay a tariff for the operation and maintenance of the projects. Under current practice, water user charges are the primary funding source for operation and maintenance of water resources projects.

As stated previously, the establishment of bulk water tariffs is one of the major pricing reforms in Brazil. Many states are implementing bulk water supply tariffs. The following section looks at some representative cases.

Water Charges in State Legislation

Since the early 1990s, several states have enacted water management legislation.[2] In every case, these laws have addressed the following issues: (a) water resources management at the river basin level, (b) state water resources management plans to guide decisionmaking about policy and investments, (c) individual water user rights, and (d) water pricing based on both quantity and quality.

Table 15.1 shows that the charges in such legislation are based on environmental quality, water availability, hydrological characteristics, and type of use. Some states, such as Minas Gerais, Bahia, and Rio Grande do Norte, include additional criteria, such as change in spatial occupation, regional priorities, and socioeconomic conditions. In at least seven states, the revenues collected from water charges for a given basin are allocated to a water management fund, from which a portion is allocated to other basins.

---

2. This section draws mainly from Seroa da Motta (1998).

TABLE 15.1
State Legislative Criteria for Water Charges

State	Application of revenue outside watershed	Revenue allocated to water management fund	Achieve better environmental standard	Change spatial occupation	Environmental quality (suitability)	Water availability and features	Type of use	Users' socioeconomic conditions	Regional economic objectives
São Paulo (1991)	x	x	n.a.	n.a.	x	x	x	n.a.	n.a.
Ceará (1992)	x	x	n.a.	n.a.	x	x	x	n.a.	n.a.
Distrito Federal (1993)	n.a.	n.a.	n.a.	n.a.	x	x	x	n.a.	n.a.
Minas Gerais (1994)	n.a.	n.a.	x	x	x	x	x	x	x
Paraná (1995)	n.a.	n.a.	n.a.	n.a.	x	x	x	n.a.	n.a.
Santa Catarina (1994)	x	x	n.a.	n.a.	x	x	x	n.a.	n.a.
Sergipe (1995)	x	x	n.a.	n.a.	x	x	x	n.a.	n.a.
Rio Grande do Sul (1995)	n.a.	n.a.	n.a.	n.a.	x	x	x	n.a.	n.a.
Bahia (1995)	x	n.a.	x	x	x	x	x	x	x
Rio Grande do Norte (1996)	x	x	n.a.	n.a.	x	x	x	x	n.a.
Paraíba (1996)	x	x	n.a.	n.a.	x	x	x	n.a.	n.a.
Pernambuco (1997)	x	x	n.a.	n.a.	x	x	x	n.a.	n.a.
Rio de Janeiro (1999)	n.a.	n.a.	n.a.	n.a.	x	x	x	n.a.	n.a.

n.a. Not applicable.
Source: Asad and others (1999).

In general, more specific water pricing calculations are left for the regulatory stage. However, no state law clearly defines the process of determining specific water charges. Rather, most laws indicate merely that state water councils will approve specific water charges proposed by user committees. The process would be more transparent if detailed regulations defined these charges. The regulations should also define the permissible degree of intervention by state water councils, the role of the water resource agency in such councils, and the determination of charges.

Rio Grande do Sul's legislation was the first to define a minimum charge, which user committees could increase, based on pre-established criteria. This is similar to the system in France. As described in this section, the São Paulo State Water Resource Council is taking a similar approach, and it seems that other states will follow.[3]

São Paulo Proposal

In October 1997, the São Paulo State Water Resources Council submitted a proposal to set specific water charges for all types of use, including irrigation, recreation, and navigation (inland shipping). The proposal advocates setting charges based on a basic unit price, or *PUB*, a maximum unit price, or *PUM*, and an average annual cost of production.

The *PUB* is estimated for water withdrawal, consumption, biochemical oxygen demand (*BOD*), chemical oxygen demand (*COD*), suspended solids (*SS*), and inorganic load.

The total amount charged to a user for use j in basin i ($CT_{j,i}$) is calculated by multiplying PUB_j by the quantity of intake, consumption, and pollutants ($Q_{j,i}$) and by coefficients specific to each ($X_{j,i}$), so that

$$CT_{j,i} = Q_{j,i} \cdot PUB_j \, X_{j,i}$$

where $X_{j,i}$ is a vector of ecological factors. The values of $X_{j,i}$ are decided by basin committees, but the $PUB_j \cdot X_{j,i}$ portion may not exceed the PUM_j.

The sum of all of a user's $CT_{j,i}$ may not exceed a specified percentage of the average annual cost of production (or an equivalent percentage of the billing). In other words, the criteria are based on the user's ability to pay. The definition of these thresholds, however, appears arbitrary and is not based on any explicit criteria of equity.

---

3. The São Paulo case is a good example of the difficulty in reaching consensus on water charges. The state has been considering this issue since 1991, but only now does it appear to be finalizing an official proposal.

The French system was used as a reference to set the amounts for the *PUB*, allocate the costs of providing and expanding the supply of water, and allocate the costs of controlling pollution (by the estimated load, and by type of use and user). For allocation purposes, consumptive use was considered most damaging to the environment, whereas diversion was considered least damaging, because it alters only the course of rivers and does not produce pollution. All other forms of water withdrawal, regardless of the level of consumption, generate some type of pollution, because they reduce flow and dilution capacity. In the case of sewage, given the limited data available, investments were distributed solely in terms of the charge for the estimated biochemical oxygen demand load in effluents.

Table 15.2 shows the proposed prices for São Paulo. The prices for water withdrawal are similar to those charged in France. For pollution charges, however, São Paulo's proposed prices are significantly lower than those charged in the French system, which, in turn, are lower than in Holland and Germany (Asad and others 1999).

With regard to $X_{j,i}$ values, the proposal suggests the gradual introduction of various factors according to the following timetable:

1. Years 1–3: type of water use, such as urban and industrial[4]
2. Years 4–6: class of river, in terms of such variables as water availability, environmental quality, and recharging zone

TABLE 15.2
Proposed Basic Unit Prices for Water Charges in São Paulo

Item	Unit	Basic unit price (R$)[a]
Water withdrawn	Cubic meter	0.01
Consumptive use	Cubic meter	0.02
Effluent discharge		
of *BOD*[b]	Kilogram	0.10
of *COD*[b]	Kilogram	0.05
of *SS*[b]	Liter	0.01
Inorganic load	Kilogram	1.00

a. US$ = R$ 1.19 (as of February 2000, US$ = R$ 1.80).
b. Term defined in the text.
Source: Asad and others (1999).

4. In 1997 the State Water Resources Council decided to postpone charging farmers until the year 2004.

3. Years 7–9: seasonal nature of water source, such as peak period and
    flooding, or excessive use area in the case of groundwater
4. Years 10 and after: additional differential factors.

The proposed incremental approach is widely accepted in Brazil as sensible, although it is still difficult to charge for all types of uses.

Regarding type-of-use charges for water consumption, the São Paulo council suggests charging relatively high prices to industry, mid-range prices to urban residents, and low prices to users of irrigated water or farmers. However, irrigation has a higher water quality charge than urban use. Rather than being based on economically efficient pricing, this overall approach seems to be based on cost-recovery objectives. Charging higher water quality prices for irrigation seems to be inconsistent with economic theory, which would argue for setting prices inversely proportionate to the price elasticity of demand for a given resource. The price elasticity in the irrigation sector is generally higher than in the industrial and urban sectors. Furthermore, even the cost-recovery objective may be difficult to achieve, because price elasticity in the water sector varies depending on the type of use. This implies that actual revenues may be significantly lower than projected.

As for rivers, the higher their environmental quality, the greater their coefficient value. This means that, as in France, the most environmentally sensitive rivers are assigned a higher price in an effort to discourage degradation.

Officials estimate that these basic unit prices will generate annual revenues of about R$ 500 million, with approximately 50 percent derived from urban consumption, 30 percent from irrigation, and 20 percent from industry. However, this estimate assumes that price elasticity is zero, which, as noted previously, is generally not the case. In reality, users will likely reduce their consumption once they face higher water charges, thereby diminishing actual revenues.

Rio Grande do Sul

Lanna, Pereira, and De Lucca (1997) is an unofficial proposal supporting the determination of a minimum price (similar to the *PUB* in São Paulo) that the state would charge for pollution. This pollution charge would vary by type of user. The study uses the Rio dos Sinos Basin as a model.

The study considers three criteria: pollution mitigation, revenue collection, and the cost of treating each water source. The pollution criterion is similar to São Paulo's environmental quality factor. As in the São Paulo proposal for basin coefficients, the state would impose higher charges to encourage greater environmental protection. The second and third criteria are similar to those used in the São Paulo proposal for calculating basic unit prices. However, the Rio Grande do Sul study is distinct in that it uses an optimization model to determine basic unit prices. This model seeks to optimize the distribution of billing costs with respect to both pollution control costs and the level of contamination in the area where the water source is located.

The study produces several simulations and analyzes the impact of charges in relation to the operational cost of the industry, with three cross-subsidy scenarios (table 15.3). In scenario 1, there is no cross-subsidy, and prices of the model are applied in full. In scenario 2, the industrial sector pays 40 percent of the costs charged to scattered rural sources. In scenario 3, industry pays for all rural costs; that is, the charges to rural sources are fully subsidized by industry.

One can see that the impact on the operational cost of industries in the different scenarios varies little, from 1.40 to 1.45 percent. Thus, leaving out the rural sector would not jeopardize the objectives of the Rio Grande do Sul model and case study. Furthermore, the political cost of rural inclusion is high, as the experiences of other countries demonstrate. As Lanna, Pereira, and De Lucca (1997) indicate, the study's results suggest avoiding charging rural users during the system's implementation phase.

Note, however, that the calculations do not take into consideration any adjustments by users in response to the new pollution charges. In addition, the prices produced by the model do not reflect optimum price

TABLE 15.3

Impact of Water Charges for Pollution in the Industrial Sector of the Rio dos Sinos Watershed, Rio Grande do Sul

(percentage of operational cost)

Sector	Scenario 1	Scenario 2	Scenario 3
Hides/skins/similar	0.2000	0.2000	0.2100
Beverages/alcohol	0.0200	0.0200	0.0200
Textile	1.6100	1.6300	1.6600
Food	1.4000	1.4200	1.4500
Chemical	0.0000	0.0000	0.0000
Metal	0.0002	0.0002	0.0002
Cellulose/paper/cardboard	0.0003	0.0003	0.0003
Public utility	1.4000	1.4200	1.4500

Source: Lanna, Pereira, and De Lucca (1997).

criteria for minimizing costs or maximizing well-being from a socio-economic perspective. There is no assurance that the model's prices are cost-efficient or include social costs.[5]

Bahia

The Bahia case study (Fernandez 1996) focuses on two of the state's most important river basins: Alto Paraguaçu and Itapicuru. The study estimates water supply charges for irrigation, urban use, and electricity generation, as well as charges for heavy metal pollution from chromium mining.

For each basin, the study identifies willingness-to-pay estimates for water services. The payments support irrigation, urban water use, and electricity generation. The estimates are based on covering all costs of water supply systems, including investments, administration, and operations and maintenance. Using a public price optimization model, which is designed to set prices inversely proportional to price elasticity demands for different water uses, the study then determines specific water charges for each type of water use in each basin.

The study focuses primarily on cost recovery, so price variations are analyzed in terms of revenue generation rather than pure economic or social efficiency. As such, for pollution, prices are not estimated for externalities but rather for financing, and only for one type of pollution and user. Table 15.4 presents the estimated charges and their respective five scenarios.

Although this section has concentrated on price variations and their effects on revenue, a comparison of these scenarios reveals various economic factors related to the impact of charging optimized prices for each use. Despite the emphasis on cost recovery, one can observe in table 15.4 price variations with respect to demand elasticities. For example, in the SE scenario, in which users that generate electricity are not charged, it is the price charged for urban use that increases. This is because the elasticity of urban use (0.04) is much lower than that of irrigation (0.39) in the Alto Paraguaçu Basin.

In the Itapicuru Basin, the estimated price for irrigation charges was higher than what users were willing to pay, when all investments were considered. Thus, in the IR scenario, which included a 25 percent charge for investment, the study considered a 75 percent reduction in these

---

5. Lanna, Pereira, and De Lucca (1997) refer to this solution as one of cost-effectiveness, because it seeks a more balanced distribution of water charge costs. In this context, the study is not defining cost-effectiveness as minimizing social costs.

TABLE 15.4

Charge Estimates in Watersheds in the State of Bahia

(US$/m^3)

Use	Alto Paraguaçu watershed			Itapicuru watershed	
	CE[a]	SE[b]	IT[a]	IR[c]	AP[d]
Irrigation	$8.00 \cdot 10^{-4}$	$8.00 \cdot 10^{-4}$	$9.91 \cdot 10^{-3}$	$2.17 \cdot 10^{-3}$	$9.86 \cdot 10^{-3}$
Urban	$2.76 \cdot 10^{-4}$	$3.13 \cdot 10^{-1}$	$1.08 \cdot 10^{-3}$	$8.80 \cdot 10^{-4}$	$1.08 \cdot 10^{-3}$
Power	$8.40 \cdot 10^{-4}$	n.a.	n.a.	n.a.	n.a.
Pollution	n.a.	n.a.	$1.52 \cdot 10^{-2}$	$2.32 \cdot 10^{-3}$	$1.80 \cdot 10^{-1}$

n.a. Not applicable.

a. Full-cost charges for all uses.

b. Full-cost charges for all uses except power generation.

c. Full-cost charges for administration, operation, and maintenance, and a 25 percent investment cost charge.

d. Full-cost charges, with higher charges for pollution.

Source: Fernandez (1996).

investments and, consequently, the new prices resulting from the charge also dropped. Nevertheless, the price reduction for irrigation was much lower than for urban use because, unlike Alto Paraguaçu, the price elasticity of irrigation (0.58) in this basin is lower than for urban use (0.99).

Note also that the price of pollution in the Itapicuru basin represents an increase of only 0.1 percent in the cost of mining and an increase of only 10 percent in the marginal cost of controlling the current level of production. As such, pollution prices based on the revenue optimization criteria may not create any significant incentive for mining companies to increase environmental controls because there is no environmental constraint for pollution in the price-setting procedure.

Similarly, if we compare the IT and AP results in table 15.4—full-cost charges versus an increased charge for pollution—there is little variation in charges for irrigation and urban users, despite the significant increase in pollution prices. This result is surprising considering that the price of pollution is relatively elastic (0.57). If pollution prices increase, one may expect water users producing pollution to substantially reduce their water consumption, which would result in reduced demand for water and, subsequently, lower water charges. The fact that the IT and AP results do not show such a variation in charges can be explained by the small amount of pollution generated in the basin compared with direct water consumption. This observation highlights the need to consider externalities and indirect water consumption (such as for hydroelectricity) when setting water charges, particularly if cross-subsidies are necessary.

Ceará

The state of Ceará has already established a bulk water tariff system (see Asad and others 1999; Kemper 1998; World Bank 1998). This has enabled the Ceará bulk water supply company, Companhia de Gestão dos Recursos Hídricos (COGERH), to establish an appropriate tariff structure, an initial tariff level, and a timetable to gradually achieve reasonable cost recovery of operation and maintenance costs and of investments in new water storage and conveyance infrastructure.

Although Ceará is one of Brazil's poorest states, with an average per capita income of about US$2,500 (compared with World Bank estimates of per capita income for Brazil of about $4,600 for fiscal year 2000), COGERH has already been able to collect annual revenues of more than US$2 million from 85 reservoirs, according to its 1997 financial statements. Although COGERH ultimately seeks to use pricing measures to adjust demand and gradually introduce water scarcity values to all users, its initial water pricing policy is explicitly based on ability to pay criteria and primarily targets industrial and municipal users.

Current Proposal for the Regulatory Framework

Three years after Congress approved the Federal Water Law, officials continue to clash over the regulatory framework that will implement the law. In accordance with Brazilian law, the framework has been prepared by the SRH and sent to the president, who may then approve it as a presidential decree. The most controversial issues under review are: (a) water rights concessions, (b) watershed committees and water agencies, and (c) bulk water pricing. The controversy about the effective implementation of bulk water pricing became so intense that the government of Brazil initially considered sending the president a proposed framework without pricing recommendations, deferring any decision on that controversial issue. It soon became obvious, however, that the implementation of the national water resources management system depended almost exclusively on water fee revenues. Therefore, the SRH, after extensive consultations with technical agencies, private and public sector groups, and public hearings, proposed rules for bulk water fees.

Recently, the SRH produced a draft regulatory framework, which was a tremendous advance forward. The framework has five principles. First, it states that all water is a public good with an economic value that should be adequately priced. Second, it calls for guaranteed, well-defined water use rights for all legitimate uses, including residential drinking and sewage, hydropower, irrigation, and navigation, while safeguarding the environment. Third, in times of scarcity, residential water supply takes priority. Other users receive allocations based on their ability to pay, and the highest bidders receive the first allocations. Fourth, the right to release effluents into bodies of water should be based on the quantity of water required to dilute the discharge, in accordance with pollution guidelines established by the relevant watershed management plan. Finally, states and watershed management agencies have the flexibility to regulate all aspects of water resources management, including planning, water pricing, revenue collection, and investment decisionmaking.

With Brazil coming off an election year in 1998, and with the government facing fiscal and administrative reforms, one may safely expect approval of the regulatory framework to take additional time.

However, a shift in political strategy led the Brazilian government to propose to Congress (September 1999—Law Proposal 1617/99) the creation of an independent National Water Agency (ANA), which would be responsible for regulating the use and conservation of water resources. In parallel, the president sent to Congress a bill (September 1999—Law Proposal 1616/99), complementary to the National Water Law, that includes the regulatory instruments for the implementation of bulk water pricing. The creation of the ANA has gained popular and political support, and the ANA bill, which has already been approved by the lower house, is currently in the Senate. The approval of the complementary bill and associated regulatory framework is, however, more complex, and the proposal is waiting for initial steps to be taken in the lower house toward its evaluation and eventual approval.

Although the delays in Brasília may slow down the overall process of water reform, they will not necessarily prevent individual states from moving more quickly. If the federal government delays persist, one may expect that states such as Bahia, Paraná, Rio Grande do Norte, and São Paulo could decide to implement bulk water pricing programs on their own. At a minimum, they will probably initiate water pricing programs for specific projects, including some financed by the World Bank. In the meantime, Ceará has implemented a bulk water pricing program that has won support from the Bank. Although the experience in the states is limited, it does highlight the improvements to water resources management, including improved efficiency and cost recovery for bulk water supply services, that can be attained in a relatively short period.

Conclusion

Brazil has recognized the need to use pricing to promote system sustainability and the efficient use and allocation of water resources, and it has quickly moved toward the establishment of water tariffs for all major user sectors in the country. However, progress is slow, and no national comprehensive framework exists to guide the formulation of specific state or municipal pricing designs. The independent efforts that this chapter describes remain isolated.

Some economists have argued that the ideal theoretical solution for bulk water pricing is to establish economic efficiency as the main objective and set prices according to full economic cost-recovery criteria. This goal, however, may be impractical for several reasons. First, it would depend partially on the daunting task of estimating opportunity costs for different water uses. Making such estimates is, at best, a complicated and expensive process, and, at worse, produces completely misleading data. Increasingly, international experts are coming to the conclusion that allowing the market to determine opportunity cost prices is more sensible. This requires creating the conditions for water markets to evolve.

The second administrative problem is that, in practice, most water agencies are doing well if they can recover operation and maintenance costs and a portion of investment costs for bulk water supply services. More typically, these services are partially or fully subsidized by public institutions. This is mainly a historical and cultural issue: water users in most countries are accustomed to paying little or nothing for bulk water. For this reason, political leaders are generally reluctant to adopt any bulk water pricing reform at all for fear of alienating powerful water user interest groups as well as individual users.

Therefore it is preferable, at least initially, to put aside the focus on economic efficiency, and instead set cost recovery as the main bulk water pricing objective. Also, regardless of whether the implementation of bulk water pricing reform is a one-time event or incremental, involving all stakeholders in the process is critical. This includes upstream involvement in the design of pricing schemes, as well as downstream involvement in the implementation of the schemes, and the involvement of both in the collection and allocation of associated revenues.

Taking the above into consideration, Brazil will be able to avoid losing the current momentum behind its bulk water pricing reform by (a) prioritizing national and state regulatory frameworks; (b) establishing clear pricing objectives, with cost recovery followed by economic efficiency; (c) justifying and creating transparent subsidies that are limited to supporting public multipurpose water resource development projects; and (d) creating conditions for water markets to evolve.

In addition, the political establishment must overcome the general public perception that the payment for the use of water resources represents another government tax. This is a difficult political obstacle to the approval of the regulatory framework because of general economic and political uncertainty in Brazil. The current drought in the Northeast adds tension to the debate, with people wondering how they may be charged for something they may not have or use. The challenge for reformers is to assure users that water supplies will be made more reliable by the establishment of bulk water tariffs, along with allocation of secure water rights, participatory and decentralized management at the basin level, and the development of adequate regulatory and institutional frameworks. The Cardoso government, as well as a number of state governments, seem to understand the importance of sustaining and broadening the water sector reforms initiated to date. The hope is that this leadership will enable Brazil to address all the challenges effectively.

References

Asad, Musa, Luiz Gabriel T. de Azevedo, Karin E. Kemper, and Larry D. Simpson. 1999. *Management of Water Resources: Bulk Water Pricing in Brazil.* Technical Paper no. 432. Washington, D.C.: World Bank.

Azevedo, Luiz Gabriel T., and Larry D. Simpson. 1995. "Brazil—Management of Water Resources" Economic Notes no. 4. Country Department 1. Washington, D.C.: World Bank.

Fernandez, J. C. 1996. "Projeto de Implantação da Cobrança pelo Uso e Poluição da Água dos Mananciais do Alto Paraguaçu e Itapicuru." World Bank-financed consultancy report submitted to secretariat, Bahia State Water Resources Agency. Salvador, Brazil.

Kelman, Jerson. 1997. "Integrated Water Resources Management in Brazil." Unpublished.

Kemper, Karin E. 1998. "Institutions for Water Resource Management." In *Brazil: Managing Pollution Problems—the Brown Environmental Agenda.* Report no. 16635-BR, Vol. II: Annexes. Washington, D.C.: World Bank.

Lanna, A. E., J. S. Pereira, and S. J. De Lucca. 1997. "Simulação de uma Proposta de Gerenciamento de Recursos Hidricos na Bacia do Rio dos Sinos—RS." Working paper, University of Rio Grande do Sol.

Seroa da Motta, R. 1998. "Utilização de Critérios Econômicos para a Valorização da Água no Brasil." Unpublished discussion text no. 556, Institute of Applied Economic Research, Rio de Janeiro.

World Bank. 1998. "Brazil Water and Sanitation Sector Strategy Note." Washington, D.C.

16

Water Pricing:

The Dynamics of Institutional Change in Mexico and Ceará, Brazil

Karin E. Kemper and Douglas Olson

In recent years, a number of World Bank projects have incorporated significant institutional components into their design. These components are aimed at complementing supply-side management with demand management. They typically include features like definition, allocation, and administration of water rights, as well as volumetric water measurement and water pricing to reflect the value of water as an economic resource. Other key components include the decentralization of decision-making to the river basin level, and the establishment and strengthening of water user associations and river basin commissions. Because typical engineering projects usually have a life span of five years, these projects are designed for five-year terms too. As this chapter will illustrate, however, the innovative designs, as well as the fact that changes in institutional arrangements are linked to political, social, and economic processes, imply the need for longer time frames to achieve the objectives of such projects.

This chapter will explore two cases: Mexico and the state of Ceará in Northeast Brazil. It will analyze, from an institutional economics perspective, the experience of implementing water resources management policies and programs. The chapter deals with three main issues: (a) the rationale for new water resources management policies, (b) the main features of the policies, and (c) the extent to which implementation has been successful and the reasons for the success. Finally, the chapter makes recommendations for fostering institutional changes in water resources management through development projects.

Institutional and Physical Background of Mexico and Ceará

Ceará is a state within a federal country, whereas Mexico is a large federal country. However, we can compare their experiences with water policies, because Ceará's water resources legislation is largely autonomous. Both cases also share an important characteristic: the water resources sectors launched significant, and similar, reforms in the late 1980s, and therefore provide rare instances in which institutional change has advanced enough to assess the results in developing countries.

Ceará has a population of about 7 million people and covers an area of roughly 148,817 square kilometers. It has a semi-arid climate with an annual precipitation of about 600 to 800 millimeters, characterized by seasonal irregularities and recurrent droughts. Most of Ceará's water supply is surface water that is stored, and the distribution of which is regulated by means of reservoirs. Groundwater use is limited, because most of the land rests on crystalline rock formations, resulting in groundwater that is in scarce supply and often has a high mineral content.

Mexico has a population of about 98 million people and a land area of 2 million square kilometers. The country's climate varies from tropical humid to semi-arid to arid. Its annual precipitation averages 780 millimeters and, like Ceará, it suffers from recurrent dry spells in the arid and semi-arid areas. Mexico, however, has major groundwater resources, and 70 percent of urban and industrial water comes from groundwater.

In both cases, water is used for irrigation. Mexico has about 5 million hectares of farmland under irrigation (of which 2 million hectares use groundwater) that account for more than 80 percent of total water usage. In Ceará, irrigation accounts for about 45 percent of total usage.

Although Ceará is almost entirely semi-arid, 76 percent of Mexico's population live in the semi-arid and arid northern and central regions of the country. This corresponds to about 70 percent of industrial and 90 percent of irrigation activity, but only 20 percent of the available water resources.

In both cases, the traditional approach to water resources management emphasized increasing supply. In Ceará, more than 8,000 reservoirs have been built in the past 100 years. The 85 most important ones are of medium and large size. These reservoirs have a total capacity of more than 10 million cubic meters (m^3), and they provide multiyear storage and about 90 percent of the state's water supply. The reservoirs have been built to ensure annual flow in the state's ephemeral rivers that otherwise dry up in the dry season from July to December. The reservoirs supply major irrigation projects and urban centers, notably the growing state capital, Fortaleza, which has more than 2 million inhabitants.

Mexico has more than 4,000 dams, defined as being more than three meters high or having a storage capacity greater than 500,000 m^3. Of these, 640 are more than 15 meters high and can therefore be classified as large dams in accordance with the International Commission on Large Dams. Mexico has about 650 aquifers, of which 100 are overexploited; some are facing critical problems.

At the same time as more infrastructure has been built, people have used water inefficiently. In the irrigation sector, efficiency sometimes hardly reaches 30 percent. In urban areas, the level of lost and unaccounted-for water reaches 60 percent. Water charges for irrigation have been very low or none, and tariffs for urban domestic water have been very low. Industrial water tariffs were higher, but industry is not a comparatively major user of water.

The Case of Ceará

In the mid-1980s, a new government came to power in Ceará with an agenda of making the use of water resources more rational. In 1986, the government created the Secretariat of Water Resources (equivalent to a ministry at the state level), which as one of its first activities produced a state water resources plan. The state followed up in 1992 by passing its first water resources law. The law incorporated most of the features associated with modern water resources management, including water use rights, pricing, and management at the river basin level.

The Reason for Change

At about this time, state officials approached the World Bank about financing new water infrastructure, particularly a number of new reservoirs that would be situated in the *vazios hídricos*, which were critical areas in the interior where urban centers regularly suffered from recurring droughts. The proposal also included the construction of pipelines from existing reservoirs that were supposed to supply urban centers with water, but had never been connected to those centers.

The Bank agreed to finance the infrastructure on the condition that the state implement and use the instruments outlined in the new water resources law. The instruments included river basin management through the proactive creation of water user associations and the introduction of tariffs for all water uses, including irrigation. The Bank also insisted on the creation of a water resources management company, which had not been part of the state's original design for its new water resources management system. Bank officials reasoned that without an implementing agency, the state would be hard pressed to carry out reforms that required improved monitoring, forecasting, and reservoir operations, as well as linkages between the operation of the system and water user participation, implementation of water rights, and tariff setting and collection. Finally, the Bank included a pilot water market in the project design. The market was to be implemented in a new, but unrelated, irrigation project. Depending on the success of the pilot, similar markets would be incorporated in subsequent projects.

Achievements and Challenges

Generally speaking, Ceará has made enormous strides. It created an official water resources management company, Companhia de Gestão dos Recursos Hídricos (COGERH), in 1994, at the same time it started the program for new infrastructure. The company has about 20 fulltime employees and is responsible for the operation of all the state's major reservoirs, including those constructed by the federal government. These reservoirs, which account for roughly 90 percent of the state's water storage, include both older facilities and an additional 14 that were built as a result of the new program.

COGERH is also responsible for decentralizing water resources management to the river basin level. Officials have helped create committees in three major river basins, the Jaguaribe, the Curu, and the Metropolitana Basin. A number of water user commissions have also begun work, and in time they will evolve into full-fledged committees. Since 1994, the decentralization process has included roughly 400 COGERH-sponsored events, involving an estimated 11,000 stakeholders of all types, such as fishermen, major irrigation farmers, irrigation district participants, and industry leaders.

Ceará is also the first state in Brazil to introduce bulk water pricing for industries, as well as for the state sanitation company, which passes on the costs to its domestic and commercial users. Up to now, however, the government has deemed it almost impossible to charge for agricultural water use. The state now plans to roll out a tentative irrigation pricing approach with a symbolic tariff.

The pilot water market has yet to materialize. One reason is that Ceará's water resources law does not permit water markets, because user rights are not tradable. In this sense, the Bank insisted on a condition that required a major philosophical change on the part of both the government and water users, and also required a change in the law. Given the other changes, this additional feature clearly was too much for Ceará to digest at the time.

In summary, the state has made enormous progress, albeit not as much as government and Bank officials had originally planned. The following sections analyze the various stakeholders in the reform process and their gains and losses. This will help explain the achievements—and the failures.

Implementing the Changes

Institutional change takes place when relative prices or power positions change. Institutions are defined as the "rules of the game" (North 1990).[1] Whenever external or internal events lead to a change in the rules, a new institutional framework is created.

As mentioned previously, in 1985, Ceará underwent a change in government. A new entrepreneur-oriented government took over after a long period of *coronel* governments, which had been dominated by large landowners who benefited from continuing low industrialization, significant subsidies for agriculture, large infrastructure projects including the construction of reservoirs on their own lands, and cheap water.

The entrepreneur-oriented government is now in its third consecutive term and is emphasizing job creation through the development of industry, tourism, and agribusiness. To succeed, this strategy requires water security. Industries will not come without guaranteed water, agribusinesses (usually linked to high-value irrigation) will not invest without a secure water supply, and tourism will not flourish if visitors lack access to safe water. The government soon realized, however, that constant investments in expanding supply would be too costly. Instead, it would also have to press for efficient water use. In this way, the goals for economic development defined the goals for water resources development.[2]

---

1. Institutional economics as a discipline is increasingly applied in the analysis of natural resources management. In this economic subdiscipline, "institutions" are commonly defined as "the rules of the game"—the laws, norms (formal and informal), regulations, and policies that influence the actions of stakeholders.

2. For example, an article in the *Gazeta Mercantil,* a national newspaper, mentioned that the state of Ceará had managed to write contracts with nearly 100 new industries that had established themselves in the Fortaleza area. If all these projects turned into reality, they would imply US$580 million in investments and more than 16,000 new jobs (*Gazeta Mercantil* 1998).

This reasoning led to the state's water resources law in 1992. The law incorporated all the features that had been recommended by such professional entities as the Brazilian Water Resources Association, as well as internationally as evidenced by the Dublin Statement (ICWE 1992). The World Bank published its own water resources policy paper only one year later (World Bank 1993).

Passage of this law represented a major step toward reform. However, one needs to take seriously the Brazilian expression *a lei não pegou*, which refers to a law that does not have any effect. Many laws in Brazil and elsewhere have little impact. But in the case of Ceará, the law is seriously being put into practice by both state and water management officials as well as by other stakeholders who now actively participate in water resources management.

To understand the current situation, we need to take a look at the various stakeholders. In the state government, these include the Water Resources Secretariat and COGERH, which is the water resources management company directly answerable to the secretariat. Other stakeholders include the federal Department for Works against Droughts (DNOCS), the state Water and Sanitation Company (CAGECE), and the various types of water users. An important issue to consider are the incentives that motivate these stakeholders to support or oppose change or to maintain neutrality. The key question is: what do they win and what do they stand to lose?

In the case of the Water Resources Secretariat, the incentives appear clear. The secretariat, as part of the government, has a strong incentive to make the program a success. However, it cannot take actions, such as imposing excessive agricultural water tariffs, that hurt the interests of important political groups, because this would jeopardize the government's standing. This is clearly one of the reasons why introducing serious water pricing in the agriculture sector has been politically difficult.

The situation for COGERH is more complex. Because its mission is to manage the state's water resources, it has a large stake in gaining control over both infrastructure and institutional change. The struggle for control over infrastructure has taken place on two fronts, one with DNOCS and one with CAGECE.

DNOCS' INCENTIVES. As a state company, COGERH can manage only state assets. However, the large strategic reservoirs in Ceará were constructed by the federal government and therefore used to be under federal (DNOCS) jurisdiction. For COGERH to manage the state's water resources effectively, it needed the federal government to transfer the reservoirs to the state. DNOCS, understandably, did not easily give up the reservoirs, because it did not want its power base eroded. The department had been losing influence since the 1970s, with its number of employees dropping from a peak of 14,000 to less than 3,000 in 1998. Furthermore, the agency's headquarters is based in Fortaleza, Ceará's capital, and most of its infrastructure was in Ceará. Losing those assets could leave it superfluous. Not surprisingly, it took almost three years of negotiations to transfer some of the management responsibility to COGERH. Since 1997, the two entities have comanaged the federal reservoirs. The new Bank-financed reservoirs were built by the state and therefore automatically are under COGERH's management.

USERS' INCENTIVES. With the water storage system under its management control, COGERH also needed to get income under its control. As mentioned previously, officials planned to introduce pilot pricing in the Curu Valley. As time went by, however, it became clear that water in the Curu Valley is used almost entirely for low-value agriculture, and consequently users have neither the willingness nor the ability to pay tariffs that would cover even COGERH's operation and maintenance costs for providing water in the valley. Indeed, one could say that the transaction cost of convincing farmers and fishermen to pay would have been extraordinarily high (for an exhaustive analysis of Curu water use, see Kemper 1996).

Instead of fulfilling the Bank demands, which did not take into account the actual local situation, COGERH is following its own strategy. It created water user commissions that joined together to form a water user committee in 1998 in accordance with the state law. During the 1998–99 drought, the committee agreed to voluntary measures to reduce its members' water use. In addition, COGERH has made funds available for municipalities involved with the committee to spend on small water-related projects. These funds, amounting to US$1 million, have two objectives. First, they give the committee a sense of real power, which is important because no tariff collection has been taking place. This increases the incentives for the valley's stakeholders to participate in the committee. Second, given the cost of investments such as wells or pipelines, and the fact that the basin has more than 12 municipalities and other stakeholders, US$1 million does not amount to much. In that sense, the funds have an educational component: they illustrate the value of the government's investments in water systems, which users historically took for granted. The next step for COGERH will be to introduce pricing of the water resources. The agency is applying the same strategy in the larger Jaguaribe Basin, which has essentially the same characteristics as the Curu Basin, although with somewhat more high-value agriculture.

In respect to charging for agricultural use, COGERH is taking a step-by-step approach. In July 1998, it signed an agreement with an association of individual irrigators near Fortaleza to provide them with water. The agreed price was R$ 0.004 per m^3 (about US$0.002). According to COGERH officials, the irrigators made the agreement, because they shared a reservoir with a nearby town and feared losing access to the water. With the gradual formalization of water rights in the state, the irrigators believed that the town and its related industries might gain priority by paying for water that the irrigators were not paying for. By making the agreement, the irrigators are on the same footing as other users with regard to water allocations.

The example shows that the introduction of water rights is having an impact on all types of users and that the increased security indeed increases the users' willingness to pay. However, the step-by-step negotiation approach implies high transaction costs for COGERH, and it is inconceivable that all individual irrigators in the state will be won over. Nevertheless, the agreement is an important first step and provides an indication of both willingness and ability to pay for water in the small-scale irrigation sector.

CAGECE's INCENTIVES. COGERH was conceived as a mixed company that was supposed to become self-financing within five years. In its search for income, it turned to the one basin in the state where users would immediately be able to make payments for bulk water: the Metropolitana Basin, consisting of Fortaleza and its industries. The industries had been paying for bulk water since becoming connected to the state water and sanitation system, operated by CAGECE. Although their willingness presented COGERH with an opportunity, the company faced a problem: CAGECE was not willing to give up its sources of funding. Again, officials had to engage in extensive negotiations. Although a temporary arrangement has been reached, a satisfactory conclusion still needs to be worked out.

CAGECE has been providing all its customers, including industries and households, with treated water and has charged them for this. However, companies such as breweries and soft drink producers did not need treated water because it contained chlorine. In fact, they faced an extra cost in removing the chlorine. The price the industries paid for water in 1997 was R$ 1.20 per m^3, rather high by international standards. When COGERH took over the Metropolitana system as part of a compromise arrangement, it started charging R$ 0.60 per m^3 for untreated water. Industries, therefore, appreciated the change in providers. As part of an arrangement, however, the state water and sanitation company remained responsible for the distribution system in Fortaleza's industrial district, Maranguape. COGERH delivers bulk water to the entry point of the industrial district, and CAGECE then distributes it within the district. For this reason, CAGECE still gets the payment for the delivery at the R$ 0.60 rate, and passes half of it on to COGERH.[3]

The 1998–99 drought further complicated the situation. When COGERH took over the Metropolitana system, CAGECE agreed to pay it R$ 0.01 per m^3. Officials thought that this tariff, in addition to the industry payments, would offset COGERH's operation and maintenance costs with enough money left over to pay into a state fund for future investments. Obviously, with industry paying 60 times as much as domestic and urban users to CAGECE, the degree of cross-subsidization is enormous. Industry currently accounts for 65 percent of COGERH's revenues, but only about 5 percent of water consumption. Table 16.1 summarizes the current bulk water tariffs for the different user groups.

Unfortunately, officials failed to take into account that, in the case of a drought, water would have to be pumped to Fortaleza. Under the 1998–99 drought, these pumping costs came to about US$270,000 per month. Because COGERH's usual costs barely enable it to break even, this extra cost could bring it to bankruptcy. CAGECE refused to pay for the extra cost and maintained that an official tariff adjustment was necessary. COGERH, however, could not increase its tariffs, because the water resources law determines that this can be done only by the state.

TABLE 16.1
Water Tariffs for Different Water User Groups in Ceará in 1998–99
(US$/m^3)

Water user category	Tariff (US$/m^3) for water measured at point of delivery [a]
Industry	0.3300
CAGECE (municipal)	0.0100
Agriculture[b]	0.0020

a. Based on 1999 exchange rates (US$1 = R$ 1.8).
b. Most agricultural users do not pay for water.
Source: Author's personal communications with various agencies in Ceará (1998–99).

---

3. The exchange rate in 1997 was about R$ 1 = US$1. Since then, the real has been losing value, and the rate is now about R$ 1.8 = US$1. The rates cited in the chapter have been kept constant in reals, but are worth less in dollars.

The state, however, was in a pre-election period, which may explain its reluctance to increase the tariffs. As a short-term solution therefore, the state assumed COGERH's electricity bill, and a tariff study is about to be undertaken that will include a mechanism to deal with such situations. It was, however, a positive step that the government, in the form of the State Water Resources Secretariat, did assume responsibility for the situation. With the current arrangement, COGERH sends its energy bill on to the secretariat, and could therefore still function as a private company would, that is, it did not receive a lump sum subsidy for its operations, but was clearly accountable for everything it did except for the electricity bill.

The three different situations COGERH faced illustrate the complexity of improving water resources management through demand management mechanisms. New management mechanisms cannot be created in a vacuum. Each country or region has its institutional framework, often consisting of longstanding agencies (however weak) and stakeholders that may have quite different incentives than reformers would expect. As the beginning of this chapter pointed out, this is often not taken into account during the design of development projects. Planners continue to view such projects as predictable engineering tasks, insufficiently assessing the institutional process.

Despite the obstacles, Ceará has succeeded in launching bulk water pricing structures for industry, irrigation, and household use; organized functioning water user committees at the river basin level; and arranged professional operational management of its supply systems. Partly as a result, Fortaleza is the only capital in Northeast Brazil that did not experience rationing because of the 1998–99 drought. A new Bank-financed project that was approved in January 2000 is expected to consolidate these gains and further emphasize demand management, promote public education campaigns to make water use more efficient, and introduce more flexible allocation policies within and between sectors.

The Case of Mexico

The World Bank and the United Nations Development Programme helped Mexico develop its first national water plan in 1975. Although the plan was well prepared and comprehensive, its focus was conventional in that it emphasized the identification of potential projects to increase the supply of water to meet projected growing demands.

As part of its ongoing economic modernization program, the government of Mexico, like the government of Ceará, confronts problems arising from growing water scarcity. It also faces the more general need to conserve the nation's natural resources. To address these problems, Congress approved the National Water Law in 1992 and the law's implementing regulations in 1994. The water law sets out broadly based mandates for the development and implementation of plans and policies related to water resources management.

Implementing the National Water Law

The responsibility for fulfilling these mandates falls on Mexico's national water authority, the National Water Commission (CNA). The CNA is a relatively young institution created in 1989. It inherited a water system and institutional mechanisms that were in desperate need of modernization. The water infrastructure was in poor repair. Individuals served by the water systems had lost confidence in top-down centralized government policies emanating from Mexico City. During its short tenure, the CNA has made remarkable strides in ameliorating, if not eliminating, many of these basic problems. Through its creation of water user organizations, the CNA has decentralized operation and maintenance activities in irrigation districts. The World Bank, through several loans, has supported the transfer of operation and maintenance responsibility to the water user organizations. Mexico's approach serves as an example to other developing countries of how to carry out the transfer process successfully.

With the water law and subsequent regulations, officials have a framework to tackle the management of scarce water resources. The law's stated objective is "to regulate the extraction, use, distribution and control of the nation's waters as well as preserve their quantity and quality in order to achieve sustainable integral development." The law recognizes the importance of water resources management and authorizes the CNA to carry out functions needed to achieve the sustainable development and use of water resources.

Water management is to be carried out with the participation of users to the maximum extent possible. The law specifically authorizes the establishment of river basin councils to coordinate activities and produce agreements between the CNA, other federal agencies, state and municipal agencies, and water user representatives on matters related to water management in the river basins. At present, the CNA's regional offices are based on state boundaries. The Mexican government recently reorganized the CNA's regional structure into 13 offices with boundaries based on river basins. This will significantly help regional offices carry out their water management responsibilities, because individual river basins will be located totally within their geographical range.

As provided by the law, the river basin councils have a key role to play in river basin planning and management. They will provide a forum for (a) identifying and evaluating problems and needs; (b) developing consensus between the various government entities, water users, and other interested parties; (c) recommending actions; (d) obtaining commitments to carry out the actions; and (e) following up to ensure continued commitment and compliance with agreed on initiatives. The river basin councils have the overall responsibility of making the planning process dynamic, participatory, and results oriented, rather than a sterile exercise, as is often the case when centralized government institutions run programs.

At present, there is one functioning river basin council, Lerma-Chapala, which started operating in 1993. In addition, about 20 more basin councils are in various stages of development. Experience has demonstrated that the establishment of functional river basin councils is difficult and time-consuming. Organizing all the different water users into functioning groups that then elect representatives on the councils with adequate communication with both users and government officials has proven to be much more difficult than officials had contemplated. Experience has shown that basins with serious water scarcity and management problems have an easier time establishing councils.

The National Water Law also permits the establishment of aquifer committees. These are similar to river basin councils, but they manage groundwater resources. The 15 aquifer committees established to date are dealing with aquifers that have severe overdraft problems. The World Bank is supporting the CNA in carrying out these activities through the Mexico Water Resources Management Project, which incorporates a new pilot project for five of the most overexploited aquifers in the country.

The government and the CNA have developed a long-term plan for water management in Mexico under which in the next 10 to 20 years river basin councils would provide the nucleus for regional companies that would assume operational and financial responsibilities for water resources management within the basins. These companies would have their own technical and administrative resources, and have financial and operational independence. The CNA would revert to being the national water authority, overseeing water rights administration and ensuring that water management is carried out in accordance with the law and regulations.

Water Pricing Reform in Mexico

To improve overall water resources management in Mexico, the law mandates the implementation of a complete system of water rights, including discharge permits. The Federal Rights Law provides the legal framework and mechanisms for the federal government to charge for the diversion and use of water, and for the discharge of water into bodies of water when the quality of the discharge exceeds predefined parameters. Mexico is in the process of implementing these laws with the objective of introducing economic water pricing and market mechanisms in a technically adequate manner.

The government, through the CNA, is currently giving priority to registering and regularizing all water users in the country. The president issued special decrees in 1995 and 1996 that allow for a waiver of fees and fines associated with water rights registry and regularization. These decrees were in effect until December 31, 1998. Anyone registering after that period is required to pay a registration fee and would be subject to the sanctions authorized by law if water was being used without a water right.

Water pricing in Mexico consists of three main components: tariffs, fees, and markets.

WATER TARIFFS. Water tariffs are charges directly related to the use of hydraulic infrastructure. They pay for operation, maintenance, and replacement costs to ensure sustainability of the system. Within transferred irrigation systems, water user organizations collect these tariffs so they can directly carry out their responsibilities. Bulk water tariffs are set to cover the costs of major infrastructure items such as dams that are not transferred to water user associations. Since 1992, Mexico has been involved in a major program of rehabilitating irrigation systems and transferring them to water user associations. Prior to this program, water tariffs covered only about 20 percent of operation, maintenance, and replacement costs. Water tariffs now cover more than 80 percent of these costs.

WATER FEES. Water fees are government charges for the use of the nation's water resources. The fees should be sufficient, at a minimum, to cover the government's costs of carrying out its water resources management roles, including resource monitoring, water quantity and quality assessments, river basin planning, and water rights administration, as well as environmental costs caused by use or contamination. The fees are set annually in the Federal Rights Law (Ley Federal de Derechos), with different rates for industrial and municipal users. Agricultural users are exempt from paying these fees. Municipal water companies often do not pay them, and they have run up huge debts. The government has forgiven past debts under the 1995 and 1996 presidential decrees with the proviso that the urban users must then begin paying the fees, which is now happening very slowly. Industrial users pay extremely high rates. Some Mexican policymakers recognize the importance of charging fees to all water users and making the fees more uniform. This, of course, is difficult to achieve politically, given the likely resistance of agricultural and urban users. Table 16.2 shows current water fees.

The government's first objective is to register and regularize all users, and then to slowly look for ways to make the fee rates more uniform. Once the water rights and fee systems are functioning, the government has the additional objective of directing a portion of the water revenues directly to the basins where the fee-generating uses are located. The purpose is to decentralize water management.

WATER MARKETS. Once the water rights systems are set up, water markets in water scarce areas will establish the market value of water, which is a reflection of the opportunity cost of water. The water rights administration procedures that the government is currently defining and implementing are designed to support the proper functioning of water markets. Since 1995, when the massive effort of registering water rights began in earnest, the CNA has approved 517 transfers of water rights, resulting in a total annual volume of water rights transferred of about 160 million m³. Because total annual water use in Mexico is estimated to be over 200 billion m³, the amount of transfers approved so far is small. However, when water can be made available to meet demand through water markets, it reduces the need for constructing costly supply-oriented infrastructure and leads to a more rational and economically viable allocation of water resources.

Establishing functioning water markets is a challenge. The markets need a strong institutional underpinning and must be related to secure water rights allocation and functioning water rights registers (which

TABLE 16.2

Water Fees for Different Water User Groups in Mexico in 1998–99

Water user category	Tariff (US$/m³) for water measured at point of delivery[a]
Industry	0.073 to 0.93
Utility[b]	0.000073 to 0.00093
Agriculture	exempt

a. Fees depend on the geographical scarcity zones as defined in the law.
b. Utilities' fees are expressed as 1,000th of industry's fees.
Source: CNA (1998).

Mexico is now establishing). They must also be related to reliable water availability, use monitoring, and low-transaction cost exchange mechanisms (see, for example, Mariño and Kemper 1999 for a discussion of the practical implementation of water markets in Brazil, Spain, and the United States). A detailed discussion of the challenges of introducing water markets in Mexico would exceed the scope of this chapter. Note, however, that for the markets to function and correctly reflect the opportunity cost of water, the water rights exchange mechanism needs to be smooth and must have low transaction costs in terms of both financing and time involved. If it becomes too difficult for users to exchange their rights, the expected incentive to move water from low- to high-value uses will not materialize.

Comparing the Mexico and Ceará Cases

For all their similarities, Mexico and Ceará present somewhat different cases. Whereas Mexico made nationwide changes, Ceará developed a statewide system. Discussions of improved water resources management at the federal level have been proceeding for a long time as a national debate in Brazil, and the president signed a national water resources law in January 1997 (see Azevedo and Asad, chapter 15 in this book). However, as mentioned previously, the new government of the semi-arid state of Ceará felt that it needed to act immediately. Under Brazilian law, a state has full jurisdiction over a river that flows entirely within its boundaries; otherwise the river is subject to federal legislation. Ceará has only one minor federal river, and therefore it could pass legislation for its waters. State officials had the power to make changes to the legislation by decree. The new water resources law changes the legal situation by setting a framework that all states must follow. It thus establishes water pricing, use rights, and river basin management by committees of users across Brazil.

Although this chapter has necessarily described Mexico's experience on a national level compared with Ceará's experience, the parallels are evident. In both cases, change seems to have been triggered by a government commitment to link the economic agenda with water management. In both cases, officials appear to perceive water scarcity, rather than pollution, as the major problem. The steps officials have taken are in line with internationally accepted recommendations for improved water resources management, including defining and allocating water rights, pricing water, and devolving power to the river basin level, along with creating water user organizations.

In both cases, the government decided to create a centralized entity—the CNA in Mexico and COGERH in Ceará—to implement this agenda. Over time, both entities are supposed to transfer a large part of their responsibilities to lower levels of self-government and are in the process of stimulating the creation of these lower-level entitites. The process seems to be rather successful, even if moving slower than anticipated.[4]

The principal challenge is, not surprisingly, water pricing. As discussed previously, entrenched interests in the form of water supply companies, industries, and irrigators make it difficult for COGERH and the CNA to insist on pricing. In both Ceará and Mexico, industry traditionally pays for surface water. Mexico is distinct, however, in that industry relies heavily on groundwater. The government does not traditionally charge for groundwater, because users are more autonomous and use is not as easily controlled.

In Ceará, the government's main challenge is to produce better estimates of tariffs that will support sustainable operation, maintenance, and replacement of the state's infrastructure, and to adjust tariffs accordingly for industrial as well as household and commercial customers. In addition, officials need to develop a strategy to deal with agricultural users.

Officials in both places are focusing on the identification of users and the allocation of water rights. This illustrates the link between changes in the overall water resources management framework and water pricing. In both Mexico and Ceará, officials believe they must first define and allocate water rights and devolve decisionmaking power to the users before they can persuade users to pay.

The risk in upcoming years is that more users may become aware of the costs of allocated rights. But users also have much to gain. Whereas formerly they were simply told about the general water allocation, the new system will grant them a voice in operations, as well as more supply security. For many water users, especially for industries, but also irrigation groups, the benefits will outweigh the costs, even with higher prices. A recent simulation conducted for the steel industry in the Mexican state of Michoacán showed, for example,

---

4. Note that Ceará, by creating a centralized entity, is taking a different approach than other Brazilian states, especially in the south and southeast, where the plan is for river basin committees to have their own operational arms. This is a viable approach in those states, because the much higher per capita income—about twice that of Ceará—means that users can finance the agencies.

5. The simulation assumes a price elasticity of –2.55. The overall study, which was carried out for seven industrial sectors (sugar, paper, chemicals, food, beverages, steel, and textiles) strongly argues that water tariffs should be differentiated to take account of the different industries' possibilities for substitution processes. Thus, the tariffs can achieve water savings without hurting the industries' profitability (IMTA 1998).

that water tariffs, currently at about US$0.032 per m^3, could be increased ten-fold without significantly affecting the industry's profit levels.[5] In the end, the entities with the most to lose may be longstanding state or federal agencies that wield reduced power with the new arrangements.

As previously mentioned, Ceará's state water resources law can be described as state-of-the-art, and officials have energetically implemented it. Ceará's water legislation is largely adequate to tackle the problems relating to water scarcity in the state. It takes into account (a) the types of water users; (b) the need to introduce water monitoring, rights, and tariffs as incentives for more efficient water reallocation and use; and (c) the need to create an agency to supply and administer bulk water. In this sense, Ceará's approach corresponds to the hydrological and socioeconomic first-best solution for the state. This is also reflected in the decision to create one agency for the entire state instead of one for every river basin. As discussed previously, other Brazilian states have created, or are planning to create, agencies for each river basin. This approach would not work in Ceará because of the limited economic activities in the state's more remote basins.

The issue of water markets remains difficult to resolve. In 1992 the general discussion in Brazil was not favorable with regard to water markets, and therefore it is not surprising that water rights in Ceará, as defined in the state's water law, are not tradable. At present, a renewed discussion about tradable water rights is taking place. More efficient reallocation of water rights and water use markets would, on the surface, surely be a first-best solution. However, one must take into account that Ceará is a state characterized by large landowners, many of whom underutilize their land, and small landholders and landless people. This raises a question: would tradable water rights actually lead to water being used more efficiently, or would the water just be accumulated by the same large landholders who are underutilizing their land? If the latter is the case, reallocation of water would fail to lead to more productive or efficient use. One could raise the issue of taxing the nonbeneficial use of water to prevent the accumulation of water rights, but Ceará's administrative capability appears too weak to implement such a policy effectively. For this reason, the government policy appears appropriate to first create water user committees in the different basins. This sensitizes all water users to the value of water, setting the stage for an eventual move to tradable water rights.[6]

---

6. For a more extensive discussion about water markets in a situation of asymmetric information and power relations between different stakeholders in Ceará, see Kemper (1996, chapter 10).

In the case of Mexico, the political and institutional structure favored a somewhat radical departure from the old way of managing water resources. The Mexican National Water Law combines all the features recommended by international experts to improve the water resources management in the country. By also actively facilitating water markets, the Mexican government went further than the government of Ceará, deciding in effect that the theoretical and practical first-best solutions coincided. This may have been due to the general liberalization of all realms of Mexican society since the beginning of the last decade.

Obviously, one may raise the same issue of the appropriateness of water markets in Mexico as was previously raised for Ceará. The difference, however, is that the water markets already existed informally before their legalization. In northeastern Mexico, water rights seem to be moving to high-value agricultural use, thus creating income for the country and local employment opportunities. The main challenge is to get the water rights registry to function smoothly, thereby guaranteeing its maintenance and providing water users with an appreciation of the security and value of their water rights as well as the certainty of unbureaucratic, low-cost transactions. This process is ongoing; time will tell if it will work as expected.

The CNA also faces the challenge of delegating decisionmaking to the local level. Although policymakers expressly created the agency with the mandate to decentralize water resources management, it is the successor of the highly centralized Ministry of Water Resources. As public choice theory tells us, all bureaucracies have a tendency to perpetuate themselves, and they experience significant difficulties in bringing about the devolution of their own power. It thus comes as no surprise that the CNA's decentralization processes are moving rather slowly. The success of decentralization will depend on water users grasping the opportunities that the law provides and taking the initiative, which is happening in various river basins in southern Brazil.

Conclusion

Given the changes that officials in Mexico and Ceará have implemented during the past 12 years, the reform efforts have clearly been worthwhile. One should also note, however, that the two cases illustrate the significant transaction costs in terms of both money and time. This should be taken into account in the design of, and expectations for, development projects.

Many times, international agencies bring about changes that were not originally contemplated by the client country. In such cases, the institutional changes may proceed at an even slower pace than in the two cases presented here where the first-best solutions, based on local and international expertise, were chosen. A general lesson is that appropriate benchmarks for success should be designed. This could mean lower benchmarks, such as second-best solutions, or consideration of a longer time frame. There is no point in criticizing clients for failing to achieve the impossible.

References

CNA (Comisión Nacional del Agua, or National Water Commission). 1998. "Ley Federal de Derechos en Materia de Agua." Mexico City.

Gazeta Mercantil. 1998. "Novos Investimentos Mudam a Face do Nordeste." August 11, p. A8.

ICWE (International Conference on Water and the Environment). 1992. *The Dublin Statement and Report of the Conference.* January 26–31, Dublin.

IMTA (Mexican Institute for Water Technology). 1998. *Aplicación de Instrumentos de Mercado Como Mecanismo para Regular la Demanda de Agua para Uso Industrial.* Final report. Mexico City.

Kemper, Karin E. 1996. *The Cost of Free Water. Water Resources Allocation and Use in the Curu Valley, Ceará, Northeast Brazil.* Linköping, Sweden: Linköping University Department of Water and Environmental Studies.

Mariño, M., and K. Kemper, eds. 1999. *Institutional Frameworks in Successful Water Markets—Brazil, Spain, and Colorado, USA.* Technical Paper no. 427. Washington, D.C.: World Bank.

North, Douglas C. 1990. *Institutions, Institutional Change, and Economic Performance.* Cambridge, U.K.: Cambridge University Press.

World Bank. 1993. *Water Resources Management: A World Bank Policy Paper.* Washington, D.C.

17

The Political Economy of Water Resources Institutional Reform in Pakistan

Joseph Makwata Wambia

The objective of this chapter is to demonstrate the difficulty of implementing a broad reform agenda in an institutionally complicated environment by examining ongoing institutional reforms in Pakistan's water sector. Under such conditions, first-best economic efficiency seems difficult to achieve. As an alternative, the chapter suggests adopting a process that leads to negotiated third-best reform outcomes.

In the real world of politics, which is characterized by competing interests, differing perceptions, unequal power relationships, and imperfect information, it is the rational interaction of supporters and opponents that determines whether reforms are implemented. Economists, in contrast, tend to view policy and institutional reforms through the prism of narrowly defined market economic models, making recommendations based on identity of objectives, enumeration and evaluation of objective alternatives, and rational selection of the best course of action.

The market economy model of rational behavior may be too simplistic in real-world situations such as Pakistan's. This is true for water sector reforms, as well as for reforms of most other economic sectors in developing countries. As previous chapters have demonstrated, economics alone cannot explain why good policy gets derailed or is not implemented at all. This chapter uses a political society or interest-group model to capture the essence of any reform program and address the struggle between economic theories and political interests.

Although both the political process and the analytical soundness of a reform proposal are necessary conditions for the reform's ultimate success, this chapter makes the case that a well-working political process is the more important determinant. Using the example of water resources reform in Pakistan, the chapter demonstrates the importance of the interaction between groups of interests (public and private), the commonality of shared problems, the adept or raw exercise of bargaining power, the manipulation of information, the levels of passion for the beliefs held by competing groups, and the loyalties that groups inspire.

In this interest-group model framework, private and public interests conflict sharply. Such a model may be used to explain the reform outcome. The next section briefly describes the economic background in Pakistan. Subsequent sections describe the irrigation system and its needs for major institutional reforms, and the proposed reform program. The fifth section provides a political economy analysis of the process, along with a political interest-group model. It also discusses the risks that the reforms pose.

Economic Background

Pakistan's annual economic growth averaged about 5.5 percent from 1985 to 1995. It slowed to about 3 percent in 1996 and 1997. Average per capita incomes have climbed in real terms by about 70 percent over the past two decades, reaching about US$490 in 1996. The percentage of residents below the poverty line declined from almost half the population in the mid-1980s to about one-third in the early 1990s. In recent years, however, Pakistan's economy has suffered from a combination of weak governance, longstanding structural problems, and persistent macroeconomic imbalances.

Agriculture accounts for more than 25 percent of gross domestic product, more than 50 percent of employment, and (indirectly or directly) 70 percent of export revenues. It has a central role in poverty issues, given the concentration of the poor in rural areas, and in environmental issues, because it is the primary user of natural resources. Agriculture contributes significantly to all other sectors and is the main engine of growth for the economy. Pakistan's agriculture sector depends heavily on irrigation. Of the total farmed area, which covers 20.8 million hectares (51 million acres), 79 percent is irrigated. Irrigated agriculture is by far the nation's dominant water user, accounting for 98 percent of direct flows and the bulk of return flows.

The Indus Basin Irrigation System

Pakistan's Indus Basin irrigation system is the largest integrated irrigation network in the world. Waters of the Indus River and its tributaries feed it. Pakistan implemented the Indus Basin Replacement Works Project, which built the irrigation system, in 1947 with the World Bank as the lead donor. The project brought 39.54 million acres under irrigation.

System Overview

The salient features of the irrigation system are three major storage reservoirs: Tarbela and Chashma on the Indus River and Mangla on the Jhelum River. In addition, the system has 19 barrages, 12 interriver link canals, 43 independent irrigation canal commands, and more than 107,000 watercourses, which are complemented with a surface drainage system.[1] The length of the canals totals 61,000 kilometers, with farm channels and field ditches covering another 1.6 million kilometers. Typical watercourse commands range from 80 to 320 hectares. The Indus is fed by melting snow and ice in the Himalayas, as well as by rainfall outside the Indus Plain. Barrages divert river water into canals. The main canals in turn deliver water to branch canals, distributaries, and minor channels. The watercourses are fed by outlets in the irrigation channels.

The distribution of water is determined by a time-share system, or *warabandi*, under which each farm gets water for a specified period. The size of a farm determines its time-share. The entire system draws an average of 106 million acre-feet of surface water each year for irrigation, supplemented by some 43 million acre-feet of groundwater. The average depth of water available at the farm level is 3.07 feet per acre. Approximately 3 million farms, with an average size of 12 acres, benefit from this system. Table 17.1 summarizes average inflows and water use.

Most system losses are due to canal and watercourse seepage, because practically the entire network is unlined. In addition to river diversions, 48 billion cubic meters of water are pumped annually from groundwater sources by about 13,500 public and about 400,000 private tubewells. Much of this is recovered water that had seeped out of the system in areas underlaid by fresh aquifers. In contrast, seepage in areas underlaid by saline aquifers is completely lost to irrigation.

Nonagricultural users extract 5.3 billion cubic meters from the system annually, of which 80 percent is returned to the system, albeit of degraded

---

1. "Command" is a term used to describe a large area served by a large canal, usually through minor off-takes known as "distributaries." Canal commands in Pakistan average 300,000 acres, but they range in size from a few thousand to 2.7 million acres. "Watercourse" is a term used to describe a minor canal that delivers water to the farm.

TABLE 17.1
Average Inflows and Water Use in the Indus Basin in the 1980s

Flows/use	Volume (billion cubic meters)	Percentage of inflows
Inflows into the system	181.37	100
Diversions to canal	131.16	72
Outflow to the sea	39.58	22
System losses	10.63	6

Source: Government of Pakistan (1993).

quality. The amount of water consumed by nonagricultural users is expected to increase from the equivalent of 4 percent of the surface water diverted for irrigated agriculture to about 10 to 15 percent within the next 25 years. Most of this water will return to the system, but its quality will be degraded. This will cause an unacceptable quality decline in the middle and lower reaches of the Indus River, threatening many of the areas that rely on the system for irrigation and domestic water supply. The quality degradation will also eventually threaten the water supply of Karachi, a city with more than 10 million residents adjacent to the mouth of the Indus River, and endanger many of the 25 wetlands in the Indus Basin that are considered a priority by international conservation groups.

Institutional Framework

Three federal ministries oversee water resources management: the Ministry of Food, Agriculture, and Livestock; the Ministry of Environment and Urban Affairs; and the Ministry of Water and Power. The latter is the most important. It operates three agencies, including the Indus Rivers System Authority, which allocates water between the provinces in accordance with the provisions of the 1991 Water Accord (WAPDA 1998).

The administrative scheme is complicated (Dinar, Balakrishnan, and Wambia 1998) by a veritable army of authorities, agencies, and councils. The Water and Power Development Authority of Pakistan (WAPDA), which has its origins in the electricity department of the Ministry of Water and Power, constructs large dams, link canals, and drainage infrastructure, as well as monitoring water levels and sedimentation. It monitors interprovincial canals with the Indus Rivers System Authority. The Ministry of Environment and Urban Affairs carries out its environmental monitoring and regulation mandate through the Pakistan Environmental Protection Agency and the Pakistan Environmental Protection Council. The Ministry of Food, Agriculture, and Livestock is responsible for watercourse development through the Federal Water Management Cell, although the Ministry of Water and Power retains lead responsibility for formulating and implementing overall water resources development policy at the national level. The Federal Flood Commission is responsible for flood control and damage rehabilitation, and it is part of the Ministry of Water and Power.

A somewhat similar setup, although with far more employees, exists in each of the four provinces that uses the irrigation system. The provincial departments of agriculture mirror the Ministry of Food, Agriculture, and Livestock with their on-farm water management directorates; the provincial environmental protection agencies mirror the federal Environmental Protection Agency; and, until 1997, the provincial irrigation and power departments mirror the Ministry of Water and Power.

Magnitude of the Water Quality Crisis

Waterlogging and salinity are the principal threats to the sustainability of irrigated agriculture in Pakistan. Some 37.6 percent of the irrigated area is waterlogged. By 1989, 15 percent of the irrigated area had become severely waterlogged, meaning that the water table was so high that irrigated agriculture was difficult or only marginally viable.[2] In addition, 14 percent of the surface water is categorized as saline (meaning it has an electrical conductivity of 8–15 ECe), of which 6 percent is categorized as severely saline (meaning its electrical conductivity is above 15 ECe).[3] The twin problems of waterlogging and salinity are most severe in Sindh Province in the lower Indus Plain, where more than half of the areas affected by waterlogging and salinity are located.

The water table in the Indus Plain was deeper than 90 feet in 1900, but rose steadily because of the irrigation for most of the 20th century. Between 1988 and 1995, however, the water table dropped from 11.7 to 23.3 feet below the surface, and it is declining by up to 5 feet in fresh groundwater

---

2. A waterlogged area is defined as an area with a water table that is within 10 feet of the surface. The critical threshold at which the water table begins to affect the productivity of agricultural land is about eight feet below the surface. In a severely waterlogged area, the water table has risen to within five feet of the surface. Irrigated agriculture becomes only marginally viable, especially when the water table has excessive salinity.

3. ECe, the electrical conductivity of the soil extract, is a measure of soil salinity.

areas. That is because of the expansion of the network of tubewells, as well as various government programs. However, it is still increasing in some saline groundwater areas (Ahmad and Kutcher 1992, pp. 52–53; Smedema as quoted in Umali 1992).

The Significance of Waterlogging and Salinity

The rise of saline groundwater tables to near the surface, and the consequent soil salinization, is becoming a serious environmental problem. The government and many independent experts blame the soil salinity for a 25 percent reduction in the production of Pakistan's major crops in SGW areas. In Sindh Province, the impact may be closer to a 40–60 percent reduction in crop production in saline groundwater areas. The critical threshold at which waterlogging and salinity begin to affect the productivity of agricultural land varies by crop, but it is especially severe for cotton, sugarcane, and wheat. The impact is less severe for rice. Similarly, waterlogging has a severe impact on yields, because high groundwater tables inhibit root growth. As the water table rises to within five feet of the surface, yields of all major crops begin to decline rapidly. For example, at a water table depth of zero to 0.8 feet, yields drop to 2 percent for cotton, 9 percent for sugar, and 21 percent for wheat (Umali 1992, table 3.7).

Origins of the Crisis and Drainage Options for Pakistan

The principal causes of waterlogging and salinity are irrigation without drainage, overirrigation, and low delivery efficiency of the irrigation system (35–40 percent from the head of the canal to the applicable farmland) and the drainage system. Groundwater pumpage, which is unregulated, further aggravates the situation by stirring up salt dissolved in the groundwater aquifer unless the effluent is properly disposed of. A widely accepted consensus has emerged in Pakistan that the lack of an effective drainage system for the Indus Basin Irrigation System is by far the principal threat to the sustainability of agriculture in the area. Analysts believe that waterlogging and salinity must be reduced dramatically by improving the irrigation system's efficiency.

The government has recognized that it has three nonmutually exclusive options for dealing with its waterlogging and salinity problems. The first is to dispose of the drainage effluent outside the irrigation system. The second is to minimize the drainage effluent by changing its chemistry, either through dilution and reuse, or through concentration and separation of dissolved salt for subsequent disposal. The third is to reduce the amount of waterlogging and salinity through source control.

The Proposed Institutional Reforms

The impetus for the institutional reforms came from the recommendation of the World Bank sector strategy report (World Bank 1994). The government approved these reforms in August 1995.

The new institutions created by the reform—provincial irrigation and drainage authorities (PIDAs), area water boards, and farmer-managed irrigation systems—are expected to reduce waterlogging and salinity by improving the efficiency of utilizing irrigation water supplies through decentralized participatory irrigation management, and by improving the efficiency by which the saline effluent from the Indus Basin is evacuated.

Experience from pilot projects in Pakistan and elsewhere has demonstrated that participatory decentralized irrigation management often results in more efficient pricing of irrigation and drainage services, better and more effective cost recovery, and reduced water waste. A basinwide focus on monitoring the condition of the river basin by WAPDA would also enable the federal and provincial authorities to obtain the necessary early warning information to pass legislation, institute appropriate incentives (especially on price), and undertake investment, with long gestation periods in anticipation of the new requirements. As opposed to the current system in which farmers are not represented in water management decisions, farmer representatives would have active roles in the board oversight of the newly formed institutions.

The reform is being phased in over 10 years. The first phase is the National Drainage Program project. It involves the enactment of laws known as PIDA Acts in each of the four provinces (which was completed in 1997), establishment of pilot area water boards in each province (completed in 1999), and the establishment of farmer organizations to manage irrigation systems (expected to be completed in 2000). In addition, WAPDA is being transformed to specialize in federal aspects of river basin management.

Pakistan's government has worked with the World Bank to formulate a strategy to deal with the crisis (World Bank 1994). The strategy takes a comprehensive approach to river basin management that includes financing an extensive research and monitoring program to identify sound technical solutions, and it seeks to reduce fiscal dependency of the provinces on the federal government for irrigation and drainage services, especially on-farm drainage.

The strategy included: (a) restructuring the provincial irrigation departments from government departments to semiautonomous PIDAs that would oversee the network of canal commands and barrages; (b) further decentralizing the four authorities into 40 or more canal commands known as area water boards; (c) privatizing irrigation systems by transferring them from the authorities and water boards to a network of farmer-managed irrigation systems organized around distributaries; (d) strengthening federal agencies, notably the water branch of the Water and Power Development Authority of Pakistan to allow them to undertake their federal responsibilities more effectively; and (e) formalizing water markets and individual water property rights. The International Development Association, Japan Bank for International Cooperation, and the Asian Development Bank supported the reform program in 1997 with external soft loans amounting to US$525 million, of which the International Development Association's share was US$285 million.

The Provincial Water Resources Institutional Reforms Program

The strategy devised by Pakistan and the World Bank may be correctly classified as the rational strategy. Concurrent with the government decentralization, farmers would be encouraged to play an increased role in managing the system at the distributary or minor canal level. A pilot approach would be used to form area water boards and farmer organizations, because the number of such organizations would be large.

Officials envisioned that the final structure would include the following:

1. Streamlined and autonomous PIDAs that would oversee the costruction, operation, and maintenance of the barrages
2. A system of regulation and adjudication for the decentralized irrgation and drainage subsector
3. Decentralization below the PIDAs to quasi-autonomous area water boards that would control the portion of the infrastructure that was previously overseen by superintendent engineers of the provincial irrigation departments on each canal command
4. Further decentralization below the area water boards to fully autonomous farmer organizations at the distributary level that would collaborate with area water boards to oversee provincial subsidies, capital grants, training, and technical assistance.

The farmer organizations, which would be completely owned and controlled by farmers, would collaborate with nongovernmental organizations to strengthen management at the distributory level and take into account the environmental dimensions of the irrigation system. These organizations were expected to assume responsibility for the portion of the irrigation and drainage infrastructure currently known as divisions.

To summarize the changes: PIDAs and drainage authorities would assume responsibility from provincial irrigation departments for operating barrages. Similarly, area water boards would operate circles, and farmer organizations would do likewise for divisions. Water user associations (WUAs) would continue to operate *warabandi* at the watercourse level.

The plan called for provincial irrigation departments to retain control over policies and regulations. They would promote the public interest and long-term institutional interests of the PIDAs, area water boards, and farmer organizations operating in the irrigation subsector at the distributory level. Eventually the regulatory functions would be carried out by an autonomous irrigation commission.

Institutional Reforms in the Water Branch of WAPDA

The government of Pakistan's institutional reform program for WAPDA's water branch consisted of strategically reorienting it to focus on federal functions; streamlining and restructuring to improve capacity utilization, operational efficiency, and effectiveness; and building capacity, including public participation and training. The strategic reorientation work program was designed to help the water branch redefine its role toward more strategically important, federally-oriented responsibilities. In particular, the strategy addressed those roles related to (a) integrated development, management, and regulation of water resources at the basin level; (b) monitoring land and water quality and environmental change; and (c) planning, construction, operation, and maintenance of interprovincial irrigation and drainage infrastructure. At the same time, the water branch would become less involved in intraprovincial construction, which would be undertaken by provincial agencies, farmers, or private companies. To meet the challenge of long-term sustainability for the irrigation system, the government provided resources to help the water branch adjust to its new role.

For its part, WAPDA was expected to prepare a strategic plan through a process approach to articulate the following key aspects. It was envisioned that the government would continue to deliver interprovincial irrigation and drainage services through construction that it would either undertake through WAPDA or with PIDAs, area water boards, or even farmer organizations. WAPDA's water branch would likely be responsible for the operation and maintenance of interprovincial infrastructure for irrigation and drainage. The government also decided that the water branch would assume responsibility for the operation and maintenance of the proposed network of interprovincial drainage facilities. This would be in addition to the operation and maintenance of environmentally sensitive effluent disposal facilities, such as evaporation ponds, and the temporary storage of drainage effluent in lakes such as Manchar and Hamal on the right bank of the Indus.

The water branch would also be responsible for receiving drainage effluent from PIDAs at designated nodal points and evacuating it from the Indus Basin to the Arabian Sea through a network of interprovincial drains such as the left bank outfall drain, trans-basin outfall drain's spinal drain, the right bank outfall drain's main Nara Valley drain, or the national surface drainage system when it is constructed. Until the national surface drainage system is completed, WAPDA's water branch would continue to operate and closely monitor a number of evaporation ponds in which PIDAs and area water boards could dispose of their drainage effluent when disposing of such effluent into the Indus River system is inappropriate.

On the irrigation side, the water branch would continue to deliver bulk water supplies from its dams and reservoirs to barrages via the link canals it manages, as well as via the Indus River and its tributaries. The water branch would also continue its responsibilities in connection with interprovincial flood control and damage rehabilitation on behalf of the federal government, and it would also continue to monitor groundwater and surface water conditions throughout the basin. If Pakistan chooses to develop a system of navigation on its vast network of canals and drains, the water branch would likely be responsible for that too, because such a task is part of WAPDA's charter. Although the provinces at present do not pay the water branch directly for such services, they will likely do so in the longer term. Another important reform is the reorientation of the water branch toward management and regulation at the basin level. Officials also want to streamline the water branch to increase its overall operational efficiency.

A Political Economy Analysis of the Reform Implementation Efforts

The Ministry of Water and Power is the lead federal agency for formulating and coordinating national water policies. However, for political reasons, including the sensitivity of the provinces to an active role by the federal government on water resources issues, it avoids being overly active. It has declined to crack down on the exploitation of water resources by the provinces. Indeed, prior to the initiation of the reform in 1995, a seemingly deliberate policy and regulatory vacuum for water resources existed at the national level.

The situation is paradoxical, because virtually all major policy initiatives in the water resources sector since Pakistan gained independence in 1947 have been overseen by the federal government, not the provinces.[4] This is the result of several factors. First, the government of Pakistan controls virtually the entire investment budget of the provinces, both because of its own resources or because it controls the provinces' access to external aid funds. Second, the federal government has tended to take a long-term view of water resources issues, in contrast to the shorter-term and more exploitative view of the provinces. Third, the provinces have evinced a greater tendency toward competition than cooperation with each other, resulting from deep-seated suspicions. Fourth, the federal government has shown more interest in drainage issues, which happen to be its constitutional responsibility, at least for investment purposes. Because of the larger scale of investment in drainage, relatively large externalities compared with irrigation, and a long payback period, drainage has been designated a federal government responsibility in Pakistan.

Design, Pace, and Sequencing of the Reforms

Although the government, the provinces, and the International Development Association agreed on the general outline of reform, they left open the pace at which the decentralization and management transfer process would be implemented. Observers, such as Pakistani and international researchers, journalists, and some farmer groups, criticized the Bank for this, maintaining that the Bank was pressing for some reforms to take place too quickly while allowing others to move too slowly. Critics preferred to see a detailed blueprint with changes spelled out in advance rather than the government's process approach of allowing details to emerge and evolve during implementation. Whereas the Bank advocated a measured pace of reforms aimed at eventually replacing the existing provincial irrigation departments with autonomous public utilities that would be regulated by provincial water commissions, federal and provincial officials instead opted for a swifter but less sweeping form of institutional change. This would be

---

4. Prominent examples include the Indus Treaty with India, the Indus Basin Plan, the 1991 Water Accord, the On Farm Water Management Program, the Command Water Management Program, the Water Sector Investment Program, the first and second Irrigation Systems Rehabilitation Programs, the Salinity Control and Rehabilitation Programs, the Left Bank Outfall Drain, the Drainage Sector Environmental Assessment, and the National Drainage Program.

modeled on the federal government's own experience with splitting up its former Ministry of Water and Power into WAPDA to implement policies and a much smaller Ministry of Water and Power to create policies and regulations and oversee their implementation.

The federal government and the provinces also chose to decentralize units of the provincial irrigation development authorities into semiautonomous area water boards, modeled on the experience of devolving WAPDA's electricity generation units into area electricity boards as a precursor to full-scale privatization. Thus, the provincial irrigation departments were to be transformed instantly into autonomous PIDAs, which in turn would be devolved rapidly into a number of semiautonomous area water boards, initially on a pilot basis.

Furthermore, rather than fully decentralize the lower reaches of the irrigation and drainage system to independent farmer organizations, federal and provincial officials opted instead for a slower pace of decentralization involving the establishment of a very few farmer organizations to test the idea, with the goal of creating more if the test proved successful. Instead of a full-fledged detailed design, the reform program was to be based on a process approach. Whereas the design was limited in details, the process was more elaborately defined and was supported by enabling legislation. Detailed implementation was left to the lessons of experience.

The success of the ongoing reforms in each province will depend on a number of factors. The first and most important will be the continuing commitment of the federal government and the provinces to implement the decentralization and management transfer process. The second will be the ability of each province to implement the decentralization process. The third will be the willingness of the affected farming population, especially the more influential landlords, to embrace the institutional reforms. Finally, success will depend on the willingness of provincial irrigation departments to embrace the reforms.

Agency Cooperation

Cooperation between, and even within, the various federal and provincial agencies that oversee Pakistan's irrigation and drainage services is almost nonexistent. On the contrary, intense interagency rivalry exists at all levels. This is particularly strong between WAPDA and provincial irrigation departments.

The concept of irrigated agriculture, whereby irrigation and agriculture are closely integrated and various federal and provincial agencies cooperate, has been lacking in Pakistan (John Mellor Associates 1994). Furthermore, federal and provincial environmental agencies have largely neglected environmental issues associated with irrigation and drainage. There is little interaction between the federal and provincial environmental agencies with any federal or provincial irrigation or drainage agency, even on environmental issues. This is a glaring omission in view of the widely acknowledged fact that waterlogging and salinity are widely considered to be Pakistan's foremost environmental problems (Government of Pakistan and IUCN 1989).

The institutional structure suggests the need for clarifying the roles of all federal and provincial agencies, not only to reduce redundant functions, but also to create mechanisms to enhance cooperation. The other significant feature of Pakistan's irrigation and drainage structure is that the government is the principal player in all matters except for fresh groundwater tubewells and watercourse-level operations.

In an effort to bridge the lack of coordination between irrigation and agriculture, the 1997 PIDA Acts provide for farmer representation at all levels of the new provincial institutional structure. Farmers dominate the farmer-managed irrigation systems and have less influence on the affairs of PIDAs and area water boards, while officials from provincial agriculture departments and on-farm water management directorates are formally designated as members of the board of directors of PIDAs and area water boards.

Subsidies for Excess Staff and Dilapidated Infrastructure

Provincial irrigation departments are seriously overstaffed, especially at the divisional levels that would be transitioned to farmer organizations. For political reasons, PIDAs, area water boards, and farmer organizations may not be able to reduce their staffing to optimal levels or increase efficiency by mechanizing or privatizing operations. Therefore, the provinces would retain transitory responsibility for financing those inefficiency costs that the new agencies may be compelled to carry.

Likewise, the new agencies are likely to inherit some infrastructure that is in a poor state of repair through no fault of their own, whereas others (such as the PIDA in Northwest Frontier Province and the area water board in Nara Canal in Sindh Province) may inherit infrastructure that is in fairly good condition. Under the new system, the new agencies would estimate the costs associated with excess staffing and dilapidated infrastructure and charge them to the provinces. The costs would not be included in charges for services provided by PIDAs to area water boards or by area water boards to farmer-managed irrigation systems. These costs would be estimated and negotiated on the basis of audited financial statements for the prior year and will include business and financing plans that reflect only the necessary levels of expenditures, including staffing and equipment replacement costs.

To offset the costs, the provinces would transfer subsidies to the PIDAs, area water boards, and farmer organizations on the basis of a transition plan to be negotiated between the provinces and the new entities that would phase out the excessive costs through retirements, reassignments, automations, or contracting out operations. This exercise would include diagnostic reviews of the operating efficiencies and costs of the new entities.

Provinces would retain temporary responsibility for funding services, such as flood control and disaster relief, and for the inefficiency costs related to overstaffing. The provinces would also retain responsibility for financing costs when the new entities inherit dilapidated infrastructure, equipment, or severely saline or waterlogged areas. Such costs would not be passed on to farmers. Efforts would be made to enable the provinces to fund these costs in a transparent manner.

Regulatory Reform

Attempts to separate policy formulation and regulation functions of the former provincial irrigation departments from the operational activities of the newly established PIDAs were not successful when the PIDA Acts were enacted. Original designs called for the establishment of a provincial regulatory commission in each province, whose task would be to regulate the newly decentralized irrigation and drainage sector.

Policy formulation and monitoring was also to remain under the purview of the secretary of the provincial Irrigation and Power Department (IPD). This was because of the justifiable political sensitivity to the establishment of a quasi-judicial apparatus outside the normal jurisdiction of the judiciary, concerns about the establishment of another bureaucratic agency, and inadequate understanding of the rationale behind the need to separate policy formulation and regulation from the PIDAs' operating responsibilities.[5]

---

5. It did not help that, at the time when officials were debating the draft PIDA Acts, tensions were rising between the federal, judicial, and executive branches of the government, as well as between the federal and provincial governments, over the separation of powers.

Because many senior officials of the provincial irrigation departments understood the proposed reforms only in terms of relieving their departments from the bureaucratic strictures of the civil service, they viewed the proposed separation of the functions from the prospective PIDAs as an attempt to reduce the powers of the new entities. After the enactment of the PIDA Acts, the World Bank agreed to the provincial government's proposal that secretaries of provincial irrigation departments may serve as managing directors of PIDAs pending the appointment of permanent managing directors from the marketplace.

This, together with the positive experience of the reforms to date, has led to a consensus on the need to separate the operational duties and authority of PIDAs from their regulatory functions, which will remain with the secretary IPD. Under the National Drainage Program, the Bank has agreed to finance technical assistance programs to beef up the capacity of the IPD secretary in policy formulation and the regulation of the new institutional structure and evolving water markets.

There is now a growing awareness among both water managers and users of the need for a separate agency to regulate the performance of the PIDAs and other new entities. In particular, the restructured IPD will ensure that, to the maximum extent possible, a level playing field is maintained between these new entities. This will involve adjudicating disputes between the entities; curbing any abuses of monopoly powers (such as passing on the costs of inefficiency to weaker members of the irrigation and drainage chain, or unreasonably denying services to smaller agencies that function at the lower echelons of the new institutional dispensation); regulating the discharge of effluent into canals and drains; regulating groundwater exploitation; and enforcing corporate behavior responsibilities prescribed in the PIDA Acts.

Although the separation of powers between residual provincial irrigation departments and the PIDAs, area water boards, and farmer organizations is likely to be achieved by 2001, an amendment to the PIDA Acts will be required to formalize this separation of powers and duties, as the Acts currently assign the responsibility for policy and regulation to PIDAs. Indications are that such amendments to the PIDA Acts would be enacted in each province within the next one or two years.

Regulation of Water Rights and Markets

So far, there is no formal explicit recognition of the existence of water markets and water rights anywhere in Pakistan. Hence regulation of such markets and rights is either lacking or at a nascent stage of development. Nevertheless, during the process of detailed preparation for the establishment of area water boards and farmer organizations, officials have undertaken detailed planning work to establish water rights as a precursor to the operation of water markets during the operational phases of the pilot area water boards and farmer organizations. Similarly, water rights are being documented around fresh groundwater tubewells, which are undergoing a transition throughout Pakistan—notably in Punjab Province under the World Bank-supported Groundwater Privatization Project.

Similar privatization efforts are set to begin. As area water boards and farmer organizations are established, water rights will be established at the corresponding levels. At the farmer organization level, water rights will be further distributed to WUAs and individual members of WUAs at the watercourse level. Thus it is expected that, by the end of the next decade, water rights will have been determined throughout much of Pakistan's irrigation system, and subsequently farmers can begin trading water rights. The medium-term expectation is that the regulatory branch of the residual IPD will register and regulate this trading.

Drainage

Drainage is the orphan issue of Pakistan's water sector. The constituency for drainage is simply absent in this irrigation-obsessed country. Everybody wants more irrigation, whether to reclaim deserts or to irrigate more farmland. Farmers always seem to ask for irrigation, unless their lands are next to natural waterways, are prone to flooding, or have lost most of their productivity because of waterlogging and salinity.

Thus, the constituency for drainage is larger in Sindh Province than anywhere else in Pakistan, and it is notably absent in the Northwest Frontier Province. Indeed, Northwest Frontier Province officials often assert during discussions with the government, other provinces, and donors, that they have no significant problem with drainage. Balochistan's interest in drainage is largely limited to its need to discharge drainage effluent from the Pat Feeder, Lasbela, and Kirthar canal commands through the right bank of the Indus in Sindh Province. Balochistan officials ardently support the proposed Right Bank Outfall Drain Project, which is designed to remove effluent from Balochistan. As salinity has become more severe in their province, Punjab officials have also developed a keen interest in drainage issues. Punjab recently expressed interest in the proposed trans-basin outfall drain, which would remove drainage effluent (largely Punjab's) from the Indus Basin to the Arabian Sea through the northward extension of the left bank outfall drain's spinal drain.

However, the Northwest Frontier Province, Balochistan, and Punjab are far more interested in developing their irrigation infrastructure. Sindh officials are showing little enthusiasm; the province has not co-operated in the construction of the right bank or trans-basin outfall drains. Indeed, in 1999, Sindh rejected WAPDA's continued role in op-erating and maintaining the completed drainage infrastructure of the left bank outfall drain, despite the significant financial advantage to Sindh that this arrangement appears to offer.[6]

Drainage Operation and Maintenance

Nevertheless, all the provincial irrigation departments had drainage orga-nizations that were responsible for operation and maintenance. But the departments fulfilled their requisite drainage function minimally. Typically, drainage operation and maintenance is far less adequately funded than irrigation operation and maintenance. Thus, the great majority of surface drains have remained neglected in all provinces, and they have conse-quently silted beyond recognition. Indeed, constructing new drains some-times may be easier than rehabilitating the existing ones.

Funding shortfalls for the operation and maintenance of saline ground-water tubewells has resulted in greatly reduced pumping hours. Rejecting the recommendations of WAPDA, donors, and drainage equipment manu-facturers, the provincial irrigation departments have performed so little maintenance that drainage facilities are often shut down within five years of beginning operations, and sometimes much sooner. The PIDA Acts, which originated in drainage, are so named because they explicitly recognize the importance of drainage as well as irrigation. Although the antidrainage bias should be reduced under PIDAs, it will be some time before drainage achieves parity with irrigation.

Operation and Maintenance of Interprovincial Drainage Infrastructure

In 1995 the federal government assigned WAPDA the responsibility for the operation and maintenance of completed interprovincial drainage projects. Funding for operation and maintenance was to be split evenly with the re-spective provinces. This decision recognized that provinces have limited

---

6. The government of Pakistan and the Sindh government would have shared 50 percent of the costs of operating the completed left bank outfall drain.

means to pay for the high cost of drainage operation and maintenance, and it also recognized that drainage has the potential to benefit neighboring provinces in the long run. The immediate impetus for this decision was the high costs of constructing the left bank outfall drain, which was estimated at Rs 670 million in 1992 prices, almost equal to the provinces' entire existing drainage operation and maintenance budgets.

Another motivating factor was the need to provide a mechanism by which the government, through WAPDA, would facilitate the operation and testing of completed drainage infrastructure to ensure its proper operation prior to handing over the facilities to provinces. This was in response to persistent complaints by provincial irrigation departments that WAPDA was handing over incomplete or poorly functioning drainage infrastructure that did not deliver promised benefits, but instead imposed heavy financial burdens.

A final motivating factor, in the specific case of the left bank outfall drain's spinal drain, was to delineate the responsibility for operation and maintenance of potential interprovincial, or federal, drainage infrastructure to a federal agency for the benefit of the entire country. The Bank supported the government's 1996 decision primarily for this reason. Pakistan's prime minister at the time was from Sindh Province, which may explain why the province accepted the new policy. WAPDA embraced the government's decision for a number of reasons. Among these were WAPDA's desire to participate in the operation and maintenance of structures that it builds and to exploit the ensuing beneficial, symbiotic relationship between design, construction, operation, and maintenance. However, WAPDA's keen interest in assuming the operation and maintenance role can also be traced to its anxieties about the deployment of surplus labor. That is because its construction activities have declined over the past decade.

Finally, WAPDA was no doubt also motivated by its frustration at the provinces' reluctance to take over completed drainage works from it, and their relative neglect of such infrastructure once they did take it over.

The Risks of Reforms

When Pakistani federal and provincial leaders, the chairman of WAPDA, and World Bank officials put together the proposed reforms, they were well aware of the risks. One of the most prominent considerations was that reforms posed many risks and opportunities for established interests in rural Pakistan, especially landowners and irrigation employees.

In particular, the reforms threatened feudal landlords with the loss of water and power. Feudal landlords dominate the legislatures of Pakistan at the federal and provincial levels. Irrigation bureaucrats with financial ties to the feudal landlords also stood to lose influence, and even their jobs. Similarly, the institutional reforms sought to transform the role of WAPDA's water branch from large-scale construction to knowledge-based river basin management, and some officials viewed the progressive transfer as a diminution of the agency.

Reform opponents spread misinformation, ran political candidates, engineered bureaucratic delays and stalling tactics, and continuously tried to whittle away at the reforms.

Reform sponsors responded in several ways. First, the federal government and provincial officials demonstrated strong political leadership through successive federal and provincial governments during a turbulent period in Pakistan's political history. The reform program was first endorsed by top federal and provincial officials on August 19, 1995, and was reaffirmed at similar forums by three successive governments in the face of mounting opposition from organized groups, such as large landholders, feudal landlords, WAPDA officials, and some provincial irrigation department staff members. Government and Bank officials engaged in extensive consultations with various stakeholders, such as organized farmer groups, chambers of agriculture, and provincial departments, to build consensus for the reform program. Interim governments gave preliminary approval to PIDA Acts, and the reforms were reaffirmed by all four affected provincial assemblies after a general election.

The extensive debates on reform strategy, wide-ranging consultations, and resulting education about the reforms helped to ease concerns about the perceived risks. These perceived risks also were mitigated by the pilot projects involving area water boards in all four provinces and farmer organizations, which were implemented with technical assistance from the International Irrigation Management Institute.

To further assess the risks, Dinar, Balakrishnan, and Wambia (1998) conducted a quantitative analysis of the implementation process. The analysis consisted of (a) evaluation of potential reform winners and losers; (b) identification of the potential reform results; (c) identification of the means by which the various parties could influence the level of achievement of each reform, and (d) identification of costs to, or required efforts of, each party to influence the achievement levels.

The analysis used the Delphi approach to estimate the probabilities of level of achievement of each reform. It indicated that the performance levels are likely to vary across reforms. The analysis showed that the most likely scenario was a medium level, or partial achievement, of reforms relating to institutional reforms in provincial irrigation departments, transferring management responsibilities of the tertiary system to farmer organizations, redefinition of the operational jurisdictions of various water resources agencies, and operation and maintenance through private sector performance contracts. The analysis, however, indicated a low level of achievement on the establishment of water rights.

Conclusion

As is the case in many reforms, policymakers in this case lack information about the political parameters of the various interest groups, making it difficult to evaluate the results. The case of Pakistan is especially complicated because, as this chapter discussed, the reform consisted of several programs, some with conflicting objectives regarding certain interest groups. The implementation process must address this, as well as the complicated political interactions between key groups.

In addition, the nature of the reform is such that each of the individual reforms, if implemented, would provide benefits. Therefore, although there are links between the various reforms, implementation could be phased in wherever necessary. The sequencing of the reform could take into account the associated social cost and likelihood of achievement. For example, reforms that have a high chance of achievement could be implemented early on, and those that have a low chance could be implemented later, following initial studies and pilot projects.

The approach suggested in this chapter aims to minimize social implementation costs, measured either by implementation time or by the transaction costs of endless discussions. Because of the broad reform agenda and Pakistan's social structure, the suggested approach will achieve a third-best solution, as opposed to a first-best solution that could have been achieved had information been available and transaction costs been negligible.

References

Ahmad, Masood, and Gary Kutcher. 1992. *Irrigation Planning with Environmental Considerations*. Technical Paper no. 166. Washington, D.C.: World Bank.

Dinar, Ariel, Trichur Balakrishnan, and Joseph Wambia. 1998. "Institutional Reforms in the Water Sector in Pakistan—Political Economy and Political Risk." Working Paper no. 1789. World Bank, Washington, D.C.

Government of Pakistan. 1993. *Drainage Sector Environmental Assessment*. Lahore, Pakistan.

Government of Pakistan and IUCN (International Union of Nature Conservationists). 1989. *Pakistan National Conservation Strategy*. Lahore, Pakistan.

John Mellor Associates. 1994. "Institutional Reforms to Accelerate Irrigated Agriculture." Unpublished consultant report, World Bank, Washington, D.C.

Umali, Dina. 1992. *Irrigation Induced Salinity.* Technical Paper no. 215. Washington, D.C.: World Bank.

WAPDA (Water and Power Development Authority). 1998. *Integrated Water Resources Management Programme for Pakistan—Institutional and Legal Matters.* Lahore, Pakistan.

World Bank. 1994: *Pakistan Irrigation and Drainage: Issues and Options.* Report no. 11884-PAK. Washington, D.C.

18

The Political Economy of Irrigation Water Pricing in Yemen

Christopher Ward

Irrigation water prices in Yemen have been formed by a delicate balance between the interests of the state, farmers, the politically powerful, and donors. The government, which originally set irrigation prices low, now is raising them. Even though the government is considered weak, it was able to subsidize both groundwater and surface irrigation for 20 years. Policies helped foster the rapid development of Yemen's water resources, enabling the government to raise farmer incomes and consolidate its alliances with many important interest groups. At the same time, however, the public policy penalized the traditional water harvesting and rainfed systems.

Now twin crises have changed the framework. First, the country has suffered severe economic and fiscal problems since the early 1990s. Second, natural resources have been exploited beyond their limit with the mining of groundwater. Conservation now suits most farmers better than a continued expansion that would only deplete groundwater further. Structural adjustment is raising the prices of inputs that made previous groundwater use cheap, participation in costs and responsibilities is being mooted in surface irrigation, and the watchword of sustainability is putting a new emphasis on traditional rainfed systems. But efficiency

Thanks are due to Tony Allan, Rozgar Baban, Ariel Dinar, Naji Abu Hatem, Andrew Macoun, and Marcus Moench for their comments and suggestions, to Ashok Subramanian for his comments and for the presentation he made of the paper at the World Bank-sponsored Workshop on Political Economy of Water Pricing Implementation, and to Matthias Schlund who carried out some of the analytical work underlying the argument.

improvements will be necessary if irrigators are to maintain their income levels. As water prices increase, the government is losing the means of patronizing powerful constituencies, creating a political risk.

The experience of Yemen is instructive in several ways. First, it shows that the combination of macroeconomic tools and donor capital can achieve very rapid development of irrigation even in a poor country with very weak public sector implementation capacity. Second, a combination of exogenous economic factors and internal economic, environmental, and political factors can lead a government to change its water pricing policy quite radically. Finally, although there is a risk to the rural economy as irrigation water prices increase, the change can encourage farmers to invest in more efficient technology. This offers the prospect of higher incomes in the longer run.

Water Management Traditions and Change

Water has always been scarce in Yemen, but the highlands at least enjoy moderate rainfall ranging from 300 to 1,200 millimeters annually. Since the days of the ancient civilization of Sheba, Yemenis have been adept at making the best use of scarce water through technology and careful husbandry. Their terraces, elaborate water harvesting structures, and adept management of springs and flood flows allowed the country to support a large population and even to grow rich at times through the export of products prized in the outside world: frankincense, myrrh, indigo, coffee. This brought Yemen the historic name of Blessed Arabia or Green Arabia.

For most of the 20th century the northern areas of Yemen underwent little economic or cultural change. Water management in the 1960s was recognizably the same as that described in the medieval almanacs. The management of springs, spate flows, and watersheds was a local affair with evolved systems of rights and responsibilities.[1] Water users usually settled disputes under traditional law. From time to time, they appealed to religious law, interpreted by local *qadis* (jurists), with the possibility of referring the matter to the law professors of the wider Islamic world. Only occasionally did disputes over water require the intervention of the *imam*, the ruler of the country, and these disputes reflected wider power struggles between tribes. Change started to come to Yemen through the influence of the colonial government of Aden and the British protectorate in southern Yemen from 1837 to 1967. Economic, technical, and sociopolitical developments began the process of modernization. First,

---

1. Spate flows are floods in *wadis* (riverbeds) that are diverted into fields for irrigation.

the economic hub of Aden spurred a market for modern products, a demand for labor, and the first flow of remittances to the rest of Yemen. As a result, people for the first time had money to spend. Second, modern technology and know-how entered the country with the introduction of motor pumps and tractors and the return of migrant workers. Finally, Yemenis who had worked in Aden or overseas returned with management ideas and organizational models that differed from the status quo that the *imam* wished to maintain.

These influences became very strong after the expulsion of the *imam* and the establishment of the republic in the north in the early 1960s. Social and political change came more easily. The oil boom allowed perhaps 1 million Yemenis to work in nearby oil-exporting countries and, through remittances, to create a second economic boom at home. An influx of capital and equipment fostered new technology and investment. Incomes went up quickly, from US$62 per capita in 1964 to US$528 per capita in 1982.[2]

Groundwater Development and Pricing

At the level of irrigation development, these changes spurred rapid development of groundwater resources. As new technologies for tubewell drilling and water pumping became available, individuals with abundant capital from remittances financed a proliferation of wells throughout the country. Under customary law, those who developed groundwater wells had the rights to the water, and government officials, despite some language in the constitution that water resources were the property of the state, lacked the technical resources, the legal instruments, and the political will to regulate well development and groundwater extraction. In practice, the government gave strong impetus to the extraction process by implementing a series of macroeconomic policies, including low-interest loans and cheap diesel pricing, and by investing in a public research and extension system that focused largely on groundwater irrigation.

As a result, over the past two decades groundwater has been priced at well below its economic cost. Until 1995, diesel—the major operating cost for groundwater extraction—was priced at US$0.02 per liter, compared with an export parity price of US$0.15 to US$0.20 per liter. The government gave credit to the agriculture sector at interest rates of 9 to 11 percent, whereas interest rates would have been 50 to 60 percent if the

---

2. Subsequent economic crises have brought a correction to this boom. Gross domestic product per capita is now estimated at only US$331 (1997 values).

credit agency had not been subsidized. Farmers sold each other water for US$0.02 to US$0.04 per cubic meter, whereas a price of $US0.05 to US$0.10 was required to cover the economic costs just of extracting and delivering the water (Moench 1998; Schlund 1998). In addition, the government did not levy a resource charge on groundwater extraction. A government ban on fruit and vegetable imports gave further impetus to groundwater development, because it made the production of fruits and vegetables far more profitable.

Finally, the government's complaisant, even supportive, attitude toward the booming production and use of *qat* has encouraged groundwater development. *Qat* is a soft drug that most Yemenis now chew regularly. The demand for *qat*, which has its origins as a sufi elixir and was used by only a few people, has skyrocketed with the economic and social developments of the last 30 years. Estimates suggest that *qat* represents 20 percent of gross domestic product and consumes 30 percent of irrigation water. Government officials have allowed this by not regulating *qat* or enforcing taxes on it, and have even encouraged production by banning its import (Ethiopian *qat* is cheaper). Farmers have taken up *qat* cultivation enthusiastically, attracted by the combination of high profitability; high returns to water; and well-organized, cash-based marketing.

The low groundwater prices and absence of regulation have stimulated a rapid expansion of agriculture irrigated with water from wells. As table 18.1 shows, areas irrigated with wells expanded from 37,000 hectares in 1970 to 368,000 hectares in 1996, which is 32 percent of the farmed area. Production of high-value crops has risen rapidly, and groundwater irrigation now accounts for two-thirds of agricultural output by value.

TABLE 18.1
Change in Yemeni Agriculture, 1970 and 1996

Category	1970	1996
Agriculture's share of GDP (percent)	45	15
Share of land cultivated by:		
Cereals (percent)	85	61
Cash crops (percent)	3	14
Total cropped area	1,266,000	1,155,000
Rainfed (hectares)	1,056,000	579,000
Well irrigated (hectares)	37,000	368,000

Sources: Government of Yemen (1970, 1996); World Bank (1999).

At the same time, however, groundwater extraction has passed well beyond the limit of sustainability (table 18.2). Aquifers are being depleted throughout the country; wells are constantly being deepened; and costs are rising while yields and quality are deteriorating. In some cases, a few individuals have been able to capture a disproportionate share of groundwater through privileged access to credit or subsidized equipment.

The explosion of groundwater use has often come at the expense of traditional spring-fed systems. As the water table declines, hill springs are early casualties. This has the effect of shifting income from one segment of the population to another, usually from the poor to the rich. On farms, the low groundwater prices are encouraging waste. Conveyance efficiencies are low (less than 50 percent on average), as water is typically conveyed through unlined channels. Few farmers have invested in water conserving distribution systems or bothered with husbandry practices to increase returns to water.

Spate Development and Pricing

In spate irrigation, a different but equally important development has occurred. Beginning with experiments under the British in the south in the early 1950s, engineers developed better technology to control flood flows and direct more water beneficially to the fields. The scale of these schemes (up to 30,000 hectares) made this kind of development more suited to the public sector than the private sector. The two Yemeni states that emerged three decades ago thus embarked on a number of large-scale, public sector, spate irrigation schemes in partnership with international development

TABLE 18.2
Yemen: Renewable Water Resources and Use, 1994
(millions of cubic meters)

Area	Renewable resource	Use	Balance (difference)
Intermontane plains	100	500	(400)
Tehama coastal plain	741	1,000	(259)
Eastern escarpment	315	540	(225)
Hadramawt	161	281	(120)
Other areas	783	466	317
Total Yemen	2,100	2,787	(687)

Source: World Bank (1997).

institutions. Government and donor funds financed these schemes, which did not recover capital costs from beneficiaries. Spate system productivity has increased enormously, and Yemenis speak of the large schemes in the Tehama region (the western coastal strip of land) as the breadbasket of Yemen.

Government agencies carry out the operation and maintenance of these schemes down to the secondary canal level. Officials have tried to devise various systems for recovering the costs of operation and maintenance, but these systems have not worked well and farmers consequently pay none of the costs at present. Spate water through public projects is thus free to farmers at the secondary canal level. However, the government's capacity to finance operation and maintenance, as well as any system improvements, has dwindled in the last few years because of the fiscal crises in the public sector. In addition, the combination of free water and the accompanying lack of organization and responsibility at the farmer level has produced less than optimal productivity on farms.

As is the case with groundwater extraction, spate development has caused equity issues. More efficient diversion of floods has meant, for most schemes, that upstream users have benefited at the expense of downstream users.

Traditional Water Control Systems

In addition to groundwater and spate irrigation, Yemen has a heterogeneous group of traditional water control systems. These include spring-fed systems, terrace agriculture, water harvesting, and watershed management systems. Government policies have neglected all of these, and even discriminated against them. The traditional systems, particularly the terrace and water harvesting systems, largely produce cereals. Yet, for two decades, the government pursued a cheap cereals policy based on importing commercial or donated grain for distribution at subsidized prices (see table 18.3). This subsidy reached 81 percent of the import parity price in 1995. The low prices have created a disincentive for domestic producers, causing a decline in production. The amount of farmland used for cereals has diminished from more than 1 million hectares in 1970 to 704,000 hectares in 1996. Again, this has created inequity, as the systems affected are predominantly used by low-income farmers.

The government policies have also led to environmental degradation, because the economic incentives to maintain watersheds and terraces have dwindled.

TABLE 18.3
Import Parity and Official Prices of Wheat, 1991–97

Category	1991	1992	1993	1994	1995	1996	1997
Import parity							
price (YRls/kg)	3.74	6.07	9.11	13.94	27.89	37.87	25.57
Official wholesale							
price (YRls/kg)	3.20	3.02	3.02	3.02	5.20	12.80	14.80
Wholesale as							
percentage of import							
parity price (percent)	86	50	33	22	19	34	58

Note: Exchange rate for rials into U.S. dollars is 25 (1991), 33 (1992), 49 (1993), 8 (1994), 121(1995), 128 (1996), and 128 (1997), according to the Central Bank of Yemen (1991–97).
Source: ADE (1998).

The Political Economy of Policies for Irrigation Water Pricing

The political economy of irrigation water pricing reflects the political system of Yemen. For the purposes of this analysis, the system of the former North Yemen is considered up to the time of unification in 1990. Thereafter, the united republic has largely followed the patterns of the former North.

The political system of the North before the emergence of the republic in the 1960s was a matter of contract between the *imam* and the tribes—the *imam* giving autonomy, the tribes returning fealty and military support. After the creation of the republic in the North, the republican system opened power to both the old and a new elite—a small but changing group of tribal leaders, military officers, rich traders, and other high-status people. The reciprocity inherent in this contract has limited the government's freedom to maneuver. Governance has remained weak, always subordinated to the need to keep control. Democracy is in its infancy, and politics generally is conducted outside the democratic institutions. After unification, the integration of the southern establishment, with its centralized planning approach and its sometimes turbulent political culture, proved problematic. Overall in the united republic, politics remains largely oligarchic in character, and the vision of government is limited to short-term reaction based on the imperative of control.

Since the creation of the modern state in the North, the government generally has focused on three development objectives: (a) legitimizing itself with both its citizens and its international partners through visible development,

(b) creating prosperity for as many families as possible, and (c) consolidating its power by ensuring that influential groups have access to wealth and prestige. For the reasons outlined earlier analysts generally regard the Yemeni government as weak. This is usually taken to mean that government can accomplish little except through agreements with powerful constituencies. However, when it came to the development of irrigation, this "weak" government achieved its objectives.

The factors that enabled the rapid spread of groundwater irrigation included the availability of abundant private capital and the introduction of the appropriate tubewell technology. The government, by adjusting the macroeconomic levers that it did control—diesel pricing, credit pricing and allocation, regulation of fruit and vegetable imports—subsidized the cost of groundwater irrigation, and thereby promoted rapid development of groundwater for an important segment of the farm population. By adjusting the same levers, particularly the credit mechanism, the government directed a large share of the benefits toward key groups that were important to its power base: *shaykhs* (tribal leaders), particularly in frontier areas where loyalty to the nation, not just the government, might be at stake; large landowners; and military and business leaders looking for profitable agricultural ventures. International lending institutions supported these developments through such steps as helping to establish the agricultural credit bank.

In the case of spate development, the government relied heavily on donor capital and international expertise for its schemes. The resulting development boosted the incomes of most users, especially the influential families whose lands were concentrated in the upstream areas with first rights on flows. The absence of capital and recurrent cost recovery, a situation that is the equivalent of free water, has been a useful element in limiting any tensions and in winning support from both ordinary farmers and the elite upstream landowners.

The neglect of traditional water control systems can be traced to one key constraint: the lack of easy technical packages that can readily lead to new productivity and attract private or public investment. The government failed to use even the one instrument that could have supported the incomes of grain producers: the price mechanism. Apparently the government's cereal policy has not been to increase the incomes of marginal cereal producers, but instead to subsidize the cost of food for the much more visible and vocal constituencies of consumers.

Past Successes and New Directions

Viewed internally, this implicit strategy for irrigation development has been successful. A reputedly weak government has promoted rapid development, substantially modernizing the agriculture sector and bringing self-sufficiency to the nation in high-value food products such as fruits and vegetables. The resulting increase in incomes has been spread across a large segment of farmers. Important interest groups have benefited disproportionately, and this has helped the government to consolidate its authority. Donors were willing partners in this strategy, seeing it as visible and productive development, and their support contributed to its success.

Food security has not been an issue. The government has access to cheap imported cereals that the market distributes efficiently. Yemen now produces only a quarter of its cereal needs, importing the rest. This has allowed the government to pursue a water pricing and agricultural development strategy that promoted high-value-added production rather than maximizing the production of lower-value basic commodities. The preponderance of cereal imports, and the government's control over them, also simplified the management of the cereal subsidies. Thus, the government's water pricing policy fitted its overall food strategy, as well as its agricultural development and political objectives.

However, after 20 years of holding down irrigation water prices, the government is now increasing them. Groundwater prices have been affected as the price of diesel shot up from US$0.02 to US$0.10 per liter between 1996 and 1999, and it is set to rise further to about US$0.16 per liter by 2001. The supply of cheap credit has dwindled and interest rates are up. Officials are dismantling controls on fruit and vegetable imports. All these actions will bring the price of groundwater closer to its economic cost. There is even talk of regulating groundwater development and extraction.

In the area of spate irrigation, the government has passed a law allowing the levying of water charges. Officials are considering involving user groups in operation and maintenance with a view to ultimately handing over the schemes to users. This would effectively get users to pay the full recurrent cost of spate water.

Moreover, the government is paying more attention to traditional water control systems. Researchers are trying to find ways to improve the traditional techniques and are conducting pilot projects to test the innovations. The government also is gradually removing the cereals subsidy. In 1997 the subsidy had dropped to about 42 percent compared with its peak of 81 percent in 1995.

The Political Economy of Higher Prices

For 20 years the government, with donor support, was able to meet important objectives and satisfy key constituencies with the help of low-priced or free water. What has changed?

First, Yemen has been in an economic crisis since 1990. Since 1995 the government has responded with a package of stabilization and adjustment measures intended to eliminate policy distortions, particularly those with fiscal repercussions. As a result, the diesel and credit subsidies for groundwater, the operation and maintenance subsidy for spate, and the cereals subsidy disincentive for traditional systems are all being phased out. Thus, the fiscal imperative is driving up water prices.

Second, the government has weakened. It can no longer shoulder the managerial and financial responsibility for spate irrigation management. Instead, officials are exploring sharing management and costs with user groups, and ultimately handing over the spate irrigation water systems to users. This process complements a structural adjustment program that calls for a reduced state role in overall economic activity.

Third, government officials have become increasingly concerned about environmental degradation, particularly groundwater depletion and damage to watersheds and terrace systems. The objective of sustainability has thus become as important as increasing income. In this regard, it should be noted that certain crops are much more efficient users of domestic resources, as table 18.4 illustrates.

Fourth, donors who had supported the old policies now are playing an important role by encouraging the government to make policy changes. In addition to strongly backing the structural adjustment program, donors would like to promote sustainability, a reduced government role in the economy, and more participation at the community level. Donors are also encouraging the use of pricing mechanisms, described previously, to manage water demand.

Fifth, the government itself has begun to change its view of how development should proceed and who should participate in development decisionmaking. Increasingly, officials are stressing community development and participation by nongovernmental organizations.

By changing its irrigation water pricing policy, the government is reacting to shifting economic circumstances and donor encouragement. But can it simultaneously pursue its longtime objectives of promoting development, generating income, and strengthening its power base?

Regarding development, the government has essentially developed irrigation resources as much as possible. The country's groundwater and surface water resources are fully harnessed and, in many cases, even overexploited. Government officials recognize that the need now is for good management of the existing projects. Most farmers will benefit more, or suffer less, from prudent management and from investment in conservation

TABLE 18.4
Domestic Resource Costs

Coastal area	Highlands	Eastern plateau
Selected crops with domestic resource costs of less than 0.5 (highly efficient users of domestic resources)		
Cotton (irrigated)	Coffee (rainfed)	Tomato (irrigated)
Oranges (irrigated)	Grapes (irrigated)	
Dates (irrigated)		
Papaya (irrigated)		
Selected crops with domestic resource costs of 0.5–1.0 (relatively efficient users of domestic resources)		
Tomatoes (irrigated)	Alfalfa (irrigated)	Alfalfa (irrigated)
Onions (irrigated)	Tomatoes (irrigated)	Tomatoes (irrigated)
Sesame (supplemental irrigation)	Potatoes (irrigated)	Potatoes (irrigated)
Sorghum (supplemental irrigation)	Onions (irrigated)	Onions (irrigated)
Millet (rainfed)	Qat (irrigated)	
	Some grains (rainfed and irrigated)	

Note: The domestic resource cost calculation measures the ratio of domestic resources used to produce a commodity against the value of that commodity at border prices. A ratio lower than 1.0 implies that the country has a comparative advantage in producing the commodity.
Source: World Bank (1997).

and irrigation efficiency than from additional development, which could only subtract water from existing uses. Thus the government is now pursuing second-generation goals of sustainability and efficiency.

However, this change in the development agenda is not easy for the government. Economic expansion is a thoroughly legitimizing activity. By contrast, the management phase (the age of the accountant that follows the age of the entrepreneur, as the historian Albert Hourani used to describe it in lectures) involves visible and unpopular changes such as price increases and regulation. Moreover, the devolution of power to user groups means that, at best, the government loses the legitimizing benefits of public water resource development. At worst, the result could be the strengthening of regional power bases, a centrifugal tendency that is everpresent in Yemeni politics.[3]

The effect of the new policies on the government's objective of creating prosperity is equally problematic. Regarding groundwater, the government is increasing the cost for farmers and trying to reduce use to within sustainable limits. For spate irrigation, farmers will have to pay costs for the first time. If nothing else changes, farmers who rely on either groundwater or spate irrigation face a decline in income. A recent study (Schlund 1998) developed a static model showing that after the application of all adjustment measures, average income declines of 13 percent for three principal agricultural products, as table 18.5 indicates. Farm incomes will hold steady only if investment or knowledge transfers can produce offsetting improvements in productivity.

TABLE 18.5
Reductions in Gross Margin of Selected Crops after Removal of Diesel Subsidies and Import Bans
(percent)

Product	Region	Current production practices	Improved husbandry
Onions	Eastern plateau	8–15	7–15
Tomatoes	Highlands	10–20	7–15
Potatoes	Highlands	11–23	8–17

Note: The gross margin is the income from the crop after the deduction of variable costs. The study shows the percentage drop in gross margin for the three crops assuming: (a) farmers continue to use their current production practices or (b) farmers adopt improved production practices.
Source: Schlund (1998).

---

3. I thank Marcus Moench for this insight.

Yemen's poor general economic prospects make the government's challenge of creating prosperity more difficult. Yemen faces a 3.7 percent annual population increase with an economy heavily dependent on oil, which accounts for about one-third of gross domestic product. In addition, rising water prices and demand management are putting an end to the benefits of patronage that previous water policies had allowed.

The government thus faces a real dilemma. As prices go up, it is hard to enhance state legitimacy, generate extra farm income, and benefit powerful constituencies. The pressures are visible. In 1993, Parliament threw out the administration's first proposal to raise diesel prices. In 1995 the government's announcement of a tripling of diesel prices triggered violent demonstrations that left about 20 people dead. Eventually the president ordered the increase to be rolled back somewhat, but the price still doubled. Further diesel price increases in 1996 sparked renewed confrontations, and the government created a fund to promote irrigation efficiency. The latest round of price increases in June 1998 provoked still more bloody demonstrations and the emergence of political rhetoric condemning certain donors for meddling in the economy.

Conclusion

Other than smoothing the process of adjustment and applying palliatives to the social costs, what are the government's options? The most attractive option is promoting irrigation efficiency through research, extension, and investment. Increasing water prices will create a need for efficiency, and farmers will adopt efficient technologies more readily. More efficient irrigation could help relieve pressure on groundwater resources and restore, or even increase, farm incomes. To be sure, farmers face costs as they gradually take over responsibility for the management of spate irrigation systems. But a decentralization policy that gives them responsibility for, or even ownership of, spate systems can contribute to increased efficiency and sustainability. Similarly, the policy of renewed support for traditional water control systems has the potential to increase production and boost incomes for poor farmers. Yemen has a comparative advantage in the many crops that it produces. The adoption of improved husbandry techniques within an undistorted incentive framework will help the country to realize its agricultural potential.

Donors can best help the transition to economic pricing of irrigation water in Yemen if they support this water conservation and efficiency program for irrigation. In addition, the government can give a powerful push to the program by redirecting public investment and subsidies away from water resources development into water conservation activities.

References

ADE (Aide à la Décision Économique). 1998. *Yemen: A Food Security Strategy.* Final Report, vol. 1, Main Report. Louvein-la-Neuve, Belgium: ADE/European Union.

Central Bank of Yemen. 1991–97. *Statistical Bulletin.* Sana'a, Yemen: Government of Yemen.

Government of Yemen, Ministry of Agriculture and Irrigation. 1970. *Agricultural Statistics Yearbook.* Sana'a, Yemen.

_____. 1996. *Agricultural Statistics Yearbook.* Sana'a, Yemen.

Moench, Marcus. 1998. "Water Markets." In Christopher Ward, Marcus Moench, and Chris Handley, eds., *Yemen: Local Water Management in Rural Areas.* Sana'a, Yemen: World Bank.

Schlund, Matthias. 1998. "Basic Facts—Economics of Crop Production in Yemen." Yemen Agricultural Policy Review Working Paper no. 1. World Bank, Washington, D.C.

World Bank. 1997. *Yemen: Towards a Water Strategy.* Report no. 15718-YEM. Washington, D.C.

_____. 1999. *Yemen: Agricultural Strategy Note.* Report no. 17973-YEM. Washington, D.C.

Index